Financial
Accounting
for
Non-Specialists

Financial Accounting for Non-Specialists

Robert Perks

The **McGraw·Hill** Companies

London   Boston   Burr Ridge, IL   Dubuque, IA   Madison, WI   New York   San Francisco
St. Louis   Bangkok   Bogotá   Caracas   Kuala Lumpur   Lisbon   Madrid   Mexico City
Milan   Montreal   New Delhi   Santiago   Seoul   Singapore   Sydney   Taipei   Toronto

Financial Accounting for Non-Specialists
Robert Perks
ISBN 0077104145

Published by McGraw-Hill Education
Shoppenhangers Road
Maidenhead
Berkshire
SL6 2QL
Telephone: 44 (0) 1628 502 500
Fax: 44 (0) 1628 770 224
Website: www.mcgraw-hill.co.uk

British Library Cataloguing in Publication Data
A catalogue record for this book is available from the British Library

Library of Congress Cataloguing in Publication Data
The Library of Congress data for this book has been applied for from the Library of
Congress

Acquisitions Editor: Mark Kavanagh
Senior Development Editor: Caroline Howell
Marketing Director: Petra Skytte
Senior Production Editor: Eleanor Hayes

Text Design by Jonathan Coleclough
Cover design by Fielding Design Ltd
Typeset by Mathematical Composition Setters Ltd, Salisbury, Wiltshire
Printed and bound in Spain by Mateu Cromo, Artes Graphicas SA, Madrid

ISBN 0077104145

Dedication

To Julia, Nikki, Stuart, Jack,
the next generation, and
greater understanding

Brief Table of Contents

Detailed Table of Contents

Preface

This book provides a fresh approach to financial accounting that emphasizes the understanding and application of the subject to the financial management of businesses. It is intended for future managers rather than for those who want to become accountants.

This may be the book for you if:

- you are not keen on studying accountancy, but it is an essential part of your course;

- you want to understand and make use of financial accounting information, but not bother with the mechanics of how it is produced;

- you take an intelligent interest in businesses, and their successes and failures, but do not want to become an accountant;

- you have previously attempted the subject, but have become lost in numerical calculations that you do not really understand;

- you want to communicate with accountants, and understand and make use of them and the statements that they produce;

- you will be studying corporate finance or financial management for which an appropriate foundation in financial accounting is necessary.

It is designed as an introductory text: no previous knowledge of the subject is required. It is particularly suitable for degree courses in management and business studies, including MBAs and other masters degree programmes. The approach is critical, analytical and evaluative, amply illustrated with real world examples. The material of the chapters, together with the questions and exercises, should meet the increasingly demanding aims and objectives of degree courses. Students are encouraged to read, understand and evaluate. There are also plenty of exercises and solutions for students to practise.

The book is based around the idea that there is a great deal of valuable information included in companies' published annual reports and accounts if only managers, analysts, financial journalists, economists, bankers, financiers and everyone with an interest in business and management takes the time and trouble to try to understand them.

Most books on financial accounting seem to be written from the point of view of those whose job it is to *produce* financial statements. They are full of complicated rules and procedures that seem only to confuse those who want to take a more general interest in the subject. This book is not a guide for bookkeepers and others who produce the financial statements. It is for those who will *make use* of financial accounting. It is particularly directed at those who may be reluctant to tackle the subject, but who can accept that it is not only valuable and useful; it is also a challenging, interesting academic subject, which is directly applicable in the real business world.

The book is intended to help those who produce projects, dissertations and reports, including journalists, who use information about companies: they need to be aware that annual reports and accounts are a valuable source of information, and to be sure that they understand them.

It is, in part, a defence of financial accounting which is intended to show the value, usefulness and applications of the subject. But it is a 'warts and all' presentation which attempts to provide a reasonable exposition of the limitations of financial accounting as well as demonstrating its value and applications. It deals with conventional interpretations of accounts by examining the financial statements of actual companies, not by presenting a series of ratios for students to memorize. It also provides a basis for some of the main issues in financial management, including how to raise additional funds, dividend policy and gearing; working capital management; and investment appraisal. Financial accounting statements are seen as a basis that indicates a company's needs in such areas, and that demonstrate the success or otherwise of a company's financial management.

It may not be necessary to understand the mechanics of bookkeeping in order to make use of financial accounting as a vehicle for financial management. But for those who want to understand basic accounting procedures a clear and straightforward exposition is provided as an optional extra: an Appendix, which includes practical exercises.

The book does not attempt to be all things to all people. It concentrates on the financial accounts of large companies rather than attempting to deal with every different type of organization. It presents the subject in a UK context, but recognizes the increasing internationalization of financial accounting. It makes no attempt to be a comprehensive or authoritative reference manual which can be used to look up the rules for dealing with complex and unusual transactions. Instead it concentrates exclusively on helping students to understand and make use of financial accounting statements, and providing an academic coverage of the subject appropriate for most degree courses where an introduction to the subject is required.

The book also provides a number of features intended to help students and lecturers. Each chapter has clear learning objectives and self-testing questions with answers provided. Assessment questions are also supplied. In addition, a wide range of discussion questions and group activities are suggested, which should be controversial, interesting and relevant to the real world; they also provide useful suggestions for coursework assignments, projects and dissertations.

The book is designed so that topics can be studied in any order after covering the first two chapters. Each chapter is self-contained, with cross-references to other chapters. The text can be used for courses which have an emphasis on financial management, or on practical financial accounting, or which are more theoretical. The order of chapters, and the extent to which each is dealt with, can be varied according to the needs of a particular course.

The Online Learning Centre that accompanies the book (www.mcgraw-hill.co.uk/textbooks/perks) provides a glossary of terms which many students will find useful, additional practice questions with answers, and some additional material and up-dating.

Guided Tour

Learning objectives

Learning objectives identify the key concepts that you should understand after reading the chapter.

Introduction

Each chapter opens with an Introduction, which sets the scene by introducing the issues that will be addressed in the chapter.

Illustrations

Each chapter provides a number of examples and balance sheets which illustrate and summarize important concepts, helping you to apply theory to accounting practice.

Summary

This briefly reviews and reinforces the main topics you will have covered in each chapter to ensure you have acquired a solid understanding of the key topics.

Review of Key Points

A brief recap at the end of each chapter is ideal for revising accounting concepts.

Self-testing Questions

These questions encourage you to review and apply the knowledge you have acquired from each chapter and can be undertaken to test your understanding. Answers are provided at the end of the book.

Assessment Questions

This section provides a multitude of questions you may be asked in an exam. They can be used as helpful revision questions or to check your progress as you cover the topics throughout the text.

Group Activities and Discussion Questions

These questions can be used to spark debate in class, and can also help readers to think around the topic.

Financial Accounting in Context

Relevant chapters end with a press item that aims to illustrate the main themes of the chapter, allowing you to appreciate how the theory applies in real life.

References and Further Reading

A list of references from the chapter, plus useful websites, can be used for further research.

Online Learning Centre (OLC)

After completing each chapter, log on to the supporting Online Learning Centre website. Take advantage of the study tools offered to reinforce the material you have read in the text, and to develop your knowledge further.

Resources for students include:

◆ Self-testing questions

◆ Useful weblinks

◆ Glossary

◆ Crosswords

Also available for lecturers:

◆ PowerPoint slides for lecture presentations

◆ Teaching Tips

◆ Artwork and illustrations from the book

◆ Guide answer to assessment questions in the book

◆ Group activities and discussion questions

For lecturers: Primis Content Centre

If you need to supplement your course with additional cases or content, create a personalized e-Book for your students.
Visit **www.primiscontentcenter.com**
or e-mail primis_euro@mcgraw-hill.com for more information.

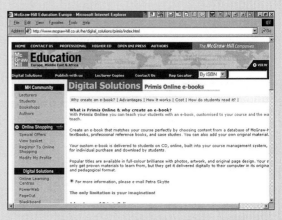

Study Skills

Open University Press publishes guides to study, research and exam skills, to help undergraduate and postgraduate students through their university studies.

Visit **www.openup.co.uk/ss** to see the full selection.

Computing Skills

If you'd like to brush up on your computing skills, we have a range of titles covering MS Office applications such as Word, Excel, PowerPoint, Access and more.

Get a £2 discount off these titles by entering the promotional code app when ordering online at **www.mcgraw-hill.co.uk/app**

Acknowledgements

My thanks go to the following reviewers for their comments at various stages in the text's development:

Kim Arnold, University of Derby
Walter Aerts, University of Antwerp
Ian Crawford, University of Bath
Julie Froud, University of Manchester
Kathy Grieve, University of Central England
Russell Kinman, University of Luton
Ruth Mattimoe, Dublin City University
Lynne Oats, University of Warwick
Syamarlah Rasaratnum, University of Ulster

The publishers would also like to thank the companies who granted permission to use material in illustrations and 'Financial Accounting in Context' boxes:

Accountancy magazine, pp 78–9, 322
David Cairns, for an extract from 'US Principles-based Accounting',
    Accountancy magazine, Sept 2003, p 78–9
The Financial Times, pp 106, 144, 171, 265, 294–5, 350–2, 380–1
PriceWaterhouseCoopers p 322
Tate and Lyle pp 117, 182
The Times, pp 106, 241

Every effort has been made to clear permission for material reproduced in this book. The publishers would be pleased to clear permission with any organization it has not been possible to contact prior to publication.

I would like to thank anonymous referees for constructive suggestions; Simon Healeas for reading a number of chapters and suggesting improvements; Alan Leong for checking much of the numerical work; and Orla Gough for support and encouragement. Remaining errors are my responsibility. I am also grateful to family and friends for putting up with me, and my irritability and neglect when the book seemed to take over my life.

1

The Balance Sheet, and What it Tells Us

Learning objectives

After studying this chapter you should be able to:

- Explain the structure and terminology of straightforward balance sheets

- Understand how balance sheets can indicate financial weaknesses and strengths

- Demonstrate how transactions and profits affect balance sheets

- Discuss the uses and limitations of balance sheets

Introduction

The word 'balance sheet' is widely used, although most people have never seen one and have little idea what it shows. This chapter provides a gentle introduction to balance sheets by showing how individuals can prepare their own personal balance sheets, and how similar these are to company balance sheets. It also gives some indication of the usefulness of balance sheets: they can give an indication of what an individual or company is worth (but with severe limitations). They also show what liabilities there are, which can help to predict future bankruptcy.

1.1 An Individual's Balance Sheet

If you want to know how much you are worth as an individual you would probably start by drawing up a list of everything that you own, and then try to put a value on each item. After working for a few years you might own a house, some furniture, a car, some premium bonds and shares which you intend to keep on a long-term basis, and perhaps some short-term investments. You might also have a good stock of food and wine in the kitchen as well as some money in the bank. But you may have debts: a mortgage owed to your bank or building society, an overdraft, money you owe on your credit card, and bills not yet paid for such things as electricity, gas, telephone and council tax.

It is easy to produce a list of what you own, and a list of what you owe. You can then deduct what you owe from what you own to show your 'net worth'. An example is given in Illustration 1.1.

We can summarize this as:

What I own − What I owe = What I am worth

If you are a full-time student this might be more difficult, or more embarrassing. It may be that the most valuable things that you own are items such as CDs, clothes, books, a stereo and a computer. You may have paid a lot for them, but their value now is questionable – especially if you suddenly needed to sell them. They would cost a lot to replace, and if they were all stolen you would probably claim quite a high value for them if they were insured. But if you try to sell them, their second-hand value would probably be very disappointing: it is likely to be only a small fraction of what you paid for them. Worse still, you may well have a student loan and an overdraft and owe other amounts of money which means that your net worth is zero, or even negative: you owe more than you own. But it is all worth it, you tell yourself, because all the time you are spending money on your education; that is an investment; and what you are really worth is your future earning power. If you go to your bank wanting to borrow money, they will

Illustration 1.1

	£
What I own	
House	300,000
Furniture	4,000
Car	10,000
Premium Bonds and shares	6,000
Food and drink	200
Cash and bank	4,800
Total	325,000
What I owe	
Mortgage	222,000
Bills (gas and electricity etc.)	1,000
Credit card	2,000
Total	225,000
What I am worth	100,000

be much more interested in your future earning power than they are in a pile of second-hand clothes and some CDs.

Three main problems arise in trying to establish what any individual or business is worth:

1 What items are we going to list? Are we going to include our 5-year-old computer, our vinyl records, all the food in the kitchen, our educational qualifications and our children? We might think of these as being some of the best things we have, but we would probably exclude them. We need some basis, or principle, for deciding what to include and what to exclude.

2 How do we establish what particular items are worth? We attempt this in several different ways, for example by looking at what they originally cost, or what the second-hand value is, or what it would cost to replace them.

3 What is our future earning power worth? Whether we look at an individual, or a company, in many cases the money that they can earn in the future is worth a lot more than a collection of bits and pieces that they own. If you want to borrow money, you could tell your bank that you expect to earn at least a million pounds during your working life, and ask to borrow the million pounds now. The bank's response is likely to be short and not very sweet.

You can, of course, make up your own rules, and decide that you are worth £100,000. But if you want to compare your own wealth with someone else's, then you need to agree how the calculation is to be made. Are you going to show your house at the amount you paid for it, or at the market value now? Are you going to show your car at the amount you paid for it, or allow for the fact that it has depreciated since you bought it? If you attempt any comparisons like this you will soon find that you need some agreed rules on what to include, and the basis of valuation to be used. You will need accounting principles.

It is difficult to know what something is really worth until you sell it. I might boast that my house is worth £500,000, but we might agree that it is more objective to show it at cost; and it cost £300,000 a few years ago. The accounting principle would be to list everything that we own, and show everything at the original cost price.

Deciding what principle to adopt for furniture and for a car is more difficult. They have only a limited life, and are likely to depreciate over time as we 'use them up'. We could decide that a car has a 5-year life and write it down by one-fifth each year.

1.2 A Company's Balance Sheet

A company's balance sheet is very much like an individual's balance sheet, except that a standard layout is used, and more impressive terminology is used.

The layout and terminology probably look quite confusing at first and it may be hard to believe that Illustration 1.2 really is the same balance sheet as Illustration 1.1. By using standardized terminology and presentation accountants say that they are making it easier to compare one company with another. You might think that they are just making it more complicated so that it is 'impenetrable' to non-accountants. But professionals can no longer hide behind their terminology, conventions and so called 'expertise'. These days many patients question their doctor's recommendations (perhaps by looking things up on the internet and being instantly more 'expert' than the doctor). Similarly, you are learning to question accountants (and other management 'experts'), and now is the time to make sure that you understand the basic terminology of financial statements.

In accountant's jargon, what a company owns and what they owe are called *assets* and *liabilities*, and the statement showing assets and liabilities (and *net worth*, or *equity*, or *capital*) is called a *balance sheet*.

In everyday English we have seen that what I am worth is the total of what I own, less the total of what I owe. In accountancy terms we would say that the balance sheet value of a company is the total of assets less liabilities.

Illustration 1.2

Balance Sheet of A. Reader Company Limited as at
31 December Year 1

Fixed assets	£	£	£
Tangible assets			
Freehold land and buildings (at cost)		300,000	
Furniture (at cost)		4,000	
Vehicles (at cost)		10,000	
		314,000	
Investments		6,000	320,000
Current assets			
Stocks		200	
Cash and bank		4,800	
		5,000	
Current liabilities*			
Creditors	1,000		
	2,000	3,000	
Net current assets			2,000
Total assets less Current liabilities			322,000
Creditors: amounts falling due after more than one year			
Mortgage			222,000
			100,000
Capital and reserves			100,000
			100,000

* 'Creditors: amounts falling due within one year' is now the correct term, but 'Current liabilities' is still widely used.

We could call this 'equity', or net assets, or capital, or net worth. Accountants sometimes talk about 'the balance sheet equation', which is simply this:

Assets – Liabilities = Equity

It is easy enough to establish the 'balance sheet value' of a company, or its 'net asset value', or 'equity', or 'net worth'. In Illustration 1.2 it would be £100,000. It is much more difficult to establish what a company is really worth – because of the same three problems already identified:

1 What items are we going to include on the list?

2 How do we establish what particular items are worth?

3 What is the future earning power of the company as a whole worth?

These problems will be addressed more fully later in the book.

1.3 Short-term and Long-term Classification

There is a standard format for balance sheets which makes it easier to compare one company with another. Both assets and liabilities are classified as being long term or short term. Anything which is intended to be around for more than a year is long term. Anything which changes within a year is short term.

Assets

Long-term assets are called 'fixed assets'. (It would be too simple just to call them long-term assets!) But there is nothing 'fixed' about them. They include cars, ships and aeroplanes, just as much as they include land and buildings which seem to be more fixed!

Within the Fixed Assets section there are three main categories:

1 Intangible fixed assets: things like goodwill, patents, trade marks, licences.

2 Tangible fixed assets: things like land and buildings; plant, machinery and equipment; vehicles; furniture, fixtures and fittings.

3 Investments, or financial assets: things like shares in other companies or loans that have been made.

We can say that things like vehicles or furniture are *usually* fixed assets, but that is not always the case. If a business intends to use them for a period of years, then they are fixed assets. But if someone is in business to buy and sell vehicles, or furniture, then any items held short term, awaiting sale, are not fixed assets.

The same arguments apply with investments. Any surplus funds invested in shares, or loaned to someone or another business, might be intended to be long term, and so are fixed assets. Or they might be intended to be short term, and so are not fixed assets.

Short-term assets are called 'current assets'. (Again, it would be too simple just to call them short-term assets!) They include:

1 Stocks of raw materials, work in progress, finished goods, and goods held for resale;

2 Debtors – money owed to the business by customers and others;[1]

3 Investments (those which are not fixed assets); and

4 Cash.[2]

One way of looking at current assets is to say that they are all cash, or things that are intended to become cash within a matter of months. We intend that our stocks will all be sold; even raw materials and components will be incorporated into things which are sold. Investments which are shown as current assets are assumed to be temporary, and so will be sold and converted into cash. And debtors should pay up within a matter of months.

Liabilities

Liabilities are also categorized as short term and long term. It might be tempting to call short-term liabilities 'current liabilities', and the term is widely used. But on published balance sheets we have the following terms:

1 'Creditors: amounts falling due within one year'. This includes most ordinary trade creditors – amounts due for goods and services bought on credit.

Illustration 1.3

<u>Simplified Balance Sheet of A. Reader Company as at
31 December Year 1</u>

	£	£
Fixed assets		320,000
Current assets	5,000	
Deduct: Creditors: amounts falling due within one year	<u>3,000</u>	<u>2,000</u>
		322,000
Deduct: Creditors: amounts falling due after more than one year		<u>222,000</u>
		100,000
Capital or equity shareholders' funds		<u>100,000</u>

---

1 And even prepayments, and accrued income, if you want to be technical!

2 Cash includes money in the bank, and petty cash in hand. Obviously the two are quite distinct, and a bookkeeper needs to account for them separately and properly. But, for the sake of simplicity and clarity, the two items will be lumped together and just called cash.

2 'Creditors: amounts falling due after more than one year'. This includes long-term borrowings such as mortgages and debentures.

The balance sheet that we have been using so far can now be shown under these four headings, which separate assets from liabilities, and long term from short term (Illustration 1.3).

The distinction between what is short term and what is long term is important in assessing the financial strength or solvency of a business – in assessing whether or not it is likely to go bust!

1.4 Balance Sheets: Financial Strength and Weakness

A balance sheet may suggest that a business is financially strong, although it does not prove it. A balance sheet may show signs of weakness – and we ignore these at our peril. Accountants are often criticized when a company gets into financial difficulty because they did not warn in big red letters, 'This company is dodgy. Avoid it like the plague'. But, in most cases, the signs of financial difficulty are there for all to see, long before a much publicized collapse, if only they take the trouble to try to understand the balance sheet.

Companies collapse in one way or another when they cannot pay what they are required to pay: when they are unable to meet their financial liabilities. Many factors may contribute to this situation: poor management, poor marketing, poor planning, trying to do too much with too little money, bad luck, dodgy customers, changes in the world economy and so on. There is usually someone, or something to blame. But, in the end, either a company can pay its bills, or it can't. The balance sheet gives a pretty good guide to what bills are due to be paid – and the resources available for paying them.

Although there may be question marks about the reliability of some figures in published accounts, the liabilities[3] figures are among the most reliable. A company needs to have sufficient funds readily available to meet its liabilities when they fall due. A company's 'current liabilities', or 'Creditors: amounts falling due within one year' should be clear from the balance sheet. The important question is: does the company have enough short-term assets to be able to pay its short-term liabilities as they fall due?

---

3 There are occasions when crooked accountants and directors omit liabilities completely, or seek to hide them as some form of 'off balance sheet finance'. This issue is examined later in relation to 'Creative Accounting'.

A company's current assets include money in the bank, debtors[4] that are due to become money in the bank within a few months, and stocks of goods which the company plans to sell and convert into money in the bank within a matter of months. If a company has a lot more current assets than current liabilities, it should be able to pay its current liabilities when they fall due. If their current assets are two or three times as much as their current liabilities, then they appear to be fairly strong; or in the terminology of accounting, they have a high current ratio.

In Illustrations 1.1 to 1.3 above, current assets are £5,000, and short-term liabilities are £3,000. The current ratio is 1.67 : 1.[5] This is not particularly high, but it looks as if there is enough cash and near cash available in the short term to be able to pay the short-term liabilities as they fall due.

It should be possible for all current assets to become cash within a matter of months, but this is more difficult with some items than others. Not all stocks of goods are easily and quickly turned into cash. A half-baked loaf will probably be finished and sold for cash within a matter of hours. A half-built house, in an area where no-one wants to live, could remain unsold for a long time. If most of a company's 'current assets' are actually stocks of goods, their ability to pay creditors quickly may be less than their current ratio suggests. A useful approach to assessing a company's ability to pay its short-term liabilities would be to exclude stocks from current assets, and assess the company's 'liquidity', by comparing their 'liquid assets' with their short-term creditors. This is known as the liquidity ratio, or acid test, or quick assets ratio.

Long-term debts are also important – a company or individual can go bankrupt because of the weight of long-term liabilities. It is difficult to say how much debt is too much – some people, and some companies, seem to manage with huge debts, whereas others (like Marconi, and a number of airlines recently) collapse. An individual who has lots of money can afford to borrow lots of money. Similarly, a company with a large amount of equity, or shareholders' funds (the company's 'own' money) can afford to borrow more money than a company with very little equity. In Illustrations 1.1 to 1.3 above the amount of equity is £100,000, so it would seem reasonable to borrow another £100,000. If a business is financed half by borrowing, and half from its own shareholders' funds, then the borrowing is high, but probably not excessive. But in the above illustrations the borrowing is much more than the equity. If we add together all of the long-term funds (shareholders' funds, plus long-term creditors = £322,000),

---

4 Debtors are customers who have not yet paid for the goods or services with which they have been supplied.

5 £5,000 ÷ £3,000 = 1.67.

then we can see that the assets of the business are mainly[6] financed by borrowing. In accounting terminology such a company is 'high geared', which usually means high risk.

But high gearing, or high amounts of long-term debt, does not particularly matter if the individual or company has a substantial amount of income with which to pay the interest, and to repay the creditors (or borrow more!) when repayment is due. Individuals who have to pay mortgage interest of £20,000 a year should have no problems if their annual income is £100,000 a year or more. Someone who has to pay £20,000 a year mortgage interest from an annual income of £25,000 is likely to have real problems! It is worth comparing the amount of interest that has to be paid each year, with the income available to pay that interest. If the interest is covered, say, 5 times by the income, then it is probably all right. But if the interest is covered only 1.25 times by the available income, then there are likely to be problems.

In assessing the financial strength of a company, or how likely it is to go bankrupt, it is worth calculating the current ratio, the liquidity ratio, the capital gearing ratio, and the interest times cover.

1.5 Depreciation and Balance Sheet 'Values'

Before looking at the published balance sheet of a real company it is useful to know that all assets are not simply shown at cost. Some fixed assets, particularly land and buildings, are revalued from time to time; and most fixed assets are depreciated each year.

If you buy a car for £10,000, you might decide that you will keep it for 4 years, and expect that at the end of the 4 years you will be able to sell it for £2,000. This is a plan, or an accounting policy. After one year you can show the car as being £8,000; after 2 years it would be £6,000 and so on. This does not mean that the car is 'worth' £8,000 after one year. What we need to do is to show three things:

(a) the car cost £10,000;

(b) after one year the cumulative depreciation is £2,000 (after 2 years it would be £4,000; after 3 years it would be £6,000);

(c) after one year the net book[7] value of the car would be £8,000 (after 2 years it would be £6,000; after 3 years it would be £4,000).

---

6   £222,000 of £322,000 is almost 69 per cent.

7   The amount shown for it in the 'books' of the company, or its balance sheet value.

It is important that *all three* of these can be found on the balance sheet, or in notes to the balance sheet: the cost of an asset, the cumulative depreciation, and the net book value. As the above example shows, the net book value is not an attempt to show what the asset is really worth now. We decided to write off the initial cost of the car, down to an estimated trade in value when we have finished with it, and to charge the same amount of depreciation each year[8] for 4 years.

In Illustrations 1.1 to 1.3 above depreciation has been ignored to simplify it. The car is shown at £10,000. If we decided that a depreciation charge, or expense, of £2,000 is appropriate, there would be two effects on the balance sheet: the car would be reduced by £2,000; and the equity, or net worth would be reduced by £2,000. We saw that the basic balance sheet equation is

Assets – Liabilities = Equity[9]

Depreciation is an expense and we can now say that assets minus expenses minus liabilities equals equity: a new equity figure emerges after expenses have been deducted. Ilustration 1.4 shows how the balance sheet changes as a result of charging expenses, earning income, and making a profit.

1.6 **Balance Sheets and Profit**

A successful individual or business is likely to show an increase in capital or equity or net worth each year.

Expenses, such as depreciation, decrease assets and decrease equity. Most expenses reduce the asset of cash when they are paid.[10] If they have not yet been paid, then there is an increase in liabilities – shown as creditors (which has the same effect as a reduction in assets). Whether they are paid out in cash or not, the effect of all expenses is to reduce equity.

Revenues, mainly from sales, increase assets and increase equity. If they come in the form of cash, then the asset of cash is increased. If the customers have not yet paid, then the increase in assets shows up as an increase in debtors. Whether they are received in the form of cash or not, the effect of all revenues is to increase equity.

In a successful business revenues should be greater than expenses, and so the net effect is to increase equity.

---

8 Depreciation does not have to be on a 'straight line' or 'equal annual instalments' basis. Businesses can choose to charge more depreciation in the early years by using a 'diminishing balance' basis.

9 The next step would be that assets minus expenses plus income minus liabilities equals equity; a new equity figure emerges showing an increase as profit. The profit is income less expenses.

10 Depreciation is an expense which reduces the fixed asset; it does not reduce the cash – it is not paid.

If we take the balance sheet at the end of one year, and compare it with the balance sheet at the end of the next year, we can get a fairly good idea of the amount of profit that was made in the period between the two dates. All we do is compare the figure for equity, or net assets, or shareholders' funds on the most recent balance sheet with the equivalent figure a year ago. This is shown in Illustration 1.4. The amount of equity or shareholders' funds has increased by £25,000 during Year 2: it looks as if the company has made £25,000 profit. The profit has shown up in additional stocks, debtors and cash: they have increased by £29,000. But fixed assets have gone down by £2,800 (depreciation), and there are additional liabilities of £1,200; the increase in net assets is £25,000.

Without more evidence we cannot always be sure that the increase in net assets is the profit for the year, for three main reasons:

1 It could be that the amount of equity has increased because shareholders have put more money into the business; there has been a new issue of shares. Any extra coming in from the issue of shares does not count as profit, and so should be deducted from the increase in equity shown on the balance sheet to arrive at the profit figure for the year.

2 All of the profits that have been made do not necessarily stay within the business. Most companies pay out dividends. They can make a substantial profit, and pay most of it out as dividends. Dividends do not reduce profits. But they do mean that any increase in equity is not the whole of the profit. Dividends must be added to the increase in equity in calculating the profit for the year.

3 Sometimes companies revalue their assets. This does not seem to have happened in Illustration 1.4. If the freehold land and buildings were really worth £350,000, the company could add £50,000 to the figure shown on the balance sheet for freehold land and buildings; and they would have to add £50,000 to equity; it would probably be separately labelled as a 'Capital reserve'. The company would then appear to be £50,000 better off, but we would probably not think of this as being profit.

A balance sheet is not the most convenient way of calculating profit, but it can be done! Profit for the year is the increase in equity during the year, minus any additional shares that have been issued, plus any dividends that have been provided.

The third of these is more problematic. Are we going to use the term 'profit'[11] for the whole of the increase in equity (after making the two

---

11 Profit is very British. The more international term is 'income'. Or you can use the term 'earnings' when you want to keep changing the terminology in order to impress, and confuse the enemy. Be careful, though; they might know more about accounting than you do.

Illustration 1.4

Balance Sheet of A. Reader Company Limited as at 31 December

	Year 1		Year 2	
Fixed assets	£	£	£	£
Tangible assets				
Freehold land and buildings (at cost)	300,000		300,000	
Furniture (at cost less depreciation)	4,000		3,200	
Vehicles (at cost less depreciation)	10,000		8,000	
	314,000		311,200	
Investments	6,000	320,000	6,000	317,200
Current assets				
Stocks	200		9,000	
Debtors	–		20,000	
Cash and Bank	4,800		5,000	
	5,000		34,000	
Current liabilities				
Creditors				
	3,000		4,200	
Net current assets		2,000		29,800
Total assets less current liabilities		322,000		347,000
Creditors: amounts falling due after more than one year				
Mortgage		222,000		222,000
		100,000		125,000
Capital and reserves		100,000		100,000
		100,000		125,000

adjustments above)? Revenues clearly contribute to equity and profit. Expenses clearly reduce equity and profit. But equity will also increase if we revalue land and buildings – provided the revaluation results in an increase. What would you think of a company that boasted of making £90,000 profit, if it had lost £10,000 on normal operations, but 'made' a surplus of £100,000 by revaluing its premises? The traditional accountant would not be impressed, and would want to see a loss of £10,000 being recorded. But much is changing in accounting, and we need to keep a careful eye on the strange ideas of the Accounting Standards Board.

1.7 A Company's Published Balance Sheet

A recent published balance sheet of Ted Baker plc for the year ended 25 January 2003 is shown in Illustration 1.5. The company's current liabilities ('Creditors: amounts falling due within one year') are as follows:

	2003 £000	2002 £000
Current liabilities	16,456	14,333

Does the company have plenty of current assets to be able to pay the current liabilities as they fall due? The amount of current assets is as follows:

Current assets	23,690	21,904

We can express the proportion of current assets to current liabilities as follows:

Current Ratio	1.44 : 1	1.53 : 1

There are plenty of current assets, which should become cash within a matter of months, to pay the current liabilities as they fall due. The ratio is lower than the 2 : 1 which some textbooks recommend, but it is in line with most retailers where current ratios tend to be lower than average.

With some current assets such as stocks it may take some months before they are turned into cash. Liquidity can be assessed by taking only 'quick assets' and comparing them with current liabilities. This is the 'acid test'. If stocks are excluded from current assets, the liquidity ratio is calculated as follows:

Current assets excluding stocks	9,753	9,586
Current liabilities	16,456	14,333
Liquidity ratio	0.59 : 1	0.67 : 1

The company's current ratio and liquidity ratio are both rather low, and have weakened since 2002. However, relatively low current ratios and liquidity ratios are fairly normal with retailers.[12]

The company's long-term debt is fairly low. The total net assets (or total capital and reserves) amount to nearly £19 million; but there is only £4 million of long-term creditors. This may be calculated as a gearing ratio as follows:

('D') Creditors: amounts falling due after more than one year	4,000	4,000
('E') Total capital and reserves	18,835	15,723
Creditors: amounts falling due after more than one year	4,000	4,000
('D + E') Total long-term funds	22,835	19,723
Gearing $\dfrac{D}{D+E}$	17.5%	20.3%

---

12 Because they have more stocks than debtors, since they sell mainly for cash, not on credit.

Illustration 1.5

CONSOLIDATED BALANCE SHEET At 25 January 2003	Notes	25 January 2003 £'000	26 January 2002 £'000
Fixed assets			
Tangible assets	11	15,375	12,167
Investments	12	349	446
		15,724	12,613
Current assets			
Stocks	13	13,937	12,318
Debtors	14	6,975	5,711
Cash at bank and in hand		2,778	3,875
		23,690	21,904
Creditors: amounts falling due within one year	15	(16,456)	(14,333)
Net current assets		7,234	7,571
Total assets less current liabilities		22,958	20,184
Creditors: amount falling due after more than one year	16	(4,000)	(4,000)
Provisions for liabilities and charges	17	(123)	(461)
Net assets		18,835	15,723
Capital and reserves			
Called-up share capital	18	2,072	2,064
Share premium	19	1,412	978
Profit and loss account	19	15,411	12,638
Equity shareholders' funds	20	18,895	15,680
Minority interests – equity	19	(60)	43
Total capital and reserves		18,835	15,723

The accompanying notes are an integral part of this consolidated balance sheet. The financial statements on pages 27 to 46 were approved by the board of directors on 24 March 2003 and signed on its behalf by:

L.D. Page   Director

The gearing is relatively low, which means that the company is not heavily dependent on long-term borrowings. The gearing has also fallen, which means that their already low risk in 2002 was even lower in 2003.

The total of capital and reserves increased by about £3 million during the year which suggests that the company's retained profit for the year was about £3 million. The profit and loss account (Illustration 2.3 in Chapter 2) shows that they made about £6.6 million profit; £3.6 million was paid out as dividends; this left about £3 million as retained profit.

The total for net assets (or total capital and reserves) is shown as being nearly £19 million. This is sometimes referred to as the 'balance sheet value' of the company. But the market value of a successful company should be much higher than its balance sheet value. The 'market capitalization' of the shares of a company is shown in the *Financial Times* on a Monday. In September 2003 the market capitalization of Ted Baker plc was about £145 million.

Published accounts show a lot more detail than the simplified balance sheets included in this chapter. A great deal of additional information is shown in notes to the accounts.

1.8 Role and Limitations of Balance Sheets

Balance sheets can be useful in a number of ways.

1 We saw that the balance sheet, or a statement of assets and liabilities, can be useful in showing what a person or business is worth. But there are problems in establishing agreed rules as to exactly which assets (and perhaps even which liabilities) should be included, and in determining the basis upon which they should be valued. There is also the problem that the value of a business as a whole is likely to be different from the value of all of its assets (less liabilities) added together. The real value of a business (or an individual) might depend more on the income that it can generate (as a whole entity) in the future than upon whatever amounts might be shown for individual assets and liabilities.

2 We also saw that, in listing the various liabilities that have to be paid, short term and long term, we can get an idea of the financial strength of a business. If its liabilities are too high, and it cannot pay them, it is likely to get into serious financial difficulties, and perhaps go out of business. Balance sheets can give a good indication of whether liabilities are too high, or whether the business is reasonably strong. The balance sheet is the basis for assessing the financial position of a company.

3 We can also measure profit using the balance sheet. There are easier ways of measuring profit, but it is useful to calculate it in two different ways so

that one checks the other. The balance sheet approach to measuring profit is one of the two main approaches, and one that may become much more important.

4 Balance sheets play an important role in 'stewardship'. Shareholders put their money into a company; directors and managers are the 'stewards' of that money; and shareholders want to know what has happened to their money. The balance sheet shows what money has been put in by the shareholders, and what retained profits have been added to it; this amount is shown as equity (or shareholders' funds). Examination of the first part of the balance sheet, the assets and liabilities, shows what that money is now financing; or, if you like, what has happened to it.

5 In order to produce a balance sheet it is necessary to produce a listing of all of the company's assets and liabilities. This can be useful in keeping track of various assets, and ensuring that all are being put to good use and are earning their keep. When a company gets into financial difficulties it sometimes seems as if they manage to find assets that they had previously forgotten about, or done nothing with. There may be investments that are not much use; sports and social facilities that are hardly used; debtors who have been neglected and have got away with not paying for too long (perhaps because of a half forgotten dispute); a workshop developing a new product that made little progress; machinery, or components and raw materials that were specially bought for a new product that was quietly abandoned; too many premises or branches; an expensive head office in the centre of London; a training centre, kitchens, computer workshops, and maintenance facilities that should have been sold or redeployed when these activities were outsourced.

Many companies do not even know what assets they own, or how many laptop computers have 'walked' out of the door, and they do not even have an up-to-date fixed assets register. The process of producing listings of assets in order to compile a balance sheet can be a useful housekeeping exercise.

6 In addition to providing a basis for assessing the financial *position* of a company, the balance sheet also provides a basis for assessing the financial *performance* of a company. The shareholders of a company are likely to be concerned about performance in terms of profitability. They are not concerned merely with the amount of profit the company makes; they are concerned with how much profit the company makes in relation to the amount of capital employed. A profit of £1 million may look good for a company with capital employed of £5 million; it would look pathetic in relation to capital employed of £100 million. It is the

balance sheet which shows the amount of capital employed. The ratio of profit to capital employed is a key ratio in assessing and improving a company's financial performance.

7 Financial accounting is a whole system, and the balance sheet is an essential part of the system in checking, balancing and controlling other parts of the system. If a company's balance sheet does not balance, there is definitely something wrong! Accountants are only (or nearly!) human, and inevitably some mistakes are made with figures. The financial accounting system is designed to show up errors, and to find where they occurred. An accounting system can also show up fraud and theft. When a balance sheet does balance, we cannot be sure that there is no fraud or error. If it does not balance we can be sure that something is wrong; and if we do make a mistake, it will probably show up during the accounting processes before producing a balance sheet. [13]

But we should not expect too much from balance sheets. They were never properly designed to achieve anything very useful. When double entry bookkeeping first became widely used, the balance sheet was just a matter of bookkeeping convenience. It was not even necessary to produce one every year. Until the eighteenth century a balance sheet was often not produced until the ledger was full; then a balance sheet was a summary of the assets and liabilities that were transferred to the new ledger. Any remaining old balances, mostly revenues and expenses, were written off. The balances shown on the balance sheet are items that are continuing, but they tend to be shown at the cost price when they are first entered in the business's books.

By the end of the eighteenth century the production of balance sheets on an annual basis became normal. During the nineteenth century it became a requirement for companies to publish annual balance sheets; and during the twentieth century legislation became increasingly specific about what should be shown on a balance sheet. Towards the end of the twentieth century accounting standards laid down more detailed requirements, and by 2005 the European Union will require the application of International Accounting Standards in the same way as many other countries.

The main limitations of balance sheets have already been referred to:

1 What items are we going to include?

2 How do we establish the value of particular items?

3 The value of a company as a whole is likely to be very different from the total net value of the individual assets and liabilities.

---

13 Mistakes usually show up in the trial balance.

Sometimes it is very difficult to decide whether or not an item should appear on the balance sheet. If a company running a number of hotels buys an additional hotel, that is clearly an extra fixed asset that would be shown on the balance sheet, and the amount shown would be the amount paid for it. If such a company pays for routine cleaning of a hotel, there is no additional asset, and the amount paid should not appear on the balance sheet as an additional asset. A payment for cleaning will reduce assets (cash) and also reduce equity. Routine redecoration, like cleaning, is an expense that does not appear on the balance sheet. Improvements, such as installing double glazing, an extension, or additional bathrooms, are 'capital expenditure': the amounts are added to fixed assets on the balance sheet. Sometimes the boundary between 'capital expenditure' (which appears on the balance sheet, and does not reduce equity) and 'revenue expenditure' (which does not appear on the balance sheet, and does reduce equity) is not clear and there may be scope for creative accounting.

Where there is a lack of clear principles to determine what should be included on a balance sheet, and the basis or valuation which is to be used for the various items, the value of balance sheets is restricted. A variety of official 'Financial Reporting Standards' has been produced to deal with this problem, and the development of financial accounting has steadily encouraged users to expect more from balance sheets. It is unrealistic to expect them to meet all of the different expectations that interested parties might have. But we cannot even begin to assess a company's financial position and performance without a good understanding of balance sheets.

Summary

A balance sheet shows the liabilities of a company, and solvency ratios can give an indication of whether a company is likely to become insolvent. Assets are not usually shown at their current value, and care is needed in using balance sheets as an indication of the value of a company. A business as a whole, as a going concern, is usually worth much more than the total of its net assets.

Review of Key Points

◆ A balance sheet shows what a company owns (assets) and what it owes (liabilities)

◆ By deducting liabilities from assets we arrive at the figure for 'equity', or 'capital', or 'net assets'

◆ Assets and liabilities are classified as being long term or short term, and in the UK are usually listed in the order fixed assets, current assets, current liabilities, long-term liabilities

◆ A successful business is usually worth more than the balance sheet figure for its net assets

◆ Balance sheets can indicate if a company has excessive liabilities

◆ Comparing this year's balance sheet with last year's can provide a basis for calculating profit

Self-testing Questions

1 Which of the following are shown on a balance sheet?
Assets; Expenses; Liabilities; Sales; Share Capital; Profit for the year

2 What is the difference between a fixed asset and a current asset?

3 Give examples of fixed assets. In what circumstances would some of the items you have listed be current assets?

4 Arrange the three main balance sheet items (Assets, Liabilities, Equity) as an equation.

5 A balance sheet appears to show what a business is worth. What are the main problems with this statement?

6 You are given the following simplified balance sheet of the Sandin Castle Company:

	£	£
Fixed assets		50,000
Current assets		
Stocks (at cost)	24,000	
Debtors	12,000	
Cash	9,000	
	45,000	
Creditors	22,000	23,000
		73,000
Share capital		50,000
Retained profits		23,000
		73,000

Self-testing Questions (continued)

(a) Calculate the current ratio.

(b) Calculate the liquidity ratio.

(c) The company sells stocks which had cost £4,000 for £8,000, which it immediately receives in cash. Show how the balance sheet would appear after this transaction.

(d) How does the above transaction affect the current ratio and the liquidity ratio?

7 You are given the following simplified balance sheets of the Windysand Company as at 31 December:

Simplified Balance Sheet of Windysand Company as at 31 December

	Year 1		Year 2	
	£	£	£	£
Fixed assets		320,000		350,000
Current assets	5,000		45,000	
Deduct: Creditors: amounts falling due within one year	(3,000)		(10,000)	35,000
		2,000		
		322,000		385,000
Deduct: Creditors: amounts falling due after more than one year		222,000		202,000
		100,000		183,000
Shareholders' funds		100,000		183,000

(a) How much profit does it at first seem that the company made during Year 2?

(b) How would your answer to (a) be affected if you found out that the company had paid £10,000 in dividends; that additional shares with a value of £20,000 had been issued; and that fixed assets had been revalued upwards by £30,000?

8 You are given the following simplified balance sheets of the Domer Castle Company and the Warmer Castle Company as at 31 December Year 1:

	Domer Castle		Warmer Castle	
Fixed assets	£	£	£	£
Tangible assets				
Freehold land and buildings (at cost)	300,000		100,000	
Furniture (at cost less depreciation)	4,000		80,000	
Vehicles (at cost less depreciation)	10,000		90,000	
	314,000		270,000	
Investments	–	314,000	44,000	314,000

Self-testing Questions (continued)

Current assets				
Stocks	8,000		19,000	
Debtors	12,000		10,000	
Cash and Bank	14,000		5,000	
	34,000		34,000	
Current liabilities				
Creditors				
	17,000		17,000	
Net current assets		17,000		17,000
Total assets less current liabilities		331,000		331,000
Creditors: amounts falling due after more than one year				
10% Debentures		100,000		200,000
		231,000		131,000
Capital and reserves				
Share capital		100,000		100,000
Retained profits		131,000		31,000
		231,000		131,000

During Year 1 the operating profit (earnings before interest and taxation[14]) of the Domer Castle Company amounted to £31,000. The operating profit of the Warmer Castle Company amounted to £32,000.

Which of the two companies appears to be financially weakest, and why? You should calculate the current ratio, the liquidity ratio, the capital gearing ratio, and the interest times cover.

9 You are given the following simplified balance sheet of the Stonefolk Company as at 31 March Year 4:

	£	£
Fixed assets		158,000
Current assets		
Stocks (at cost)	110,000	
Debtors	120,000	
Cash	20,000	
	250,000	
Creditors	120,000	130,000
		288,000
Share capital		250,000
Retained profits		38,000
		288,000

14 'EBIT' is a widely used measure. It is not always the same as operating profit.

Self-testing Questions (continued)

(a) The following transactions took place in April Year 4. Show how each would affect the balance sheet. (Each transaction must affect two or more figures, and the balance sheet must continue to balance.)

    (i) A building which had cost £80,000 was sold for £100,000 which was immediately received in cash.

    (ii) Stocks which had cost £30,000 were sold to Mr Spliff for £80,000. Mr Spliff agreed to pay for the goods by the end of May Year 4.

    (iii) The company paid £40,000 of the amount that it owed to creditors.

(b) Show how the balance sheet would appear after these transactions have been recorded.

Assessment Questions

1 What are the main functions of a balance sheet?

2 You are given the following simplified balance sheet of the Hackin Company as at 30 June Year 9:

	£	£
Fixed assets		250,000
Current assets		
Stocks (at cost)	60,000	
Debtors	40,000	
Cash	120,000	
	220,000	
Creditors	100,000	120,000
		370,000
Share capital		250,000
Retained profits		120,000
		370,000

(a) Calculate the company's current ratio and liquidity ratio.

(b) The following transactions take place during July Year 9:

    (i) New fixed assets are bought for £80,000, and payment is made in cash.

    (ii) Additional stocks of goods are bought for £15,000; it is agreed that they will be paid for in August.

Prepare a revised balance sheet after these transactions have been recorded.

(c) How do these transactions affect the current ratio and the liquidity ratio?

Assessment Questions (continued)

3 You are given the following simplified balance sheets of the Fourpine Company as at 31 December:

Simplified Balance Sheet of Fourpine Company as at 31 December

	Year 1		Year 2	
	£	£	£	£
Fixed assets		520,000		450,000
Current assets	45,000		55,000	
Deduct: Creditors: amounts falling due within one year	(30,000)		(35,000)	
		15,000		20,000
		535,000		470,000
Deduct: Creditors: amounts falling due after more than one year		200,000		100,000
		335,000		370,000
Shareholders' funds				
Share capital		300,000		310,000
		35,000		60,000
		335,000		370,000

(a) How much profit does it at first seem that the company made during Year 2?
(b) How would your answer to (a) be affected if you found out that the company had paid £25,000 in dividends?

4 You are given the following simplified balance sheets of the Port Andrew Company and the Port Edward Company as at 31 December Year 1:

	Port Andrew		Port Edward	
Fixed assets	£	£	£	£
Tangible assets				
Freehold land and buildings (at cost)	100,000		200,000	
Machinery (at cost less depreciation)	200,000		100,000	
Vehicles (at cost less depreciation)	100,000		100,000	
	400,000		400,000	
Investments	200,000	600,000	30,000	430,000
Current assets				
Stocks	70,000		40,000	
Debtors	50,000		90,000	
Cash and Bank	10,000		60,000	
	130,000		190,000	

Assessment Questions (continued)

Current liabilities		
Creditors	70,000	80,000
Net current assets	60,000	110,000
Total assets less current liabilities	660,000	540,000
Creditors: amounts falling due after more than one year		
10% Debentures	300,000	100,000
	360,000	440,000
Capital and reserves		
Share capital	300,000	300,000
Retained profits	60,000	140,000
	360,000	440,000

During Year 1 the operating profit of the Port Andrew Company amounted to £61,000. The operating profit of the Port Edward Company amounted to £40,000.

Which of the two companies appears to be financially weakest, and why? You should calculate the current ratio, the liquidity ratio, the capital gearing ratio, and the interest times cover.

5 You are given the following simplified balance sheet of the Whiting Company as at 31 August Year 6:

	£	£
Fixed assets		350,000 +10000
Current assets		
Stocks (at cost)	90,000	−50000
Debtors	80,000	−10000
Cash	30,000	+90000
	200,000	
Creditors	130,000	70,000
		420,000
Share capital		380,000
Retained profits		40,000 +40000
		420,000

(a) The following transactions took place in September Year 6. Show how each would affect the balance sheet. (Each transaction must affect two figures, and the balance sheet must continue to balance.)

(i) A new machine costing £10,000 was purchased and paid for in cash.

(ii) Stocks which had cost £50,000 were sold to Mrs Fish for £90,000 and paid for immediately in cash.

(iii) £30,000 was received from debtors.

(b) Show how the balance sheet would appear after these transactions have been recorded.

Group Activities and Discussion Questions

1 Each individual in the group should attempt to answer the question 'How much am I worth?' There is no need to disclose actual figures or personal information. The objective is to determine – and for members of the group to agree – the way in which the question would be answered. What principles or rules would you use?

2 Each member of the group should choose two listed companies, and obtain their published balance sheet (from the companies' websites; or by using the *Financial Times* Annual Reports Service). Try to assess how financially strong each company is (or is it likely to collapse?). The group should rank each of the companies that members have examined from the strongest financially, to the weakest. The group should discuss, and try to agree, criteria to form the basis for this assessment.

3 Is it possible to calculate the value of a company? If not, why not? If so, how?

4 Which of the following should be included as assets on a company's balance sheet: money which is owed to the company; the cost of an advertising campaign; machinery which is over 20 years old but which is still used occasionally; key employees who have a high market value; money paid as 'commission' to a government minister in Wayawayaland which has helped to secure a lucrative contract; brand names; profits that will be earned next year on a contract which was signed yesterday; machinery which the company does not own, but for which they have signed a 5-year lease.

References and Further Reading

Glynn, J., M. Murphy, J. Perrin and A. Abraham (2003) *Accounting for Managers*, 3rd edn, Thomson Learning.

Pendlebury, M. and R. Groves (2003) *Company Accounting: Analysis, Interpretation and Understanding*, 6th edn, Thomson Learning.

Wood, F. and A. Sangster (2002) *Business Accounting Volume 1*, 9th edn, Pearson Education.

www.tedbaker.co.uk (select: £, share info, investor relations)

2

The Profit and Loss Account
(The Income Statement)

Learning objectives

After studying this chapter you should be able to:

◆ Explain the structure and terminology of straightforward income statements

◆ Understand that there are different reasons for measuring profit, and different views of what profit is

◆ Describe the main categories of expenses

◆ Assess some possibilities for 'creative accounting' in measuring profit

◆ Discuss the role and limitations of income statements

The term 'profit and loss account' has been widely used for many years, but following international accounting standards the term 'income statement' is increasingly used instead.

Introduction

In Chapter 1 we saw that the amount of profit a company makes during a year can be calculated by comparing the balance sheet at the beginning of the year with the balance sheet at the end of the year. Some additional information may be needed, and it is not the easiest way of calculating profit. Income statements (or profit and loss accounts) provide more straightforward presentations of profit figures. But even a brief examination of the published income statement of a company shows a complex assortment of different profit figures, and it can be difficult to know where to start.

At first sight the notion of profit seems very straightforward. If you buy something for £6 and sell it for £10, you have made £4 profit. But accountants would say that this is 'gross profit', which is the first of the profit figures shown on an income statement. We need to deduct expenses before we arrive at operating profit, and more deductions and a variety of profit figures appear later.

To begin with, we need to be clear about (a) terminology, and (b) the usual formats for presenting the information. Most people are clear that they want to know the profit figures, but they are much less clear about exactly what profit means, and what the profit figures are to be used for. If we are clear about the function(s) of profit figures, we can then see what principles for measuring profit are appropriate.

2.1 **Terminology and Format**

Income statements show income for the year.[1] Profit and loss accounts show profit for the year. Unfortunately these are just different words for the same thing!

An income statement shows the calculation on the basis that expenses are deducted from revenues.

Revenues – Expenses = Profit

Revenues and turnover and even 'sales' are much the same thing, but unfortunately some people also use the term *income* as if it means the same. So we have to be careful. Sometimes the word income seems to mean profit. Sometimes it seems to mean revenues, or turnover. The word expenses and costs mean much the same thing, but payments (of cash) are quite different. It sometimes seems as if accounting terminology is designed to be confusing!

---

1   An income statement can be for a year, or a month, or any period you like. A balance sheet is never for a period – it is always 'as at' a particular date.

One thing we need to be very clear about is that the word 'receipts' is nothing to do with income or profit; it means receipts of cash. Similarly the word 'payments' is nothing to do with expenses or profit measurement; it means payments of cash. The differences between cash flow and profit are essential to an understanding of financial accounts. They are demonstrated in the Appendix to this book using numerical examples. The problem is also addressed in Chapter 7.

The format of an income statement shows profit in several stages. A more detailed study of income statements can show that there is almost no limit to the number of different profit figures that can be identified, and may be useful for different purposes. A simplified version shows four different profit figures, plus a fifth figure which is misleading and rather useless.

First, there is 'gross profit' which is the difference between the sales figure and *the cost of the goods which have been sold* – and that is a very important phrase.

Secondly, there is 'operating profit' which is arrived at after deducting the main categories of expenses, which are distribution costs and administrative expenses. Operating profit is an important figure: it shows how much profit has been made from the normal operations of the business before deducting any interest payable and adding such things as income from investments.

Thirdly, there is 'profit on ordinary activities before taxation', which is arrived at after various bits and pieces such as income from investments and interest receivable and interest payable.

Fourthly, there is 'profit on ordinary activities after taxation', which obviously comes after deducting the company's tax charge for the year.

Each of the above four versions of profit may be useful in assessing different aspects of a company's performance. The fourth figure shows profit available after taxation that is the basis for the amount of dividend to be paid. The dividend for the year is then deducted to show the amount of profit that has been retained in the business for the year. This fifth 'profit' figure gives no indication of what has been earned; it is a left-over figure, largely useless and misleading, and it should be avoided in most exercises interpreting financial statements.

Although company income statements can be almost infinitely complex, it is also possible to have versions that look relatively simple, as shown in Illustration 2.1.

Each of the different figures has its own uses, but the two shown in bold are, perhaps, the most important and useful in assessing a company's performance.

Extra care is needed with the last few figures on an income statement. For most purposes the amount of profit that happens to have been retained in

Illustration 2.1

Simple Company Ltd: Profit and Loss Account for the Year Ended 31 December Year 3

	£000
Turnover	100
Cost of sales	60
Gross profit	40
Distribution costs	(12)
Administration expenses	(9)
Operating profit	**19**
Interest payable	(3)
Profit before taxation	16
Tax on profit for year	(4)
Profit after tax for the year	**12**
Dividends paid and proposed	(5)
Retained profit for year	7

a particular year is of little consequence. How much profit was earned is very important; how much dividend was paid is of some importance. The relationship between profit earned and dividend paid is interesting. But the amount that happens to be left over may look important – it is the final figure – but it is of little significance, and should be ignored for most purposes. If you start trying to assess the performance of a company on the basis of how much profit they retained during the year, you know you are going seriously wrong. This is sometimes made even worse where companies choose to add the previous year's retained profits to this year's retained profits to produce a figure which is no more than a distraction.

After the final figures on the income statement itself the 'earnings per share' figure is shown. An income statement might show what looks like a healthy 50 per cent increase in profits, but this is not much use if the number of shares has doubled! Earnings per share is sometimes seen as being the most important figure in assessing company performance. Shareholders expect to see it increase year after year, and some companies even aim for 'double digit' growth in earnings per share – they want it to increase by at least 10 per cent each year. Not many companies manage to achieve this for more than a very few years.

2.2 Reasons for Measuring Profit

There are many good reasons for measuring profit. It is a symbol of success for companies and their managers. A company that shows steadily increasing profits is likely to go from strength to strength. A company that shows losses, or falling profits is likely to find itself in difficulties.

More specifically, the main reasons for measuring profit, or functions that profit measurement may serve, are as follows:

1 It is a measure of *performance*; shareholders want to know how well the directors and managers of a company are doing, running the company for the owners.

2 It is a guide to dividend policy. A company chooses how much profit is paid out as dividends. Occasionally a company pays out more dividends than it earns in profits, but it cannot do that for very long. A company must earn profits if it is to continue paying dividends.

3 Directors and managers may have a direct interest in such performance for their own reasons: they are often shareholders themselves, and they may have some sort of performance-related pay which means that they get extra salaries or bonuses if profits[2] achieve specified levels.

4 It is a measure of the *efficiency* of a company. Efficiency is about the relationship between inputs and outputs. To maximize efficiency is to minimize the cost per unit of output; or to maximize the outputs per £ of cost. For a company the inputs are shown as costs; outputs are shown as sales; the difference between sales and costs is shown as profit. Maximizing profits therefore maximizes efficiency.

5 It is a measure of the *effectiveness* of a company. Effectiveness is about the relationship between outputs and objectives. An effective organization (or individual) is one that achieves what it is intending to do. If we assume that companies intend to maximize profits,[3] then maximizing profits maximizes effectiveness.

6 It is a guide to the financial strength of a company. A company that is profitable is more likely to survive, and be able to pay its dues, than one which is loss making.

7 It is a basis for taxation. The government lays down various rules for taxation purposes (for example, what rate of depreciation or 'writing

---

2 Or they may be 'fat cats' who get good bonuses even when the company does badly. Or their bonuses may depend on the share price achieving a particular level. Or they may have share options which are valuable only when the share price achieves particular levels. As directors are supposed to be accountable to shareholders it is worth considering the effectiveness of accountability arrangements; these will be discussed later.

3 That is an oversimplification; maximizing 'profitability', or return on capital employed is more important.

down allowance' should be used), which means that the profit figure shown in a company's published accounts may be quite different from the figure used in calculating the amount of corporation tax payable.

8   It is relevant in pricing decisions. In most circumstances prices are determined more by what the market will bear, and the company has to find ways of keeping costs below the market price (and/or ways of pushing up what the market will bear). In some circumstances (for example, in public utilities which were previously publicly owned) there are official restrictions on price increases that are related to profits.

9   Employees have an interest in profits. They may believe that a profitable company is the best guarantee of long-term employment. They may also believe that good profits present an opportunity for pressing for increases in wages and salaries.

10 Profits are sometimes seen as being the key to a successful economy and a successful country. Companies that are most profitable find it easiest to raise capital, at lowest cost; and so resources in the country flow into the most profitable companies, which are also the most efficient and effective. Companies that are least profitable find it hardest to raise capital, have to pay more for it, and so the least efficient and effective companies tend to decline.

Some of the above may be questionable, or political, and you are, of course, free to take very different views. You may believe that profit is a measure of the success of the strong in exploiting the weak; that big business makes too much profit; that more should go to the workers; that profit fails to measure social costs; and all of the above ignores issues such as health and safety, child labour, damage to the environment, and non-sustainable development. You can, if you wish, take the view that profits are a 'bad thing'. It is probably a 'good thing' if this book encourages you to think about these issues!

It is, however, worth being explicit about the general assumptions that seem to lie behind the measuring and reporting of profit. Many different people and groups in society are likely to be in favour of companies making good and increasing profits for many different reasons. In some circumstances governments may try to restrict the amount of profit that monopolies (or near monopolies) are allowed to make. But increasing profits are generally favoured by shareholders, managers (and the Treasury who are usually happy to rake in more in taxation), and the company's bankers and professional advisers (whose fees seem to keep going up), the financial press, many employees, and anyone else who can jump on the gravy train.

There is enormous pressure on managers to perform, and to produce profits. And if they cannot, they are liable to be replaced by others, sometimes by managers who can produce profits out of thin air,[4] like magicians. There are always some who can make use of creative accounting techniques for their own advantage. But, like magicians, such managers do not want to be watched too closely, and the more successful ones move on rapidly to other companies to display their tricks and illusions.

Given that profit figures are likely to be used for many different purposes it is not surprising that there are different approaches to profit measurement.

2.3 What is Included as Revenues and Income

The income statement begins with the figure for turnover, which could also be called sales. It includes all of the sales that have been made during the period, not just of goods, but, depending on what kind of business it is, also of services, and it can include rents receivable. The turnover figure is shown net of such things as value added tax.

It includes all sales that have been made during a period, even if the money for those sales is not received until a later period. This principle is important. It means that a rapidly expanding business might be making very good sales each month, and good profits, but the amount owed by debtors will increase each month, and the cash that comes into the business lags behind the profits that are being earned. This could mean that a rapidly expanding and profitable business runs out of money.

It is also important because it is sometimes not clear exactly when a sale has been made. It could be that a sale is initially agreed by telephone; a few days later an order is received; then a few weeks later the goods are completed ready for dispatch; then, a few days later, the goods are received by the purchaser; then the seller sends out the invoice. Payment for the goods is probably not made for another month or two. There is a need for a clear accounting principle that determines the exact point, or the critical event, at which a sale is recognized. In practice, an accounting system usually recognizes a sale when the invoice is sent out. But it is easy to see that temptations can arise to recognize sales at an earlier date. When sales are below target, perhaps in the last month of the year, and a manager sees his bonus disappearing, or even his job disappearing, it is not difficult to create a few extra sales by bringing some forward, or sending invoices out early; they can be reversed the following month. It is a bit like a shop assistant

---

4 Such 'creative accounting' is examined more fully later in the course.

borrowing from the till, with the intention of paying back before the final reckoning comes: you can get away with it for a while, but eventually it will catch up on you. You can bring forward your revenues one year, but you cannot bring them forward more and more each year.

Other items of income are included in published income statements such as profits on sales of fixed assets, investment income, interest receivable, and any share of profits from associated companies.

2.4 What is Included as Expenses

There are more problems with defining and measuring expenses, and no shortage of accounting standards or principles attempting to deal with them. Expenses are recognized in accordance with the *accruals concept*, which means that it is not the amount of cash paid out during a period that is counted; it is the amount incurred in earning the revenue that is recognized during the period. This is also about *matching*, after recognizing the turnover for a period, we match against it those expenses that have been incurred in earning that turnover. This is particularly important with cost of sales and with depreciation.

Cost of Sales

The first expense on the profit and loss account is cost of sales, or cost of goods sold. This means that if you buy 100 items, but sell only 70 of them, only the 70 count in the cost of sales. The other 30 are 'closing stock' (stock remaining at the end of the period), and are carried forward to be treated as an expense in the following period (see Illustration 2.2).

As the calculation of gross profit (or any other profit) is dependent on the closing stock figure, the way in which this is determined is important. If Raj had made a mistake, and his closing stock figure was really £3,000, then his cost of sales would be only £8,000, and the gross profit would be £7,000. If his real closing stock figure was only £1,500, then his gross profit would be only £5,500.

If a higher closing stock figure is shown, then the profit figure will be higher, and the assets[5] and equity figures on the balance sheet will be higher. If a lower closing stock figure is shown, then the profit figure will be lower, and the assets and equity figures on the balance sheet will be lower. This has important consequences: if Raj overstated his closing stock figure by £1 million, his income statement and his balance sheet would look better by £1 million. Clearly we need some clear rules and principles

---

5   Closing stock is shown as a current asset on the balance sheet.

Illustration 2.2

At the beginning of March Raj's shop had stocks of goods amounting to £1,000. During March he bought goods for resale costing £10,000.[6] His sales figure for March was £15,000.

Raj therefore had £11,000 worth of goods available for sale. But that is not the cost of sales figure. Some of the goods he had available for sale were not sold, and we cannot calculate the cost of sales or the gross profit until we know the closing stock figure.

His stock of unsold goods at the end of March was £2,000.

The cost of the goods which he sold can now be calculated as follows:

Opening stock	£1,000
Purchases	£10,000
Cost of goods available for sale	£11,000
Deduct closing stock	£2,000
Cost of goods sold (or cost of sales)	£9,000

The cost of sales figure is then compared with the sales figure, and the difference, £6,000, is the gross profit.

for determining closing stock figures. The general rule is that stocks of goods are shown at cost price.[7]

In a retailing business it is relatively easy to establish the cost price of goods. In a manufacturing business it is more difficult because we need to establish the cost of manufacturing the goods, which involves some difficult decisions in allocating overheads.

The cost of sales figure includes only the costs of buying, or producing goods and services. It includes an appropriate share of production overheads, including the costs of running the factory or other production facilities (including rent, lighting, heating, depreciation and maintenance of machinery, and factory supervision costs). Cost of sales does not include the general administration costs of the business, or the selling and distribution costs.

Depreciation

Figures for depreciation are less obvious on the income statement; they may be included under several headings with the detail hidden away in the notes

---

6 That is what he bought during March. He probably did not pay for them until April. But receipts and payments of cash are quite distinct from profit measurement.

7 Or, more precisely, stocks are shown at the lower of cost and net realizable value. They should not be shown at selling price.

to the accounts. When a business buys a fixed asset, such as a piece of machinery, it is not immediately treated as an expense. The asset is shown on the balance sheet; the business decides how long the useful life of the asset is expected to be; and the figure is written down, or depreciated, each year. Depreciation is an expense in calculating profit which sounds straightforward enough. But it causes problems to students of accounting because:

(a) they often think that expenses are paid out in cash; but depreciation is not paid out in cash. The fixed asset has already been bought, and the cash has already flowed out. Depreciation is a bookkeeping entry, not a flow of cash. Profit is always calculated *after* charging depreciation. If we want to know what cash flow a business is generating, then we have to add depreciation back on to profit. Some people say that a business's cash flow is its profit plus depreciation, which is roughly right.[8] Some people say that depreciation is an inflow of cash, and that is completely wrong: depreciation is something that, in calculating profit, we treat as if it is paid out as cash (but it is not) so we add it back as if it is an inflow of cash (which it is not).

(b) they see depreciation as part of a process of valuing assets, which it is not. The objective is to write down the cost of a fixed asset, year by year, as the useful life of the fixed asset is being used up. Usually[9] this results in asset figures being shown on the balance sheet that are closer to current values, but that is incidental. The main point is to charge, as an expense in calculating profit, the amount of the fixed asset that has been used up.

(c) they think that a provision for depreciation is a pool of money that can be used to replace fixed assets when they come to the end of their lives. But there is no money in a provision (or in 'reserves'). If you want to know what money there is in a business you have to look in current assets. The provision for depreciation is a bookkeeping entry, not an allocation of cash. It reduces profits, and as companies usually relate dividend decisions to the level of profits, the fact that depreciation is charged may limit the amount of dividends paid out – a way of achieving 'capital maintenance'.

Even for sophisticated users of accounts there are problems with depreciation. Different companies have different depreciation policies, and we never really know how long a fixed asset will last, or how long we will keep it, or how much it will be sold for when we have finished with it. We might

---

8 But for more detail you should look at Cash Flow Statements.

9 But not always. Companies are expected to depreciate buildings as their effective lives are 'used up', even if they are increasing in value.

buy a car for £10,000, and *plan* to keep it for 4 years, and then to sell it for £2,000. But that might change; we might keep it much longer, or sell it much earlier; and the amount we sell it for might be much more, or less, than we planned.

The easiest approach to depreciation is to use the 'straight line' method. If we buy a car for £10,000, and plan to sell it for £2,000 after 4 years, then the total amount to be depreciated is £8,000, which works out at £2,000 a year for 4 years.

Slightly more complicated, but still reasonably popular, is the 'diminishing balance' method.[10] If we charged 33 per cent[11] per annum on this basis, the figures would be as follows:

Initial cost of car	£10,000
Year 1 Depreciation 33% of £10,000	3,300
Balance at end of Year 1	6,700
Year 2 Depreciation 33% of £6,667	2,211
Balance at end of Year 2	4,489
Year 3 Depreciation 33% of £4,489	1,481
Balance at end of Year 3	3,008
Year 4 Depreciation 33% of £ 3,008	993
Balance at end of Year 4	2,015

This method of depreciation results in higher depreciation in the early years, and lower depreciation in the later years.

Occasionally depreciation is calculated in more obscure ways. A vehicle could be depreciated in relation to the number of miles it does each year.

If a company suddenly changed its policy and planned to keep its vehicles (or ships, or aeroplanes, or machinery) for twice as long as they had previously planned, that could halve their depreciation charges, and produce a very significant increase in profits. Such a change in policy, and its financial effects, would have to be disclosed in a note to the financial statements. But there is inevitably some scope for individual judgement or manipulation as there is no certainty in the future lives, or residual values, of fixed assets.

Depreciation figures and policies should be disclosed fully in the notes to the financial statements, but they do not usually appear on the face of a published income statement. The three main categories of expense (cost of sales, distribution costs, administration expenses) may all include some depreciation as there may be fixed assets involved in producing the goods and services, in selling and distributing them, and in the administration of the business.

10   Also known as the reducing balance method.

11   The figure used is 33 per cent, not $33\frac{1}{3}$ per cent which would produce a different answer!

Amortization of Goodwill

When one company buys another business the amount of money they pay is partly for the net assets of the business, and partly for their 'goodwill', a term which covers a multitude of attributes of a business that enable it to earn profits. If a company buys a business with excellent prospects, they may pay a lot for 'goodwill', and the amount must be shown on the balance sheet as a fixed asset; and like any other fixed asset, it must be depreciated over its useful life. The term 'amortization' is used in relation to the depreciation of goodwill.

Goodwill and its amortization are controversial areas in accounting. The traditional view was that if goodwill is an asset, its value is dubious and it should be written off as soon as possible. A more current view is that, provided the business is well run, goodwill should last indefinitely, and there is no need to amortize it each year – especially as this can lead to massive reductions in reported profits. The official requirement is that goodwill should be depreciated, but it could be over a very long period.[12] Some subjectivity is inevitable, and the door is wide open for creative accounting. Regardless of the requirements of Financial Reporting Standards, many companies and investment analysts choose to emphasize profit figures which have not been charged with amortization of goodwill.

Classification and Disclosure of Expenses

A business can produce a profit and loss account showing as much detail as they wish – with separate figures for wages and salaries, repairs and maintenance, cleaning, rent and rates, lighting and heating, insurance, telephones, stationery, postage, newspapers, directors' fees, auditors' fees, lawyers' fees, and many other things. But the published accounts of companies are in standardized formats, as shown in Illustration 2.1 above, which group most expenses under the general headings 'Cost of sales', 'Distribution costs', and 'Administrative expenses'. The income statements (or profit and loss accounts) included in the published annual reports and accounts of companies probably look more complicated, but the basics are the same as shown in Illustration 2.1.

If you plough through the notes to the accounts, and the Directors' Report, you will find lots more detail of expenses, including wages and salaries, directors' remuneration, interest payable, costs of hiring plant and machinery, auditors' remuneration, depreciation and amortization, charitable and political donations. Other items disclosed include exceptional

---

12   Not usually more than 20 years, but companies can use a longer period if they carry out an annual impairment review to check that the value of goodwill is maintained.

items such as profits or losses on disposals, the results of discontinued operations, and of new acquisitions, and an analysis of results classified as different segments.

As long as an expense is clearly recognized as such, which heading it is included under may not be particularly important. The chief executive may spend part of his time dealing with production issues (arguably part of the cost of sales), part dealing with distribution issues, and part dealing with administration. But there is no need to bother with allocating the costs of employing him to these different headings, and it is acceptable to treat the whole cost as being administrative expenses. Gross profit ratios[13] may be important, but it is sometimes difficult to be clear about just which expenses have been included in cost of sales.

2.5 A Company's Published Income Statement

The profit and loss account for Ted Baker plc is shown in Illustration 2.3. It is called a 'consolidated' profit and loss account because it includes the results of subsidiary companies that the Ted Baker Company owns.

The main feature to note, from the shareholders' point of view, is that the 'Profit for the financial year' has increased from just over £6.5 million to nearly £6.6 million. This is a very small increase, particularly in the light of the substantial increase in shareholders' funds (from profits being retained – see Illustration 1.5). The company is expanding fairly rapidly: turnover has increased by 13 per cent. Shareholders must be hoping for a comparable increase in profits.

Relatively little detail about expenses is disclosed on the face of a published profit and loss account. More detail can be found in the notes to the accounts. The only categories of expenses shown, apart from interest payable are:

- ◆ Cost of sales

- ◆ Other operating expenses (including distribution costs and administrative expenses)

Each of these includes a whole range of expenses such as rent, rates, lighting, heating, stationery, telephones, maintenance, depreciation, salaries, wages, advertising and so on. The notes to the accounts show a few of these in detail.

---

13 Gross profit as a percentage of sales.

Illustration 2.3

FINANCIAL STATEMENTS		52 weeks ended 25 January 2003	52 weeks ended 26 January 2002

CONSOLIDATED PROFIT AND LOSS ACCOUNT

For the 52 weeks ended 25 January 2003	Notes	£'000	£'000
Turnover	2	70,188	62,095
Cost of sales	2	(28,252)	(27,166)
Gross profit	2	41,936	34,929
Other operating expenses (net) before impairment	3	(30,475)	(24,974)
Impairment of fixed assets	3	(1,551)	–
Other operating expenses (net)	3	(32,026)	(24,974)
Operating profit		9,910	9,955
Interest receivable		55	62
Interest payable		(480)	(581)
Profit on ordinary activities before taxation	2,4	9,485	9,436
Tax on profit on ordinary activities	7	(3,033)	(2,942)
Profit on ordinary activities after taxation		6,452	6,494
Minority interest – equity		104	21
Profit for the financial year	8	6,556	6,515
Dividends paid and proposed	9	(3,600)	(3,220)
Retained profit for the period	19	2,956	3,295
Earnings per share	10		
Basic earnings per share		15.9p	15.9p
Adjusted basic earnings per share		18.6p	16.5p
Diluted basic earnings per share		15.6p	15.5p

STATEMENT OF TOTAL RECOGNISED GAINS AND LOSSES

For the 52 weeks ended 25 January 2003	£'000	£'000
Profit on ordinary activities after taxation	6,452	6,494
Exchange rate movement	34	(1)
Prior year adjustment recognised in the 52 weeks ended 26 January 2002	–	(456)
Total recognised gains relating to the year	6,486	6,037

The accompanying notes are an integral part of this consolidated profit and loss account.

There are no differences between the Company's historical cost profit and that recorded in the profit and loss account (2002: £nil).

A statement of movements on reserves is given in note 19 to the financial statements. The profit for the current and prior period was entirely derived from continuing activities.

The gross profit ratio is calculated as follows

	2003	2002
	£000	£000
Turnover	70,188	62,095
Gross profit	41,936	34,929
Gross profit ratio	59.7%	56.3%

This seems fairly high, and has increased. It would be interesting to compare it with other clothing retailers.

Other operating expenses can be expressed as a percentage of sales. It is not difficult to see that these have increased substantially (from about £25 million to about £30 million) – much more than would be justified by the increase in sales. From the notes to the accounts other information about expenses, and some explanation of the increases, can be found.

2.6 Income Statement Detailed Items

Examining the published income statement of a company usually reveals more complexities than have been outlined so far.

Acquisitions, Discontinued Operations, Continuing Operations

Large companies often sell off parts of the business, and buy new businesses. If you want to assess the future performance of a business, it is not much use doing so on the basis of information that includes parts of the business that have been closed down or disposed of. If you want to assess the past performance of a business, it is not much use comparing last year's figures with this year's figures if there has been major acquisition; in that case we would expect to see a significant increase in this year's figures. To make meaningful comparisons we need to separate out the figures for new acquisitions from continuing operations, and we need to separate out the figure for operations that have been discontinued or disposed of.

Income statements provide the information under the three headings for sales and for operating profit.

Segmental Reporting

Many large companies combine together a number of different businesses, perhaps with very different products, or with very different geographical areas. International accounting standards (IAS 14) require companies to disclose their revenues, profits and capital employed for each major geographical and business segment. This can be very useful if you are trying to forecast a company's future performance and you believe that one area of business is going to perform better than another in the future. It can also be useful in assessing whether the management of one company has been as successful as others in dealing with areas of growth, and areas of decline.

Extraordinary and Exceptional Items

Companies used to like to hide away any nasty losses as 'extraordinary items' which did not affect their earnings per share figures. But extraordinary items have been virtually abolished, and, in the very unlikely event that there are any, they do affect the earnings per share figure. It may be best to quietly forget that they ever existed.

Exceptional items are really just ordinary items (such as selling a fixed asset at a loss) which are particularly large, and/or to which the company wishes to draw attention. Sometimes a company presents two earnings per share figures, one of which excludes the exceptional items. Investment analysts often accept this if the item really does seem to be exceptional.

2.7 Subjective Measurement and Creativity Problems

Creative accounting is an important subject in its own right, but even an introductory look at income statements reveals several areas where subjective judgements are required, and where there may be scope for creative accounting.

Capital Expenditure and Revenue Expenditure

Capital expenditure adds to the amount for fixed assets which are shown on the balance sheet; its effect on profit figures is delayed, and spread over a number of years as depreciation. Revenue expenditure is an immediate charge against profit. Buying a new car, premises, or machinery are capital expenditure. Maintaining them, and the costs of using them, are revenue expenditure.

If a company can make most of its 'repairs and maintenance' expenditure look more like improvements and additions to fixed assets, they can avoid charging them as expenses on the income statement, boost profits, and show higher asset figures on the balance sheet.

There are areas, such as research and development, where research-based companies can capitalize large amounts of development expenditure in this way. It is also possible, when constructing a fixed asset (perhaps building a new hotel) to treat interest payments on this as being capital expenditure rather than revenue expenditure.

Depreciation

There is inevitably scope for differences of view on the lives of fixed assets, likely values at the end of their lives, and in choosing what method of depreciation to use.

Stock Valuation

The value of stocks at the end of the year affects profits: if closing stocks are overstated, then profits and assets are overstated. Although the general rule is that stocks are shown at cost price (or net realisable value if it is lower), there may be some room for manoeuvre, especially when the company has itself manufactured the unsold stocks.

Timing

The rules on when sales should be recognized are not very clear and there is sometimes scope for bringing forward the recognition of sales, and so boosting the sales figure for the year.

2.8 Role and Limitations of Income Statements

The main role of the income statement is to set out the profit that a business has made during the period, and its component parts. The term 'profit and loss account' may still be preferred because it shows the profits and losses from the various activities undertaken by the company. There are many good reasons for measuring profit, as set out in Section 2.2 above.

The income statement also has a role in indicating how and where profits might be increased. Comparing this year's results with last year's is a useful monitoring exercise. Most businesses expect their sales figure to increase each year, with an increase in cost of sales and an increase in gross profit. But they hope also to at least maintain their operating margins: that gross profit as a proportion of sales will be maintained or increased. The same kind of analysis should be applied to the main categories of expenses. As sales increase, expenses might also be expected to increase. But management should be monitoring the various expenses as a proportion of sales, and trying to ensure that expenses, as a percentage of sales, do not increase. Sometimes, as a matter of policy, a business might decide to increase particular items of expense (spending more on marketing for example). But, more generally, a business should expect some economies of scale as it expands, and monitor the results to see if each category of expense really is declining as a proportion of sales.

The information shown in the income statement can be useful in comparing this year's results with last year's as part of the financial control.[14] It can also be useful comparing one company's results with another. Of course a large supermarket chain makes more profits than a small one; but detailed analysis of the income statement, looking at the various expenses as a proportion of sales, can show where one company is doing better than another, and where there is room for improvement.

In comparing one company with another we need to look carefully for explanations of difference in performance. One company might lease all of its premises and equipment while another owns them. One might have very old fixed assets, and so have very low depreciation charges, while another has much newer fixed assets. One company might be financed wholly by shareholders' funds, and so have no interest charges, while another is largely financed by borrowing (i.e. it has high gearing). There might also be different accounting policies, and where there is scope for 'creative accounting', it may be difficult to make meaningful comparisons between one company and another. One of the functions of International Accounting Standards is to aid comparisons between different companies, and different countries.

It is also important to realize that profits are not the same as cash flow. A company might do very well in selling equipment and civil engineering products to what the Americans call 'rogue states'; but there could be massive delays in receiving the money from these sales which rather takes the shine off the performance. Income statements should be interpreted together with cash flow statements. Indeed, the three principal financial accounting statements should be taken as a whole. Making profits is not enough. Profits need to be enough, when compared with the amount of money invested in the business, to justify that investment. Companies need to make a good return on capital employed, and assessing the performance of a company requires the use of figures both from the income statement and from the balance sheet.

Summary

A profit and loss account, also known as an income statement, shows the profit for a period, typically a year. Profit is based on the difference between

---

14 The exercise is usually also carried out comparing budgeted (or planned) income statements with the actual results.

sales (or turnover), and the costs incurred in earning those sales. Profit figures are useful in many different ways, and care is needed in interpreting the information. Profit is calculated after charging cost of sales (which requires a value to be put on closing stock), and depreciation; these are examples of expenses where there is an element of subjectivity.

Review of Key Points

◆ The profit and loss account (or income statement) shows the profit for a period by deducting from sales (and any other revenues) the costs incurred in earning those revenues

◆ It is useful to measure profit as an indication of a company's performance and as a basis for dividend decisions

◆ Profit figures are also useful to a range of different groups in society

◆ There is some subjectivity in profit measurement, for example in depreciation and in valuing closing stocks

◆ Profit figures are most useful in making comparisons

◆ Profit is different from cash flow

Self-testing Questions

1 What are the main differences between a balance sheet and an income statement?

2 What is an expense? How does an expense differ from an asset? Can an asset become an expense?

3 How is closing stock valued? Why does it matter? Would it be a good idea to show closing stocks at selling price?

4 Why is depreciation charged?

5 What is the difference between capital expenditure and revenue expenditure?

6 Which of the four (or five!) profit figures shown in a simplified income statement (Illustration 2.1) are shareholders likely to be most interested in, and why?

7 The Kingsdun Company buys a delivery van for £25,000, and a boring machine for £25,000. They decide that the delivery van should be depreciated at 25 per cent per annum on a diminishing balance basis, and that the boring machine should be depreciated at 10 per cent per annum on a straight line basis. Calculate the depreciation charge for each of the first four years of the assets' lives, and the net book value of each at the end of Year 4.

8 The Dargate Retailing Company sells a range of different products, some with modest gross profit margins, and some with much higher gross profit margins. For example, they buy Fargs for £100 each, apply a 25 per cent mark-up, and sell them for £125 each; the gross profit on Fargs is therefore 20 per cent (£25 gross profit is 20 per cent of the selling price). Employees

Self-testing Questions (continued)

often confuse percentage mark-ups with percentage gross profit. To avoid confusion you are asked to produce a definitive list showing the cost, mark-up percentage, selling price and gross profit percentage of each product by completing the gaps in the table below:

Product	Cost price	Mark-up	Selling price	Gross profit
	£	%	£	%
Fargs	100	25	125	20
Gargs	100	10		9.09
Hargs	50		100	
Jargs	40		80	
Kargs	80			$33\frac{1}{3}$
Largs		20	60	$16\frac{2}{3}$
Margs		30	40	
Nargs			50	10
Pargs	75			25

9 Banterbury Company Ltd:

Income Statement for the Year Ended 31 December

	Year 3	Year 4
	£000	£000
Turnover	100	120
Cost of sales	60	73
Gross profit	40	47
Distribution costs	(12)	(14)
Administration expenses	(9)	(12)
Operating profit	19	21
Interest payable	(3)	(3)
Profit before taxation	16	18
Tax on profit for year	(4)	(3)
Profit after tax for the year	12	15
Dividends paid and proposed	(5)	(6)
Retained profit for year	7	9

The Chairman of the company boasts that sales, profits and dividends are at record levels and that the amount of shareholders' funds in the business has increased to £300,000 at the end of Year 4.

Critically assess the performance of the company.

Assessment Questions

1 The Broadstores Company

Income Statement for the Year Ended 31 December

	Year 7	Year 8
	£000	£000
Turnover	200	220
Cost of sales	120	131
Gross profit	80	89
Distribution costs	(22)	(24)
Administration expenses	(40)	(41)
Operating profit	18	24
Interest payable	(10)	(18)
Profit before taxation	8	6
Tax on profit for year	(3)	(2)
Profit after tax for the year	5	4
Dividends paid and proposed	(4)	(0)
Retained profit for year	1	4

The chairman of the company states that the management of the company have performed well in a very difficult economic climate, and that increased profits have been retained within the business to finance profitable expansion.

A shareholder at the Annual General Meeting of the company claims that the reduction in profits, and the absence of dividends prove that the management of the company is a disaster.

Assess the evidence for each point of view.

3 The Billygate company operates with a 40 per cent mark-up on the goods that it buys, what is their gross profit ratio?

The Sillygate company operates with a 40 per cent gross profit margin, what percentage mark-up do they use?

4 Roger, a graduate of the University of South East England, has been running a business called 'SuperSoftService' since he completed his IT degree six years ago. He sells software and prides himself on providing fast delivery using his sports car, and he has an extensive stock of software, catering for the latest developments as well as meeting demand for software for old operating systems – he still can still supply most things for Windows 95 and makes the occasional sale of old software.

About half of his sales are on a cash basis, and about half are on credit. He sells on credit only to friends, graduates and people he knows, and has no experience of bad debts.

The business is very profitable, and is almost entirely financed by borrowing from his father. But his father is concerned that Roger keeps borrowing more and more money to keep the business afloat.

Assessment Questions (continued)

His profit and loss account for the year ended 31 December Year 6, and balance sheet as at that date are summarized below:

Sales		£100,000
Cost of goods sold		
Opening stock	60,000	
Purchases	40,000	
	100,000	
Less closing stock	80,000	20,000
Gross profit		80,000
Administration and distribution expenses		50,000
Net profit		30,000
Drawings for personal expenditure		29,000
Retained profit for year		1,000
Fixed assets		
Car at cost 1 January Year 1		18,000
Less provision for depreciation		9,000
		9,000
Current assets		
Stocks at cost	80,000	
Debtors	80,000	
	160,000	
Current liabilities		
Creditors	3,000	
Overdraft	3,000	6,000
		154,000
Loan from father		(150,000)
		13,000
Roger's capital		6,000
Retained profits		7,000
		13,000

(a) Comment on the financial position and performance of the business.

(b) How 'real' are the profits?

Group Activities and Discussion Questions

1 Profit figures are wanted by so many different groups of people for so many different purposes that it is not possible to define and measure profits in such a way as to meet all of those different needs. Discuss.

Group Activities and Discussion Questions (continued)

2 Attempt a definition of 'profit'. You can use other books. Can all members of the group agree on the definition? Is the definition clear and robust enough to provide a basis for measuring profits in all businesses? You could have a formal debate with two people arguing in favour of a particular definition of profit, and two arguing against that definition. Or two could argue that it is possible to produce a workable definition, and two arguing that it is not.

3 Last year a company's balance sheet showed freehold land and buildings at cost, the amount being £4 million. This year the properties have been revalued at £7 million. Is the company £3 million better off? Have they made £3 million profit?

4 Why do companies aim to earn profits? Should all organizations attempt to earn profits? If you think that some organizations should not attempt to earn profits, on what basis would you decide which organizations should earn profits, and which should not?

5 Do companies have too much freedom to determine the methods and rates of depreciation that they use for their published accounts? Where governments specify methods and rates of depreciation to be used to calculate profits for taxation purposes, should companies be required to use those same rates in their published accounts?

6 You are a shareholder in a listed company and are told that last year the company's net profit after tax increased from £100 million to £130 million, and that the management of the company are therefore performing extremely well.

   (a) What additional information would you want in order to assess the effectiveness of management? (Produce a list, and don't look at (b) until you have done that!)

   (b) Obtain the published annual report and accounts of a listed company. How much of what you wanted to know does it tell you?

7 Examine Ted Baker's results since 2003. Has the expansion of the company been successful in leading to a big enough increase in profits?

8 Compare the gross profit ratios of a number of different retailers. Are the differences very substantial? How do you explain or justify such differences?

References and Further Reading

Glynn, J., M. Murphy, J. Perrin and A. Abraham (2003) *Accounting for Managers*, 3rd edn, Thomson Learning.

Pendlebury, M. and R. Groves (2003) *Company Accounting: Analysis, Interpretation and Understanding*, 6th edn, Thomson Learning.

Wood, F. and A. Sangster (2002) *Business Accounting Volume 1*, 9th edn, Pearson Education.

www.tedbaker.co.uk (select: £, share info, investor relations)

3

The Context of Financial Accounting

Learning objectives

After studying this chapter you should be able to:

- ◆ Understand how financial accounting has been shaped by its historical development

- ◆ Explain the main influences on the historic and current development of accounting

- ◆ Discuss the idea of company objectives, how they are achieved, the measurement of how far they have been achieved

- ◆ Assess the role of financial accounting in making companies accountable

- ◆ Consider how financial accounting is likely to develop in the next few years

Introduction

It is easy to criticize financial accounting for failing to do whatever it is that you think that it is supposed to be doing. There seem to be endless financial scandals, companies (unexpectedly?) getting into financial difficulties, and cases where companies' financial statements are incredible or incomprehensible. And there are always accountants involved. It is a similar story with traffic jams, crime and football hooliganism: the police always seem to be around. But it is not the police who are to blame for all that goes wrong in society. It is their job to get involved and to try to sort things out. Similarly, accountants are not to blame for all company financial scandals; but they are usually involved in trying to sort them out.

But what is it that financial accounting is supposed to achieve? Why do things so often seem to go wrong? Whatever definitions of its 'objectives' are produced, financial accounting is usually found wanting. In part this is due to unrealistic expectations. Financial accounting cannot predict all financial scandals and corporate collapses;[1] it cannot prevent rogue directors from bending rules or being outright crooks; and it cannot show the 'true value' of a company, because that depends on future performance which no-one knows.[2] We have come to expect a lot from financial accounting, and, if we are to understand it as it operates today, we need to examine its origins: how it came about. We also need to understand which interest groups in society influence accounting, and how their power is exercised. Accounting emerged and developed over hundreds of years in response to the needs of business and the pressures of various interest groups.

3.1 **Historical Development**

Financial accounting as it exists today was not designed by anyone, or any group of people, to meet any specific objectives. It has evolved over hundreds of years, mainly to meet the needs of various businesses. We cannot understand accounting as it exists by reading the official pronouncements of the Accounting Standards Board and then deciding what 'improvements' are needed for it to meet a particular set of objectives today. It is important to understand that accounting has evolved in response to the needs and objectives of a range of different interest groups, and will probably continue to do so.

---

1   Although it can, and does, provide lots of evidence which can help to predict such events – if investors and others could be bothered to try to understand it, and/or stop believing that things which go up will continue to go up!

2   No-one – not even the so-called experts!

Financial accounting has developed from double entry bookkeeping which was first described by Luca Pacioli, a Franciscan monk/friar in Italy in 1494. He did not invent the system – nobody did. It emerged naturally from the practices of international traders, particularly in medieval Italy, who needed to keep records of their cash, sales, expenses, debtors, creditors and so on. They kept accounts of their various ventures, such as voyages or consignments of spices. The priority was record keeping; the idea of annual financial reports came much later.

Business in medieval Italy was international and relatively complex. There were voyages around Europe and to the East. There were partnerships, many of which were short term for a particular voyage or venture. Much of the business was done on credit. It was essential to keep records not just of cash, but of debtors, creditors and other assets and liabilities. The results of particular ventures also needed to be worked out: what revenues it generated, what expenses were incurred and, when it came to an end, who owed how much and to whom. Almost everything that double entry bookkeeping required was recorded anyway. It became a matter of convenience to complete the double entry. Every transaction was recorded twice: once as a debit, and once as a credit. The total of debits could then be compared with the total of credits to see if it balanced, and to find errors.

The British did not take kindly to the new Italian system of double entry bookkeeping, and the old English systems ('charge and discharge') and single entry bookkeeping, continued declining for several hundred years. But the 'Italian System' spread steadily from Italy; Pacioli's book was translated into English and Dutch early in the eighteenth century; it became a standard system throughout the business world. Its main functions were to record transactions and to keep a record of who owed what and to whom. Accuracy was its most important attribute.

Bookkeeping was, of course, originally done in books or ledgers, and books eventually become full. When the book is full, it is necessary to transfer all of the balances which still matter to a new book. Everything that was to go into the new book would be summarized on a 'balance sheet'. Old balances that were finished with were written off to a 'profit and loss account' which showed all of the profits and losses on the various activities that had been undertaken. At first, balance sheets and profit and loss accounts were produced only when necessary: when the book was full. By the end of the eighteenth century, it had become normal to produce these statements annually, and managers and others were starting to see accounting as being more than mere record keeping; it could provide useful statements.

Following the industrial revolution, the nineteenth century saw the next major development of financial accounting with the establishment of companies. The cost of financing major industrial enterprises and railways required more capital than individuals and their partners[3] could provide. It was necessary to find a larger number of investors, and partnership was not the best way of attracting investors. All partners are liable for the debts of the business, and a partner could lose everything if the business went wrong. Individuals who had modest sums to invest, and who knew little about the business or the people running it, would want to be sure that their potential liability (the maximum amount that they could lose) was limited to the amount that they had invested.

The vehicle for more substantial investment became the limited liability company. Investors' potential liability was limited to the amount that they had invested in the company, and they could be relatively passive investors. But they needed to be able to trust the company's directors to take proper care of their money: directors had 'stewardship' responsibilities for shareholders' funds. This had several important consequences:

1 Company shareholders had annual general meetings and the annual report and accounts became the major vehicle by which directors were accountable to shareholders. Management and directors became separated from ownership (with large companies), and there was a need for directors to be accountable to shareholders.

2 Shareholders wanted to see what had happened to the money that they had invested, and the balance sheet was the easiest way of showing this. On one side the capital that shareholders had invested was shown; on the other side were shown the assets in which it had been invested – perhaps a railway line from London to Warmington-on-Sea. In a successful company the assets side would steadily increase, and the increase in net assets was reflected on the other side of the balance sheet as 'reserves', which became part of shareholders' funds.

3 The establishment of companies with 'limited liability' made the position of creditors less secure. When creditors are owed money by an unincorporated business (a sole trader or partnership) with unlimited liability, if the business does not pay them what is due, they can, when all else fails, recover the amounts from the personal assets of the proprietors. With small businesses, banks are often keen to secure any loans on the private property (particularly houses) of the proprietors. With companies there is no recourse to the private assets of the directors or shareholders. Limited liability may be seen as a privilege which government

---

3 Even their 'sleeping partners'. It was common for an older partner to more or less retire from a partnership, but to leave his money invested, and to get an income, without taking an active part in the business. Young and thrusting entrepreneurs would be happy to have an older partner who could finance them, and provide experience and contacts, while being essentially passive.

legislation has established, and creditors have to accept if they want to do business with companies. In return for that privilege, companies' financial information is opened up to the public: annual reports and accounts are deposited at Companies House for all to see.

4 Shareholders also wanted the company to do well and to pay an annual dividend. Directors could easily find the money to pay a dividend to shareholders – perhaps by borrowing,[4] or issuing more share capital. But dividends should come out of profits, not from share capital, and this is a basic principle of accounting. By today's standards it would be a fairly unsophisticated[5] fraud to pretend that a company is making profits, and to pay dividends simply by raising more share capital. As long as new shareholders can be conned into investing in a company that appears to be doing well, the company could keep going. But companies are not allowed to pay dividends out of capital, and the principle of 'capital maintenance' is central to modern accountancy.

5 If capital is to be 'maintained' before any dividends can be paid, that is not a problem for a railway company. Most of their capital was invested in the railway line; the railway line had to be maintained; and a railway line can be assumed to last for ever – if it is properly maintained. But some fixed assets have only a limited life, and a company cannot be said to have made a profit unless provision is made for depreciation of fixed assets. Thus it became necessary to charge depreciation as an expense, and to separate capital expenditure (which adds to fixed assets) from revenue expenditure (which reduces profits) in order to determine profits; this is to help to assure investors that dividends were paid out of profits, not out of capital.

6 Another important consequence of the development of companies is that financial accounting practices came to be based on new company laws, and company laws came to reflect accounting practice: they were intended to reflect the better accounting practices of the day, not the worst! From time to time various financial and accounting scandals arise, and governments need to be seen to respond to these in various ways, such as setting up committees of inquiry and developing proposals for more rigorous company laws and more effective implementation and enforcement.

---

4 Many still do.

5 It is at least worth asking the question: are some companies today (in a much more sophisticated way) paying dividends and appearing to be successful, although the company does not seem to be generating sufficient 'real' profits and cash flows to justify the dividends?

7 Following the development of companies, and increases in their accounting requirements[6] there was lots more work for 'accountants' to do, and professional accountancy bodies were established to add to the credibility of accountants, and to represent their interests. Although governments took responsibility for revising company law, the professional accountancy bodies increasingly came to be seen as the 'experts', and in many ways governments left regulation of accountancy to the professional bodies.

In the second half of the nineteenth century governments had a 'laissez faire' attitude to businesses and accountancy: let them get on with it in their own way. By about 1900 governments started to (and continue to) take a more active role in the development of accountancy. But changes in accounting practice are not the result of any single dominant person or force. They result from the interplay of a range of interested parties, including accountants and auditors; bankers and creditors; companies and their directors; governments and the law; the standard setters; academics and theorists; investors and stock markets.

3.2 **Accountants and Auditors**

The status of a profession seems to depend partly on its antiquity, and in this respect accountants are way behind doctors, priests and lawyers. The first professional accountancy body in the world was established in Scotland (1854) with England and Wales, Canada, Australia, the USA, Ireland, New Zealand and the Netherlands following by 1895. The early development of professional accountancy bodies in these countries is associated with a distinctive development of accountancy which differs from most of continental Europe. Sweden was the first of the other European countries to develop an accountancy profession; Germany and France came much later.

Another peculiar feature of the UK accountancy profession is that it has far more members[7] (per head of the population) than any other country. In the 1980s, predictions were made that, if present tendencies continued, by the middle of the twenty-first century every man, woman and child in the UK would be an accountant! There are a number of possible explanations for the UK having so many accountants. UK accountants are not just auditors.

---

6 And increases in the amount of work available in dealing with liquidations and bankruptcies.

7 Members of professional accountancy bodies. Anyone can call themselves an accountant. But you have to be a member of one of the professional bodies to be a 'chartered accountant'.

We include as 'accountants' members of professional accountancy bodies who are engaged in a wide range of different financial and management positions. Professional accountancy qualifications are also highly regarded. As criticisms of some educational standards has increased, the respect for tough professional examinations has been further strengthened.

Fifty years ago accountants were not a particularly impressive bunch and were relatively poorly educated. Equipped with just a few GCE 'O' levels they would pay to become articled to a chartered accountant, and study for their modest examinations by correspondence course. But other managers were even less impressive, typically having no professional training, limited numerical ability, and little knowledge or understanding of accountancy. Accountants of reasonable ability soon gained promotions and senior management positions. In the last 20 years or so the calibre of accountants has increased substantially. The large professional firms require a very high standard in the trainees they recruit. Personality is important, and most recruits have good A levels, and a good degree from a good university. Those who also manage to pass the tough professional accountancy examinations and get into senior positions with major professional firms are generally people of formidable ability.

Professional accountancy firms have become important and powerful organizations, not least because of their size, ability and economic resources. Power also lies in the professional accountancy bodies

Illustration 3.1

Firm	Number of UK offices	Fee income 2002–3 £million	Audit/accounting fees	Tax fees	Insolvency fees
PriceWaterhouseCoopers	36	2,304			
Deloitte & Touche	23	1,245	358	365	199
KPMG	22	1,018	422	265	82
Ernst & Young	20	754	298	283	
Grant Thornton	36	216	66	69	42
BDO Stoy Hayward	30	194	96	52	21
Baker Tilly	32	157	74	52	20
PKF	28	107	46	26	11
Smith & Williamson	11	100	16	21	9
Tenon Group plc	28	92	48	6	16
Moore Stephens	24	77	47	15	8
RSM Robson Rhodes	9	67	24	13	11

Source: *Accountancy Age*, 26 June 2003. Detailed figures for PriceWaterhouseCoopers are not available. Separate figures for consultancy, corporate finance and 'other' have been excluded. Some large firms have disposed of their consultancy activities

Illustration 3.2

	Expectation	More realistic
1	The financial statements are prepared by the auditors; the auditors agree with everything in them and are responsible for them	The directors are responsible for preparing the financial statements. Auditors agree only that they represent one of perhaps several possible 'true and fair' views
2	The financial statements are correct and accurate; a different auditor would produce the same financial statements from the same basic information	The auditors do not prepare the financial statements, and as there are many areas requiring judgement, different accountants would probably come to different conclusions (e.g. on rates of depreciation; or the appropriate provision for bad debts). The decisions belong to the directors
3	The financial statements show what a company is worth; assets have been properly valued	Most assets are shown at some variation of historic cost. Even if they were shown at some sort of current value, the value of the business as a whole would almost certainly be very different from the value of the separable assets less liabilities
4	The auditors have checked and ascertained that no significant fraud or irregularities have taken place	The auditors are on the look-out for fraud, but they are not responsible for finding it all. And even if they find some, provided it is not too enormous, they will still say that the financial statements show a true and fair view
5	The business is a going concern and is not likely to collapse or fail in the foreseeable future	The auditors check to see if there are any doubts about the business being a going concern, and report accordingly. But there can be no guarantee that it will not collapse in the near future
6	The management of the company are reputable, competent, efficient and effective	Auditors are usually happy to take fees from even the most hopeless managers and are not likely to disclose any incompetence!
7	The audit report draws attention to any doubts about the company's finances	If there are doubts about the company's immediate financial survival, the auditors should comment
8	Auditors are independent and cannot be got rid of by directors	In theory auditors have great security and independence. But directors can easily put an audit out to tender, and replace existing auditors.
9	Auditors are controlled and disciplined by a professional body which clearly specifies what is required of them	This is a reasonable expectation
10	Auditors are more concerned with their duty to the public and their reputation than with maximizing their own remuneration	This is more a matter of opinion!

themselves[8] – various organizations where accountants have effective representation (such as the Accounting Standards Board and the International Accounting Standards Board). The large professional accountancy firms are powerful – and on a worldwide basis. Illustration 3.1 shows that there are only three or four major players (and they do the audits of the vast majority of listed companies in the UK). Their resources and skills are enormous and their ways of seeing and operating in the worlds of business, accounting and finance tend to predominate.

The power, prestige and status of professional accountants should not be underestimated. Governments and regulatory bodies that try to 'interfere' in the sphere of professional accountants are likely to find themselves up against very tough opponents who can run rings around them and argue them into a corner. It may be that professional accountants act mainly in the interest of the public – to ensure true and fair financial reporting, the proper operation of capital markets, and so the efficient allocation of resources in society. But, sometimes, it may be that the self-interest of accountants predominates.

In spite of the strength and prestige of many large firms of auditors, and their professional bodies, there are also many examples of disappointment with auditors. Every time a company gets into financial difficulties, or there is a fraud or a scandal, the auditors seem to come in for criticism. Many have unrealistic expectations of what auditors could or should do. Some of these 'expectations' are listed in Illustration 3.2, together with comments indicating what would be a more realistic expectation.

Some of these issues are explored more fully in Chapter 8.

3.3 **Bankers and Creditors**

Although financial statements are said to have many different 'users', including employees, customers and competitors, the two most important groups are shareholders and creditors.

It is usual to make a distinction between short-term creditors (trade creditors who supply goods and services; overdrafts), and long-term creditors (loans and debentures). Both have a similar interest: will they get their money back when they are supposed to?

8 The Institute of Chartered Accountants in England and Wales (ICAEW); the Institute of Chartered Accountants of Scotland (ICAS); the Institute of Chartered Accountants of Ireland (ICAI); the Chartered Association of Certified Accountants (ACCA); the Chartered Institute of Management Accountants (CIMA); and the Chartered Institute of Public Finance and Accountancy (CIPFA).

Ideally, what creditors want to see is a business with lots of valuable assets, very few liabilities, and one which generates lots of 'free cash flow'[9] with which to make necessary repayments. In Illustration 3.3, the Dodge Company has lots more assets and lots more equity than the Wadge Company, but it also has lots more liabilities. The Wadge Company looks safer from the point of view of creditors. We can express liabilities as a percentage[10] of net assets. In the Dodge Company 65 per cent of net assets are financed by liabilities; in the Wadge Company only 30 per cent of net assets are financed by liabilities. It may seem unlikely, but if the companies get into financial difficulties, and the assets are difficult to sell (or if they have been overvalued), there might not be enough funds in the Dodge Company to pay all of the creditors. If the net assets could realize only 60 per cent of their book value (£1,200,000), the creditors could not be paid in full, and there would be nothing left for the shareholders. In the Wadge Company, if net assets realized only 60 per cent of their book value (£540,000), the creditors could be paid in full, and there would be a decent amount left over for the shareholders.

This leads to an interesting question: how reliable are asset values as shown on the balance sheet? When a business gets into difficulty any forced sale of assets is likely to result in low prices. Creditors want to know that the assets are really worth *at least as much* as the balance sheet shows. That is their security. They have an interest in *prudent* asset values. This is true of all creditors, and banks are important in this respect. Conservatism, or prudence, was for long a fundamental concept of financial accounting, particularly in much of Europe where banks have been more important sources of finance for businesses than stock markets. In the UK and similar countries,

Illustration 3.3		
	Dodge Company	Wadge Company
	£000	£000
Net assets	2,000	900
Liabilities	1,300	270
Equity	700	630

9   This is explained in Chapter 7.

10   This is comparable with calculating a gearing ratio. But gearing ratios usually exclude short-term liabilities from debt. If you want a simple life, you could just learn a standard set of ratios to interpret financial statements. But life is not simple! When interpreting financial statements, you need to be clear exactly what question you are asking, and then select data that answers the question most directly.

conservatism has now been de-emphasized. The basis of accounting is moving away from giving priority to the information needs of creditors; the equity investors' view is becoming dominant.

3.4 Companies and their Directors

Accountancy has evolved mainly to meet the needs of businesses; companies have become the dominant form of business organization; accountancy has therefore developed mainly to meet the needs of companies. We could say that financial accounting exists mainly to meet the needs of companies; or of shareholders; or of company directors. We could say that it exists primarily to serve the needs of companies. Unfortunately the words 'company', 'shareholders', and 'directors' are sometimes used as if they mean the same thing. Each should be considered separately.

Objectives of Companies

If accountancy is to serve the needs of companies, we need to be clear what the objectives of companies are – if companies can have objectives. A company is an organization of different individuals, each with their own particular aims, interests, powers and priorities. The directors are the most powerful, but employees, shareholders and others also affect what a company does. Companies succeed in operating cohesively by maintaining the myth that they all have an interest in achieving objectives such as those considered below.

1 Survival; avoiding going bankrupt or into liquidation, or being taken over by a 'predator' – another company which intends to close down the business. Financial accounts can show if a company appears to have excessive liabilities and if it is generating sufficient cash flows to meet its obligations.

2 Maximizing profits. It is often assumed that this is the primary objective of companies. But the *amount* of profit a company makes is much less important than their return on capital employed, or their *profitability*. If a company increases its profits from £10 million to £12 million, the increase in profits of £2 million might at first seem impressive. But if, at the same time, the company's capital employed has increased from £100 million to £140 million, the return on capital employed has fallen.[11] It is easy to make lots of profits if there is lots of capital employed to play around with.

---

11 It falls from 10 per cent to 8.6 per cent.

3 Maximizing profitability, or return on capital employed is a better objective in terms of improving performance. If profits increase from £10 million to £12 million, and at the same time capital employed is reduced from £100 million to £90 million, that is a much better result.[12] The test of good management is whether they can increase profits by a bigger proportion than any increase in capital employed.

4 Growth often seems to be the objective of companies. Many act as if increases in sales will, in due course, be followed by increases in profits. But there are too many examples of companies that succeed in increasing turnover at too high a cost. In reading Chairman's Statements it is worth looking to see if they are too keen on pursuing growth – at the expense of the 'bottom line' (profit). It is also worth looking to see if increases in sales are matched by increases in profits. With new ventures it often takes a while for profits to build up; but it is not hard to find examples of companies where profits never catch up.

5 Dominating an industry. Some companies take pride in being the biggest operator in a particular industry. Tesco dominates the supermarket industry; Asda has overtaken Sainsbury, and so it goes on. If a company can become the dominant force in a particular industry it is in a more powerful position to make profits; it also appeals to the vanity of chairpersons and directors.

6 Meeting the needs of customers. Few companies claim to be interested only in making as much profit as possible (even if they are!), and claim to be doing all sorts of good for society, employees, customers, the environment, disabled people, and anything else that puts them in a good light. We may each have our own opinions regarding the ways in which companies present themselves. It seems likely that, to be successful and to continue in business, companies do have to meet the needs of customers. If they are to continue to do this, they also need to survive financially.

7 'Satisficing', or balancing the needs of different interest groups around the company. A company cannot fully meet everyone's objectives. Customers might want better products at a cheaper price. Employees might want higher wages and salaries for working fewer hours. Suppliers might want to charge higher prices and be paid more quickly. Shareholders might want as much dividend income as possible. And the directors might want increases in their fees and fringe benefits. A company cannot give everyone what they want. They have to find some sort of balance that 'satisfices' all of the different demands.

---

12   £12 million as a percentage of £90 million is $13\frac{1}{3}$ per cent.

8 Maximizing shareholder wealth. This is usually assumed to be the objective of financial management. Shareholders' wealth comes from two (related) sources: dividends, and the share price.

Maximizing Shareholders' Wealth

At first sight the idea of maximizing shareholders' wealth seems fairly straightforward. If a company maximizes profitability, then it is in a position to maximize dividends payable to shareholders, and it is a reasonable expectation that the share price would be maximized. But, unfortunately, life is not so simple. We can never be sure exactly what determines share prices,[13] but companies appear to act as if they can influence share price in ways other than maximizing profitability.

1 Listed companies tend to have Shareholder Relations Departments, which may be seen as companies' 'spin doctors'. Careful presentation can make a company's record and prospects look better than the statements that a boring accountant would produce. Companies that tell a good story are likely to have more highly rated shares than those which have a good story to tell, but which give insufficient attention to the telling, the presentation, and to 'spinning'. Sometimes when companies believe that their shares are under-rated they launch a 'charm offensive': making presentations to institutional shareholders in the hope of improving the performance of their shares.

2 Much rests on the reputation of management: management must appear to be in control, to know what they are doing, to have sensible plans, and to be able to implement them and achieve the results that investors have been led to expect. A company that announces that it expects profits to increase by 5 per cent in the coming year, and then, 12 months later, finds that they have increased by 30 per cent does not look very credible. An unexpectedly good year could easily be followed by an unexpectedly bad year – and the share price is likely to suffer.

   If management announce a reorganization programme that will lead to a 2 per cent reduction in profits in the coming year, followed by a 6 per cent increase the following year, then 'double digit' growth thereafter, the share price is not likely to suffer – as long as they maintain credibility and deliver what they have said.

3 In real life, profits do not always increase in line with management expectations, and there is a temptation to indulge in some form of

---

13 A company's share price is determined by the interplay of supply and demand for the company's shares on the stock market. The difficulty is knowing what determines the supply and demand; what influences investors, when, and why.

'creative accounting'[14] to give the impression that they do. The idea of 'income smoothing', if it can be pursued with credibility, is likely to benefit the share price. Investors seem to like to see a pattern of steadily increasing profits every year. If management can succeed in hiding away some of the profits in the good years (the idea of 'secret reserves' used to be popular), they can boost profits in the lean years and maintain the image of steadily increasing profits.

4   Jumping on bandwagons may also be seen as a good way of maximizing shareholder wealth – at least in the short term. In the 1990s, when share prices were booming (a 'bull' market), companies had to be seen to be involved in e-business if they were not going to lose out. Some companies sought re-classification from boring, under-rated sectors into more highly rated sectors. A glance at the *Financial Times*[15] indicates which sectors are most highly rated at a given time. The P/E ratio shows how expensive shares are in relation to profits. Even after the decline in TMT[16] shares, Information Technology, Media and Entertainment, and Telecommunications were still among the highest rated sectors in autumn 2003.

5   Much emphasis is given to maximizing earnings per share, and, obviously, increasing profitability helps with this a lot. But if a company is struggling to make good profits, arithmetically there is a simple solution to increasing earnings share: reduce the number of shares. Companies can buy their own shares on the stock market and cancel them. Reducing share capital is also a way of increasing return on capital employed. A company needs to have the money to be able to buy a significant number of shares. Sometimes this seems to be the best use of surplus funds – more effective (in maximizing shareholders' wealth) than increasing dividends.

6   One way of finding the money for the company to buy its own shares is to borrow; or to have a sale and leaseback[17] arrangement on its properties. Such arrangements are fairly common practice among large retailers.

7   Companies also use dividend policy[18] to try to influence share price. If a company has a record of steadily increasing dividends, not marred by short-term fluctuations, it is likely to be beneficial to their share price.

---

14   Creative accounting is explored in Chapter 8.

15   FT Actuaries Share Indices UK Series.

16   Technology Media Telecommunications.

17   Explained more fully in Chapter 12.

18   Explained more fully in Chapter 12.

8 Careful use of gearing[19] is also often seen as having an effect on share price. Modest use of borrowing, when profits are steadily increasing, can 'gear up' the return earned for ordinary shareholders. But excessive borrowing can make a company look too risky, and have an adverse effect on share price.

Whatever we think that companies are doing, or attempting, financial accounting can help them to achieve their objectives. It also indicates to shareholders and other interested parties how successful or otherwise the company has been in achieving many of those objectives. Most shareholders may care more about the share price than they do about the financial accounts. Financial accounts do not explain fully what happens to share prices, but they are an essential part of the story.

Accountability

The directors of companies are supposed to be accountable to the shareholders who own the company, and they are required to give an annual account of their activities. They are free to embellish these accounts with whatever additional information they wish, which they often do to show themselves in a more favourable light. In some ways they are like politicians seeking re-election, and a company's annual report and accounts may be seen as being their election address. But politicians somehow manage to avoid most of the really difficult areas of their performance, and to include only the most favourable aspects of their performance (with some loss of credibility as a result). It is harder for directors to avoid the difficult questions because there are very specific disclosure requirements, and the share price is there for all to see; and the arrangements for the accountability of directors are more thorough than they are for politicians.

Companies Acts lay down the information that a company has to disclose each year in its annual report and accounts, and these requirements are generally effective. In addition, 'accounting standards'[20] specify additional disclosures, although these are not always meticulously followed. The information that is disclosed also has to be audited – directors cannot just make it up, as politicians sometimes seem to! It is also made public: the annual reports have to be filed at Companies House for all to see; and they are very easy to see using the Companies House website.[21]

---

19 Explained more fully in Chapter 12.

20 Now Financial Reporting Standards, and International Financial Reporting Standards.

21 For a small fee. Most large companies have their own websites and the annual reports can be accessed free of charge.

But if shareholders do not like what they read, their options are limited. How many shareholders really read the annual report and accounts is not clear, but they usually know about their company's performance, especially the share price. If the company is doing badly, the annual report and accounts usually provide plenty of information to demonstrate why this is the case, and perhaps even to show how the directors are to blame.[22] But it is the directors who have produced the annual report, and who are responsible for the contents. They have usually made sure that, in addition to the information that is required by law, there is also plenty of information intended to demonstrate what a good job they have done, and to justify their re-election.

It is not easy to get rid of directors. Contested elections are almost unknown; directors are usually re-elected unopposed. Directors usually have some shares themselves; many shareholders sign proxies to allow directors to vote on their behalf; and financial institutions, who have enormous potential voting power, tend either to support directors or to avoid being involved at all. Sometimes institutions do take an active role in changing the management of a company: that usually spells trouble for the existing chairperson and chief executive! But sometimes company directors (Unilever in 2003) complain that institutional investors are too inactive.

The *Financial Times* (6 August 2003) reported that:

> Unilever has turned the corporate governance debate on its head by asking 10 of its major shareholders to account for their failure to register their votes at the last annual general meeting.
>
> The Anglo-Dutch group's unorthodox questioning of its own shareholders will add to the pressure on institutional investors to be more active custodians of their clients' money.

This was immediately after Unilever had reported disappointing half year results. Their 'Path to Growth' plan, concentrating on their strongest brands, had resulted in a fall in sales, profits and share price. This would seem to be a good time to be glad that institutional shareholders are keeping quiet. But perhaps attack is the best form of defence!

Shareholders have little chance of carrying a resolution against the wishes of the directors at an annual general meeting; and even if they do, directors can just ignore it. If shareholders find that the performance of their company is unsatisfactory there is not usually much they can do other than bail out, and sell their shares. The trouble is that when it becomes clear that a company is doing badly, the share price has already fallen; if many

---

22 Try finding an example of directors admitting that they are to blame for poor results. Directors usually take credit for good results, but the blame for poor results usually lies elsewhere!

shareholders sell when the price is falling, it is likely to fall further, and they can lose out badly. Eventually share prices fall until someone thinks that they are good value and starts buying them.[23] Directors are not usually keen on seeing 'their' company being bought up, on the cheap, by operators who may have very different ideas about the future of the company – or about the future of the existing directors! Existing directors usually do their best to maintain the share price, partly for their own survival, and partly because they probably have lots of shares in the company themselves, and perhaps they also have favourable options to acquire more shares.

3.5 Governments and the Law

Governments have long been involved in the regulation of companies. Prior to the 1844 Joint Stock Companies Act there were very few companies, and most of them were incorporated by special Act of Parliament. The important change introduced in 1844 was that companies could be incorporated simply through registration. The Act also brought in the requirement to maintain books of account; and to produce a full and fair balance sheet, which had to be audited, presented to annual general meetings, and filed with the Registrar of Companies. Little was laid down about the content of the balance sheet; and almost anyone could be an auditor. The 1856 Act introduced model articles of association for companies, which were more thorough and prescriptive than the requirements of the 1844 Act, but the adoption of them was voluntary. Indeed, the attitude of governments until the end of the nineteenth century was very much 'laissez faire': leave companies to carry on their businesses as they saw fit. The relationship between directors and shareholders was a matter for them, not for governments.

The pattern in the twentieth century was rather different. There was a major Companies Act roughly every 20 years; each Act strengthened the accounting and auditing requirements; and some of the requirements of each Act were responses to abuses and scandals where previous Acts had proved inadequate. Governments no longer accepted that the accountability of directors to shareholders and others was a private matter for them to agree among themselves; governments became increasingly involved in the specification of accounting and auditing requirements. But a lot of the detailed implementation was left to accountants, auditors and their professional bodies who operated within the framework of the Companies Acts.

The 1900 Companies Act required an annual audit for registered companies; and the 1908 Companies Act required the publication and audit of balance sheets. These reversed the laissez faire approach since 1856.

---

23   Unless the company is a total disaster.

The 1929 Act brought in important new requirements, including the publication of the profit and loss account. But little detail on the content was specified – disclosure of turnover came much later.

The 1948 Companies Act established the basis for a whole generation of accountants. It established the main disclosure requirements. Consolidated accounts (for groups of companies) were required. Auditors had to have specified qualifications. And the audit report had to state if the published financial statements showed *a true and fair view*, which has become a key phrase in financial accounting.

The 1967 Act continued the trend with additional disclosure requirements, including turnover. Additional disclosures were also specified for the Directors' Report (such as exports, charitable and political donations, and the market value of investments).

The 1981 Companies Acts clarified rules for determining distributable profits, specified additional disclosure requirements (including cost of sales), and implemented the EEC's 4th Directive, specifying formats, principles and valuation rules. It also ensured that *a true and fair view* became the overriding consideration.

The 1985 Companies Act was a major consolidating piece of legislation. It also did a little to reverse previous trends of constantly strengthening accounting and auditing requirements: small and medium-sized companies were allowed to disclose less information.

The 1989 Companies Act implemented the EC's 7th and 8th Directives (group accounts; qualifications for auditors), and allowed companies the option of distributing only summary statements to shareholders.

At times governments seem only to have flirted with the idea that they should be involved with determining financial accounting requirements, but, increasingly often, they have been forced by events to become actively involved. Since 1981 major changes have been very much influenced by Europe, with a more prescriptive approach to measurement and disclosure. There has also been a tendency to concentrate on increasing the accounting requirements for larger companies while allowing some exemptions for smaller companies.

The Labour Government (since 1997) seems to be continually discussing the possibility of new companies legislation, but is heavily involved in negotiations with the accountancy profession and any legislative changes are likely to come as a result of agreement. In the meantime the role of self-regulation remains undiminished, and the Accounting Standards Board, and the International Accounting Standards Board are continuing to develop, promulgate and perhaps even enforce[24] Financial Reporting

---

24   By the autumn of 2003 proposals for the well-respected Financial Reporting Review Panel to review the accounts of hundreds of listed companies were well advanced.

Standards which define accounting terminology and specify methods of measurement, and information to be disclosed.

3.6 **The Standard Setters**

History; Scandals; the Conceptual Framework

Long ago when accountants were not sure how to account for particular items, they had nothing to rely on but a few well-worn accountancy text books. The early ones seemed to be modelled on Pacioli's 1494 work, but better books like the well-known 'Spicer and Pegler' acquired authority, and, in due course, the ICAEW produced its 'N' series: Recommendations on Accounting Principles (1942–69).

A major change came at the end of the 1960s with a series of well-publicized accounting scandals, including the GEC–AEI takeover, and Pergamon Press. In October 1967, when AEI was defending itself from a takeover by GEC they produced a profits forecast for the year 1967. As 9 months of the year had already passed, they should have had a pretty good idea of what the results for the year would be. But GEC's takeover succeeded, and AEI's 'actual' profits for 1967 were published. Instead of being a substantial profit it turned out to be a substantial loss. It was announced that the differences were due partly to matters of fact, and partly to matters of judgement. The public could be forgiven for thinking that there were no accounting principles at all. It seemed that different accountants, using the same basic data, could come up with entirely different profit figures; and losses could be turned into profits, just by using different 'principles'. Robert Maxwell proved to be very successful at this. A Department of Trade report on a Pergamon Press takeover included some amazing examples of how accounting practices could be selected to produce the required result. It was as miraculous as turning water into wine; accounting had moved a long way since it did no more than record transactions and then summarize them as balance sheets and profit and loss accounts; and accountancy has never looked back.

The professional accountancy bodies set up the Accounting Standards Steering Committee at the end of 1969 which was intended to narrow the areas of difference and variety in accounting practice by promulgating a series of 'accounting standards', or Statements of Standard Accounting Practice (SSAPs). Twenty-five SSAPs were produced.[25] They started off as

---

25 Three were withdrawn (Numbers 7 and 16 dealing with changing prices; and 11 on deferred tax) and many were revised.

Exposure Drafts (EDs) for consultation, and, when agreed by the main professional accountancy bodies, they became authoritative statements. They did much to clarify definitions and alternatives, and to improve disclosure practice. But too often they allowed more than one treatment; and there was no effective enforcement mechanism. By the 1980s they were losing credibility as 'creative accounting' became well known.

A new accounting standards regime was established in 1990. The Accounting Standards Board produces Financial Reporting Exposure Drafts (FREDs), which, after consultation, become Financial Reporting Standards (FRSs). By 2003, 19 FRSs had been produced, and 30 or so FREDs. The Accounting Standards Board works under the supervision of the Financial Reporting Council, alongside the Financial Reporting Review Panel (FRRP). In addition there is an Urgent Issues Task Force to provide guidance on problems as they arise, without the formality of issuing a whole new FRS. Overall the new arrangements work better than the old Accounting Standards Committee. The FRSs (together with the SSAPs which they have adopted) have more legal backing, and auditors are required to state if they have been followed; attempts are being made to reduce the number of permitted alternative treatments; and the FRRP is gradually developing an enforcement role. Where questionable accounting treatments have been referred to the FRRP they have insisted on the accounting statements being revised; and by 2004 they are likely to start systematically reviewing samples of financial statements to check that accounting standards are being applied properly.

Internationally, the International Accounting Standards Committee has been superseded by the International Accounting Standards Board (IASB), and in the European Union it has been agreed that International Financial Reporting Standards (IFRSs) will be applied to listed companies by 2005. The IASB is working with the UK-based Accounting Standards Board, and the USA's Financial Accounting Standards Board for greater harmonization of accounting standards. There is still a substantial gulf between US requirements on the one hand, and continental European accounting traditions on the other. But there is enormous force behind current proposals for internationalization, and it seems likely that the idea of countries having their own accounting standards will soon be a thing of the past. This will probably be only a minor problem for countries like the UK: the IASB is based in London; its chairperson is Scottish, the previous chairperson of the Accounting Standards Board; and IFRSs seem to follow the UK and US practice of prioritizing the needs of shareholders. It is likely to be a significant problem in some European countries with different accounting traditions. IFRSs will, no doubt, be applied to listed companies; but significant changes to accounting traditions in the bulk of smaller businesses will take longer to be effective.

3.7 **Academics and Theorists**

Financial accounting has mostly been a practical subject rather than a theoretical one, but it does have some respectable academic roots. In Scottish universities it tended to develop in law faculties, and the subject may have been seen differently in England. Perhaps the practice of accountancy was primarily the application of legal concepts. In English universities the subject has developed more within an economics framework, with a London School of Economics' view rapidly spreading and predominating since the late 1940s.

The ad hoc nature of financial accounting served well enough until financial statements came to be seen as hopelessly unrealistic as a result of the ravages of high inflation in the 1970s. One theoretical solution to the problems was found in the work of Sweeney (1936) who advocated general price level adjusted financial statements. This became the accountancy profession's favoured solution in the ill-fated 'Provisional' Statement of Standard Accounting Practice number 7. Replacement Cost Accounting was a more radical solution, and modified versions of this (Current Cost Accounting) came to be favoured. This used 'deprival value' in measuring assets and profits, and it became the basis of the accountancy profession's (equally ill-fated!!) SSAP 16. But the approach is still favoured by economists, and still permeates the thinking of accounting standard setters. The idea is to move financial accounting away from being a system that merely records transactions and summarizes them: balance sheets (and profit measurement) are to be based on attempts to value assets.

The idea that assets should be shown at some sort of current value, rather than historic cost, emerged over a long period. Fixed assets have long been shown at cost less depreciation. Stocks of goods are shown at the lower of cost and net realizable value. Debtors are shown after deducting a provision for bad debts. All of the early moves away from pure historic cost were in the direction of conservatism or prudence. Although investments on balance sheets are still generally shown at some sort of 'book value', the current market value is also shown. But, increasingly, there are revaluations of land and buildings to show current (higher) values. Gradually, prudence is going out of the window.

Accountants have long sought some sort of 'conceptual framework': a statement of principles that could be seen as underlying all financial accounting. The idea is presented as if accounting is a subject something like economics, or mathematics. If we had a basic set of principles, then all accounting standards and rules could be built upon the implementation of these principles. Where a detailed standard has not yet been produced, then the principles would serve as guidance in the absence of a standard. Such principles could also reduce the need for offering detailed guidance on every new problem and issue that arises: accountants and auditors would just have to follow the principles. The Accounting Standards Board could present itself as having an orderly approach to the steady application of principles. In recent years they have been criticized for what is seen as being more like a 'fire fighting' approach: rushing in to deal with problems and crises as they arise, and neglecting many issues when they do not seem to be urgent. The existence of principles would also reduce the effectiveness of 'political' lobbying in the accounting standards setting process. There is wide consultation in the process of developing accounting standards and it is clear that the standards setters are under pressure to allow accounting treatments that favour the interests of powerful lobby groups.[26]

The idea of having answers to fundamental questions is also appealing: what is the definition of profit, and how is it measured? What is an asset, and how do we measure its value? The credibility of accounting statements, and of the accountancy profession would be enhanced if people believed that their work is all based on a sound theoretical framework. Such a framework would also enhance the respectability of accounting as an academic subject.

There have been many attempts to develop such a framework.

In the 1940s and 1950s the American Institute of Certified Public Accountants produced a series of Accounting Research Bulletins, and this work was consolidated by the Financial Accounting Standards Board in the 1970s and 1980s. In the UK the 1975 Corporate Report was a remarkable and liberal framework that was respected for many years.

The early parts of developing a conceptual framework are not very difficult. There is usually agreement on the objectives of financial reporting by businesses, and on the desirable characteristics of financial information. Financial reporting is intended to provide information about the company's financial performance and position that is useful to users (mainly investors) for assessing management's stewardship of the company, and for making economic decisions. The information should be relevant, reliable, comparable and understandable; other characteristics which contribute to this are that the information should be neutral, accurate, complete, prudent and consistent.

The Accounting Standards Committee's SSAP 2 specified four fundamental accounting concepts: accruals, consistency, going concern and prudence. Although a whole generation of accountants was brought up on this idea it did not provide a very satisfactory basis for the development of

---

26 We could argue all day about whether, or when, development expenditure creates a fixed asset, or is an expense in calculating profit. But it is clear that many companies with substantial development expenditure want to be able to capitalize it, and they will use whatever 'political' influence they can muster in the standard-setting process to achieve this.

accountancy. The four seemed to conflict with each other, but prudence was supposed to prevail. The Accounting Standards Board's *Statement of Principles* has de-emphasized these four concepts and now the debate is more about *reliability* versus *relevance* in accounting information, and deciding which should prevail.

In the 1970s it seemed that effort was put into producing long lists of desirable characteristics (or accounting concepts, or doctrines, principles), and long lists of 'users'. The UK's 'Corporate Report' (1975) listed just about everyone as a user of a company's accounts, including competitors, journalists, and all *potential* shareholders and potential employees.

The next stage in developing conceptual frameworks was quite easy too: it is assumed that what all of these users want is a balance sheet, an income statement, and probably a cash flow statement and a few other bits and pieces. It is rather more difficult to define exactly what should be included in these statements. But the stumbling block was (and probably still is) determining on what basis these should be measured. While academic theorists favoured some sort of current cost accounting, traditional accountants preferred historic cost and have usually managed to block the compulsory replacement of historic cost accounting by some form of current cost accounting.

The Accounting Standards Board published its 'Statement of Principles' in December 1999, and that is deemed to be the basis of financial reporting standards. It is a formidable document which should effectively discourage non-accountants from questioning the adequacy of the theoretical basis of financial accounting. It is significant in examining the ways in which profits and assets are defined and measured. These issues are explored in Chapters 5, 10 and 11.

3.8 Investors and Stock Markets

Those countries which were first to develop professional accountancy bodies also tend to be the ones where stock markets are most important. The countries with the largest number of listed companies are the USA, the UK, Japan, Canada and Australia. Although France and Germany are much larger countries, they have only about half the number of listed companies as Canada, and less than a third of the number in the UK. The message seems to be that accounting has developed in this group of countries very much based on the supposed needs of shareholders, under the eye of stock markets, and with the aid of professional accountants.

At times the organized stock exchanges have been influential in pressing for more and better disclosure of financial information for investors. Their influence is less obvious today, but their importance may be seen in their support of the work of the accounting standards setting bodies, and in the push for international financial reporting standards.

Summary

Financial accounting is based on a myth (perhaps many myths): it exists primarily to provide financial information for investors and creditors. But what investors really want to know about is the future. What will future profits, dividends and share prices be? Will creditors all be paid on time, or will the company get into financial difficulties? But we cannot know the future, and any estimate of value, or even (last year's) profit,[27] rests on assumptions about the future. Perhaps there is a natural human need to have faith that someone can help us to predict the future. If prophets and religion are declining, it may be that the need for faith in accountant's profits and other figures is increasing. But if accountants are now expected to fill this human need for guidance about the future, there are bound to be problems with credibility. We have the Accounting Standards Board, and even the International Accounting Standards Board to help us to have faith in complex financial reports. Published financial statements can provide valuable information. But we should be realistic about what we can expect from a system which, in its essence, has done little more than record and summarize transactions.

---

27   We cannot measure profit without making assumptions about the future of assets: we need a figure for closing stock at the year end; we need to estimate how long fixed assets will last, and how much depreciation is appropriate.

Review of Key Points

- ◆ Financial accounting has evolved in response to the needs of businesses; it was never designed as a whole

- ◆ Its development has been effectively influenced by accountants and auditors; bankers and creditors; companies and their directors; governments and the law; the standard setters; academics and theorists; and investors and stock markets

- ◆ The accountability of directors to shareholders is central to financial accounting

- ◆ The Accounting Standards Board has produced a Statement of Principles upon which financial reporting standards should be based

Self-testing Questions

1 Who are the main users of financial accounting, and what are their information needs?

2 To what extent and in what ways is the financial accounting information that creditors want different from that which shareholders want?

3 Who determines what is to be included in company annual reports and accounts?

4 Why does there seem to be a lot of criticism of auditors?

5 What have been the main influences on the development of financial accounting in the UK?

Assessment Questions

1 Compare the idea and practice of the 'accountability' of governments with that of companies.

2 In what ways, and to what extent, can financial accounting indicate the extent to which companies have achieved their objectives?

3 For what reasons might financial accounting for listed companies differ from financial accounting for unlisted companies?

4 Explain the meaning of 'relevance' and 'reliability' and discuss the importance of each in financial reporting.

5 In what ways is it helpful to understand the historical development of financial accounting?

Group Activities and Discussion Questions

1 Making use of your knowledge of other subject areas (perhaps the armed forces; the church; the British constitution; the transport system; universities; football), discuss the view that we cannot understand how something operates today without knowing about its historical development.

2 The chapter referred to the interests of a number of different groups in society. With the legal and medical professions we can say that there is also a 'public interest' (in justice; in health). Is there a 'public interest' in accountancy?

3 As a group, make a list of about 10 to 15 professions. You may wish to discuss what you mean by a 'profession'. As individuals rank each of the professions with the best at the top of the list; be aware of what criteria you are using to rank the different professions. As a group try to agree which criteria you want to use to rank professions. Is accountancy the best profession? If not, why not?

4 Select two or three businesses that you know something about (perhaps Manchester United, the University of Buckingham, Scottish Power, EMI, Severn Trent Water, BP). To whom should they be accountable, and for what, and how? To what extent would you expect accountants to be able to implement accountability in a form that you would like to see?

5 (For groups of students from different countries.) How has the historical development of accountancy in your country/countries differed from the UK? Discuss the relative importance of the government, bankers, stock markets and the accountancy profession in that development. What are the main problems to be overcome in implementing International Accounting Standards in all countries?

Financial Accounting in context

Discuss and comment on the following item taken from the press:
US Principles-based accounting
accountancymagazine.com
September 2003

The Securities and Exchange Commission (SEC) has issued a staff study recommending that accounting standards should be developed using a principles-based approach. It proposes they should:

◆ be based on an approved and consistently applied conceptual framework;

◆ clearly state the accounting objective of the standard;

◆ provide sufficient detail and structure so that the standard can be applied on a consistent basis;

◆ minimize the use of exceptions from the standard; and

Financial Accounting in context (continued)

♦ avoid use of percentage tests ('bright-lines') that allow financial engineers to achieve technical compliance with the standard while evading the intent of the standard.

The standards would clearly establish the objectives and the accounting model for the class of transactions, while providing management and auditors with a framework that is sufficiently detailed for the standards to be operational.

The staff acknowledges that the FASB has begun the shift to this approach and suggests that the approach also requires the FASB to:

♦ address deficiencies and inconsistencies in the conceptual framework;

♦ address current standards that are more rules-based;

♦ redefine the GAAP hierarchy; and

♦ continue efforts on convergence of US, foreign and international accounting standards.

References and Further Reading

Accounting Standards Board 1999, Statement of Principles for Financial Reporting.

Accounting Standards Steering Committee 1975, The Corporate Report.

Lewis, R. and D. Pendrill (2004) *Advanced Financial Accounting*, 7th edn, Pearson Education.

Perks, R.W. (1993) *Accounting and Society*, Chapman and Hall.

Spicer, E. and E. Pegler (1908) *Book-keeping and Accounts*, 1st edn; 16th edn by W.W. Bigg, H.A.R.J. Wilson and A.E. Langton (1964) HFL Publishers Ltd.

Sweeney, H.W. (1936) *Stabilized Accounting*, Harper and Row.

www.asb.org.uk

www.iasb.co.uk

4

Conventional Interpretation of Financial Statements

Learning objectives

After studying this chapter you should be able to:

◆ Calculate and interpret four solvency ratios from a company's published financial statements

◆ Understand different ways of calculating and interpreting gearing

◆ Calculate and analyse a company's return on shareholders' funds based on its published financial statements

◆ Use financial statements to indicate how a company could increase its profitability

◆ Enhance the usefulness of accounting ratios and appreciate different approaches and their limitations

Introduction

This chapter shows how financial accounting provides information that can be useful to managers in assessing the financial strength of a company, and in analysing and improving its performance in terms of profitability.

Financial accounting also provides information that helps in making decisions to buy or sell shares, and in interpreting the performance of a company's shares on the stock market. These issues are covered in Chapter 6.

Interpretation of accounts is not about memorizing a number of ratios and then calculating them. It is about examining a set of accounts, with some clear questions in mind, and then carefully arranging the evidence to answer those questions. The first part of this chapter is concerned with financial strength and solvency – its ability to survive.[1] The second part is concerned with measuring and improving profitability.

4.1 Financial Strength/Solvency

A balance sheet shows what a company owns (assets) and what it owes (liabilities). Unless the company is a complete disaster it should have more assets than liabilities, and the excess of assets over liabilities is called 'equity'. If someone owns a house worth £200,000, and has a mortgage of £120,000, their 'equity' in that house is £80,000.

A company can collapse in many different ways: bankruptcy, liquidation, receivership, winding up, reorganization, takeover. Many different reasons are put forward to explain what went wrong, including bad management and bad luck. But, in the end, a company collapses if it is unable to pay its liabilities as they fall due. Balance sheets show liabilities clearly, and it is worth trying to assess if those liabilities are excessive – if the company owes so much that it is likely to get into financial difficulties.

The balance sheet clearly separates short-term assets and liabilities from long-term assets and liabilities, and the assessment can be done in two stages.

Short term

The key question is: can a company meet its short-term liabilities as they fall due? Current liabilities are more usually shown as 'Creditors: amounts falling due within one year', so it is clear what liabilities are due to be paid within the short term. If a company has current liabilities of £1 million, and

---

1 Some books use the term 'liquidity' to describe the assessment of financial strength; but liquidity is only part of the assessment.

they have £2 million in the bank, then there should not be a problem. There are companies with so much money in the bank that they do not know what to do with it, but that is not the norm. Even if a company does not have lots of money in the bank, it is worth looking at their current assets as a whole. Current assets include cash, and things like stocks and debtors that should become cash within a matter of months. If a company has lots more current assets than current liabilities, then they look reasonably strong.

If we look at the Solverham Company balance sheets in Year 1 (Illustration 13.1 on p. 351) we see current liabilities amount to £120,000. If all of their current assets are turned into cash there should not be a problem: current assets amount to £175,000. The position would look stronger if current assets were twice as much as current liabilities. This relationship between current assets and current liabilities is called the current ratio.

Closer examination of the current assets reveals another problem: there is no cash, and more than half of the current assets are stocks. We can be reasonably sure that debtors *should* pay up within a matter of months. We are usually less sure about how long it will take for stocks to be converted into cash. Stocks of food in a supermarket should be sold and turned into cash within a few weeks. But, in some companies, stocks can include raw materials and components that have not yet been incorporated into saleable products; there may also be work in progress that could take weeks or months to complete; and there may be excessive stocks of goods ready and waiting for sale, but for which demand is currently slack. To get a clearer picture of whether or not a company has enough 'liquid' assets to meet its current liabilities, we can exclude stocks from current assets. If we do that with the Solverham Company we can see that there are not enough 'liquid assets' to cover the current liabilities. This relationship between liquid assets and current liabilities is called the liquidity ratio.

It looks as if the management of Solverham were concerned about their liquidity position, and by the end of Year 2, a year later, both their current ratio and their liquidity ratio look much stronger.

Long term

It can be more tricky to find exactly which figures to use to assess long-term solvency. There is a clear heading on the balance sheet which shows 'Liabilities: amounts due after more than one year'. That seems to show clearly what we owe, but careful examination of the notes to the accounts often reveals that this includes strange things like 'Provision for deferred taxation' and 'Deferred income', which it is not clear whether we owe or not. The easiest thing is to concentrate on long-term borrowings – things like debentures, on which interest is paid. 'Obligations under finance leases' should also be included as being much the same as long-term borrowings.

Many companies have found themselves in serious financial difficulties – or have collapsed – because they have borrowed too much, or more than they can afford. But how do we decide when borrowings are too high?

It is easier for a millionaire to borrow money than for someone who has nothing. Banks would prefer to lend to those who already have plenty of 'equity'. Indeed, the greater the equity, the greater the security for the bank or other lender. It can be very revealing to relate a company's long-term liabilities or 'debt' to the amount of equity. If we look at the Solverham Company for Year 1 we can see that they have a lot more debt (£110,000) than equity (£85,000), which can be a worrying sign.

Another way of looking at this is to see how the company is financed, particularly the long-term financing. In Year 1 the company has fixed assets and current assets of (£140,000 + £175,000 =) £315,000; this is partly financed by current liabilities of £120,000, which means that the remaining £195,000 is financed on a long-term basis. The long-term financing is made up of debentures of £110,000, and equity of £85,000. We can express debentures as a proportion of long-term funding as follows:

$$\frac{\text{Debentures}}{\text{Debentures} + \text{Equity}} \qquad \frac{£110,000}{£195,000} \times \frac{100}{1} = 56.4\%$$

This is usually referred to as 'gearing', or 'capital gearing', or 'leverage'. In Year 1 Solverham's gearing is more than 50 per cent, which is a bit worrying. But it is even more worrying the following year.

Gearing is very often measured as shown above. If a company has less than about 20 per cent gearing it is regarded as being low geared, and low risk. When it gets much above about 50 per cent the gearing is relatively high, and this means relatively high risk. When measured in this way, 90 per cent gearing would be extremely high; and it can never reach 100 per cent.[2]

Unfortunately for the student of accountancy there are many different ways of measuring gearing, including the following variations:

1 Debentures are sometimes measured as a proportion of equity. With Solverham, for Year 1, this would give a gearing ratio of over 100 per cent. It expresses exactly the same thing in a slightly different way.

$$\frac{\text{Debentures}}{\text{Equity}} \qquad \frac{£110,000}{£85,000} \times \frac{100}{1} = 129.4\%$$

---

2 Unless the company had no equity at all, which is most unlikely. A company *could* have less than no equity, if accumulated losses are greater than share capital – but then it really is in the knacker's yard.

Gearing of over 100 per cent can be serious. But it is important to be clear about how it has been calculated.

2   Often we use 'debt' rather than debentures, and this could mean including short-term debt, such as overdrafts, and even normal trade creditors.

3   Debentures are a form of long-term financing that requires a fixed return (interest) to be paid each year. Preference shares fall into the same category: the preference shareholders must be paid a fixed dividend each year before any dividends go to ordinary shareholders. If a company does not pay its preference dividend, that is a sign of real financial difficulties (although it is less serious than not being able to pay debenture interest – that is a sure sign of near financial collapse). Capital gearing is often measured by adding preference shares to debentures, and relating that total of long-term funding (which requires a fixed return) to equity.

4   Where both equity and debentures are quoted on the stock market, gearing is sometimes measured using the stock market values of these securities, not the book value shown on the balance sheet. This makes sense in relation to debentures, because the company can buy them on the stock market at the listed price: the market value of debentures is a proper indication of the amount of the liabilities at any given date. But, in relation to equity, it is more questionable, but it can flatter gearing. When a company's share price is very high, the gearing might look very low. But when the company's share price falls, the gearing steadily looks bigger (as a proportion of equity), and more worrying, even when there has been no change in the real assets and liabilities of the company. BT's infamous £30 billion debt mountain did not look too serious when the market value of their equity was over £100 billion; but it looked much more serious when the market value of their equity fell to less than £20 billion.

There is no single 'correct' way of calculating gearing. The important thing is to compare like with like: when making comparisons from year to year, or from company to company, make sure it is being calculated in the same way for each. It is also important to keep in mind the question you are really asking: is the company too much in debt? We should not allow some technically 'correct' definition of gearing to lead us to ignore worrying amounts that the company might have to pay, but fall outside some textbook definition. Companies might appear to have very low gearing, provided we ignore massive (supposedly short-term) overdrafts, scarcely understood provisions for deferred taxation, and 'contingent liabilities' which might (or might not) have to be paid.

Long-term debt is not a problem if an individual or company is easily able to service that debt – to pay the interest and to repay the capital when it falls due. A person who has a mortgage of £500,000 will probably be able to sleep at night if they have a house worth at least £1 million, and if their income is secure, and plenty big enough to live on and to make the mortgage repayments each month. If their annual mortgage payments are £35,000, and their annual income is £40,000, they have problems! If, however, their annual income is £210,000, they should be able to sleep at night because their annual mortgage payments are covered six[3] times by their annual income.

In assessing whether or not a company has too much debt, it is important to look at the amount of interest that they have to pay each year, and compare it with the income they have available to pay that interest. The appropriate lines on a profit and loss account are easily located: immediately above the interest payable figure is a figure equivalent to 'earnings before interest and tax (EBIT)', which is often much the same as the operating profit figure.[4] Interest cover is calculated by dividing EBIT by the amount of interest payable.

But we should not be deceived by mere arithmetic! In any particular year the EBIT figure might be distorted by strange, exceptional things.[5] We need to have some idea of what the regular EBIT pattern is, preferably by looking at the pattern over several years. It is also worth relating the interest figure to the amount of borrowings. At the time of writing we would expect annual interest payments to be between about 5 per cent and 9 per cent of borrowings. If the figure is very much more than we would expect, say 18 per cent, it might mean that the company is being ripped off by their bankers. But it is more likely to mean that there were more borrowings during the year than were shown at the year end: the company has managed to reduce its debts by the year end. If the figure is significantly less than about 5 per cent, it could mean that the company has found a kind-hearted banker; but it is much more likely to mean that the borrowings are fairly recent, a full year's interest is not yet due, and the bad news is yet to come.

An Overall View

The approach so far has been to calculate four widely used 'ratios':

1 Current ratio (or working capital ratio)

2 Liquidity ratio (or quick assets ratio, or acid test)

---

3 £210,000 ÷ £35,000 = 6.

4 Various 'exceptional' items may be added to or deducted from 'operating profit' before arriving at something like 'profit on ordinary activities before interest', though the terminology is by no means standard. These 'exceptional items' may include profits or losses on sales of fixed assets, and various 'provisions'.

5 Such as profits or losses on sales of fixed assets; or there might be profits from parts of the business which have since been disposed of.

3 Capital gearing ratio

4 Interest times cover

The first three of these were calculated based on the 2003 balance sheet of Ted Baker plc in Chapter 1 (Illustration 1.5). The fourth, using the profit and loss account provided in Chapter 2 (Illustration 2.3) can be calculated as follows:

	2003	2002
	£000	£000
Operating profit	9,910	9,955
Interest payable[6]	480	581
Interest times cover	20.6 times	17.1 times

Interest payments look safe as the cover is high, and has increased. A figure of less than about 3, and a declining trend, would be a cause for concern.

This conventional approach separates short-term liabilities from long-term liabilities. It may also be important to look at the total of all liabilities in forming an assessment of a company's financial strength and survival prospects.

In assessing the financial strength of a company there are many other factors to take into consideration, many of which can be found in the financial accounting statements. The balance sheet alone will not tell us all we want to know. We also have to look at the income statement in order to calculate interest cover. Profit is by no means a guarantee of survival, but creditors of a profitable company are likely to be much more secure than creditors of a loss-making company. From the point of view of managers, a company that is making profits is much more likely to survive than one which is making losses.

Moreover, in terms of survival, it may be that cash flow matters more than profit, or any of the above ratios. As long as a company is generating lots of cash it can pay its liabilities and survive.[7]

We should not necessarily take the ratios we have calculated at face value, as the following examples show:

1 **Retailers**

Most retailers have low current ratios, but that is not necessarily a problem. Retailers hold stocks of goods; they hope to turn them over within a few weeks; but they do not pay their creditors for them for at least a month. This means that their creditors figure is often higher than their stocks figures. Their customers tend to pay by cash or credit card,

---

6 In Ted Baker's financial statements there is also a sum for interest receivable. There is a case for adding this to operating profit; or it could be deducted from the interest payable. The most important things are to make calculations in a consistent way; to look at the overall picture; and to look for trends. In interpreting financial statements don't be put off by relatively small figures that you are not very sure about.

7 But if it is to survive *and prosper* it needs to make profits as well.

so they have few debtors. This means that their current assets figure is often lower than their current liabilities figure. But they usually have strong cash flows, which means that there is no problem in meeting their current liabilities as they fall due.

2 Property Companies

Most property companies borrow large sums of money to buy property, which makes their gearing look high. But that does not necessarily indicate high risk. The loans are secured on properties which tend to maintain or increase their value. The interest cover may look low, but rental income is relatively secure.

4.2 **Profitability**

In 2001 Hays plc made after-tax profits of £94 million, which might sound impressive, but it means nothing, except by comparison. We could compare it with the previous year's profits, which were £131 million, which makes the performance much less than impressive.

But perhaps the most important comparison, at least from the shareholders' point of view, is the amount of profit in relation to the amount of money that the shareholders have tied up in the business. If total shareholders' funds are £100 million, any fool could make at least two or three million pounds profit a year by making sure that the business had no assets other than cash, and putting all of it in a deposit account earning 3 per cent or 4 per cent per annum. Such a return is pathetic, and if that is the best that a company can do, the shareholders would be better off keeping the money themselves, and putting it in a high interest deposit account. Investors buy shares accepting that there is some risk, but hoping for a return on their capital[8] of a lot more than 3 per cent or 4 per cent, and preferably more than 10 per cent.

Hays plc

	2001 £m	2000 £m
Profit on ordinary activities after taxation	94	131
Total shareholders' capital and reserves	485	408
Return on shareholders' funds	19.4%	32.1%

Hays plc has a high return on shareholders' funds, but the substantial reduction in 2001 is a serious concern.

8 This is a measure of profit (not dividends) in relation to shareholders' funds. It should not be confused with 'dividend yield', which relates dividends (not profits) to the market value of the shares (not the balance sheet value of the shareholders' funds).

Profitability should be seen in relation to capital employed. This is the really important point, before we get bogged down in detail – such as how to work it out! If you don't like the section on how to work it out, then jump to '*Its Importance*'.

How to Work it Out

From a shareholders' point of view, the amount earned for them is net profit after tax[9] – a figure easily found on the income statement. This is then expressed as a percentage of shareholders' funds – the final total figure on the balance sheet which includes share capital and all retained profits. It is usually calculated as a percentage return on *ordinary* shareholders' funds,[10] may also be called 'return on equity'.

Unfortunately for the student of accountancy there are many different ways of measuring profitability, or return on capital employed, and many of them are wrong. It does not really matter whether the return is measured before or after tax, as long as the approach is consistent, and comparisons are made only like with like. But it does matter very much that the numerator and the denominator are consistent with each other. With return on ordinary shareholders' funds, it is clear that the numerator is the profit attributable to the ordinary shareholders, and the denominator is the total of ordinary shareholders' funds. A different approach would be to take total long-term capital employed: this means adding debentures and loans to shareholders' funds to give the denominator. If loans are included as part of capital employed, then the interest on those loans must be included as part of the return on capital employed.

This second approach is usually called return on net assets, or return on long-term capital employed, or even (confusingly) return on capital employed. The calculation is then most easily calculated before taxation: the numerator is profit *plus* interest (which is much the same as earnings before interest and taxation); the denominator is shareholders' funds *plus* debentures and other long-term borrowings. If borrowings are included as part of capital employed, then interest must be included as part of the return on that capital employed.

It is easy to find the profit before interest figure[11] on the income statement, but it is much harder to find the figure for the borrowings to which

---

9   Or 'Profit on ordinary activities after taxation'.

10 If there are any preference shares, this calculation is best described as return on *total* shareholders' funds. Return on ordinary shareholders' funds is then calculated by deducting the preference dividend from after tax profits, and deducting the preference share capital from the shareholders' funds.

11 Immediately before the interest figure.

that interest relates. The amount shown on the income statement as the company's interest for the year is likely to include interest on debentures, and other borrowings such as overdrafts; and it is probably not possible to separate overdraft interest from interest on long-term borrowings. If the numerator and the denominator really are to be consistent, then it is necessary to include overdrafts as part of long-term capital employed (which they are not) when using profit before interest as the numerator (the return).

There are other approaches to calculating return on capital employed, such as trying to use market values for capital employed figures. But then it gets really messy.

Its Importance

If management are primarily concerned with trying to maximize shareholder wealth, it may be that maximizing return on equity is the best way of achieving this.[12] There are two distinct approaches to increasing profitability, and most people have a pretty good idea about the first approach – which concentrates on increasing profits by increasing sales, and/or reducing costs. In an expanding company the best policy is probably to increase both costs and sales, but to make sure that sales increase a lot more than costs.

Obviously it is usually a 'good thing' to increase profits. But if this is done with a massive increase in capital employed (e.g. lots more premises, equipment, stocks and debtors), then the effect on profitability will not be so good – it might even be negative. Just as too little profits have a bad effect on profitability, so too much capital employed has a bad effect on profitability. The second approach to increasing profitability is to concentrate on utilization of capital employed, with an emphasis on the utilization of assets.

This approach to increasing profitability may be seen as being based on a 'pyramid of ratios'. At the top is the single key ratio: return on capital employed. At the second level down there are two ratios, representing the two approaches to increasing profitability: the profit/sales ratio, and the ratio of sales to capital employed. Then, at the next one or two layers down, each of these two ratios is analysed in increasing detail.

Profits/Sales

It is not difficult to analyse an income statement and identify ways in which profits might be increased. It is simply a matter of expressing each expense,

---

12 It could be argued that maximizing earnings per share would be more effective, or even using creative accounting and/or financial engineering (and perhaps more dubious practices) to increase the company's share price.

and each measure of income and profit, as a percentage of sales, and then comparing this year's results with last year's results to see where there is room for improvement. Other comparisons are possible: one company can be compared with another; a company's actual results can be compared with its planned, or target or budgeted results; comparisons can be made over 5- or 10-year periods; and average figures for a particular industry might be available[13] so that one company's results can be compared with the average for the industry.

It is simply a matter of working down the income statement: cost of sales is expressed as a percentage of sales; gross profit is expressed as a percentage of sales; distribution costs are expressed as a percentage of sales; administrative expenses are expressed as a percentage of sales; operating profit is expressed as a percentage of sales; net profit before and after tax are expressed as a percentage of sales. Various other expenses (such as depreciation, amortization, wages and salaries) are shown in the notes to the accounts, and each of these can be expressed as a percentage of sales. The purpose in each case is to identify where improvements can be made.

If this exercise is applied to the Solverham Company (Chapter 7 Assessment Question 2) we can see that the position is deteriorating under almost every heading. It shows the difficulty of keeping expenses under control when the volume of sales is declining. In most companies there are areas where improvement has taken place, and areas where improvement is needed. Often useful hypotheses can be formed which are worth investigating: an increase in depreciation usually means that additional fixed assets have been bought, and it could be that there is a reduction in the cost of wages and salaries as a result, but this is offset by additional interest costs if money has been borrowed to finance the additional fixed assets. Significant expansion often leads to increases in expenses (as a proportion of sales) in the short term, but the intention is that expenses (as a proportion of sales) will decrease as the additional volume of business flows through. But in some businesses expenses as a proportion of sales just keep increasing, and the economies of scale that they hoped would come with expansion fail to materialize. It is not difficult to use financial accounts to see whether expenses are being kept under control.

Utilization of Capital Employed

If profitability is measured by taking profit as a percentage of capital employed, it is simply a matter of arithmetic that it can be increased either by increasing profits, or by reducing capital employed (or both). An effective financial manager must keep the amount of capital employed under control and ensure that it is all used profitably. Everything must earn its keep.

---

13 From the Centre for Interfirm Comparison, for example: www.cifc.co.uk

Any reduction in fixed assets, stocks or debtors is likely to show up as an increase in cash (as assets are sold off, or debtors pay up), but this does not change the total capital employed. If we define capital employed as including borrowings, then the extra cash can be used to reduce borrowings. If we define capital employed as including only shareholders' funds, the extra cash can be used to pay extra dividends to shareholders; this reduces retained profits, part of shareholders' funds. Or a company can buy its own shares and cancel them. It is not unusual for companies to pay extra dividends to shareholders, or to purchase their own shares, sometimes in an attempt to increase share prices.[14] It is less usual for companies to admit that they have surplus cash; that they can't think of any profitable ways of using it; and that it would be better to return the money to the shareholders and let them make their own investment decisions with their own money.[15]

An actual reduction in capital employed is unlikely in a reasonably successful, expanding business. As sales increase, so capital employed is likely to increase. But one of the aims of financial management should be to ensure that capital employed increases by a smaller proportion than the increase in sales. This is easily measured: we can divide annual sales by the amount of capital employed at the year end, and hope the figure increases each year. In other words, we want to ensure that we get more sales[16] out of our capital employed.

These measurements should, ideally, be monitored over a number of years. When a company makes a significant investment (in a new branch or factory or machinery, a new product, a new line of business) it might take a year or two for this to pay off in terms of additional sales. The pressure is always on large, listed companies to produce results very quickly, but there are some companies that invest for years without seeing much return.[17]

Detailed analysis of each item of capital employed can then follow. We can relate sales to fixed assets, and then to current assets to see if each is under control. This is often described as 'asset utilization', or 'turnover of assets', and analysts want to see improvements, or increases, preferably

---

14 Managers, directors and chief executives are often motivated to increase earnings per share, and the share price, by their own 'incentivized' remuneration packages.

15 Companies are more likely to hang on to surplus cash and use it to expand by buying new businesses abroad, or jumping on the latest bandwagon (it was e-commerce in the 1990s). Financial accounts can be used to monitor the success or otherwise of some of these (ad)ventures.

16 And, of course, we want those sales to be increasingly profitable, which is what we were monitoring in the section on Profits/Sales above.

17 Some small drugs companies, for example. They may one day make a fortune; or they may burn up cash for years, and get nowhere.

every year. More detailed analysis can then follow, relating sales to each category of fixed asset, and to each category of current asset.

Sometimes this analysis is easier to understand if we convert annual sales into daily sales (divide by 365), and then express items such as debtors in 'days sales' (divide the debtors figure by the daily sales figure). The meaning is clear if we say that debtors represent 56 days sales; or debtors, on average, are taking 56 days to pay. In other words, the debtors/sales ratio is 6.5.[18]

Stocks can be shown as being 'turned over' four times a year, or as representing 91 days' supplies. But, technically, we should relate the stocks figure (which is shown at cost) to the cost of sales figure – not to the sales figure. Like should always be compared with like. Stocks are at cost, so compare them with cost of sales. Debtors are at selling price, so compare them with sales.

A comparable analysis can be made of current liabilities, particularly creditors. The creditors figure can be related to cost of sales, and expressed in days, to work out how long, on average, it takes to pay creditors. But, in terms of profitability and utilization of capital employed, there is no hurry to pay creditors: creditors and other current liabilities are deducted from assets to give the capital employed figure: a larger creditors figure leads to a smaller capital employed figure, and so an improved return on capital employed. There are good reasons for paying creditors on time; but in terms of profitability, delaying payments to creditors improves the utilization of (net) assets.

– C. liabities – assets
= Capital employed

Most of these calculations, or 'ratios',[19] are useful only by comparison, usually with previous years, or other companies. But sometimes we can see that figures are way out of line, either with the company's expectations, or with anything reasonable. A company may aim to collect money from debtors within a few weeks, or within a month or two; if debtors on average are taking 3 months to pay, something is seriously wrong. An antique shop may have stocks on average for many weeks or several months; but if a fish shop has stock levels representing much more than a week's sales, then something definitely smells; similarly, with a flower shop, we would not expect to see stocks of flowers around for several weeks.

In the Solverham Company we can see that the ratio Sales ÷ Capital employed is 'heading south',[20] which is definitely a bad sign. But that does not mean that it is all bad news. Detailed analysis of utilization of capital

---

18   6.5×56 days = 365 days (approx) = one year.

19   Accountants are inclined to divide anything by anything, and call it a 'ratio'.

20   That does not mean they are moving from Yorkshire to the Isle of Wight. In City speak that just means going down.

employed shows that control of stocks and debtors has improved: each represents a smaller proportion of sales than in the previous year.

Management of working capital is dealt with in a separate chapter (Chapter 13). The chapter on investment appraisal (Chapter 14) deals particularly with fixed assets.

4.3 Interpretation of Accounts: Maximizing the Benefit

If you want to get maximum benefit from interpreting the financial statements of companies, consideration needs to be given to the following:

Comparisons

The figures and ratios from an analysis of financial statements are meaningful only by comparison with something. The easiest thing, in all companies' accounts, is to compare this year's results with last year's; they are presented side by side for that very purpose. We can immediately see whether a company's financial position and performance is improving or deteriorating, as a whole, and in detail, using many different figures and approaches.

[handwritten margin note: Reason why use horizontal analysis]

Comparisons with the financial statements of other companies in a similar sector of the economy can be more revealing.

There are also conventional assumptions, although these should be interpreted with care. Many textbooks suggest that a current ratio of 2 : 1 is desirable, but there can be great variations, and it does depend on the kind of business involved.

We might suggest that if debtors, on average, pay up within 20 days, that is pretty good; but we probably do not know what proportion of sales are on credit, and what proportion are for cash; if almost all sales are on a cash basis, comparing the debtors figure with the total sales figure does not mean much.

If we want to assess the performance of management, it is useful to compare their stated plans and objectives with their actual performance. Internally, budgeted income statements and balance sheets are usually produced, and the comparisons can be made. Companies do not usually publish their detailed budgets, but they often make public statements of their expectations in terms of growth in sales and profits. Investment analysts then concentrate on evaluating the success of management in achieving their stated aims. The company that declares that it will continue with 'double digit' growth in profits may find its share price badly dented if they manage only 9 per cent growth. A company that forecasts difficult trading conditions, but then achieves only a small reduction in profits, may find that the stock market is so relieved that the share price increases when a profit reduction is announced. Managing expectations is important.

With some ratios we can look at what 'the market' expects, particularly the stock market. Current market interest rates are also relevant in interpreting performance.

Different Types of Business

It is difficult to interpret the financial statements of one company without having assumptions, based on knowledge of other companies, about what sort of financial position and performance you would expect. But the results of retailers are likely to be very different from manufacturers or service providers. In a large company there are often different businesses all contributing to the same total figures on the financial statements, and it can be useful to separate these out into their component parts where the information is available.

Different Financing Policies

Some companies are financed almost entirely by equity shareholders' funds; and some are heavily dependent on borrowing. Some even manage to finance a large part of their operations through short-term credit. Some companies have bought large amounts of fixed assets whereas others have rented most of their fixed assets, or even sub-contracted or 'out sourced' many of their operations, and so manage with relatively few fixed assets. Different financing policies can have major effects on the interpretation of financial statements.

Accounting Policies

In comparing one company with another we should try to identify where differences arise because of different accounting policies. Although international accounting standards are steadily reducing the areas of choice available to companies, there can still be differences in many areas. These include depreciation policies; the useful life assumed for various categories of fixed asset; whether any interest payable during a construction project is capitalized; whether software and other development costs are capitalized; the use of FIFO (First In First Out) or weighted average; and the capitalization of leased assets. The most meaningful comparisons and analyses of performance are achieved when the financial statements of the companies are adjusted so that they are on the same basis. Comparisons between financial statements of companies in different countries are particularly problematic, but, gradually, the development and implementation of International Accounting Standards will improve comparability. Sometimes comparability is improved by requiring additional disclosures which enable the person analysing the financial statements to adjust them to a common basis.

4.4 **Some Complications**

If you manage to understand what a textbook tells you about interpretation of financial statements, and apply it to the simplified illustrations provided, the next step is to look at a company's real set of published accounts. Most of them immediately look more complicated than the textbook leads you to believe. The important things are to try to be confident about what you are looking for, to be clear about general principles, not to get distracted by detail and complications, and to go for consistency, always comparing like with like from year to year.

Management's Version

It is also worth concentrating on the formal financial statements rather than being distracted by the particular gloss that companies choose to put on them. However badly a company is doing, they usually manage to find some peculiar version of earnings that shows them doing well. There is an officially approved version of 'earnings per share' figure, but companies are free to use a second measure of their own choosing, which enables them to use a whole variety of tricks. Ways of flattering performance (all within the rules) include giving emphasis to figures which:

- exclude interest
- exclude taxation
- exclude depreciation
- exclude amortization of goodwill[21]
- exclude losses on sales of fixed assets, or discontinuing parts of the business
- include profits on sales of fixed assets, or selling off parts of the business
- include the results of newly acquired businesses, if they are doing well (but excluding them if they are doing badly)

---

21 'EBITDA' is often emphasized: earnings before interest, taxation, depreciation and amortization.

- include the results of businesses they have disposed of, if they were doing well (but excluding them if they were doing badly)

- exclude the costs of setting up new parts of the business

- exclude any extra redundancy or reorganization costs, and any extra government levies, or fines, or settlements of legal claims

- exclude almost anything which management do not like the look of, if it can be presented as being exceptional, unusual, or not their fault.

All of these items are clearly disclosed, and it is an unwise analyst who ignores them – or does not understand them. There can be endless debate about which version of earnings is most appropriate for which particular purpose, but, as always, there is no certain, 'right' answer, and it is important to be absolutely clear about what is included and what is excluded; to ensure consistency from year to year; and to compare like with like.

Some annual reports include apparently useful 5- or 10-year summaries, but these are in no set format, and companies are free to include whatever figures they wish, calculated in whatever way they consider most appropriate. The ways in which the figures have been calculated should be disclosed, and easily reconciled with the formal accounting statements. Companies do not need to include any ratios in such summaries of previous years. The cynic may take the view that figures which flatter management's performance are more likely to be included than those that do not. A company may be more inclined to show a dividend per share figure that steadily increases each year, than an earnings per share figure that fluctuates a lot. They may be more inclined to show turnover figures, and shareholders' funds figures, which increase each year than they are to show return on capital employed figures that fluctuate or are decreasing. The important thing is not to be misled by the picture to which management is trying to give credibility: analyse the original statements and try to provide your own answers to the questions that you are asking.

The above is not intended to imply that management are always trying to mislead investors and analysts. It is only natural to emphasize the more favourable aspects of performance, and it is quite proper that unusual items in the financial statements are disclosed.

Consolidated Financial Statements

In interpreting the financial statements of a large company we should look at the consolidated balance sheet, not just that of the holding company. The group accounts include the results and assets and liabilities of all of the companies owned or controlled by the group.

In calculating ratios we should be looking at the group as a whole, which, fortunately, means making use of the figures that are easiest to find. The 'profit on ordinary activities after taxation' already includes all of the profits of any subsidiary companies which the group controls (there is no need to deduct the minority interest share of these profits), and the group's share of any profits in associate companies or joint ventures. In calculating the return on equity, we must make sure that the equity figure also includes the capital employed of subsidiaries, and the group's share of the capital employed of any associates or joint ventures. Again, fortunately, this figure is easy to find: it is simply the balance sheet total of shareholders' funds, or capital and reserves; the minority interest should not be deducted. If the profit figure we use includes the minority interest's share of that profit, then the capital employed should also include the minority interest shareholders' funds.[22]

Similar arguments apply to associated companies: their share of profits is included in the return figure; so their share of capital employed must be included in the capital employed figure.

In more detailed analysis it can be useful to separate out the minority interest and the associated company results so that the profitability of those investments can be determined.

Disaggregated Information/Segmental Reporting

Most large companies are combinations of different businesses, dealing with different products and services, in different markets, at home and abroad. A thorough evaluation of a company's performance should involve analysis of the performance of the different segments that make up the company as a whole.

If we examine the annual report and accounts of Hays plc, we can see that they provide some separate or disaggregated information for each of three segments: commercial; personnel; and logistics. They also identify three geographical segments: UK; other Europe; rest of the world. For each segment they provide the turnover figure, the operating profit, and the operating net assets. We can therefore calculate three of the most important profitability ratios for the company as a whole, and for each segment: return on capital employed (in this case operating profit as a percentage of operating assets); Operating profit as a percentage of sales; and sales ÷ operating assets. We can also determine the rate of growth in the last year of each of these segments, and the relative importance of each to the business as a whole.

---

22 Alternatively 'Profit for the year' can be compared with 'Capital employed', with minority interests excluded from both. A 'return on equity' should exclude preference dividends and preference share capital.

We can also get a pretty good guide to the performance of (the total of) subsidiary companies and associated companies.

There is a great deal of information available if we can be bothered to dig it all out and analyse it properly.

4.5 An Easy Guide to Assessing a Company's Solvency/Financial Strength

It might be easiest to do the following just for one year, but it is best to do it for two years because it produces more useful information, and because you are more likely to do the calculations in a consistent way if, as you do each calculation, you do it for each year.

Short term

1 How much does the company have to pay out within the next year?

   Current liabilities =

2 How much does the company have that is expected to become cash within the next year?

   Current assets =

3 Are there a lot more current assets than current liabilities? If there are twice as many current assets as current liabilities, the company looks strong. Divide current assets by current liabilities.

   $$\frac{\text{Current assets}}{\text{Current liabilities}} =$$

4 Are the current assets really likely to become cash within a matter of months? What would happen if stocks proved difficult to sell? If we exclude stocks from current assets, how much would be left ('liquid assets' = debtors[23] and cash)?

   Current assets excluding stocks =

5 Will these liquid assets be enough to cover the current liabilities? Divide liquid assets by current liabilities.

   $$\frac{\text{Current assets excluding stocks}}{\text{Current liabilities}}$$

---

23 Short-term investments are also included as liquid assets.

6 Compare this year with last year. If the 'cover' of current liabilities (calculated in 3 and 5 above) has increased, the company's short-term financial position looks stronger. If it has decreased, then the position looks weaker.

Long term

1 What long-term liabilities does the company have? There are probably several different figures that you could use. Choose one, such as long-term borrowings (you can call it 'debt'), and stick to it.

2 How much equity is there? It is usually simply the last total figure on the balance sheet, which includes share capital, plus all reserves, retained profits, share premium and any other odd items grouped under the same heading. The only bit to exclude is preference shares. 'Equity', or ordinary shareholders' funds, is the total of all shareholders' funds minus any preference share capital.

3 Compare the figure you have chosen for debt with equity. This can be done by expressing debt as a percentage of long-term capital (long-term capital is debt + equity). A very safe company will have a lot more equity than debt. The higher the debt figure is, as a proportion of long-term capital, the higher the risk.

4 How much interest did the company pay last year?

5 How much of earnings (EBIT) was available to pay that interest?

6 Compare EBIT with interest payable: if it is not at least 3 or 4 times as much, and preferably 10 times as much, it is a worrying sign.

4.6 An Easy Guide to Analysing and Improving a Company's Profitability

Again, it is better to do 2 years at a time as you do each calculation.

1 How much profit after tax did the company earn for the company's ordinary shareholders? ('The return'.)

2 What is the total amount of ordinary shareholders' funds invested in the company? ('The ordinary shareholders capital employed'.)

3 Calculate the return on ordinary shareholders' capital employed. (Number 1 as a percentage of number 2.)

4 Decide if you want to (or have to) bother with other versions of return on capital employed.

5 Analyse profits by expressing each item on the income statement as a percentage of sales.

6 Analyse utilization of assets by expressing each category of asset in relation to sales. In most instances this means dividing sales by the amount of assets. Debtors can be shown as representing a number of days sales (debtors ÷ average daily sales). Creditors and stocks can be shown as representing a number of days purchases (divide each of them by average daily purchases).

For a company to increase its profitability it should aim to do some, or all, of the following:

♦ increase gross profit as a percentage of sales

♦ decrease each category of expenses as a percentage of sales

♦ increase the utilization of assets.

The utilization of assets can be measured as the number of times they 'turn over' in a year, as shown in the example below with debtors:

	Year 1	Year 2
Sales (from the profit and loss account)	£24,000	£36,000
Debtors (from the balance sheet)	£6,000	£6,000
Number of times turned over	3	6

Alternatively, assets can be measured in terms of the number of days sales that they represent. The above illustration can show debtors as follows:

$$\frac{\text{Debtors}}{\text{Sales}} \times 365 \qquad\qquad 91 \text{ days} \qquad 61 \text{ days}$$

The objective is to identify where there is scope for improving profitability. This can be done by comparing the results of a company over a number of years, or by comparing it with other companies' results. Many companies are divided into a number of divisions, or branches; the results of each can be compared, relative weaknesses identified, and policies put in place to produce improvements.

Summary

There are a number of conventional ratios that can be calculated from balance sheets and profit and loss accounts which give a good indication of a company's solvency and profitability. Care is needed in selecting and interpreting the most appropriate figures, and the exercise is more useful if comparisons are made over a number of years. Companies need to be solvent to survive. But profitability is also important, and is best indicated using figures for return on capital employed. Careful analysis of gross profit, operating profit, and various costs as a percentage of sales can indicate where improvements may be made. But utilization of assets is also an essential part of profitability: there should not be excessive assets in relation to the amount of sales generated. Management of working capital, and investment appraisal (particularly in relation to fixed assets) are essential elements of profitability and are examined in Chapters 13 and 14.

Review of Key Points

◆ The current ratio, liquidity ratio, capital gearing ratio, and interest times cover can be used to assess a company's solvency, but care is needed in calculating and interpreting them

◆ There are two main ways of calculating return on capital employed; each can be used to assess a company's profitability and how it might be improved

◆ One side of return on capital employed can be used to assess all costs as a proportion of sales

◆ The second side of return on capital employed can be used to assess the utilization of each group of assets by relating them to sales

◆ Accounting ratios are most useful when used in making comparisons, but care is needed in comparing different types of business which may have different financing policies and different accounting policies

◆ Published financial statements often contain a lot of detail that is hard to understand; it is important to be clear about the key figures that you are looking for and to focus on those.

Self-testing Questions

1 Describe how to calculate

(a) Current ratio
(b) Liquidity ratio
(c) Capital gearing ratio
(d) Interest times cover

2 Why are stocks excluded from current assets when calculating a liquidity ratio?

3 How is the return on ordinary shareholders' capital employed calculated?

4 If debentures are included as part of capital employed, what figure is used for 'return'? How and why does it differ from the 'return' figure used for calculating return on ordinary shareholders' capital employed?

5 If a company's gross profit ratio has increased, what does that tell us about the volume of sales, and selling prices?

Self-testing Questions (continued)

6 You are given the following information about the Nikkigra Company:

Balance Sheet as at 31 December

	Year 1			Year 2		
	£000	£000	£000	£000	£000	£000
Fixed assets at cost less depreciation			1,000			900
Current assets						
Stocks		1,200			1,000	
Debtors		600			500	
Cash		68			600	
		1,868			2,100	
Current liabilities						
Creditors	294			451		
Taxation	60			65		
Proposed dividends	80	434	1,434	84	600	1,500
Fixed assets plus net current assets			2,434			2,400
Long-term liabilities						
10% debentures			1,000			900
			1,434			1,500
Shareholders' funds						
Ordinary 50p shares			1,000			1,000
Retained profits			434			500
			1,434			1,500

Profit and Loss Account for the Year Ending 31 December

	Year 1		Year 2	
Sales		3,600		3,780
Cost of goods sold		3,225		3,396
Gross profit		375		384
Distribution costs		(50)		(48)
Administration expenses		(30)		(31)
Operating profit		295		305
Interest payable		(100)		(90)
Net profit before tax		195		215
Taxation		(60)		(65)
Net profit after tax		135		150
Dividends				
Paid	35		35	
Proposed	45	80	49	84
Retained profit for year		55		66

You are required to comment on the financial performance and position of the company, making use of appropriate ratios.

Assessment Questions

1 Why would you expect retailers to have lower current ratios than manufacturers?

2 What information (in addition to the current ratio, liquidity ratio, capital gearing ratio and interest times cover) would you want to assess a company's solvency?

3 Accounting ratios are said to be most useful when making comparisons. If you had a set of ratios for a company, what comparisons would you make?

4 What are the main limitations of accounting ratios?

5 How could a company increase its profitability when sales are falling (assuming that they are unable to increase sales)?

6 You are given the following information about the Jackdan Company:

Balance Sheet as at 31 December		Year 1			Year 2	
	£000	£000	£000	£000	£000	£000
Fixed assets at cost less depreciation			300			330
Current assets						
Stocks		70			90	
Debtors		50			70	
Cash		30			40	
		150			200	
Current liabilities						
Creditors	38			45		
Taxation	32			40		
Proposed dividends	30	100	50	35	120	80
Fixed assets plus net current assets			350			410
Long-term liabilities						
8% debentures			(100)			(150)
			250			260
Shareholders' funds						
Ordinary 50p shares			200			200
Retained profits			50			60
			250			260

Profit and Loss Account for the Year Ending 31 December		
Sales	492	550
Cost of goods sold	369	410
Gross profit	123	140
Distribution costs	(12)	(12)
Administration expenses	(10)	(9)

Assessment Questions (continued)

Operating profit		<u>101</u>		<u>119</u>
Interest payable		(8)		(12)
Net profit before tax		93		107
Taxation		<u>(32)</u>		<u>(40)</u>
Net profit after tax		61		67
Dividends				
Paid	20		22	
Proposed	<u>30</u>	<u>50</u>	<u>35</u>	<u>57</u>
Retained profit for year		11		10

You are required to comment on the financial performance and position of the company, making use of appropriate ratios.

Group Activities and Discussion Questions

1 Which is more important: increasing return on capital employed, or increasing earnings per share, and why? Can a company increase its earnings per share year after year, although its return on capital employed is steadily falling?

2 In what circumstances can a substantial improvement in a company's position result in a reduction in their return on capital employed?

3 In what circumstances can a steady increase in a company's return on capital employed be a symptom of a company being in decline?

4 Most companies' profitability is lower than it should be because they have too much money tied up in assets. They should aim to have a zero level of assets. This would lead to a return on capital employed of infinity. Discuss the practicability of these suggestions.

5 Most efforts to reduce the amount of funds tied up in assets are wasted because one type of asset is turned into another: stocks and surplus buildings become debtors and cash. The total capital employed, and the total profitability is unaffected. Discuss the validity of these statements.

6 The Executive Service Company has high levels of stock, and fine premises; their sales/net assets ratio is 1 : 1.

The QuickValue Service Company has low levels of stock, and backstreet premises; their sales/net assets ratio is 2 : 1

Does that mean that the QuickValue Service company is more profitable?

Making use of this example, discuss the idea that the use of ratios shows the effects of companies choosing to do business in different ways; ratios do not indicate how businesses *should* be run.

Financial Accounting in context

Discuss and comment on the following items taken from the press:

Reuters relocates by Martin Dickson

Financial Times, 24 September 2003

For any journalist who began their working life, as I did, at Reuters' Lutyens headquarters building in Fleet Street, there is an end of era sadness about the company's decision to relocate to Canary Wharf – even though the company's editorial staff were moved out of 85 Fleet Street many years ago.

But sentimentality has no place in business and the move by Tom Glocer, chief executive, as part of his £440m cost-cutting programme makes a great deal of sense.

Instead of occupying 10 buildings across London, Reuters will relocate to a single leased property at Canary Wharf. There should be property cost savings of £5m a year, while the sale of 85 Fleet Street and an adjoining building to Canary Wharf Group will release £32.3m of capital.

There should also be savings on travel time and duplicated facilities, and, if one is cynical, the move east could also help Reuters' headcount reduction programme, since some staff could find the extra commute off-putting.

In addition, the relocation could serve as an important symbol of cultural change, as it has for other companies: Marks and Spencer's decision two years ago to move its headquarters from Baker Street to Paddington signalled a big cultural shift. Indeed, Reuters' move makes so much sense that the wonder is that its management did not quit Fleet Street years ago, with the rest of the newspaper industry. But the long bull market of the 1990s bred complacency at the company and Mr Glocer is still struggling with its painful legacy.

For Canary Wharf Group, the deal also seems positive, though too few details of the terms are known to make any definitive judgments. Apart from the usual move of buying the Fleet Street buildings, it is taking on Reuters' leases on buildings equivalent to 2.5 years rent free at Canary Wharf, a fairly standard period for these depressed City property markets.

The building Reuters will be occupying is one of the older ones in the Canary Wharf portfolio and the news organisation will have won keen terms. However, the deal will fill a building from 2005 with a quality tenant from a sector other than pure financial services, and that is a positive.

Analysts yesterday suggested the deal would have little impact on the group's net asset value, but the timing is interesting, with Canary Wharf in what appears to be the final stages of private equity takeover negotiations. It could give a fillip to independent directors trying to squeeze out a slightly higher price.

UK plc 'less profitable'

The Times, 8 September 2003

British companies were less profitable in the latest financial year than at any time in the past decade, according to Experian, the business information provider. The rate of profit ran at little more than a third of its 1998–99 peak. Experian's Corporate Health Check, which analyses the audited profits of the UK's 2,000 biggest companies, found that the average return on capital fell from 6.35 per cent in the year to March 31, 2002, to only 5.76 per cent a year later. Profitability fell for 16 consecutive quarters. Peter Brooker, who compiled the Experian report, said 'This is a longer period of sustained decline than in either of the past two recessions.'

References and Further Reading

Lewis, R. and D. Pendrill (2004) *Advanced Financial Accounting*, 7th edn, Pearson Education.

Pendlebury, M. and R. Groves (2003) *Company Accounts: Analysis, Interpretation and Understanding*, 6th edn, Thomson Learning.

Walton, P. (2000) *Financial Statement Analysis: An International Perspective*, 1st edn, Thomson Learning.

www.cifc.co.uk (select: benchmarking and interfirm comparison)

5

Profits: Definitions, Role and Measurement

Chapter contents

Learning objectives

After studying this chapter you should be able to:

- Explain the main functions of profit measurement

- Appreciate that there are different ways of defining and measuring profit

- Relate profit measurement to economic theory

- Understand how the balance sheet approach to profit measurement can differ from the income statement approach

- Identify different elements of profit in published accounts and appreciate their relevance in predicting profits

- Understand the limitations of historic cost accounts in a period of rising prices

- Evaluate proposed changes including CPP and CCA

Introduction

Nearly everyone seems to believe that profit is important, even if they are not sure why. But they do not seem to know what 'profit' means, or how to define it, or how to measure it. This chapter explores these issues. The first section explains why profit figures are important: there are several good and different reasons for measuring it and reporting it. The second part of the chapter examines in more detail two main ways of measuring profit: the income statement approach; and the balance sheet approach. In practice, at present, the two different approaches produce the same figure. But profit figures often do not provide the information that people want or expect from them. Any attempt to provide 'better', or more useful profit figures ought to be based on some clear theoretical basis if we are to have credible profit figures that are comparable from one organization to another.

5.1 Functions of Profit Measurement

The widespread belief that profit is important is based on the idea that profit figures tell us something useful. Profit figures may be useful in many different ways.

As a Guide to Dividend Decisions

The more profit a company makes, the more it can pay out as dividends. The idea of capital maintenance is important: dividends are paid out of profits, not out of shareholders' capital. Profits must be calculated after making provision for depreciation so that, as the useful life of assets declines, the amount of shareholders' funds invested in assets does not. Charging depreciation ensures that an equivalent amount stays within the business, whether in the form of cash or other net assets, and is not paid out as dividends.

When companies decide how much of their profits to pay out as dividends they consider other factors, not just the current year's profit.[1] In some years, even if profits are very low, they may maintain, or even increase dividends. But they cannot do this indefinitely. In the long run, profits are the main guide to dividend decisions. The 1985 Companies Act limits the amount a company[2] can distribute as dividends to the total of accumulated, realized profits, less accumulated losses.

---

1   Dividend policy is discussed in Chapter 12.

2   If you want to be technical it is slightly less strict in a private company where it is necessary to deduct only accumulated realized losses. In public limited companies it is necessary to deduct accumulated losses both realized, and unrealized.

Measuring the amount of profit available for distribution as dividends may also be seen as measuring how much can be consumed during a period without reducing the amount of capital at the beginning of the year, that is without 'living off capital'.[3]

To Indicate Cash Generated

Many people talk about making money as if it is the same as making profits. The differences between cash flow and profit are central to financial accounting, and are illustrated in the examples in the Appendix to this book, and explained in Chapter 7. To some extent we could argue that it is mainly a matter of timing: in the end, all profits should eventually show up as cash. Profits may be tied up in stocks and debtors, but, in due course, the stocks are sold, and the debtors pay up. But profits may also be tied up in additional fixed assets and used up in other ways (such as paying off long-term debt; or reducing the company's own share capital). Although we can say that profits do generate cash, there is no reason to expect profits will still be around as cash at any given time.

The Companies Act requirement that dividends should be paid only out of *realized* profits goes along with the idea that profits turn up as cash, and are 'available'. Profits are realized when a sale is made. Unrealized profits, such as those which result from revaluing buildings and other fixed assets, are not available for distribution as dividends – until the assets are sold, and the profits are realized.

Even the idea of profits being 'available' for distribution as dividends implies that profits are a pool of cash that can be used either to pay out as dividends, or to spend on more fixed assets, or whatever the company chooses to do with them. It is one of the hardest things for non-accountants to understand: reserves or retained profits are not cash. The fact that reserves are not usually available as cash is shown in Illustration 5.1.

The company has made £90,000 profit,[4] but none of it is 'available' to pay out dividends because, as the profit and cash flow was generated, it was all paid out, and more cars were bought. Legally, £90,000 is 'available' to pay out as dividends; but in cash terms there is nothing available – only cars.

Although the idea of using profit figures to indicate the amount of cash that a company has generated may have some popular appeal, it must be rejected as misleading, impracticable and simply wrong. It is more useful to

3   Harold Macmillan famously referred to living off capital (or governments selling off assets to meet current revenue needs) as selling off the family silver.

4   It probably made a lot more, much of which was paid out as dividends; the £90,000 is retained profits (after paying dividends).

Illustration 5.1

The Quirkar company was established on 1 January Year 1 with £10,000 capital. The business bought and sold second-hand cars. All profits generated were either paid out as dividends, or used to increase the stocks of cars. At the end of Year 3 the company's balance sheet was as follows:

	£
Stocks of cars	100,000
Share capital	10,000
Reserves	90,000
	100,000

examine cash flow statements to see what has happened to the profits that have been generated.

To Indicate How (Un)successful the Management of the Company is

Companies are expected to make profits. Shareholders elect directors to run the company for them. If the directors manage the company successfully they will make lots of profit for the shareholders. If they do not make decent profits, then they are failing and should be got rid of. This might be a bit simplistic, but it is essentially what companies are about.

A more sophisticated version would be that the aim of the financial management of companies is to maximize shareholder wealth; shareholder wealth is made up of dividends and the value of the shares; maximizing profits is likely to maximize dividends and share price.[5] It is easy to make lots of profits if the company has lots of capital employed; profits as a proportion of capital employed[6] are therefore most important.

It might be possible to think up circumstances where directors succeed in maximizing shareholders' wealth without making much profit. This was happening during the 'dot.com' bubble as share prices went up to unsustainable levels. But it is difficult to maximize shareholders' wealth for very long without making profits. In most circumstances, directors have to deliver good and increasing profits if they are to be seen as performing well. We should not be surprised if we find that directors sometimes try to manipulate profit figures to make their performance look better.

5   This is examined more fully in Chapter 12.

6   Return on capital employed.

Some naïve economists seem to believe that there are such things as 'correct' profit figures, and if we have proper accounting and auditing standards, directors would not be able to indulge in such creative accounting. But, as will become increasingly clear, there are no 'correct' profit figures; there are many difficult areas in profit measurement; and profit figures in practice are, at least in part, the result of negotiation rather than 'economic reality' (whatever that is!).

As a Basis for Taxation

Governments expect companies to pay corporation tax on their profits and so have an interest in the way in which profits are measured. In the UK the Inland Revenue lays down rules for profit measurement for taxation purposes, and these rules are different from those used for financial reporting. This sometimes surprises people from some other countries where companies had to follow the rules laid down by taxation authorities for financial reporting purposes. It does not surprise those who just assume that there is something dishonest about it: some profits are hidden from the tax authorities. But there is nothing dishonest about it; there are two distinct regimes for profit measurement, and two sets of rules.

Current trends for the harmonization of accounting standards on an international basis are likely to end the system in those countries where government taxation rules have to be followed for financial reporting purposes. But, one day, the argument could be turned on its head. At present the International Accounting Standards Board seems to be making a good job of producing International Financial Reporting Standards. But the history of these things is not encouraging. The day may come when the accounting standard setters lose credibility, and there is a call for the rules for profit measurement to be laid down by governments and tax authorities.

To Guide Investors in Deciding to Buy or Sell a Company's Shares

The main users of financial accounts are supposed to be investors, particularly (a) those who are thinking of buying shares in the company; and (b) those who already have shares in the company and are considering selling them, or deciding whether to retain the ones they already have. These investors want to know about future performance and hope that the profits of the last few years will provide the appropriate guidance. The priority is therefore to find profit figures which have predictive value. One way of forecasting future profits is to analyse previous years' profits into various elements, some of which are likely to continue along with known trends, some of which are one-off, some of which are coming to an end. In recent years official disclosure requirements have specified increasingly detailed analysis of the various different elements of profit, as shown in Section 5.2 below.

To Guide Creditors

Creditors may be more interested in the balance sheet, to calculate current ratios, liquidity ratios and gearing ratios. But, in assessing a company's ability to pay amounts due to creditors, it is not just the assets available at the balance sheet date that matter; it is also the company's ability to generate assets, particularly in the form of profits. If a company is making losses, the security which creditors see in assets can soon disappear as the assets are diminished by losses.

We could say that investors and creditors are mainly interested in the future cash flows that the company will generate, and that principles for profit measurement should be selected to provide the best basis for prediction. Perhaps the companies themselves should provide more predictions.

Profit figures are used as a survival indicator. A company that makes profits is more likely to survive than one that makes losses. Various sophisticated versions of 'Z scores' have been developed to predict corporate failure which incorporate measures of working capital, debt and equity; but the biggest single element is usually some measure of profitability.

To Indicate Economic Efficiency

Efficiency is concerned with the relationship between inputs and outputs. An organization which maximizes the ratio of outputs to inputs is maximizing efficiency. There are of course difficulties in defining the inputs and outputs which should be counted, and how to measure them. In a company, the simplest approach is to say that the main output is sales or revenues; and the main input is costs. The difference between sales and costs is profit. Maximizing profit therefore maximizes efficiency. Efficiency can be increased by (a) increasing sales; (b) reducing costs; (c) increasing sales and costs, but increasing sales by more than the increase in costs; (d) reducing sales and costs, but reducing costs more than the reduction in sales. This is all very simplistic, and the overall approach could ignore many inefficiencies. It also ignores costs to society, and costs to employees and other interested parties. This idea does, however, underlie much of our thinking: a profitable company is efficient; an unprofitable company is inefficient. In organizations that are not primarily intended to make profits it is more difficult to assess efficiency.

A profitable company is also assumed to be an effective company. Effectiveness is concerned with the relationship between outputs and objectives. An effective organization is one that achieves its objectives. If we assume that profitability is a primary objective of companies, then it is also a measure of effectiveness.

Profits are also assumed to be concerned with efficiency in the economy as a whole, particularly the allocation of resources in the economy. The most profitable companies will attract investment and resources most easily; companies which are not profitable will have difficulty in finding funds for investment. Investment in the economy therefore goes to the most profitable, and so the most efficient organizations.

This idea is also rather simplistic; but in attempting to understand what goes on in the economy, and how it is justified, these arguments about efficiency and effectiveness should not be ignored.

To Indicate Anything You Like

Profit figures seem to be quoted in many different contexts to indicate a wide variety of different matters of concern to individuals, groups or society. Employees and their representatives are likely to look at profits as an indicator of how much companies can afford to pay out in wage increases, or as an argument against closures and redundancies. Socialists may see profits as an indicator of how much companies exploit others. Profits are also relevant in any government imposed price controls, for example with privatized utility companies. Such companies are usually allowed to make a reasonable return on capital, but are not expected to use their monopoly or near monopoly positions to make excessive profits.

Different profits figures seem to be required for different purpose. It is reasonable to expect financial statements to identify different versions of profit to meet the needs of the various different users of financial statements.

5.2 Different Elements of Profit

Companies generate profits in different ways, and from different sources, some of which might be expected to continue, and some of which are more exceptional, or are derived from parts of the business which have since been disposed of. Financial reporting standards require these different elements to be identified in three main ways.

'Reporting Financial Performance'

It is not unusual for companies to change the range of products and services which they offer; to sell off substantial parts of their business; and to buy new businesses. With some companies it sometimes seems that it is a story of constant change: underperforming parts of the business are disposed of; new parts are acquired and developed. If investors are trying to predict future profits, figures for the year which has just ended may be very misleading. It is not much use basing profit predictions on figures which include products that the company no longer provides. Care is also needed with predictions based on newly acquired lines of business; they may grow more quickly than existing lines of business; and last year's profit figures may include only a month or two of the new line of business.

In Illustration 5.2 the Oke Company has one line of business which is discontinued; one line of business which is continuing; and one newly acquired line of business. Without the detailed analysis the picture is one of a modest decline (1 per cent) in sales, and a slightly larger decline (4 per cent) in operating profit. A potential investor might reasonably assume that the pattern will continue. In a situation like this good management will try to halt the decline in sales, and to increase the profits. One way of doing this is to discontinue the declining parts of the business; and to move into more successful areas. A profit figure based on more detailed analysis would suggest a very different picture.

In the UK there is a requirement[7] that company profit and loss accounts show separate figures for continuing operations, discontinued operations and acquisitions. The analysis should show, for each, turnover, cost of sales, gross profit, operating expenses and operating profit. The equivalent

Illustration 5.2

The Oke Company makes Bokes and Cokes. Bokes are not very profitable and the company ceased producing them in the autumn of Year 8. On 1 December Year 8 they bought a Doke manufacturing business and they believe that the demand for Dokes will increase rapidly. Their results for the years ending 31 December Year 7 and Year 8 may be summarized as follows:

		Year 7	Year 8
Sales (of Bokes, Cokes and Dokes)		£1,000,000	990,000
Operating profit		£ 100,000	96,000
Sales of Bokes		500,000	440,000
Sales of Cokes		500,000	510,000
Sales of Dokes		–	40,000
Operating profit	Bokes	35,000	20,000
	Cokes	65,000	68,000
	Dokes	–	8,000

7   FRS 3 Reporting Financial Performance.

International Accounting Standard (IAS 35) required comparable disclosures for discontinuing operations, but not for acquisitions.

The group profit and loss account of Tate and Lyle for the year ended 31 March 2003 is shown in Illustration 5.3. The first half of the statement, down to 'Profit before interest' is analysed between 'Continuing activities' and 'Discontinued activities'. The figures for the business that has been discontinued are fairly small, but such information could be vital to the analysis of some companies. GUS, for example, has recently disposed of its home shopping division. Where a business has made 'Acquisitions' during the year, equivalent information is also separately disclosed.

Tate and Lyle's annual report and accounts includes several pages of further detailed analysis of the above information. Their Segmental Analysis shows their turnover, net operating assets and profit before taxation analysed in two ways:

(a) By class of business

The breakdown shows £2,832 million of turnover for sweeteners and starches, and £335 million for animal feed, bulk storage and other businesses. The one main class of business dwarfs everything else that they do.

(b) By geographical segment

The breakdown shows £1.331 million of turnover for Europe, £1.147 million in the Americas, and with the 'Rest of the world' contributing a relatively small amount to turnover.

In Tate and Lyle's profit and loss account there is also reference to 'exceptional items'. There was a loss of £39 million for 'impairment of assets', which is rather like some extra depreciation; a loss of £12 million on writing down the balance sheet value of a business that they planned to sell; and a loss of £1 million on selling fixed assets. These were offset to some extent by a profit of £4 million on selling a business.

Some elements of the previous year's profit (or loss) need to be regarded separately in making predictions of future profits. There are often exceptional, extraordinary or one-off items that are not likely to be repeated. Examples might include profits or losses resulting from the disposal of a major part of the business; costs of a significant reorganization; the results of war and terrorism; uninsured losses; damages payable or receivable as a result of a legal case; the effects of epidemics; losses or gains resulting from changes in exchange rates. The list could go on forever. Some Chairman's Reports seem to put forward an endless variety of 'exceptional' causes of poor results: the Central Line was not working; a flu epidemic; a health or safety scare; the sales manager broke her leg while skiing; the lorry broke down; Mary had a headache; the cat had kittens.

Illustration 5.3

Group Profit and Loss Account , Tate and Lyle

Notes		Continuing activities £ million	Discontinued activities £ million	Total £ million	Year to 31 March 2002 £ million
			Year to 31 March 2003		
	Group sales	2758	91	2849	3616
	Share of sales of joint ventures and associates	318	–	318	328
	Total sales	3076	91	3167	3944
	Group operating profit:				
	Before goodwill amortisation and operating exceptional items	220	(1)	219	180
	Goodwill amortisation	(8)	–	(8)	(8)
5	Operating exceptional items – impairment of assets	(39)	–	(39)	–
4	Group operating profit	173	(1)	172	172
	Share of operating profits of joint ventures and associates	35	–	35	36
	Total operating profit	208	(1)	207	208
	Non-operating exceptional items:				
5	Write-downs on planned sales of businesses	(12)	–	(12)	–
5	Profit/(loss) on sale of businesses	4	15	19	(5)
5	(Loss)/profit on sale of fixed assets	(1)	–	(1)	13
	Profit before interest	199	14	213	216
7	Interest receivable and similar income			31	47
8	Interest payable and similar charges			(60)	(102)
	Share of net interest receivable/(payable) of joint ventures and associates			3	(2)
	Profit before taxation			187	159
9	Taxation			(57)	(39)
	Profit after taxation			130	120
	Minority interests – equity			2	(2)
	Profit for the period			132	118
10	Dividends paid and proposed – including on non-equity shares			(86)	(85)
	Retained profit for the period			46	33
	Earnings per share				
11	Basic			27.8p	24.7p
11	Diluted			27.7p	24.6p
	Before goodwill amortisation and exceptional items				
	Profit before taxation			228	159
11	Diluted earnings per share			33.0p	22.1p

There is no material difference between the Group's results as stated above and its results prepared on a historical cost basis.

Some of these 'exceptional' items are, of course, very genuine, and it is helpful for investors to be able to identify them and to quantify the financial effects of them. FRS 3 specifically requires the disclosure of (a) profits or losses on the sale or termination of an operation; (b) costs of a fundamental reorganization or restructuring; and (c) profits or losses on the disposal of fixed assets. But, inevitably, companies have enormous discretion over what they disclose as 'exceptional'. In the end, the final earnings per share (EPS) figure must take into account all of these so-called exceptional items, whether they are favourable or unfavourable. There should be no hiding of them. But companies are free to disclose more than one version[8] of their EPS. Their basic EPS figure should follow all of the accounting rules to make sure it is after charging (and crediting) just about everything. Many companies also disclose an alternative measure[9] of EPS. It is always worth looking at the justification for such an alternative. Sometimes it seems that companies are saying that (their version of) EPS increased from 10 pence to 12 pence because of good management. But if we take into account the loss on disposal of their premises in Amblebridge, the costs of a reorganization, depreciation of premises and amortization of goodwill (as the accounting rules say we should), their EPS actually fell to 4 pence.

Analysts seem unclear and inconsistent in how they treat alternative measures of EPS. Sometimes sophisticated analysis is build up on the basis of very dubious earnings figures.

Segmental Reporting

It is sometimes surprising what different business segments a company is in. British Gas supplies electricity. Marks and Spencer sells pension schemes. GUS[10] owns a major credit rating agency.

Where a company operates in a number of different sectors they are required by IAS 14 and SSAP 25 to disclose the turnover, operating profit and assets of each segment. The two standards differ slightly on the technical definition of what constitutes a separate segment, and exactly what information has to be disclosed. But most companies provide sufficient information about the performance of the different segments of their business to enable investors to make better predictions than they could in the absence of such 'disaggregated' information.

---

8   In addition to the 'fully diluted' basic earnings per share.

9   Which FRS 14 permits provided it is done properly, is consistent, is explained and justified, reconciled with the standard figure, and given no more prominence.

10   Formerly Great Universal Stores, the home shopping company.

Investment Income, Subsidiaries, Associates, Joint Ventures

Large companies usually have investments in other companies and the shareholders of an investing company are provided with information on the performance of these investments in three main categories:

1 *Subsidiary companies.* Where the investing company has a controlling interest in other companies, all of the revenues, expenses, assets and liabilities are included in the consolidated (or group) income statement and balance sheet. If a proportion of the subsidiary company belongs to outside shareholders, this 'minority interest' is also shown.

2 *Associates and joint ventures.* Sometimes the investing company has 'significant influence' over companies in which it has invested, but not enough influence to control those companies. Typically this would be a shareholding of between 20 per cent and 50 per cent. With these investments the group accounts include the group's share of the profits (or losses) of the associates and joint ventures. The group balance sheet shows the investment as an asset which increases as the companies make and retain profits (but the investment is reduced if they make losses).

3 *Simple investments.* Where the investing company has shares in another company, but exercises no control or significant influence, the position is simpler. The investing company takes credit for dividends receivable (not profits or losses; they have no influence over these); and on the balance sheet the investment is usually shown at cost, with a note of its current market value.

The financial performance of each of these categories of investment can be noted. A return on capital employed can be calculated for each category, and trends can be monitored.

Accounting disclosure requirements in recent years have required increasingly detailed disclosure of the items that make up profit for the year. Users of financial statements are able to select particular figures and, in effect, define profits in their own way. There can be no single measure of profit that suits all purposes and the standard setters have developed the idea that profit figures are made up of many very different elements, and discouraged the idea of a single figure that suits all purposes. But, somehow, journalists, analysts and others seem to be attached to the idea of a single, correct figure which tells us all that we want to know. Over the years, income statements have steadily provided more detail, and more analysis. But they always finish with the EPS figure – a single figure that is presented as if it encapsulates everything.

5.3 **Two Approaches to Profit Measurement**

There are two basic approaches to profit measurement.

In the first approach, the *income statement* could take priority. The emphasis would be on reporting revenues, and carefully determining the costs that should be matched against those revenues in order to determine the amount of profit. The balance sheet would then be a statement of left-over balances with no pretence that they represent the current *value* of assets.

When we measure depreciation, the emphasis is on profit measurement: we allocate the cost of the asset over its estimated useful life. There is no pretence that the balance left over after a few years' depreciation represents the current value of the asset.

Profit may be defined as sales and any other revenues earned during a period, minus the costs incurred in earning those sales and revenues. This seems straightforward enough. Sales are not very hard to identify,[11] and most costs are obvious. Both are shown on a profit and loss account or income statement. It starts off with showing the sales figure, then the cost of goods sold is deducted to give a gross profit figure; then various other expenses are deducted to give net profit figures (before tax, then after tax).

Determining exactly which costs should be 'matched' against the revenues of a period is, in most cases, done with little difficulty, although it does mean dealing with asset values, or 'unexpired costs'.

If a company buys goods for £100, and sells half of them for £120 they have made £70 profit. The cost of goods was £100, but half of the costs are 'unexpired', or unsold: those stocks are still there to be shown as assets on the balance sheet. The gross profit requires the 'cost of goods sold' to be deducted from sales.

There can be problems when valuing the closing stocks. They may be difficult to sell, and they may eventually have to be sold for less than the cost price of £50. Accountants should be prudent. The figure for closing stock needs to be assessed carefully and it may not be acceptable simply to show it at cost price. Christmas trees sell well in December, but not in January. A hit record may be almost impossible to sell a few months after it has peaked. It is not conservative enough to show stocks always at cost. When the net realizable value of the stocks is less than the cost price, the closing stock must be written down. In the above example, if the net realizable value of the closing stock which had cost £50 was only £35, then the cost of

---

11   Some problems are examined in Chapter 11.

goods sold[12] would be £65, and the gross profit would be £55. If the closing stock value falls by £15, then profit falls by £15.

There are also problems in the treatment of fixed assets, and calculating depreciation based on estimates of how long the asset's useful life will be, and what its scrap value will be at the end of its life. There may also be problems with debtors (and estimating provisions for bad debts) and other assets or unexpired costs.[13]

Most revenues and expenses can be established with reasonable certainty and accuracy, but there are inevitably some difficult or subjective areas in profit measurement.

In the second approach the *balance sheet* could take priority. The emphasis would be on correct definition and valuation of assets and liabilities. Any increase in a company's net asset value[14] would be the profit figure. This is an 'all inclusive' version of profit. The emphasis of financial accounting would change from being mainly the recording and summarizing of transactions (at cost price) to being mainly concerned with the valuation of assets. The income statement would be downgraded, but would provide some detailed breakdown of the elements that have made up the overall gain.

Profit is calculated as the increase in net assets during a period (after deducting any additional share capital subscribed, and adding back any dividends paid), as shown in Illustration 5.4.

Conventional accounting uses both approaches at the same time. The retained profit for the year calculated on the income statement

Illustration 5.4

Net assets at 31 December Year 4	£45 million
Net assets at 1 January Year 4	£35 million
Increase during year	£10 million
Minus additional proceeds of share issue	(£5 million)
Plus dividends paid	£7 million
Profit for year	£12 million

---

12 Cost of goods sold is opening stock (zero), plus purchases (£100), less closing stock (£35) = £65.

13 Sometimes the benefit from paying for something (advertising, development expenditure) may extend over several periods and it is necessary to determine how much is to be treated as an expense in the current period, and how much is to be carried forward as an asset.

14 A company's net asset value (or shareholders' funds) would increase if additional share capital is subscribed; it would reduce if any dividends are paid. The increase in net assets must be adjusted to allow for these in calculating a profit figure.

(after deducting dividends payable) is the same as the increase in retained profits during the year that is shown on the balance sheet. At present some accounting figures are an uneasy compromise between income measurement and asset measurement.

Unfortunately it is not possible to measure profits without having to decide on the amount to be shown for some assets. To measure cost of goods sold an amount for closing stock has to be shown.

The requirement to charge depreciation also means that some value for fixed assets has to appear on the balance sheet.

Similarly, in an income statement credit is taken for all sales, even if payment has not yet been received for them. The amounts yet to be received from sales are shown on the balance sheet as debtors. But it is likely that a proportion of debtors will not pay up, and a provision for bad debts is made, and this, in effect, becomes a revaluation of debtors.

Even if we decide that the income statement is most important, we cannot avoid having to determine some asset values for the balance sheet.

Cash Flow Statements

It is important to be clear that the definition and measurement of profit is very different from cash flow. Many people talk about making money and making profits as if they are the same thing. However, we saw in Chapter 2 that profit is not cash flow; this becomes clear in some of the exercises in the Appendix; and it is clear from cash flow statements, as shown in Chapter 7.

If a business buys some goods for £6, and sells them for £10, it has made £4 gross profit, even if not a penny has changed hands. It is normal business practice to buy goods on credit, and to sell goods on credit. The payment for the goods follows about a month later. But the profit has still been made before any cash has flowed.

If a business buys some goods and pays £6 cash for them, and then sells half of them for £10, which it receives in cash, they have generated a net cash flow of £4. But the gross profit is £7. Gross profit is the difference between sales (£10) and the cost of the goods which have been sold (£3).

A business can generate profits, but if the profits are tied up in debtors and stocks, it can take some time before they materialize as cash. In some circumstances it might be only a matter of time before profits turn up as cash. But a company that is continuing to expand, and to invest in more assets, may find itself short of cash year after year. Profits are used as a guide to dividend decisions. But even if a company makes good profits which appear to justify good dividends, they do not necessarily have enough cash to pay dividends. Cash flow statements indicate what has happened to the cash which profits are supposed to generate, and neatly reconcile profit figures to available cash balances.

5.4 Economic Theory and Profit

Profits cannot be measured without requiring some assets to be valued. The move towards emphasizing asset values and the balance sheet in profit measurement is also influenced by economic theory.

We saw in Chapter 3 that profit and loss accounts originally emerged more as a convenience of bookkeeping than as any serious attempt to measure profit. But with the development of companies the idea of 'capital maintenance' became essential. This involved no very complex theory. The main change was that fixed assets had to be depreciated: no dividends could be paid except out of profits; and there was no annual profit unless annual provision for depreciation had been made. With high inflation in the 1970s depreciation provisions had proved to be insufficient, and various ad hoc solutions to this problem had been around for 30 years or more. But the great and the good of the accountancy profession sought something more sophisticated: a theoretical basis was required for profit measurement.

The Hicks (1946, p. 172) definition of profit or income can be applied to the dividend decision. He stated that 'The purpose of income calculations in practical affairs is to give people an indication of the amount which they can consume without impoverishing themselves'. The idea of companies 'impoverishing themselves' may seem a little obtuse, and the quotation has been adapted to mean that profit is the amount that a company can pay out as dividends without making itself less 'well off' at the end of the year than it was at the beginning. The emphasis is on how well off a business is – the net worth of its net assets – not how much income it has earned. The idea is that income measurement is based on periodic valuation of assets.

The Hicks definition is derived from ideas expressed by Fisher (1919, p. 38) who stated that:

> Income is derived from capital goods, but the value of the income is not derived from the value of the capital goods. On the contrary, the value of the capital is derived from the value of the income. Not until we know how much income an item will probably bring us can we set any valuation on that capital at all. It is true that the wheat crop depends on the land which yields it. But the value of the crop does not depend on the land. On the contrary, the value of the land depends in its crop.

In a sense this is no more than a statement of the obvious. The value of an asset depends on what you can get out of it. If we want to establish the value of something we need to estimate the future cash flows that it will produce, and then 'discount'[15] those cash flows to arrive at a net present value.

---

15 To allow for the loss of interest during the periods that we have to wait for the cash flows. Obviously the value *now* of a cash flow receivable in 5 years' time is less than the same cash flow receivable today.

This approach to the valuation of assets (net present value; sometimes called economic value) is increasingly important in financial accounting. It is based on *future estimates*, not on recording past transactions.

As we have seen with closing stock, debtors, and depreciation of fixed assets, it is not possible to measure profits without some estimates of the future benefits that assets will generate. Any measure of profit is, to some extent, dependent on assumptions about the future.

The distinction between the two approaches to profit measurement is not as stark as it might at first appear. The income statement approach depends on asset values. The balance sheet approach necessitates an analysis of the total change in 'well-offness' that an income statement provides. Both approaches have theoretical and practical problems. Chapter 10 deals with problems in the definition and measurement of assets and liabilities; Chapter 11 deals with revenues and expenses. In any attempt to decide which approach is 'better' it may be a question of emphasis. The need for accuracy, reliability and verifiability might lead to a preference for the income statement approach: if revenues and expenses can be reliably measured, reliance on asset valuation can be minimized. The need for a theoretically robust definition of profit (based on measure-ment of 'well-offness' – with all its subjectivity) might lead to a preference for a balance sheet approach to profit measurement.

5.5 Adjusting Financial Statements for Rising Prices

Financial accounting has always been based on the recording of transac-tions; transactions are recorded on the basis of costs; and balance sheets and profit and loss accounts are traditionally based on these 'historic cost' figures, not current values. But prices change, the value of assets changes, and it has long been recognized that cost figures need to be modified in particular ways. Creditors feel safer if they know assets are worth *at least as much* as the balance sheet shows, and prefer a prudent approach to asset valuation. Fixed assets are depreciated; stocks of goods are shown at the *lower* of cost and net realizable value; and it is recognized that all debtors may not pay up and so a provision for bad debts is created which reduces the debtors figure accordingly. Companies can continue to show any investments they own at cost, or 'book value'; but they also have to show the current market value at the balance sheet date. It would therefore be wrong to suggest that we ever had a 'pure' historic cost system. It has been modified in various ways to reflect changes in prices and values, and to make financial statements more prudent or conservative. As the level of inflation steadily rose after the 1960s, the usefulness of financial statements was increasingly affected, and various ad hoc ways of dealing with it were adopted. But there were also pressures to develop different systems of accounting, moving away from historic cost.

The Problem

Price increases affect the usefulness of traditional historic cost financial accounts in a number of important ways.

1 The cost of sales is understated.[16] If a company buys oil at $20 a barrel, and sells it at $23 a barrel, it seems to have made $3 a barrel profit. But if prices are rising, by the time they come to replace the oil that they have sold, it may cost them $22 a barrel to buy. Most of their so-called 'profit' will be used up merely to continue operating at the same level as they were before; they are only $1 a barrel better off; in real terms they have made only $1 a barrel profit.

The same argument is true with all companies where prices are rising and they need to replace the goods they have sold. It is most obvious with a trading company or a retailer. Part of their 'profits' are needed simply to replace what they have sold because the replacement cost has increased. If they paid out all of their profits as dividends, they would not be able to afford to finance[17] the same level of operations. They would not have maintained capital in real terms.

Another way of looking at this is to say that there are two kinds of gain. In the oil company above they made a *holding gain* of $2 a barrel and an *operating gain* of $1 a barrel. We could say that the $1 a barrel operating gain is profit that could be paid out as dividends without reducing the operating capacity of the business. But the holding gain of $2 a barrel is needed to continue to finance existing stock levels.

2 Depreciation is understated.[18] Depreciation is an expense which reduces profits by the amount of fixed assets that is deemed to have been consumed during a period. It is usually based on the original cost of the fixed assets. When the asset comes to the end of its life, the cost of buying a new one is likely to be much higher than the amount of depreciation that has been charged. Depreciation is understated, and profits are overstated.

If all profits are paid out as dividends, a company would not be able to afford[19] to replace the fixed assets at the end of their lives, and they would not have maintained capital in real terms.

---

16 A numerical illustration of the effects of this is provided in Self-testing Question 6 at the end of the chapter

17 They could borrow the money they need.

18 A numerical illustration of the effects of this is provided in Self-testing Question 7 at the end of the chapter.

19 Again, they could borrow the money needed.

3 Debtors. The amount of debtors increases in line with prices. An additional charge can be made against profits to allow for the extra cost of financing debtors.[20]

4 Overstated profits. The effect of rising prices on historic cost accounts is that profits are overstated because they do not allow for the extra cost (due to price rises) of replacing assets. If dividends are based on profits, then dividends are likely to be excessive. If corporation tax payments are based on profits,[21] then corporation tax payments are likely to be excessive. The effect of these, together with the additional cost of replacing assets at higher prices, means that companies are likely to suffer liquidity problems. If companies distribute all of their profits as dividends they will probably need to borrow quite a lot of money if they are to carry on financing the same level of activities.

5 Asset values understated. If assets are shown on the balance sheet at cost (or some modified version of cost), as prices rise, so the amounts shown for assets become increasingly unrealistic. Attempts to use the balance sheet to indicate what a company is worth are, to say the least, difficult.[22] Creditors may be reassured by low asset values if they can be sure that assets are worth *at least as much* as the balance sheet shows. But company directors might like to see higher asset valuations in order to support additional borrowing.

6 Return on capital employed is overstated. If profits are overstated, and asset values are understated, both factors will lead to a company's return on capital employed being overstated, as shown in Illustration 5.5.

We can generalize from this during a period of rising prices. A company may be showing a reasonable return on capital employed, but if profits and assets are restated, the return on capital employed will be significantly lower. It depends on the rate of inflation, and the circumstances of particular companies, but Illustration 5.5 could be typical: a company's 'real' return on capital employed might only be about half of what the conventional published accounts show.

20   This would be for net debtors (debtors less creditors), and is explained more fully as the Monetary Working Capital Adjustment which is used in Current Cost Accounting.

21   Although the Inland Revenue's rules for calculating profits are different from the basis on which profits are calculated for the purpose of published annual reports. The Inland Revenue usually specifies writing down allowances which are greater than companies' depreciation charges. The effect is that profit for taxation purposes is less likely to be overstated than profit for annual reporting.

22   Balance sheets can only give an idea of what a company might be worth. Attempts can be made to update the figures shown for fixed assets by estimating their average age (divide the amount of each category of fixed assets by the year's depreciation charge for that category), and then estimating the average price increase since they were bought. It is a bit crude, but might be better than having no idea at all.

Illustration 5.5

Last year the Luxgud Company had a return on capital employed of 12 per cent, calculated as follows:

	£000
Fixed assets plus current assets less current liabilities	100
Shareholders' funds plus long-term liabilities	100
Earnings before interest and taxation	12

The company's auditors, RiceSlaughterhouse, estimated that profits were overstated by £4,000 because of the effects of rising prices; and that asset values were understated by £33,333.

The return on capital employed, after adjusting for rising prices, was

$$\frac{8}{133} \times \frac{100}{1} = 6\%$$

7 There are other practical and theoretical problems with historic cost accounts. The idea of adding together items expressed in different units of currency is, to say the least, dubious. Not many would find the following extract from a balance sheet acceptable:

Fixed assets	Land and buildings	€10 million
	Plant and machinery	$ 5 million
	Vehicles	£ 2 million
	Total	17 million

It is usually acceptable to add together all items expressed in pounds, even if the items were acquired at very different dates, and the value of the pound was very different at those dates. If the land and buildings had been bought 20 years ago, and the plant and machinery 10 years ago, we would happily add the two together if they were both expressed in pounds. But the value of a US dollar or a euro is closer to the value of a pound, than the value of a pound 20 years ago. One solution to this problem would be to express everything in an inflation adjusted unit of currency: this came to be called pounds of current purchasing power (as at the balance sheet date).

8 Conventional historic cost accounts also fail to show the gain that a business can make by borrowing lots of money. If a business borrows money, it usually has to pay interest, and that is properly shown in the financial accounts. But if they borrow £1 million to invest in tangible, non-monetary assets (such as land, buildings, machinery, stocks of goods) these assets are likely to go up in line with inflation. The assets will increase to,

say, £1.1 million, while the amount of the loan stays the same. There is a gain to the company of £100,000.

Many assets can be expected to increase roughly in line with inflation. But money sitting in the bank does not. If a company has no borrowings, but has a spare £1 million in the bank, it will earn interest, and that will be properly shown in financial accounts. What will not be shown is the fact that, after inflation of say 10 per cent, they will not be able to afford to buy the same amount of assets that they could one year ago. They still have their £1 million, but what they could have bought for £1 million a year ago will now cost £1.1 million. In real terms they have lost £100,000.

Conventional historic cost accounts do not reflect the gain that is made by holding more monetary liabilities than assets; or the loss that is made by holding more monetary assets than liabilities.

Most of the time companies can live with the effects of inflation on their financial statements, especially when inflation levels are modest. They may also like to see their profits and return on capital employed exaggerated if it makes their performance look better. Companies like to boast that each year they have made record sales, and record profits. But they are not so keen on paying excessive taxation, or having serious liquidity problems. When inflation levels are very high the effects on conventional financial statements can be serious.

Some Solutions

Accountants have long been aware that the effect of changing prices is to limit the usefulness of conventional financial statements and the ICAEW has given advice on the subject since as far back as 1949. They recognized that the usefulness of conventional profit figures was severely limited by the effects of rising prices, and recommended caution in interpreting the figures, and that companies should not pay out all of their profits as dividends.

During the 1950s and 1960s various ad hoc ways of dealing with the problem were used. Some helped to produce more realistic balance sheet figures. Some helped to produce more realistic profit figures. The use of current values on balance sheets increased, and a requirement was introduced to show the market value of investments in addition to the book value.

Fixed assets could also be revalued, although there was little agreement on how this should be done. Many companies were happy to show more healthy looking balance sheets, with higher asset values, and so higher equity figures. But if fixed assets are revalued upwards, the depreciation charge should be increased accordingly; and this reduces profit figures. Companies were less inclined to implement higher depreciation charges.

LIFO[23] was another partial[24] solution. During a period of rising prices, if the cost of sales figure is based on the most recent purchases it will be higher;[25] profits will be lower, and closer to being based on current costs. But the use of LIFO means that the items left in stock (and shown on the balance sheet) are at old, low, irrelevant prices.

By the early 1970s a more thorough-going solution was required. Inflation was extraordinarily high; and the credibility of the accountancy profession was extraordinarily low. A number of different suggestions have been made, including a pure replacement cost accounting system; and systems based on using net realizable values. But, as is so often the case, the solution to the problem depends upon the way in which the problem is defined. It came to be seen as a problem of capital maintenance. Profit for the year is seen as being the maximum amount that a company can pay out as dividend without being less 'well off' at the end of the year than it was at the beginning. Maintaining 'well-offness' means maintaining capital. The debate has been dominated by three versions of capital maintenance:

1 Money capital or financial capital. If a company starts the year with net assets of £100, and ends the year with £120,[26] it has made £20 profit. Inflation is ignored. This is traditional historic cost accounting.

2 General purchasing power. If a company starts the year with net assets of £100, and ends the year with £120, but there has been 12 per cent inflation during the year, distributable profits are only £8. To maintain the original capital, in terms of general purchasing power, it must go up in line with inflation to £112 before there are any distributable profits. This is current purchasing power (CPP) accounting.

3 Operating capability. A company might start the year with £100 invested in operating assets. By the end of the year the balance sheet shows a total of £120 (historic cost – HC). But the cost of financing the same level of operating capability might have increased to £108. In current cost terms their profit is £12. This is based on the specific price rises that affect the company, not the general level of inflation. This is current cost accounting (CCA).

---

23 Last In First Out: pricing stocks that are used on the basis of charging them out on the basis of the most recent price at which the same items have been purchased. It is widely used in the USA but is not acceptable to UK standard setters, or the Inland Revenue.

24 Perhaps all solutions are partial.

25 Higher than FIFO (First In First Out) which is the usual UK method.

26 In these three examples it is assumed that there were no dividends paid and no additional capital subscribed.

As inflation faded, and interest in adjusting accounts to reflect changing prices faded with it, the Accounting Standards Committee came up with a compromise solution that combined CPP with CCA in their 1988 document *Accounting for the Effects of Changing Prices: A Handbook.*

5.6 Inflation: Current Purchasing Power

The accountancy profession's first set of proposals to deal with the problems was to require, in addition to conventional historical cost accounts, a set of inflation adjusted accounts using CPP accounting. The accountancy profession's Provisional Statement of Standard Accounting Practice No. 7 CPP used the Retail Price Index to adjust accounts.

In principle it is very simple. All items[27] in the financial statements are multiplied up by the rate of inflation since the item first arose to express them in pounds of current purchasing power as at the balance sheet date.

The effects on the income statement are shown in Illustration 5.6. We can assume that most transactions (sales, purchases, expenses) take place on average in the middle of the year. We convert them to year end prices by multiplying them by the year-end index, and divide by the mid-year index; most items are simply multiplied up to year end prices by the rate of inflation since mid-year. Depreciation has a much bigger uplift because fixed assets were bought some years ago. Opening stock (an expense) has a bigger uplift than most items, because it was bought at least 6 months before mid-year. Closing stock (a deduction from expenses) has the smallest uplift because it was bought not long before the year end.

The effect of applying CPP in Illustration 5.6 is to convert a historic cost profit of £10,000 into a loss of £92,410. CPP accounting also requires the calculation of a gain or loss on holding monetary items. If a company has net monetary assets (e.g. lots of cash in the bank), its purchasing power declines during the year, and a loss on holding net monetary assets is shown. If a company has net monetary liabilities (e.g. they have borrowed lots of money) there is a gain because the assets in which the borrowings have been invested are assumed to go up in line with inflation, but the amount of the borrowing stays the same.

The distinction between monetary and non-monetary items is also important on the balance sheet. Non-monetary items (mainly fixed assets and stocks) are multiplied up in line with inflation. With monetary items

---

27 No change is required to monetary items (such as cash, debtors, liabilities) on the balance sheet at the year end: they are already expressed in pounds of current purchasing power at the balance sheet date.

Illustration 5.6

The Retail Price Index was at 100 on 1 January Year 1. By 31 December Year 1 it had risen to 120.

Summarized Income Statement for Year Ended 31 December Year 1

	£HC 000	Conversion	£CPP 000
Sales	1,500	$\frac{120}{110}$	1,636.36
Opening stock	100	$\frac{120}{98}$	122.45
Purchases	1,100	$\frac{120}{110}$	1,200.00
	1,200		1,322.45
Deduct			
Closing stock	(110)	$\frac{120}{118}$	(111.86)
Cost of goods sold	(1,090)		1,210.59
Gross profit[28]	410		425.77
General expenses	(200)	$\frac{120}{110}$	(218.18)
Depreciation	(200)	$\frac{120}{80}$	(300.00)
Net profit	10		(92.41)

Opening stock was bought before the beginning of the year, so we need to estimate when it was bought, and what the index was then. In this instance we assume that the index was 98 when it was bought.

Closing stock was bought before the end of the year; we estimate[29] that the price index was 118 when it was bought.

Fixed assets were bought some years ago; in this instance we assume that the price index was 80 when they were bought. Depreciation is multiplied up in line with the amount of inflation since the assets were bought.

---

28 In this instance the adjustments increase sales by more than the cost of sales, and so a higher gross profit figure is shown. It will often be the case that the adjustments increase cost of sales more than sales, resulting in a lower CPP gross profit.

29 It could all be established much more accurately in practice. This illustration is intended to be simple.

(such as cash, bank, creditors, debentures) there is no change. Perhaps the most important figure is share capital: it is multiplied up in line with inflation: this is intended to maintain capital in terms of general purchasing power. Profits are regarded as being available for distribution as dividends only if the total amount of shareholders' funds has increased more than in line with inflation.

A CPP balance sheet does not show the 'real' value of tangible assets: it shows historic cost (less any depreciation), multiplied by the rate of inflation since they were purchased. The market value at the balance sheet date might be higher or lower than the £CPP figure (but 'prudence' suggests that if CPP values are significantly in excess of current value, they should be written down).

CPP had many advantages. It is relatively easy to implement because it does not mean that we need to change all existing financial statements and systems. It introduces a supplementary statement expressed in pounds of current purchasing power. It is a fairly credible and effective system. It deals with the main problems that arise from the effects of inflation on financial statements. Indeed, it is the only real 'inflation accounting' system. It appealed to accountants because they could just about understand it, while at the same time it baffled most non-accountants. Moreover it does not introduce any additional subjective judgement. The historic cost figures are taken as given, and multiplied up for inflation. This also means that the figures can be as easily verified by auditors as historic cost accounts.

CPP is a system that should 'maintain capital' in a very particular sense. Profits are not regarded as distributable unless equity has been maintained in real terms.

The main drawback is that it does not reflect the specific price changes that affect particular businesses. The Retail Price Index is based on the price of bread and butter, steak and kidney pies, rents and council tax, shoes and socks, and all of the things that make up the cost of living for a household. This is not very relevant to an oil company when the price of oil has just doubled, or halved. On average CPP might produce relevant figures for average companies. But the figures are of questionable value to particular companies dealing with particular price changes.

In practice the main problem with CPP accounting was that the government(s)[30] at the time were not happy with it. They were afraid of the idea of general indexing. They were trying to control prices and incomes and did not want either to go up automatically in line with inflation.

---

30   There was a change of government in 1974 from Conservative (Heath) to Labour (Wilson).

That might be a recipe for still worse inflation. And they certainly did not want to see government borrowing indexed so that they had to repay inflation adjusted amounts.

5.7 Maintaining Operating Capability: CCA

Just before SSAP 7 was issued the government appointed the Sandilands Committee on Inflation Accounting to consider whether, and how, company accounts should be adjusted to allow for price changes. It was asked to look at the profession's CPP proposals and other possible accounting methods. They were requested to take into account the financial requirements of investors, creditors, employees and the public; the efficient allocation of resources through the capital market; and management decision making and the efficiency of companies. In addition they were required to consider some of the economic concerns of the government, including the need to restrain inflation, and the taxation of company profits and capital gains.

The Sandilands Report was published in 1975 and recommended against CPP. Instead current cost accounting should be adopted. Current cost accounts should be the main published accounts, not supplementary statements. Assets should be shown at *value to the business*, which in most (but not all) cases would be the written down replacement cost. The profit for the year would be *operating profit*, which would be calculated by charging against sales the 'value to the business' of the assets consumed in generating that revenue. Holding gains and losses would be shown separately from operating profit. The report was clear and well written; its recommendations seemed realistic; they were based on a system of replacement cost accounting that had been used by the Dutch electrical company, Philips, for many years. The Report was widely welcomed. Perhaps Sandilands' neatest move was to pass it to the accountancy profession to produce the detailed recommendations on how the system should be implemented.

The Accounting Standards Committee (ASC) established the Morpeth Committee to work on the detailed implementation of CCA, and their recommendations were published in October 1976 as ED18. At first this, too, was widely welcomed: at last there was a solution to the problems of price changes and financial statements! But that was before people read the detailed recommendations. Most accountants found it far too complicated, and they did not want to move away from historic cost accounting. It was like asking a vicar to give up the Bible, or a toddler to give up its security blanket: it may be full of holes, but it had served them well for a long time, and how could they cope in a world without that which they know best?

A large proportion of the ICAEW's members were against the proposals. An Extraordinary General Meeting was called; a vote against the proposals was carried; and the accountancy profession was left with egg on its face. The only answer was for the ASC to set up another committee. This time it was under William Hyde, and it produced the 'Hyde Guidelines' as an interim measure. These recommended retaining historic cost accounts as the main accounts; large companies should in addition publish a supplementary statement which made a number of current cost adjustments to arrive at current cost profit. These guidelines became the basis of SSAP 16 which was issued in 1980.

The basic principle is that current cost operating profit should be calculated after allowing for the effect of price changes on funds needed to continue the business and maintain its operating capability. It is the specific price changes that affect the business that matter, not the general level of inflation. When prices increase, a business needs the funds to finance more assets. Even if the business is not expanding, or increasing its operating capability, the cost of replacing the existing level of assets increases. They need to replace stocks of goods as they are sold; they need to replace fixed assets as they are used up; and they probably need to finance a higher level of debtors.[31]

Current cost adjustments are made to historic cost profit to allow for the extra funds needed to finance the higher amount of assets that is due to price increases. A company cannot afford to distribute all of its historic cost profits as dividends; they need to retain some of those so-called profits to finance the additional cost of replacing assets.

There are four adjustments to HC profit, and the first three are very similar. We can assume that most items on an income statement (sales, purchases, most expenses) take place, on average, in the middle of the year. The current cost of most of these items is therefore matched against current revenues, and so no adjustment is required. The three exceptions where adjustment is required are:

1 Cost of sales adjustment. Opening stock is increased to mid-year prices – which increases the amount charged against profit. Closing stock is reduced to mid-year prices – which reduces the credit to profit. The effect of both of these is to reduce HC profit.

2 Depreciation adjustment. The depreciation charge is increased in line with the change in the price of the fixed assets concerned since the date that they were acquired.

3 Monetary working capital adjustment. It is easiest to think of this in terms of amounts for debtors.[32] As prices increase, so the amount of

31 In some businesses debtors are financed by creditors. It is the amount of 'net debtors' (debtors less creditors) that matters.

32 Net debtors, i.e., debtors less creditors.

debtors increases; and the business needs to finance that higher level of debtors. Debtors are treated in the same way as stocks and fixed assets: all need more finance because of price increases; an appropriate charge is made against profit to allow for the maintenance of operating capability, and to ensure that the necessary part of profits are retained in the business and not paid out as dividends.

If debtors are wholly financed by creditors, there is no need for such an adjustment. We can assume that as prices increase, creditors go up in line with debtors, and there is no need for a monetary working capital adjustment to allow for the financing of additional debtors.

If a company has more creditors than debtors, the creditors are not only financing the debtors; they are also financing other assets. The effect of inflation would be to increase the creditors, and reduce the amount of funding the company needs to finance other assets. A monetary working capital adjustment would then be a *credit* which offsets the effect of the cost of sales adjustment.

The total effect of the first three adjustments is a reduction in historic cost profit to allow for the increased cost of financing assets. The assumption so far is that it is shareholders' funds (or retained profits) that have to do all of the financing. But many companies are partly financed by borrowing. If a company is financed two-thirds by shareholders' funds, and one-third by borrowing, we can assume that this will continue to be the case. Any increase in assets will be financed partly by shareholders' funds (two-thirds), and partly by borrowing (one-third). The effect of the first three adjustments is to charge shareholders' funds with *all* of the financing of the additional assets. A fourth adjustment allows for the fact that part of the financing is likely to be from borrowing.

4 Gearing adjustment. The proportion of the business financed by monetary items is calculated.[33] If only two-thirds of the business is financed by shareholders' funds, then only two-thirds of the first three adjustments remain as a charge against profit. One-third is credited back in arriving at current cost operating profit; this is the gearing adjustment.

The use of liabilities to finance assets usually involves an interest cost; the benefit of the gearing adjustment is shown after the cost of borrowing (interest), as shown in Illustration 5.7. The amount available for distribution as dividends is shown after charging interest and taxation, and after crediting the gearing adjustment.

---

33 Borrowings and any other monetary liabilities not already included in monetary working capital. This is expressed as a proportion of all shareholders' funds. The proportion is calculated as at the beginning of the year, and as at the end of the year, and an average of the two is taken.

Illustration 5.7

Income Statement of the Currant Quest Company for the Year Ended
31 December Year 3

	£000	£000
Historic cost profit before interest and taxation		100
Deduct		
Cost of sales adjustment	20	
Monetary working capital adjustment	15	
Depreciation adjustment	25	
		60
Current cost operating profit		40
Deduct		
Interest payable	12	
Taxation	23	
	35	
Add Gearing adjustment	20	15
Current cost profit attributable to shareholders		25
Deduct Proposed dividends		30

The Currant Quest Company paid a dividend of £30,000 which seemed to be well covered by historic cost profits after interest and tax. HC accounts showed £65,000[34] as being available for dividends. The dividend was covered 2.16 times. But after making the current cost adjustments we can see that too much dividend was being paid. The company was failing to maintain their operating capability.

A current cost income statement is based on mid-year prices. A current cost balance sheet is based on year-end prices; or, to be more exact, it is based on value to the business at the year end. The main differences between a historic cost balance sheet and a current cost balance sheet are in relation to fixed assets, stocks and the current cost reserve.

The first step in calculating current cost[35] of fixed asset and stocks is to establish their replacement cost. What would it cost to buy an equivalent asset at the balance sheet date? This could be established very specifically by looking at suppliers' price lists. With fixed assets allowance must be made for depreciation: obviously it costs more to buy a new asset than the amount that would be shown on the balance sheet for an old one. The nearest equivalent asset must be established, and an allowance made for

---

34 £100,000 less interest (£12,000) and taxation (£23,000).

35 Or value to the business; or deprival value.

(say) 3 years' depreciation if the asset is (say) 3 years old. An easier way to get at an appropriate replacement cost is to apply a price index, but it must be a specific price index dealing with that type of asset, not a general price index such as the retail price index.

But current cost accounting is not the same as replacement cost accounting. In most circumstances the use of replacement cost is appropriate. But sometimes the replacement cost is too high; the business would not want to replace an asset.

Illustration 5.8

The Stainleigh Company bought a machine 4 years ago for £10,000. Its book value is now £6,000. An equivalent new asset would cost £20,000 today; the written down value would be £12,000. But the company does not use the asset very often and it would not be worth buying a replacement. The existing machine could be sold for £4,000; but the company prefers to keep it as it still generates some revenues. The company estimates that, over its remaining life, the economic value[36] of the machine to the business is £5,000.

The company will not sell the machine for £4,000 because it is worth £5,000 to them. They would not replace it: the cost (even the written down replacement cost) is more than the machine is worth to the business. The value to the business of the machine is £5,000; that is the amount at which it would be shown on a current cost balance sheet.

When the replacement cost of an asset is more than the asset is worth to the business, the 'value to the business' is not the replacement cost; it is the 'recoverable amount'. With the Stainleigh Company above its economic value (continuing to use it) was more than its net realizable value. The value to the business is therefore its economic value. Sometimes it is not worth continuing to use an asset: its economic value is less than it could be sold for;[37] in this situation the value to the business is the net realizable value.

We could think of an asset as being worth what we can get out of it. This might be what we can sell it for (net realizable value), or how much we can make out of it by using it (economic value). The 'recoverable amount' for an asset is the higher of net realizable value and economic value. If the replacement cost is so high that we would not replace the asset, then the value to the business is the recoverable amount.

---

36 The net present value of the future cash flows that it will generate.

37 This is often true with assets (such as stocks) that the company intends to sell.

After making all of the above alterations to historic cost accounts, the resulting balance sheet will not balance. The easiest thing is to put in 'Reserves' as the balancing figure – but that is cheating! It is useful to separate out what has happened to the historic cost balance sheet:

(a) retained profits for the year have been reduced by the current cost adjustments;

(b) asset values have been increased to a current cost basis.

The current cost balance sheet will show two categories of reserves: retained profits (on a current cost basis); and a current cost reserve which includes unrealized surpluses on revaluation of assets.[38]

Current cost accounting has a number of advantages compared with historic cost accounting. It deals with most of the problems with historic cost accounting that were identified in the first part of Section 5.5. It provides a more defensible measure of profit and indicates the amount that could be distributed as dividends while still maintaining the operating capability of capital. But full and detailed implementation is complex, expensive and time consuming. It is also very dependent on subjective judgement about valuations, and is therefore open to manipulation. It also puts auditors in a difficult position: most historic cost figures are a matter of fact that can easily be verified. But companies can easily defend a wide range of different figures for the value of assets; this can make it difficult for auditors to verify the figures with any real certainty.

5.8 A Compromise: Real Terms Accounting

The ASC's 1988 *Handbook* outlined a number of approaches to dealing with the problems of the effects of changing prices on financial statements, but is best known for suggesting a voluntary, compromise proposal combining CPP and CCA. It seemed like the accounting profession's last attempt to deal with the problem before interest in it faded away.

The proposals involve using current cost balance sheets (based on the idea of value to the business), and calculating profit by comparing the net assets at the beginning of the year with the net assets at the end of the year.[39] As the intention is to maintain capital in 'real terms' (allowing for inflation), the opening balance is multiplied by the amount of inflation during the year. If the net assets figure at the end of the year is more than the opening balance (after adjusting for inflation), then a profit in real terms has been made. This profit will include realized operating gains;

---

38   Offset by the current cost adjustments to the profit and loss accounts.

39   After adding back any dividends and deducting any additional share capital.

it will also include unrealized gains from revaluing assets. The system may be seen as implying that such gains are regarded as being distributable as dividends; but normal accounting rules (and company law) do not regard unrealized gains as being distributable. They are, however, an indicator of the performance of a company.

In many cases the amount by which shareholders' funds have to be uplifted to allow for inflation will more than offset the amount of unrealized holding gains. In Illustration 5.9, unrealized gains on fixed assets and stocks amount to £80,000. But as there was 20 per cent inflation during the year shareholders' funds needed to increase by £200,000. There was therefore no real holding gain. The historic cost profit was reduced from £150,000 to £30,000 because of a real holding loss.

Illustration 5.9

Balance Sheet Extract as at 1 January	£000
Net assets at current cost	1,000
Share capital	500
HC reserves	400
Unrealised holding gains (on fixed assets and stocks)	100
	1,000

Balance Sheet Extract as at 31 December	
Net assets at current cost	1,230
Share capital	500
HC reserves	550
Unrealized holding gains (on fixed assets and stocks) (100 + 80)	180
	1,230

Income Statement Extract for Year Ended 31 December	
Historic cost profit after taxation	150
Add	
Unrealized holding gains (on fixed assets and stocks during year)	80
Deduct	
Inflation adjustment to shareholders' funds	200
Real holding loss	(120)
Total real gain	30

The balance sheet shows that total shareholders' funds have increased by £230. But £200 of this was needed just to keep up with inflation. The total real gain was only £30.

In some instances there will be a real holding gain (when the current cost of fixed assets and stocks increased by more than the rate of inflation) which is added to the historic cost profit. Whether such unrealized holding gains should be regarded as being part of profit for the year is debatable. But clear identification of the various elements that make up any increase in 'well-offness' during the year should provide more useful information to the careful user of financial statements.

Summary

There are many different reasons for measuring the amount of profit that a company has made during the year; and there are at least as many different profit figures. The idea that one single figure can tell us most of what we want to know about a company is unrealistic. It is as unrealistic as pretending that we can measure the performance of an individual in a single figure (such as IQ, or GCE A level points). As individuals we are each a combination of strengths and weaknesses, and our performance varies from time to time. Companies are similar to individuals in this respect. A single 'correct' earnings per share figure, the final figure on the income statement, a neat summary of company performance, is an appealing idea, but over-simplistic. It is easy to criticize financial accounting for failing to provide just what we want. But if we took the trouble to be very clear and specific about what we want to know about a company's performance, we will find that there is a wealth of information in published financial statements that gives as good an indication of what we want to know as it is realistic to expect.

Review of Key Points

- Profit figures are useful as a guide to dividend decisions, the success of management, as a basis for taxation, to guide investors and creditors, to indicate economic efficiency and to provide information to other users of accounts

- Different elements of profit such as segments, exceptional items and investments can be monitored

- The income statement approach to profit measurement emphasizes revenues generated and the costs incurred in generating them

- The balance sheet approach emphasizes asset valuation

- Financial statements based on historic cost have serious limitations; if they were adjusted for price increases they would show lower profits

- Historic cost accounts can be adjusted using current purchasing power, or current cost accounting

- It is unrealistic to rely on a single profit figure; different figures may be useful for different purposes

Self-testing Questions

1 What are the main reasons why profit is measured?

2 Explain how profit can be calculated using balance sheets. How does this approach differ from profit measurement using income statements?

3 There are likely to be different rates of growth in the profits of the various activities that a company undertakes (and different levels of risk). What detail is given in published financial statements of the performance of the different activities of a company?

4 Explain why it is not possible to measure profit without making predictions about the value of assets in the future.

5 What are the main differences between CPP and CCA?

6 (*Do not attempt this question unless you are good at basic statements – and can manage the Appendix to this book. You could look at the answer: it illustrates some important points.*)
Mary runs a small business buying and selling Bibles. All transactions are on a cash basis. She started last year with 100 Bibles which had cost her £10 each. During the year she bought 1,000

Self-testing Questions (continued)

Bibles for £11,000; and she sold 1,000 Bibles for £15,000. At the end of the year she had 100 Bibles in stock which had cost her £1,200. She decided to give all of her profits to charity.

Required:

(a) The balance sheet at the beginning of the year.
(b) The income statement for the year.
(c) The balance sheet at the end of the year before giving profits to charity.
(d) How much could the business afford to give to charity?
(e) How would the results have been different if she had used LIFO?

7 Jackie received £30,000 compensation for unfair dismissal and plans to set up in business running a taxi. The vehicle will cost £30,000 and will have a trade in value of £3,000 after nine years. Taxi fares, all received in cash, will amount to £40,000 per annum. Expenses (petrol, road tax, insurance, repairs), all paid in cash, will amount to £20,000 per annum. Jackie plans to take all of the profits out of the business, as cash, each year.

Required:

(a) The balance sheet at the beginning of the business.
(b) The income statement for a typical year.
(c) How much will Jackie draw out of the business each year?
(d) The balance sheet at the end of nine years.
(e) What does this tell us about capital maintenance?

Assessment Questions

1 Using Illustration 5.2, produce a prediction of profits for Year 9.

2 Using the profit and loss account of Tate and Lyle (Illustration 5.3), how many different versions of profit can you identify for the year ending 2003? Which of these figures is likely to be most useful, and why?

3 On 1 January Year 5 Smele Ltd was set up with 250,000 fully paid 50 pence shares. On the same day the company bought a freehold property for £100,000, and purchased 12,000 items of stock for £24,000.

On 31 December Year 5 two-thirds of the stock that had been bought on 1 January 1995 was sold for £40,000; 2,000 units of identical stock were purchased for £5,000; and the total expenses for the year of £12,000 were paid.

There were no other transactions during the year. All items were settled in cash on the date of the transaction.

The company uses FIFO. Freehold property is depreciated on a straight line basis over 50 years. The relevant index for property prices is:

| 1 January | 120 |
| 31 December | 150 |

Required:

(a) Prepare an income statement for Smele Ltd for the year ended 31 December Year 5, and a balance sheet on that date, using replacement cost accounting.

(b) Explain how and why the results differ from using historic cost accounting.

4 The Floatus Car Company has a car showroom and is in business to sell sports cars. They decide to use current cost accounting. In their window they have, as an advertising gimmick, a 1936 Rolls-Royce, and they are unsure what amount should be shown for it on their balance sheet. It originally cost them £10,000, five years ago. It has no engine in it, and it would cost about £8,000 to make it sellable; with an engine it could be sold for about £25,000. If it needed to be replaced it would be extremely difficult to find exactly the same model; it could probably be obtained from a specialist collector for £150,000. As an advertisement they reckon it is worth £10,000 a year for the next 5 years after which it would have a net realizable value of £20,000.

Since they bought the car the retail price index has increased by 100 per cent; the average price of second-hand cars has increased by 80 per cent. The company's cost of capital is 12 per cent per annum.

Outline the principles for asset valuation using current cost accounting, and attempt to apply them to Floatus's Rolls-Royce.

5 The following is a summary of the balance sheet of the Flaxey Company for the last two years:

	Year 6	Year 7
	£000	£000
Fixed assets at cost	500	500
Provision for depreciation	300	350
	200	150
Stocks	100	140
Debtors less creditors	50	80
	350	370
Debentures	100	100
Share capital and retained profits	250	270

The price index of equivalent fixed assets has increased from 80 to 240 since the fixed assets were bought. The price index applicable to stocks, debtors and creditors increased by two points a month from 84 at the end of October Year 5 to 112 at the end of December Year 7.

You are required to calculate the following, making and stating appropriate assumptions:

(a) Cost of sales adjustment
(b) Depreciation adjustment
(c) Monetary working capital adjustment
(d) Gearing adjustment

Group Activities and Discussion Questions

1 (a) Profit is an essential indicator of company performance. Accounting standards setters are steadily improving its reliability and we will soon have reliable, consistent and comparable company profit figures on an international basis.

   (b) The meaning of 'profit' changes as often as accounting standards change and companies find new ways of bending the rules for profit measurement. Undue importance is attached to a figure that is no more reliable than predictions by astrologers, weather forecasters, and experts who tell us what will happen to house prices.

   Present a case in favour of each of the above views. A group could be divided into two parts, one to present a case in favour of each. Or there could be a third sub-group which assesses the cases presented by each of the other two sub-groups.

2 Inflation makes a company's performance look better, and this is to everyone's advantage. Discuss this statement. You should consider the point of view of (i) directors, (ii) share-holders, (iii) creditors, (iv) employees, (v) the government, (vi) the public. The discussion could take the form of a formal debate. Alternatively role play could be used, with each member of the group representing the interests of one group of users of financial statements.

3 Why has inflation accounting (and CCA and all its variants) generally fallen into disuse? What would be likely to revive it?

4 Profitability is a good measure of efficiency and effectiveness in companies. It is very difficult to measure efficiency and effectiveness in 'not-for-profit' organizations. Governments do not want to be responsible for organizations that make losses and are criticized for being inefficient and ineffective. Governments are increasingly privatizing organizations so that their activities can be seen to be efficient and effective.

   Explain and assess the above argument.

Financial Accounting in context

Discuss and comment on the following item taken from the press:
Reckitt starts raising returns to shareholders by Alison Smith
Financial Times, 27 August 2003

Reckitt Benckiser is raising its dividend by 10 per cent and beginning a share buyback programme as it increases shareholder payments for the first time since the merger that created it in late 1999.

Reckitt, one of the world's largest household goods groups, is increasing the interim pay-out from 12.5p a share to 14p, and embarking on a rolling buyback that could mean spending £250m a year.

Bart Becht, chief executive, rejected the suggestion that the planned buyback, announced yesterday, made it less likely that the group would make a big acquisition.

Financial Accounting in context (continued)

He said: 'We are continuing to look at acquisition opportunities, and can run both of these things in parallel.'

Reckitt, whose brands include AirWick, Dettol and Vanish, is seen as a potential bidder for SSL International, maker of Durex condoms and Dr Scholl footcare products, which said earlier this summer that it had received an approach.

Mr Becht would not comment on this, but some analysts believe parts of SSL would fit well with Reckitt's ambition to increase its presence in the health and personal care category.

Mr Becht said Reckitt would be interested in buying a new multinational brand in this category because 'launching entirely new brands in FMCG [fast-moving consumer goods] is largely a thing of the past. It's very risky and very expensive unless you have a blockbuster idea'.

Reckitt also announced pre-tax profits up 14 per cent in the first half and set itself new targets for the full year.

The increase in net revenues is now expected to be at the top of the 4–6 per cent range announced in February, while net income would be 14 per cent higher – ahead of the earlier 10–12 per cent target.

Operating profit in North America slipped 11 per cent to £58m over the half, as the group continued to raise its marketing spending on key brands. Mr Becht said the benefits would show in the second half.

Group sales in the six months to June 30 rose 4 per cent to £1.83bn, while pre-tax profit rose from £173m to £199m, and earnings per share were up 14 per cent to 28.1p.

The full-year dividend last year was 25.5p, and the expectation is that it will be 28p this year. The share price rose 32p to 1162p.

References and Further Reading

Fisher, I. (1919) *Elementary Principles of Economics*, Macmillan.

Hicks, J.R. (1946) *Value and Capital*, 2nd edn, Oxford University Press.

Lee, T. (1996) *Income and Value Measurement: Theory and Practice*, 3rd edn, Thomson Learning.

Lewis, R. and D. Pendrill (2004) *Advanced Financial Accounting*, 7th edn, Pearson Education.

UK and International GAAP, 8th edn, 2003, LexisNexis (Butterworths Tolley).

www.asb.org.uk

www.iasb.co.uk

6

How the Stock Market Assesses Company Performance

Learning objectives

After studying this chapter you should be able to:

- ◆ Discuss various factors that influence share prices

- ◆ Understand the main information shown by the *Financial Times London Share Service*

- ◆ Calculate and interpret P/E ratios, dividend yield and dividend cover

- ◆ Explain why cash flows may influence share prices

- ◆ Understand the relationship between share prices and balance sheet values

- ◆ Critically assess the possible influence of a variety of other factors on share prices.

Introduction

The performance of companies' shares on the stock market is part of our everyday news agenda, but it is difficult to be sure about what really influences share prices, and why it is important. Share prices are determined by supply and demand for a company's shares; this in turn is influenced by a number of factors, and the information revealed in financial accounts is perhaps the most important. It is easy to see which companies are doing well, but by the time this is obvious, their shares are usually already quite expensive. Similarly, by the time a company's performance is obviously poor, the share price has already fallen. Unfortunately this chapter cannot teach you how to 'beat the market'; but it does a lot to explain what happens.

6.1 Investing in Shares

When we talk about investing in shares we usually mean buying shares that are listed on the London Stock Exchange, or other leading international stock markets. There are many thousands of private companies in the UK, most of them very small, typically with only about two shareholders; their shares are not available on any stock market. There are also many public companies, some quite large, which are also not listed on stock markets. You may be invited by friends or family to buy shares in an unlisted company; you may set up your own company; you may inherit some shares. But unless the company is a listed one, buying and selling the shares is usually difficult because there is no ready market.

The shares in listed companies are bought and sold frequently, sometimes every few minutes or seconds, on the stock market, and it is easy to buy and sell them. If you want to buy or sell shares in listed companies you need to have a stock broker; or you could ask your bank to act for you; or you could register with a stockbroker who arranges for you to deal directly on the internet. In the bull[1] market of the 1990s many private individuals became 'day traders', buying and selling shares on the same day, and making more profit than they could earn by working for a living. It is not difficult to make profits when share prices are rising.

Companies do not buy and sell shares themselves. If you go to Marks and Spencer, or to Boots and ask to buy some shares, you will be referred elsewhere. Shares are, in effect, bought and sold by investors (companies, institutions and individuals), via an established stock market. The price or current value of the shares is not calculated, or determined by the company

---

1 A bull market is a rising market; a bear market is a falling market.

or individual. It constantly changes as a result of supply and demand for a particular company's shares. If demand for a share is very high, the price will be marked up; this will encourage some investors to sell their shares so that others can buy. When the price goes up too high, demand for the company's shares will slacken, and an equilibrium is reached. If a company's shares are not in demand, the price will fall until some investors decide that the shares have become good value.

Sometimes there are exaggerated short-term effects on share prices. If there is a rumour that there will soon be a takeover bid for a particular company, demand for those shares might increase rapidly until the situation is resolved. When a company has some bad news, or there is bad news from comparable companies, there might be a sudden, exaggerated decrease in the share price which may prove to be only temporary.

6.2 **What Influences Share Prices?**

Many different factors influence share prices. Some have nothing directly to do with the company itself but are more to do with general sentiments about investing and the economy. Such factors include expectations about interest rates, growth or recession in the economy, and exchange rates. To some extent stock markets in different countries move in line with each other, and it often seems that the UK stock market follows the USA.

The most widely used measure of share price performance is the FTSE 100 ('Footsie'). This is the *Financial Times* index of the share prices of the hundred largest companies, based on their market capitalization. The FTSE 250 covers the next 250 largest companies and the FTSE All Share is the index for all listed companies. The constituent companies of the index change slightly on a regular basis as the value of their shares change. During the 1990s there were substantial increases in share prices and the index reached an all time high on the last trading day of the century. The first 3 years of this century saw falls in share prices generally, but, at the time of writing, there were signs of recovery with the FTSE 100 reaching around 4300 in September 2003.

The FTSE 100 is widely used, and some 'tracker' investment funds simply buy shares in the companies that make up the index; and the performance of these funds is often better than funds where the managers use their own expertise to select the best investments. Inclusion, or non-inclusion in the index can affect a company's share price. It may be partly a matter of prestige and status. It is also a result of increased demand for shares that are going into the index; the managers of tracker funds have to buy them. And when companies are about to be removed from the index (because of a relative fall in their market capitalization), the share price is hit by the need for tracker funds to sell those shares.

A company's share price is also influenced by what is happening to other companies in the same sector. When one retailer reports relatively poor results, the share prices of many retailers may suffer too because it is anticipated that their results will also be poor. It also seems that sectors go in and out of favour.

Other factors influencing a company's share price are more directly to do with the company itself. Fundamentals of solvency and profitability are important, and so is growth. The (perceived) quality of management can also affect share prices. When a company has been through a bad time, chief executives often lose credibility, and their jobs. When new chief executives are appointed they, and the company's share price, often enjoy a honeymoon period while the market awaits the delivery of improved results.

Share prices are also influenced by the reputation of the company, by actual or rumoured takeover bids, and by all sorts of rumours, scandal and gossip.

There may be individuals who really understand how the various factors operate. If such individuals exist, they are likely to keep their advice to themselves, and to act on it, and to become extremely rich. When you read advice from investment analysts, bankers and other 'professionals' you may be tempted to believe them. But you might also wonder why they are giving you this advice, or selling it to you so cheaply. Why do they not simply take their own advice and make more money that way? There are a number of possible explanations for this:

1 Investment analysts are fair-minded individuals, solely interested in pursuing the truth, with no interest in making money for themselves, and with more interest in helping others to make money

2 They do not really know. Like journalists, they are just writing for a living and putting out any credible stories for which they get paid

3 For some reason they want you to follow their advice and buy and sell shares when they suggest that you should

There are infamous tales of financial journalists who offered share tips to readers. They would choose a company with a credible story about its future prospects; then they would buy themselves a few thousand shares at the current price, say £1 each. Then they would recommend readers of the Daily Whatsit to buy the shares at £1 each. Once such a recommendation is published (unless it is total rubbish) the share price is likely to go up immediately – even prior to publication. By the time the poor readers of the Daily Whatsit get their shares, the price has gone up to, say, £1.10, and they are likely to stay at this increased level for at least a few days. The journalists then sell their shares at, say, £1.10, having made a nice little profit. They can then boast to readers that the share price increased, as they predicted it would.

If such journalists write for a minor newspaper, and few people act on their advice, there is likely to be no effect on share prices. If they write for a major daily newspaper it might be different. If we are talking about a major investment bank, or the chief executive of the company concerned, what they say, and what is reported in the financial press, may have a significant effect on share prices.

At any one time there are likely to be hundreds or thousands of theories around about which shares are going to do particularly well in the future. And, of course, some of those theories will prove to be correct, while most will be quietly forgotten.

Most investors want to buy shares when they are cheap, and sell them when they are expensive. If you think that the true value of a particular share is £2.00, and you can buy it for £1.80, you are doing well. If you still think it is worth £2.00 and you can sell it for £2.20, you are doing better still. The problem is determining what a share is really worth.

Unfortunately there is no 'true value' with which the market price of shares can be compared. It does not mean much to say that a share with a market value of £2.50 is cheaper than a share with a market value of £3.00. We can, however, say that a share price is expensive or cheap in relation to key information such as the amount of earnings, or dividends, or net assets per share.

6.3 Accounting Information and Share Prices

Investors and investment analysts make their investment decisions and recommendations using financial accounting information – and whatever other relevant and/or credible information they are able to find. Share prices reflect the information that is available to investors, and financial accounting information is central to this. Share prices may be influenced by any information that a company discloses, but the most important figures are probably:

1 The profits earned by a company

2 The dividends paid out by the company

3 The net asset (or balance sheet) value of the company

4 The cash flows generated by the company.

Each of these can be related to the most recent share price which gives an indication of whether a share is 'expensive' or 'cheap' in relation to that information. Investors are guided by the most recent figures for each of these; predictions are also sometimes available, which is what investors really need; but predictions have varying degrees of credibility, and should be compared with the actual results when they become available.

Profits

From the shareholder's point of view, the most relevant profit is the amount that was earned for them in the most recent financial year. It is the figure after all expenses, including interest and any exceptional items, have been deducted, and after charging taxation for the year. It usually has a straightforward label such as 'profit for the financial-year', and that is the amount that has been earned for the shareholders during the year. Some of it is paid out as dividends; the rest remains in the business and is called retained profit for the year.

If there are preference shareholders, then part of the profit earned for the year belongs to them; preference dividends have to be deducted from profits for the year to arrive at the amount earned for ordinary shareholders.

There is a relationship between the value of a company, and the amount of profits that the company earns. If a company earns £1 million a year, the company might be worth, say, £10 million or £15 million. The relationship is called the 'Price[2]/Earnings Ratio', which, in this example, would be 10 or 15. It can be calculated by relating the company's *total* earnings for the year to the *total* market value for all of its shares.[3] Alternatively, it can be calculated by relating the earnings *per share* to the market price *per share.*

Dividends

Some shareholders may be more interested in the dividends that a company actually pays out than in how much profit the company makes. If a shareholder needs the income, profits are all very well, but it is the cash dividend that the shareholder actually receives that helps to pay the bills.

Companies usually declare dividends in pence per share, perhaps 4 pence per share. This means that the shareholders receive 4 pence dividend for each share that they own. The amount varies from year to year, and companies usually try to increase it a little each year.

A company usually pays a dividend twice a year: an 'interim' dividend, and a 'final' dividend. The shareholders are most interested in the total amount for the year.

---

2   The 'price' is the price of one share: in this example it is worth 10 or 15 times the amount of profits earned per share.

3   The total market value of all of the shares is called the *market capitalization.*

There is a relationship between the value of a company's shares, and the amount of dividend paid. If a company pays a dividend of 4 pence per share, and each share is worth, say, £1.00, then the 'dividend yield' is 4 per cent. If the share was worth £2.00, the dividend yield would be 2 per cent. The same dividend yield figure would be produced if the company's total dividends for the year are expressed as a percentage of the company's market capitalization.

There is also an important relationship between the amount of profits a company earns, and the amount that they choose to pay out as a dividend. If a company pays out a lot less than half of its profits as dividends, then the dividend looks reasonably secure: the dividend is well covered by profits. If a company pays out nearly all of its profits as dividends, then the dividend looks less secure. Analysts divide the profit by the dividend and say, for example, that the dividend is covered 1.6 times by profits. If a company earned £100 million profits, and paid out £62.5 million as dividends, then the dividend is covered 1.6[4] times by profits.

'*Dividend cover*'[5] can be calculated using earnings and dividend figures for the company as a whole, or on a per share basis.

Net Asset (or Balance Sheet) Value

A company's balance sheet clearly shows the amount for 'Equity share-holders' funds' (which is the same as the amount for 'Net assets').[6] But the total value of the company's shares on the stock market is likely to be very different from what the balance sheet shows. Share prices result from the interplay of supply and demand for shares, rather than the result of recording financial transactions within the business. If a company's prospects are seen to be very good, there is a strong demand for the shares, and the share price tends to increase. Generally, with a successful company, the market price of the shares is much higher than the net asset value per share (based on balance sheet values).

Cash Flows

Many analysts do not rely on profit information alone, but also analyse the company's cash flow statement, and are likely to have more confidence in a company that has healthy cash flows.

---

4   £62.5m × 1.6 = £100m

5   Dividend cover should not be confused with interest cover.

6   Where there are preference shares, the amount of preference shares should be deducted from the total of shareholders' funds to give ordinary shareholders' funds, or equity.

6.4 **The *Financial Times***

The *Financial Times* shows key figures and ratios in respect of each listed company on the London[7] Stock Exchange, on a daily basis. On Tuesdays to Saturdays the P/E ratio and the dividend yield is shown for each company together with the following additional information (see Illustration 6.1):

Illustration 6.1

Company	Closing price on previous day (pence)	Change in pence since previous day	52 week high	52 week low	Yield %	P/E	Volume '000s
Marks & Spencer	315	+6	384	258	3.3	15.2	17,440
United Utilities	467	−1	563	449	9.2	10.4	4,893

On the day that these figures were published[8] the average yield for the FTSE 100 companies was 3.34 per cent, and the average P/E ratio was 17.4.

(i) Name of company, usually abbreviated

(ii) Various notes. The most useful is the ♣ symbol which indicates that the *Financial Times* will supply a copy of the company's annual report and accounts if you telephone 020 8391 6000. If the ♣ symbol is not shown, the annual report and accounts can be obtained by contacting the company directly

(iii) Share price at close of business on the previous day (closing mid price[9])

(iv) Amount by which the share price changed during the previous day

(v) The highest the share price has been during the previous 52 weeks

(vi) The lowest the share price has been during the previous 52 weeks

(vii) Yield: the latest known dividend per share expressed as a percentage of the share price

(viii) P/E: the price/earnings ratio: expresses the relationship between the share price and the latest known profit, or earnings, per share.

(ix) Volume. The number of shares traded in thousands

---

7 Comparable information is shown on preceding pages for many other shares and markets in the world.

8 16 September 2003.

9 There is always a 'spread' between the buying price and selling price: the mid point is shown.

On Mondays, as there was no previous day's trading, the *Financial Times* shows different information as follows, and as shown in Illustration 6.2

(i)   Name of company, as above

(ii)   Various notes, as above

(iii) Price, at the close of business on the previous Friday

(iv)   The percentage change in the share price during the previous week

(v)   The amount of the last known annual dividend, expressed in pence per share

Illustration 6.2

Company	Closing price on Friday	% Change during last week	Dividend in pence per share	Dividend cover	Market capitalization £million	Date when share last became ex-dividend	City line telephone
GUS	721	5.4	23.3	2.0	7,275	9.7	2740
Sainsbury	273	−1.0	15.58	1.4	5,289	28.5	3904

First, the percentage by which a share price changed during the whole of the previous week is shown. In the above week, GUS shares increased by 5.4 per cent while Sainsbury's shares went down in price by 1 per cent.

The amount of the previous year's dividend is then shown, in pence. The amount of dividend does not mean much by itself. On other days the dividend is shown in relation to the share price to give a dividend yield.

The company's dividend cover is then shown, which can give some indication about the prospects for future dividend increases. The dividend of GUS is covered twice by profits which makes it look more secure than Sainsbury's.

The market capitalization is a measure of the size of a company. It is the current share price multiplied by the number of shares in issue.

When a company declares a dividend it is payable to all who own the shares on a particular date. Anyone buying the shares after that date will not receive the company's most recent proposed dividend. If the dividend is, say, 20 pence per share, we can expect the share price to drop by 20 pence on the day that it becomes ex-dividend. It is important to know the date that a share becomes ex-dividend (and the amount of the dividend), if we are to make sense of share price movements.

The city line telephone number is a service provided by the *Financial Times*. For up-to-the-second share prices anyone can call 0906 003, or 0906 843 followed by the four digit code provided for each company.

(vi) The dividend cover: earnings per share divided by dividend per share[10]

(vii) Market capitalization: the share price multiplied by the number of shares that the company has in issue

(viii) The date when the share became 'ex dividend'. The most recent dividend was payable to whoever owned the shares on the day before the 'xd' date. If the dividend is 4 pence per share, we might expect the share price to fall by about 4 pence on the 'xd' date, because whoever owns the share on that date will not receive the 4 pence dividend, and will probably have to wait 6 months before another dividend is due.

(ix) City line. This is a four digit telephone number which gives live, up-to-the-second share prices, if you dial 0906 003, or 0906 843, followed by the four digit number. Normal trading hours are 8.00 a.m. to 4.30 p.m.

For information about net asset values and cash flows it is necessary to look at the annual report and accounts; alternatively information produced by investment analysts and in the financial press can be examined.

6.5 Price/Earnings Ratios

Calculating the Price/Earnings Ratio

The 'P/E' ratio is perhaps the most widely used stock market indicator. It shows clearly the relationship between the last known earnings per share figure and the most recent share price. The calculation, for two companies, may be shown as in Illustration 6.3.

What the P/E Ratio Can Tell Us

In the example in Illustration 6.3, Cronky plc has a P/E ratio of 10. If we pay £2.00 for a share, and the company earns 20 pence per share each year, the share will have paid for itself[11] in ten years. That seems rather a long time for an investment to pay for itself. But the position with Voddy plc is even worse – it would take 20 years. These figures are not unusual. At the time of writing

---

10 Or, if you prefer, the total profits earned for ordinary shareholders, divided by the total dividends payable to ordinary shareholders. It should give the same answer whether the calculation is done for the company as a whole, or on the basis of the amount of profits and dividends per share.

11 In terms of profit that the company earns, not in terms of dividends that the company pays out.

Illustration 6.3

		Cronky plc	Voddy plc
(a)	Number of ordinary shares	1,000,000	1,000,000
(b)	Current share price	£2.00	£3.20
(c)	Market capitalization (a × b)	£2,000,000	£3,200,000
(d)	Total profits after taxation attributable to ordinary shareholders	£200,000	£160,000
(e)	P/E ratio (c ÷ d)	10	20
→ (f)	Earnings per share (d ÷ a)	£0.20	£0.16
(g)	P/E ratio (b ÷ f)	10	20

the average P/E ratio on the London Stock Market was about 16. This could mean that most shares are hopelessly overpriced, that they still have a long way to fall, and an average P/E ratio of around 10 is more sustainable. It is more likely to mean that investors expect earnings per share to increase significantly in the coming years. The share price looks high in relation to current earnings, but (hopefully) not in relation to future earnings.

If share prices seem high it is because demand for them is high; and if demand is high it is usually because investors are optimistic about the future prospects of the company. Investors in Voddy plc do not assume that the earnings per share will remain at 16 pence for the next 20 years: they expect – or demand – *growth* in earnings per share.

If earnings grow at a constant rate of 10 per cent per annum, they will double in less than 8 years. If they grow at 15 per cent per annum, they will double in just less than 5 years. Not many companies manage to maintain such rates of growth in earnings, but they may be needed to justify high share prices, that is, to justify high P/E ratios. We can assume that, generally, a high P/E ratio means that investors are expecting high rates of growth, although they may, of course, be disappointed. In the late 1990s many share prices were very high, with high P/E ratios, particularly Technology, Media and Telecommunications, together with Computing, and anything vaguely connected with the 'dot com' bubble. But most companies failed to deliver the rapid growth in earnings that was needed to justify the high P/E ratios, and many high share prices crashed. In the 1990s many investors jumped on the bandwagon of high P/E ratios, only to be disappointed. In 2003 more modest P/E ratios, and more realistic expectations of growth were the order of the day.

We can get a feel for P/E ratios by looking at the back pages of the *Financial Times*. It gives the average for the London Stock Market as a whole, the average for the top 100 companies (the FTSE 100), and the average for about 35 different sectors. At the time of writing the average P/E ratio for the FTSE 100 was 17. Sectors with high P/Es included Telecommunications, and Health. Sectors with low P/Es included Mining, and Construction.

We can generalize that high P/E ratios are associated with expectations of high rates of growth. If the average P/E is 16, then any company with a P/E of much more than 20 is expected to deliver high rates of growth if investors are not to be disappointed. A company with a P/E of less than about 9 is not expected to produce so much growth in earnings per share.

Most companies have a P/E of between about 9 and 25. But care is needed in interpreting these, especially if the P/E is unusually high or low. The P/E ratio of a number of water companies is shown in Illustration 6.4; they fall within the normal range.

Illustration 6.4

P/E ratios of selected water companies	
AWG	11.7
Dee Valley	22.0
East Surrey	18.3
United Utilities	12.2

The fact that investors seem to expect more growth from Dee Valley, and from East Surrey *could* mean that Dee Valley has a brilliant record in increasing profits every year. It is, however, more likely to mean that last year's profits were so awful that they are bound to be a lot better this year!

The fact that AWG and United Utilities have much lower share prices (in relation to last year's earnings) means that investors' expectations of growth from those two companies is more modest. The fall in the P/E ratio of United Utilities between the two dates on which it is quoted in this chapter was due to a fall in their share price following an announcement that they were going to make a substantial rights issue.[12]

12 Existing shareholders are invited to buy additional shares because of the company's capital needs, ostensibly at a favourable price. The market often reacts badly when a company seeks substantial additional sums from shareholders.

Sometimes P/E ratios are abnormally high – so high as to be meaningless. The *Financial Times* does not publish P/E ratios that are higher than 80. In Illustration 6.5 Sudndip plc had four very successful years. Profit increased each year by more than 10 per cent, and at an increasing rate. This raised expectations, and the P/E ratio went up from 12 to 18 during the period. Then, in Year 5, earnings collapsed; earnings per share are minute. We could be fairly sure that the share price would collapse too. Maybe it would go down to £1.00 or even to £0.80. But with a tiny earnings per share figure, even at £0.80 the P/E ratio would still be 160, which is so far out of the normal range as to be misleading. It still means that the share price is very high in relation to the latest earnings per share; but the explanation is more to do with exceptionally low earnings than it is to do with a high share price.

The drop in earnings shown in Illustration 6.5 is rather extreme, but it is often the case that a high P/E ratio signifies that the previous year's earnings were unusually low, and better results are expected soon. Many hotel companies suffered a loss of business in 2003 (partly due to the SARS epidemic and the Iraq war), but their P/E ratios stayed fairly high: the shares were expensive in relation to last year's earnings, but not in relation to anticipated earnings.

Although Financial Reporting Standards and International Accounting Standards lay down clear rules on how earnings per share should be calculated, it is not always clear which earnings per share figures have been used in calculating the P/E ratio, particularly in the financial press. Unusual P/E ratios are often the result of unusual earnings figures – such as exceptional profits or losses on the sale of a subsidiary, or write offs of goodwill. Companies often produce two different earnings per share figures, choosing to exclude particular items for one of them. In the financial press use is sometimes made of P/E ratios based on future forecast earnings; these are sometimes called prospective or forward P/E ratios.

Illustration 6.5

Sudndip plc has 10 million ordinary shares in issue. Their total profits after tax, earnings per share are shown below. The share price and P/E ratio shortly after the results were published are also shown.

	Year 1	Year 2	Year 3	Year 4	Year 5
Net profit after tax	£1 million	£1.1 million	£1.25 million	£1.45 million	£50,000
Earnings per share	£0.10	£0.11	£0.125	£0.145	£0.005
Share price	£1.20	£1.43	£1.87$\frac{1}{2}$	£2.61	
P/E ratio	12	13	15	18	

6.6 **Dividend Yield**

Calculating the Dividend Yield

The dividend yield is another widely used stock market indicator. It shows clearly the relationship between the last known amount of annual dividend, and the most recent share price. It can be calculated on a 'per share' basis, by dividing the most recent annual dividend by the most recent share price.[13] Alternatively it can be calculated for the company as a whole, by dividing the company's total dividends payable for the most recent year[14] by its 'market capitalization' (the most recent share price multiplied by the number of shares that the company has in issue).[15]

The calculation, for two companies, is shown in Illustration 6.6.

In this example, Cronky has a significantly higher dividend yield than Voddy, but care is needed in interpreting this. It does not mean that Cronky's dividends are higher than Voddy's; both companies are paying the same dividend per share, that is, 10 pence. Cronky's higher dividend yield means that it has a lower share price than Voddy. A high dividend yield means that the share price is low (in relation to dividends); a low dividend yield means that the share price is high in relation to dividends.

Illustration 6.6		Cronky plc	Voddy plc
(a)	Number of ordinary shares	1,000,000	1,000,000
(b)	Current share price	£2.00	£3.20
(c)	Market capitalization (a × b)	£2,000,000	£3,200,000
(d)	Total ordinary dividends	£100,000	£100,000
(e)	Dividend yield (d ÷ c × 100)	5%	3.1%
(f)	Dividend per share (d ÷ a)	£0.10	£0.10
(g)	Dividend yield (f ÷ b × 100)	5%	3.1%

13   And multiplying by 100 to express it as a percentage.

14   After deducting any preference dividends.

15   And multiplying by 100 to express it as a percentage.

What the Dividend Yield Can Tell Us

In the 1990s, little attention was given to low dividend yields. The average dividend yield on shares was only around 2 per cent at a time when it was possible to get 5 per cent or more from a bank or building society deposit account. Dividend yields looked very low, partly because share prices were very high. Although interest rates can vary, there is no 'growth' in the amount of interest paid on deposit accounts. But the hope and expectation is that dividends will increase, year after year, and in the majority of companies they still do. If someone invests £100 in shares, and the only dividend they get is £2.00, that looks miserable. But the following year it might be £2.15, then £2.35 the next year, then £2.55; and, after a number of years (hopefully before the investor retires!) the dividend might look very respectable in relation to the original £100 invested, with every prospect that it will continue to increase, at least in line with inflation. With a successful investment, the share price also increases, which means that the dividend yield still looks low: it is the *amount* of dividend which increases each year, not the dividend yield.

It was 'normal'[16] for the average yield on shares to be lower than interest rates on deposit accounts, because investors expect there to be growth in dividends on ordinary shares. But in recent years interest rates on deposit accounts have steadily fallen; and, in the last two years, as share prices have fallen, dividend[17] yields have increased. Shares on average were yielding nearly 4 per cent in 2002–2003; but as share prices rose in mid 2003, the average yield fell to about 3.3 per cent which is comparable with what can be obtained from a deposit account at a bank.

Low dividend yields are mainly the result of high share prices, and low dividend yields go hand in hand with high P/E ratios. Shares that are expected to deliver rapid and sustained growth have high prices, and therefore high P/E ratios, and therefore low dividend yields. But many of the growth portfolios of the 1990s did not deliver, and share prices collapsed as the twentieth century ended.

In the early years of this century investors' faith in growth stocks[18] steadily evaporated, and there has been more focus on shares that represent real value: low P/E ratios, and higher dividend yields.

---

16   Though normality steadily changes. At the time of writing the fashion for institutional investors is to buy corporate bonds because they have relatively high yields, with reasonable security. But as these bonds become more popular, so their price will increase, and their yield will fall. And a few more big collapses (Enron, WorldCom, Marconi, Telewest, Energis, Parmalat) may soon show this 'profitable' strategy to be just as dubious a bubble as previous ones.

17   Dividends have not generally fallen; share prices have fallen.

18   Stocks or shares – much the same thing.

It might be a rational strategy for investors to choose companies with high dividend yields, provided they can be sure that the dividends will continue to be high. We do not know what future dividends will be. For a time in 2002/2003 Abbey National had a high dividend yield (10 per cent), but there was no guarantee that this level of dividend would continue. The dividend yield looked high in relation to the previous year's dividend, partly because the share price had collapsed,[19] and it was rumoured that the following year's dividend would be reduced.

At present, interest rates are low: it is difficult to get more than about 3.5 per cent from a deposit account. Although the average yield on shares is only 3.3 per cent, there are plenty of shares with yields higher than 4 per cent which look reasonably sound, and have prospects of steadily increasing dividends. But yields of more than about 6 per cent may be suspicious: the share price is low in part because investors think that there may be problems with future dividends. Many individual and institutional investors are attracted to 'good value' shares with a reasonable dividend yield. It is possible to get some guidance on how sound such an investment might be by looking at the company's record over a number of years (profits and dividends), and by looking at their cash flow statements.

6.7 Dividend Cover

The easiest and most widely used indicator of how likely it is that a company's dividend will be maintained and increased is 'dividend cover'. This is the relationship between profits and dividends. If a company pays out only a small proportion of its profits as dividends, then the dividend looks reasonably secure: even if profits fall in the following year, there should still be more than enough to pay the dividend.

Dividend cover is calculated by dividing earnings per share by dividend per share. It can also be calculated by dividing the total profits attributable to ordinary shareholders by the total amount of ordinary dividends payable for the year.

The calculations for Cronky plc and Voddy plc are shown in Illustration 6.7.

On this basis, Cronky's dividend looks more secure than Voddy's. We must expect profits to fluctuate from time to time. Cronky can afford a bigger percentage reduction in profits before the dividend looks threatened

---

19 The P/E ratio was down to 4.6, one of the lowest on the stock market. Investors were really pessimistic about the company's growth prospects.

Illustration 6.7

		Cronky plc	Voddy plc
(a)	Total profits after taxation attributable to ordinary shareholders	£200,000	£160,000
(b)	Total ordinary dividends	£100,000	£100,000
(c)	Dividend cover (a ÷ b)	2 times	1.6 times
(d)	Earnings per share	£0.20	£0.16
(e)	Dividend per share	£0.10	£0.10
(f)	Dividend cover (d ÷ e)	2 times	1.6 times

than Voddy. If each company suffered a 40 per cent reduction in profits, the earnings per share would be:

	Cronky plc	Voddy plc
Earnings per share	£0.12	£0.096

If each company continued with a 10 pence per share dividend, the dividend cover would be:

	Cronky plc	Voddy plc
Dividend cover	1.2 times	0.96

Although it is acceptable for a company to pay out more in dividends than it earns in profits from time to time, perhaps when there is an unusually bad year, clearly this cannot continue for very long. A dividend that is not well covered by profits looks insecure. The average company on the stock market at the time of writing had a dividend cover of about 1.7 times. Many companies try to maintain the amount of dividend, even in years when profits are not good; their dividend cover then looks weaker.

6.8 Net Asset (or Balance Sheet) Value

It is easy to calculate the net asset value of a company, or the value of its equity, from the balance sheet. In most cases this is simply the total of shareholders' funds, which is the same as the total amount of net assets (fixed assets + current assets − Current liabilities − Long-term liabilities). The amount for preference shares (if there are any) should be deducted because we are usually assessing only the value of the ordinary shareholders' funds.

This amount can then be compared with the 'market capitalization' – the total value of all of the company's shares, using the most recent share price.

The comparison can be made using these total figures for the company as a whole. Alternatively, it can be made on a per share basis, comparing the net asset value per share with the share price.

In most cases the market value of a company is much higher than the net asset value shown on the balance sheet. This is for two main reasons:

1 Balance sheet values may be understated, often being based on historic cost rather than current values; and some assets are not shown on the balance sheet – human assets, skills and any 'internally generated'[20] goodwill.

2 Share prices are determined by supply and demand for the shares, and the balance sheet usually has a minor influence on demand for shares. The major influence is expectations of future profits, and expectations that the share price will rise in the future.

Some traditional manufacturing companies may have huge amounts of assets, and their market capitalization may not be very much more than their net asset value. Many modern companies have relatively small amounts of tangible assets, and their value lies in their skills, expertise, reputation, brands, and other intangibles not shown on the balance sheet. Such companies might easily be worth five or ten times their net asset values – especially at the height of a bubble!

The *Financial Times* does not regularly publish net asset values – which might be taken as an indication that they are not seen as being particularly important. They can easily be calculated from a company's balance sheet, and usually feature in reports by investment analysts, and are published by journals such as the *Investors Chronicle*.

In a minority of cases the net asset value of a company falls below its market capitalization. If the difference is substantial, this might invite an asset stripping takeover bid: it may be possible to buy up the company at a bargain price, and then sell off all of the separate parts of it at a profit. Investment analysts often assess the market value – not just the balance sheet value – of the separate parts of a business, and when this falls below the market capitalization, there are danger signs for management: another management team may be able to take over and do a better job for the shareholders.

In some cases, such as property companies, the market capitalization is usually significantly less than the market value of the underlying assets. In part this may be because the balance sheet shows properties at fairly full

---

20 When a company buys another business, any amount paid for 'goodwill' has to be shown. But when a company generates its own goodwill, this is not shown on a balance sheet.

current valuations, and it may be difficult to sell the properties at those prices. It may also be because it is difficult to generate much growth in profits: rental income is relatively stable, and safe, but does not produce 'double digit' growth in profits.

6.9 Cash Flow

Cash flow may be a better indicator of a company's performance than profit. A company that generates substantial profits on paper, but cannot back them up with cash flows, raises serious questions. A company which makes profits year after year, but has to keep raising more money (by borrowing or making rights issues) may be unpopular with investors. Cash flow statements explain how and why a company's cash flow differs from its profit, as explained in Chapter 7.

The first question is: does the company generate cash from its normal operations? If it does not there is a need to establish why not.

The second question is to do with expansion. Is the company investing in more fixed assets, and buying other businesses? This is clearly shown on the cash flow statement. Such expansion may require additional borrowing, or the issue of more shares. Amounts invested in expansion can be compared with the amounts raised as additional share capital and borrowings. It is a danger sign if the company is raising lots more capital, without any evident increase in profitable investment. It is more healthy if a company is investing in additional capacity, but this is partly financed from operating cash flows, and not totally dependent on raising additional funds.

A cash flow statement is arranged roughly in order of the importance of the figures in giving an indication of the company's strength in generating cash. It starts with the most important figures: cash generated from operations. Then interest and taxation are deducted to give a figure that indicates how much the company has generated (if any) – it is free to decide how to use this amount. It may be invested in fixed assets, or other businesses; it may be paid out as dividends.

The final figures on the cash flow statement, the increase or decrease in cash during the year, is not particularly important. It is more important to analyse the various factors that have given rise to that increase or decrease in cash.

Some analysts emphasize profit plus depreciation and amortization as being the key figure. Others look for 'free cash flow' which can be deduced from somewhere in the middle of the cash flow statement, by estimating how much of the amounts paid for additional fixed assets is essential, and how much is for expansion.

6.10 **Other Indicators/Predictors of Performance**

There is no shortage of investment analysts, experts and charlatans giving advice on how to pick winners when investing on the stock market. Most accountants are more cautious – but not all! It is difficult to be clear about who is an expert, who is a charlatan, and who is advising investing in particular shares for reasons of self-interest. Even the 'experts' do not seem to be able to get it right, and are often carried along with the fashionable conventional wisdoms of the day. In the late 1990s it was not difficult to spot that shares in telecommunications companies were overpriced as the bubble went up and up. But institutions who did not invest in telecommunications companies saw their results compared unfavourably with others who were more successful in investing in shares that continued to increase in value. They, and almost everyone, invested in telecommunications shares until the bubble burst, and share prices collapsed. The effects were serious for many, including pension funds.

All financial accounting information can be analysed with a view to guiding investment decisions. Many different ratios can be calculated, and an examination of trends over a number of years can be revealing.

The relationship between a company's turnover figure and its market capitalization is one of many ratios that might be worth following. The idea is that if a company's market capitalization is higher than its turnover, the shares are overpriced. If a company's turnover is very much higher than its market capitalization, the shares are good value. The theory is that if a company has a high level of sales (in relation to share price), profits will follow. The hardest thing is to achieve a high level of turnover. If the present management cannot make good profits from a high level of sales, a future management will. This may be no more than a hypothesis. It would probably turn out to be a good basis for investment in some companies, in some years; but not for other companies in other years. This is probably true for most decision rules which are supposed to form the basis for investment decisions.

During the period of enthusiasm for shares in telecommunications companies, emphasis was given to measures such as earnings before interest, taxation, depreciation and amortization.[21] Decision rules emerged that a company should be worth about three times this figure. But ideas like this can be quickly abandoned when the market changes.

The more fully past data is analysed, the more models can be developed that appear to predict future share prices. It is not difficult to find past data

---

21   Known as EBITDA.

which, if analysed in a particular way, would have predicted share prices. But we cannot assume that such relationships will hold good in the future. In choosing between different accounting policies accountants often favour those policies which have most predictive value; but we can know only those which would have had most predictive value in the past. Markets are constantly changing. Companies and activities that did well in the 1990s may be a disaster in the 2000s. Past performance is no guide to the future.

The same arguments apply with technical analysis: it is difficult to believe that graphs of share prices over time show patterns which enable us to predict future share prices.

Although financial accounting cannot give us all of the answers that we might like, the information that it provides is central in making investment decisions, and in monitoring how successful those decisions turn out to be.

6.11 A Further Illustration

The main stock market ratios are shown in Illustration 6.8. The figures suggest a typical, average company, and may be used to make comparisons with other companies and to see how the ratios have been calculated. The P/E ratio, the dividend cover, and the dividend yield may all be calculated using figures for the company as a whole, or on a per share basis.

The figures for Stoutmouth plc are in many ways typical of a listed company. At the time of writing, the average P/E ratio of the 100 largest

Illustration 6.8

	Stoutmouth plc
Share capital (25 pence shares)	£ 5,000,000
Reserves	£31,000,000
	£36,000,000
Net profit after tax for year	£6,400,000
Dividends for year	£4,000,000
Number of shares	20,000,000
Market price of shares	£5.44
Market capitalization	£108,800,000
Earnings per share	£0.32
Dividend per share	£0.20
Price/Earnings ratio	17
Dividend times cover	1.6 times
Dividend yield	3.7%
Net assets per share	£1.80

companies quoted on the London Stock Exchange was 17.6; the average dividend yield was 3.3 per cent; and the average times cover for dividends was 1.7. The market capitalization of each of the companies in the largest 100 is between £1 billion and £100 billion. But the market capitalization of most listed companies is nearer to that of Stoutmouth plc.

Summary

One of the main objectives of financial management is to maximize shareholders' wealth. Dividends, which are dependent on profits, contribute to this. But the main element of shareholders' wealth is the value of their shares. Directors and chief executives are usually well motivated to maintain and increase their company's share price: they own shares themselves; they may have options to buy shares at predetermined prices; and their remuneration may include substantial incentives related to share price performance. If they fail, and the share price languishes, they risk the wrath of shareholders, and leave themselves open to a hostile takeover bid with a new management team replacing them.

Accounting measures of solvency and profitability are central to the performance of share prices. If a company is seen as having excessive debt, the share price will suffer. Profitability is essential to maintaining and increasing share prices, although more attention seems to be paid to earnings per share than to return on capital employed. Growth, and expectations of future growth in sales, profits and dividends make a major contribution to increases in share prices. Sometimes it seems that expectations of share price increases are the main cause of share price increases. Share prices are influenced by expectations, rumours and many other factors which are difficult to define and measure, particularly in the short term. In the long run, sound finances, and growth in earnings per share are likely to be the main contributors to increasing share prices.

Review of Key Points

- Many different factors influence share prices

- A company's price/earnings ratio, dividend yield, and dividend cover are widely used measures of share price performance

- Growth and expectations of growth of sales and profits help to boost share prices

- Many influences on share prices are difficult to quantify

- Company directors and shareholders have an interest in maintaining and increasing share prices

- Claims to be able to predict share prices should be treated with caution

- Financial accounting information helps to explain changes in share prices

Self-testing Questions

1 Explain the meaning, calculation and significance of each of the following:
   (a) Price/earnings ratio
   (b) Dividend yield
   (c) Dividend times cover

2 Is a company's balance sheet value (net asset value) likely to be higher or lower than its market value? Explain.

3 If a company currently has a dividend yield of 10 per cent, does that mean that someone investing £100 today will receive £10 dividend in the coming year? Explain. Reference should be made to United Utilities, Illustration 6.1.

4 You are given the following information about two companies. You are required to fill in the missing items for Beermouth plc.

	Alemouth plc	Beermouth plc
Share capital (20 pence shares)	£1,600,000	£ 2,000,000
Reserves	£3,200,000	£18,000,000
	£4,800,000	£20,000.000
Net profit after tax for year	⁻£3,520,000	£1,200,000
Dividends for year	£3,200,000	£ 800,000

Self-testing Questions (continued)

Number of shares	8,000,000	10,000,000
Market price of shares	£4.40	£1.80
Market capitalization	£35,200,000	£18,000,000
Earnings per share	£0.44	£0.12
Dividend per share	£0.40	£0.08
Price/earnings ratio	10	–
Dividend times cover	1.1 times	–
Dividend yield	9.09%	–
Net assets per share	£0.60	–

5 Comment on the dividend yield of Alemouth plc.

6 Comment on the relationship between the net assets per share of Beermouth plc and its share price (or on the relationship of the total of shareholders' funds to the market capitalization).

Assessment Questions

1 What is the level of the FTSE 100 today? What is the average P/E ratio of the top 100 companies? What is their dividend yield and dividend cover?

   On 16 September 2003 the FTSE 100 stood at 4299; the average P/E of the top 100 companies was 17.6; the average dividend yield was 3.3 per cent; and the average dividend cover was 1.72. What do you think are the main causes of the changes since September 2003?

2 You are given the following information about two companies, partly extracted from their most recent balance sheet and profit and loss account, and partly taken from the financial press. You are required to fill in the missing items for Drinkmouth plc.

	Cidermouth plc	Drinkmouth plc
Share capital (20 pence shares)	£ 4,000,000	£1.200,000
Reserves	£14,000,000	£2,400,000
	£18,000,000	£3,600.000
Net profit after tax for year	£3,400,000	£1,800,000
Dividends for year	£2,000,000	£ 900,000
Number of shares	20,000,000	6,000,000
Market price of shares	£3.40	–
Market capitalization	£68,000,000	£45,000,000
Earnings per share	£0.17	£0.30
Dividend per share	£0.10	–

Assessment Questions (continued)

Price/earnings ratio	20	25
Dividend times cover	1.7 times	–
Dividend yield	2.9%	2.0%
Net assets per share	£1.80	–

3 You are given the following information about Swin Gin plc:

	Year 1	Year 2	Year 3	Year 4	Year 5*	Year 6	Year 7
Earnings per share	£0.50	£0.55	£0.62	£0.01	£1.20	£0.83	£0.90
Share price	£6.00	£7.70	£9.92	£6.00	£7.20	£12.45	£15.30

(after publication of results for year)

* In Year 5 the company sold their head office building in London making a profit which amounted to £0.45 per share.

You are required to calculate the P/E ratio for each year, and comment on how the market appears to have reacted to changes in earnings per share.

4 Assess the usefulness of P/E ratios and suggest how they might be misleading.

5 Select a recent takeover bid (e.g. the 2003 bids by William Morrison and others for Safeway). Assess the various factors that determined the price that was eventually agreed for the company which was taken over.

Group Activities and Discussion Questions

1 Look at the shares listing in the *Financial Times*. What is an average P/E ratio? Select some companies with high P/E ratios. Do they seem to have anything in common? How useful are the P/E ratios given for different sectors in the 'FTSE Actuaries Share Indices'? Select some companies with low P/E ratios. Do they seem to have anything in common?

2 Look at the shares listing in the *Financial Times*. What is an average dividend yield? Select some companies with high dividend yields. Do they seem to have anything in common? How useful are the dividend yields given for different sectors in the 'FTSE Actuaries Share Indices'? Select some companies with low dividend yields. Do they seem to have anything in common?

3 Each member of the group selects one or two companies in which they believe the shares are likely to increase in price during a selected period. A long period may be preferable, but in a 12-week module the selection could be made in week 4; the shares monitored for 6 weeks; and the 'final' results assessed in week 10.

   Each member of the group is required to give a justification for selecting a particular share in week 4. Then, in week 10, each member should present an explanation of what has happened to their company's share price.

Group Activities and Discussion Questions (continued)

There would be a competitive element (who would have made most money?). There should also be an assessment of the quality of the presentations; this assessment could be done partly or wholly by the students themselves.

4   Each group forms one or more hypotheses about how to select companies where the increase in share prices is expected to be higher than the average for the FTSE 100 companies. Examples might include (with variations) such things as:

   (i)   companies with a dividend yield of between 4 per cent and 5 per cent where the cover is not less than 2;

   (ii)   companies where sales have increased by more than 20 per cent per annum (over a given number of years), but profits have not (yet) increased;

   (iii) companies where profits have increased by more than 10 per cent since last year, but the share price is lower.

This exercise might be more fun if it is done live. But it is difficult to complete it during the 12-week period of a typical module. It is easiest to do it historically. The decision rules are selected first; then they are applied to a sample of companies.

Some competition between different groups can produce interesting results. The results produced by the winners might need careful scrutiny.

5   Each group chooses three different sectors (e.g. Pharmaceuticals and Biotech; Construction and Building Materials; Transport; Retailers). The key stock market indicators are found for each sector and compared with the average for the FTSE. These are shown in the *Financial Times* as 'FTSE Actuaries Share Indices'. Suggest factors which make each sector different from the FTSE average.

Financial Accounting in context

Discuss and comment on the following item taken from the press:
BA's pessimism could hit hopes of Footsie return by Kevin Done
Financial Times, 9 September 2003

Rod Eddington, chief executive of British Airways, warned yesterday that 'a real recovery in air travel was still some way off'. The aviation market had bottomed out but there was 'little evidence of significant recovery', he said.

Mr Eddington's pessimistic assessment could undermine BA's hopes of being reinstated this week in the FTSE 100.

BA's share price has more than doubled in the last six months on hopes that airlines were coming through the worst of the crisis in the aviation industry.

Financial Accounting in context (continued)

The strong recovery has propelled BA to the brink of reinstatement in the FTSE 100, but its shares closed yesterday 10p lower at $190\frac{1}{4}$p. Last night's ranking of 92 amongst listed UK companies would not guarantee it readmission, when the index undergoes its quarterly adjustment, based on tonight's closing prices.

Mr Eddington also made a strong plea in a speech to the UBS transport conference for a third runway to be built at Heathrow. Delays and congestion at the airport, BA's main base, were costing the group £67m a year and a third runway was 'vital' for the group. Playing down recent suggestions that a recovery in the aviation industry was already under way, he said that volumes in the airline's crucial UK/US business class market were still 20 per cent below those of 2000.

Mr Eddington said the propensity to travel premium class on long-haul services, as measured by industry surveys, was at a record low, and he ruled out any chance of a longer-term recovery of business class flying on short-haul services, where there had been a structural change in the market.

Mr Eddington said industry yields on long-haul services were at record lows, below even the level of the three months following the September 11 2001 terrorist attacks in the US. Yields on European short-haul services were also 'unlikely to improve', said Mr Eddington, because of the heavy competitive pressures from the fast-growing low-cost airlines.

References and Further Reading

Berger, D. and J. Carlisle (2002) *The Motley Fool UK Investment Guide*, Boxtree.

Brett, M. (2003) *How to Read the Financial Pages*, Random House Business Books.

Rees, B. (forthcoming) *Financial Analysis*, 3rd edn, Pearson Education.

Investors Chronicle (weekly magazine)

www.ft.com

www.londonstockexchange.com

7

Cash Flow and Profit

Learning objectives

After studying this chapter you should be able to:

♦ Understand the differences between cash flow and profit

♦ Explain the accruals concept

♦ Understand and interpret cash flow statements

♦ Prepare simple cash flow statements

♦ Understand and interpret cash budgets

♦ Prepare simple cash budgets

♦ Explain how 'incomplete records' are converted into income statements and balance sheets

♦ Prepare straightforward income statements and balance sheets from incomplete records

♦ Appreciate the importance of having both accruals based, and cash flow based financial information

Introduction

It is tempting to say that the performance of a company should be judged by the amount of cash that it generates. A successful company generates lots of cash. An unsuccessful company runs out of cash. The accountant's job would be very easy: there is no need to do more than record all receipts and payments, and to report on a regular basis which is higher. The analyst's job would be easy: the company which generates most cash is most successful.

There would be no problems of credibility or subjectivity, or manipulation of asset values and exaggeration of profits. Everything could be easily checked by looking at the company's bank statement.

But generating lots of cash is not necessarily a sign of success. Few of us would be impressed by a company that massively increased its cash balances simply by selling off assets and borrowing lots of money. A company that succeeds in generating large amounts of cash is not necessarily a successful company.

Similarly, a successful company might pay out far more cash than it receives. A profitable company might be paying out substantial sums of cash to buy assets that are going to be even more profitable in the future. The company could be seen as performing well – even though it is using up lots of cash.

It may be that, in many companies, profit and cash[1] flow go hand in hand and tell a similar story. But they can also tell very different stories, and the distinction between cash flow and profit is vital to an understanding of financial accounting – and to the survival of many businesses.

Many people go into business in order to 'make money', even though they are not very clear what 'making money' means. Does it mean making profit, or do they mean generating cash? And what is the difference?

This chapter explains and illustrates the differences between cash flow and profit. The distinction is not easily understood and is dealt with in four parts:

1 The accruals concept

2 Cash flow statements

3 Cash budgets

4 Incomplete records.

You may study any one of these sections independently: the explanations and illustrations should be sufficient. If you choose to read all four sections at a

---

1 The word 'cash' is used to include both petty cash (coins and notes) and money in the bank.

single sitting (and you manage to stay awake), you will find that there is some repetition, but the distinctions should become clear in your mind, and you will understand different contexts in which the distinctions are important.

1   The *accruals concept* is the theoretical basis of the distinction between cash flow and profit.

2   A *cash flow statement* provides a reconciliation between the amount of profit generated during a period, and the amount by which cash balances have increased or decreased during that period.

3   A *cash budget* is a plan of receipts and payments of cash, typically prepared for the next coming year. It shows the cash generated each month, and the balance remaining (or overdraft) at the end of each month. It can be compared with a budgeted income statement or profit and loss account to show how profit differs from cash flow.

4   *Incomplete records* are often kept by small businesses. They do not have a full set of double entry accounts, but a summary of receipts and payments of cash can be constructed from bank statements. The process of converting receipts and payments into an income statement, the calculation of profit, and the production of a balance sheet, illustrate how cash flow differs from profit.

7.1 The Accruals Concept

Balance sheets and income statements are based on the *accruals concept*, which means that profit is the difference between the Revenues earned during a period (regardless of when the money is received), and the costs incurred in earning those revenues (regardless of when cash is paid out).

The accruals concept has long been regarded as a *fundamental accounting concept*.[2] It requires that revenues and costs are accrued, and matched with one another so far as their relationship can be established or justifiably assumed. They are dealt with in the profit and loss account of the period to which they relate, which is often not in the period when cash is received or paid.

The profit figure for a particular period is therefore likely to be very different from the amount of cash generated in that period. A naïve, non-accountant might think that:

Profit   =   Receipts of cash   less   Payments of cash

But they would be seriously mistaken.

---

2   SSAP 2 specified four fundamental accounting concepts: going concern; accruals; consistency; and prudence (or conservatism).

Financial accounting is based on the accruals concept which means that, for a particular period:

Profit   =   Revenues earned   less   Costs incurred in earning those revenues

The words are important. Receipts and payments apply to cash. Revenues or income and costs or expenses apply to profit calculation.

The accruals concept is applied throughout financial accounting. Gross profit is the difference between sales and the cost of goods sold. In calculating profit, it is the amount of sales revenue earned during a period that matters, not when the money is received. The cost of goods sold uses the purchases figure, which is the total amount purchased during the period, regardless of when they are paid for. The cost of goods sold figure also adjusts for stocks. The expense is based on the cost of the goods which were actually sold. Unsold stocks from last year become a cost for this year. Unsold stocks at the end of this year become a cost for next year.

Any payment made to buy fixed assets that is made this year (or which it is agreed will be paid in another year) is not an expense for this year. The cost is spread out over the life of the fixed asset and is charged as depreciation each year. The timing of cash paid out for buying fixed assets is very different from the timing of the expense charged in calculating profit.

It is important to be clear that:

1 Not all payments of cash are expenses; some payments are not a charge against profits

2 Not all receipts of cash are revenues; some receipts do not add to profits

3 Not all expenses are payments of cash; some expenses are charged against profits although no payment of cash is required in the year that the expense is charged

4 Not all revenues are receipts of cash; some revenues are added to profits although there is no receipt of cash in the year that credit is taken for the revenue.

There are examples of each of the above four differences. But, in interpreting financial statements, it is important to look for the big differences. The biggest inflows of cash are likely to come from borrowings, issuing share capital, and selling off assets;[3] none of these count as revenues for the purpose of calculating profit. The biggest outflows of cash are usually for buying fixed assets; but such payments are not charges against profit for the year. The biggest expense, which is not paid in cash, is depreciation – and that can easily cause confusion!

---

3 Any profit on selling a fixed asset counts towards profit for the year, the full amount of the sale proceeds does not.

Some of the examples of differences are relatively minor timing differences. But they are all important in explaining the difference between cash flow and profit. And, in some circumstances 'minor' items can become very significant.

1 *Payments of cash that are not expenses*: purchase of fixed assets; investing in other companies; repaying loans; payments to buy stocks of goods which are not sold until the next period; payments to creditors for expenses incurred in the previous period.

2 *Receipts of cash that are not revenues*: sale of fixed assets; borrowing money; proceeds from issuing shares; receipts from debtors this period in respect of sales for the previous period.

3 *Expenses that are not payments*: depreciation and amortisation;[4] expenses incurred this period but which are not paid for until the next period; creating a provision; increase in a provision for bad debts; discount allowed to customers for settling their accounts promptly.

4 *Revenues that are not receipts*: sales that are made during this period, but the money is not received until the next period; discount allowed by suppliers for settling accounts promptly; reduction in a provision. There are also examples where the cash receipt is very different from the revenue figure. When a fixed asset is sold, all of the cash received is credited to the cash account. But in calculating profit, only the difference between book value and the sale proceeds is credited to profit, as shown in Illustration 7.1.

It is sometimes argued that cash flow would be a better basis for accounting than the accruals concept because it is more objective. But total cash flows (including receipts from borrowing, and payments to acquire

Illustration 7.1

The Floughin Company has a small assembly plant at Jurbeigh which originally cost £30,000; cumulative depreciation is £6,000. The government decided to develop an international airport nearby, and the company was able to sell their plant for £40,000.

The receipt of cash is £40,000. The net book value of the plant is (£30,000 − £6,000 =)£24,000. Only the profit of £16,000 is credited towards profit for the year.

4 Amortization is really the same as depreciation, but the word is usually applied to leasehold property, and to intangible fixed assets such as goodwill.

fixed assets) mean little unless there is some classification of the receipts and payments. The need for classification would remove the supposed objectivity. Almost all accountants agree that profit measurement[5] and the use of the accruals concept are essential.

7.2 **Cash Flow Statements**

A *cash flow statement* provides a reconciliation between the amount of profit generated during a period, and the amount by which cash balances have increased or decreased during that period. The idea is that profits do generate cash; but cash tends to flow away. The statement shows where it has gone.

It starts off by showing how much operating profit was generated during the period; then it shows what happened to the profits. Some of it may be tied up in additional stocks and debtors; some may have gone in paying interest and taxation; some may have gone in buying more fixed assets, or repaying loans. The final figure shows how much cash is left. The cash left at the end will be the same as the cash figure shown on the balance sheet at the year end.

The statements are produced in a standard format, using standard headings, to facilitate comparisons between companies. A simplified cash flow statement is shown for Pei Lun as Illustration 7.2. The standard headings are shown in Illustration 7.5 although most do not apply in this simplified example.

Statements always start off with a calculation of the cash inflow from operating activities. Users may want to know how much cash the business is generating from normal operations. It is then necessary to add the year's depreciation charge back to the operating profit. Depreciation is an expense that was charged in calculating operating profit, but as (unlike other expenses) there was no cash paid out, it has to be added back in calculating operating profit.[6]

Operating profits can be used up in financing additional working capital (stocks and debtors); or they can be supplemented by reductions in working capital (cash from selling stocks; debtors paying more quickly; and increases in creditors).

The net cash flow from operating activities is based on operating profit, plus depreciation, adjusted for any changes in working capital. It gives an indication of whether a company is generating cash from its operating activities; or whether its operating activities are using up cash.

5   The reasons why profit is measured are explored in Chapter 5.

6   Sometimes the phrase 'cash flow' is used loosely to mean profit plus depreciation.

Illustration 7.2

A Simplified Cash Flow Statement: Pei Lun

		£000
Cash inflow from operations		
Profit		32
Depreciation		5
		37
Deduct: Increase in working capital		
Increase in stocks	20	
Increase in debtors	5	
Decrease in creditors	2	27
Cash inflow from operating activities		10
Deduct purchase of fixed assets		
Vehicles		45
Cash outflow		35

Pei Lun started the year with £10,000 in the bank. By the end of the year she had an overdraft of £25,000. In total £35,000 had flowed out of the business, as shown on the cash flow statement.

In the case of Pei Lun (Illustration 7.2), most of the operating profit is used to finance increases in working capital. The cash inflow from operating activities is still positive (£10,000), but additional fixed assets (vehicles) are bought for £45,000. The result is that there is £35,000 less cash at the end of the year than there was at the beginning.

Illustration 7.2 is a much simplified example. The published cash flow statement of Ted Baker plc is shown in Illustration 7.3.

The calculation of the cash inflow from operations is very much as shown above, although in published accounts it is usually hidden away as a note.

Consolidated Cash Flow Statement

The first part of a cash flow statement, where the cash flow from operations is calculated, is normally shown as a note to the accounts. In Illustration 7.2, the note has been added to the main cash flow statement.

The net cash inflow from operations at Ted Baker for the year to 25 January 2003 was nearly £14 million, a significant increase on the previous year.[7] But the company ended the year with a decrease in cash of just over

7   From £12,250,000 to £13,632,000, an 11 per cent increase.

Illustration 7.3   Ted Baker

21. RECONCILIATION OF OPERATING PROFIT TO OPERATING CASH FLOWS	52 weeks ended 25 January 2003	52 weeks ended 26 January 2002
	£'000	£'000
Operating profit	9,910	9,955
Impairment of fixed assets	1,551	–
Depreciation charges	3,093	2,319
Loss/(profit) on sale of tangible fixed assets	9	(2)
Decrease in own shares	97	–
(Increase)/decrease in stocks	(1,654)	338
(Increase)/decrease in debtors	(1,135)	121
Increase/(decrease) in creditors	1,761	(481)
Net cash inflow from operating activities	13,632	12,250

CONSOLIDATED CASH FLOW STATEMENT For the 52 weeks ended 25 January 2003	Notes	52 weeks ended 25 January 2003 £'000	52 weeks ended 26 January 2002 £'000
Net cash inflow from operating activities	21	13,632	12,250
Returns on investments and servicing of finance			
– Interest received		55	62
– Interest paid		(502)	(579)
		(447)	(517)
Taxation			
UK corporation tax paid		(3,215)	(2,705)
Overseas tax paid		–	(32)
		(3,215)	(2,737)
Capital expenditure and financial investment	22	(7,949)	(2,651)
Equity dividends paid		(3,313)	(3,012)
Cash (outflow)/inflow before financing		(1,292)	3,333
Shares issued		225	30
Debt due after more than one year		–	4,000
(Decrease)/increase in cash in the period	22	(1,067)	7,363

The accompanying notes are an integral part of this consolidated cash flow statement.

£1 million.[8] There were three main reasons why the large cash inflow from operations disappeared. Taxation was more than £3 million and dividends paid were more than £3 million. But the main item was capital expenditure and financial investment of nearly £8 million.

In the previous year Ted Baker's capital expenditure was more modest: £2.65 million. Their operating cash flow was more than enough to cover this, and taxation, and dividends; and they ended the year with a substantial increase in cash.

Tate and Lyle's group statement of cash flows is shown in Illustration 7.4. It begins with the net cash flow from operating activities, the detail of which is shown in a note to the accounts. Compared with the previous year there has been a substantial reduction in the net cash flow from operating activities; to some extent this has been offset by a reduction in the amount of interest that the company paid. But there was still a decrease in cash during the period; this was mainly because substantial borrowings were repaid (£245 million + £104 million repaid, offset by new borrowings of £195 million).

It is tempting to think that the cash inflow from operations is the money that the business has generated; it can then choose what to do with it. But not all of the operating cash flow is freely available like this. Some of it has to be paid out in interest, and some has to be paid in taxation.

The first four sections of a cash flow statement are usually:

1 Net cash inflow from operating activities

2 Dividends received from joint ventures and associates

3 Returns on investment and servicing of finance. The main item is usually interest paid;[9] there may also be interest received[10]

4 Taxation paid.

The company can usually do more or less what it likes with the cash flow figure produced after these first four headings. They can use it to buy more fixed assets, to buy other businesses, to pay dividends, or to repay loans.

It is tempting to think of this figure as being 'free cash flow'. But no such figure is highlighted on cash flow statements although it is important, and widely used by analysts. The reason is that most companies, in most years, have to buy some fixed assets. It may just be replacing cars, computers,

---

8   The previous year their cash balances had increased by over £7 million.

9   Interest actually paid is what appears on a cash flow statement. In calculating profit the amount of interest *payable* is shown, as required by the accruals concept.

10   Plus any preference dividends paid; and dividends paid to minority shareholders in subsidiary companies.

Illustration 7.4

Tate & Lyle annual report 2003
group statement of cash flows

Notes		Year to 31 March 2003 £ million	Year to 31 March 2002 £ million
29	Net cash inflow from operating activities	323	445
	Dividends received from joint ventures	10	7
	Returns on investments and servicing of finance		
	Interest paid	(51)	(109)
	Interest received	30	48
	Dividends paid to minority interests in subsidiary undertakings	(2)	(1)
		(23)	(62)
	Taxation paid	(7)	(35)
	Capital expenditure and financial investment		
	Purchase of tangible fixed assets	(75)	(76)
	Sale of tangible fixed assets	1	15
	Purchase of fixed asset investments	(15)	(12)
	Sale of fixed asset investments	4	12
		(85)	(61)
	Acquisitions and disposals		
	Sale of subsidiaries	55	103
	Net overdrafts of subsidiaries sold	–	2
	Sale of interests in joint ventures and associates	–	7
	Refinancing of existing joint ventures	–	(3)
		55	109
	Equity dividends paid	(84)	(85)
	Net cash inflow before financing and management of liquid resources	189	318
	Management of liquid resources		
	Increase in current asset investments	(67)	(2)
	Net cash inflow before financing	122	316
	Financing		
	Repayment of borrowings due after one year	(245)	(246)
	New borrowings due after one year	195	220
	Decrease in short-term borrowings	(104)	(272)
	Net cash outflow from financing	(154)	(298)
31	(Decrease)/increase in cash in the period	(32)	18

Net cash inflows of £56 million were received in respect of exceptional items.

machinery and furniture as they become worn out or obsolete. But there is usually little choice but to spend *something* extra on fixed assets.

We could estimate that perhaps one-third of the spending on fixed assets is essential, and two-thirds is optional. There is no real basis for this: it is just a guess. But it can be useful to estimate how much 'free cash flow' (if any) a company generates. It gives an indication of financial performance, and also of the company's flexibility to change direction and improve opportunities.

The fifth heading on a cash flow statement is 'Capital expenditure and financial investment' which refers mainly to money paid to acquire additional fixed assets. The heading also includes any money received for disposals of fixed assets. Capital expenditure is usually seen as being 'a good thing': capital expenditure should add to the value of a company. But there are also examples of companies which seem to go in for never ending borrowing and investing in fixed assets, with little or no benefit to shareholders, until they collapse under the weight of the debt they have accumulated.[11]

The sixth heading is 'Acquisitions and disposals', which is similar to the fourth heading except that it refers to payments to acquire businesses, not just fixed assets. It includes payments for whole businesses, and for part ownership of a business. This may be a partly owned subsidiary, an associate, or a joint venture. The heading also includes any money received from disposing of businesses.

The seventh heading is 'Equity dividends paid'. An income statement indicates the extent to which dividends are justified by profits. A cash flow statement can indicate to what extent the dividend is justified by the cash flows that the company is generating.

After the seventh heading a sub-total is shown: 'Cash inflow/outflow before use of liquid resources and financing'. The first three headings may be seen as showing how much cash the business has generated. The next three show what they have chosen to spend it on. They may spend less than they have generated, which means that they build up their cash balances, or repay loans.[12] Or they may spend more than they have generated, which means that they reduce their cash balances, or have to find more money by borrowing or issuing more shares.

The eighth and ninth headings show what has happened to any surplus from the previous six headings; or if there is a deficit from the previous six headings, how it has been financed.

---

11 Recent collapses of airlines and telecommunications companies come to mind, but it is a danger to look out for in any company.

12 Or even buy back their own shares.

The eighth heading, 'Management of liquid resources' shows how any short-term cash surpluses have been dealt with. Surplus cash may have flowed out into short-term deposits and other liquid resources. And cash may have flowed in by withdrawals from short-term deposits or redemption of any liquid investments.

The ninth heading, 'Financing', is much more important. There may be major cash inflows from issuing shares and/or debentures. There may also be outflows from redeeming debentures or shares, and for the expenses involved (such as commission) in such financing activity.

The final figure shows the increase or decrease in cash during the year. This can be reconciled with the figures shown for cash on the balance sheets at the beginning of the year and at the end of the year.

Cash flow statements illustrate very clearly the differences between cash flow and profit. In Illustration 7.2 Pei Lun makes a reasonable profit, but ends up with a net cash outflow because additional fixed assets have been paid for. In Illustration 7.5, the opposite has happened: the business made a loss in normal accounting terms; but by reducing stocks and debtors, and selling some fixed assets, they ended the year with a lot more cash than they started with. Illustration 7.5 shows the nine headings described above, but most do not apply in this simplified example. A fuller example for practice is provided as Self-testing Question 5 (Penuham).

Preparing a cash flow statement

A cash flow statement can be produced from the published income statement and balance sheets of companies. The figures can be selected or calculated to fit in with the nine standard headings shown in Illustration 7.5. The first of these, net cash flow from operating activities, is the most difficult.

1 *Net cash flow from operating activities.* This starts with operating profit which is easily identified on the profit and loss account. It is usually the group operating profit, before crediting share of profits from associates and joint ventures, and before deducting interest and taxation.

Then the depreciation charge for the year is added. This may be harder to find. There should be a note to the accounts dealing with tangible fixed assets; the first part deals with their book value; the second part reconciles the provision for depreciation at the beginning of the year with the provision at the end of the year: part of this reconciliation is the depreciation charge for the year.

There may also be amortization to add. This is similarly tucked away in a note to the accounts dealing with intangible fixed assets.

The figures for stocks, debtors and creditors are found on the balance sheets. Any decrease in stocks and debtors, or increase in creditors, adds to

Illustration 7.5

Cash Flow Statement of Pressda Ltd for Year Ended 31 December Year 1

		£000
Operating profit (loss)		(13)
Depreciation		5
		(8)
Reduction in stocks	20	
Reduction in debtors	13	
Increase in creditors	8	
Profit on sale of fixed assets[13]	(1)	40
1. Net cash flow from operating activities		32
2. Dividends from joint ventures and associates		0
3. Returns on investment and servicing of finance		0
4. Taxation paid		0
5. Capital expenditure and financial investment		
Proceeds of sale of fixed assets		3
6. Acquisitions and disposals		0
7. Equity dividends paid		0
Cash inflow before use of liquid resources and financing		35
8. Management of liquid resources		0
9. Financing		0
Increase in cash during year (45 – 10)		35

the cash inflow; any increase in stocks and debtors, or reduction in creditors reduces the cash inflow.

When a company sells fixed assets they usually make a profit or a loss on the sale.[14] These are normally shown on a profit and loss account as an exceptional item, not as part of operating profit. On a cash flow statement they should be included under the fifth heading as part of the proceeds of sale of fixed assets.

13 The profit on sale of fixed assets must be taken out of operating profit because it is included in heading number 5 as part of the proceeds from the sale of fixed assets.

14 The difference between the net book value of an asset, and the amount for which it is sold, is the profit or loss on sale.

2 *Dividends from joint ventures and associates.* The profits or losses of joint ventures and associates are usually shown in published accounts as if they are part of operating profits. But in a cash flow statement it is important to show only the cash received from dividends, not the profits.

3 *Returns on investment and servicing of finance.* The main item here is interest paid. There may also be interest received. It may not be possible to find these figures elsewhere in the published accounts. The profit and loss account shows interest payable and receivable during the period, which is slightly different from interest paid and received (that is the accruals concept).

Dividends paid on preference shares are also included under this heading.

4 *Taxation paid.* The profit and loss account shows the amount of tax payable for the year. But the cash flow statement must show the amount actually paid. This can usually be calculated from the accounts. We can find from the balance sheet notes the total liability for taxation at the beginning of the year (which may be under short-term or long-term liabilities or both); the tax charge for the year is added to this; then the total liability for taxation at the end of the year is deducted. The remaining figure should be the amount of tax that was actually paid during the year.

5 *Capital expenditure and financial investment.* The amount spent on buying additional fixed assets should be clear from the balance sheet notes on fixed assets. Where there is incomplete information, and there have been both acquisitions and disposals of fixed assets, care is needed to separate these two. Both the amount spent on acquiring fixed assets, and the proceeds of any sale of fixed assets should be shown on a cash flow statement

6 *Acquisitions and disposals.* This deals with acquisitions and disposals of businesses, not individual tangible fixed assets, and it should be clear from a separate note to the accounts dealing with fixed asset investments.

7 *Equity dividends paid.* As with taxation, the amount of dividends payable for the year is easily seen on the profit and loss account. But the amount actually paid during the year is likely to be different, and not shown separately; but it can be calculated. We can find from the balance sheet notes the liability for 'proposed dividends' at the beginning of the year; the dividend payable for the year is added to this; then the liability for proposed dividends at the end of the year is deducted. The remaining figure should be the amount of dividend that was actually paid during the year.

Cash inflow before use of liquid resources and financing. This is a subtotal of the previous items

8 *Management of liquid resources.* Where there are transfers between cash and short-term investments these may be difficult to trace in a set of published accounts. There should be some information in the notes to current assets in respect of investments that are included as current assets.

9 *Financing.* It is usually clear from the balance sheet and notes what has happened here. The share capital (and share premium) figures show how much has been raised from issuing shares (but look for any issuing costs: these must be deducted to arrive at the amount of cash actually received). The figures for long-term liabilities show whether there has been any cash raised from additional borrowing, or cash paid out to reduce such borrowing.

Increase (or decrease) in cash during year. The final figure on the cash flow statement can be found by comparing the amount of cash shown on the balance sheet at the beginning of the year with the amount shown at the end of the year.

Sometimes, when full information is not available, a reasonably accurate cash flow statement can be put together from what is available from published financial statements, and by making reasonable assumptions.

It can be a little difficult to sort out what has happened with fixed assets, especially if the information given is not complete. Sometimes fixed assets have been sold; sometimes additional fixed assets have been bought. It is necessary to sort out what has happened in stages. Figures should be provided for:

1 Fixed assets at cost (or valuation). The figure for the beginning of the year should be reconciled with the figure at the end of the year. The following may have happened:

   (a) additional fixed assets have been bought – this is normally a straightforward figure to be included under the sixth heading as payments to acquire fixed assets;
   (b) fixed assets have been revalued – this is not a cash flow, and it should not be included on a cash flow statement;
   (c) fixed assets have been disposed of – the figure here is what the assets cost, not the amount of cash they raised.

2 Depreciation. This is the cumulative figure of provision for depreciation. The figure for the beginning of the year should be reconciled with the figure for the end of the year. The following differences are likely:

   (a) additional depreciation has been charged during the year – this is added to operating profit in the first part of the cash flow statement;
   (b) some of the depreciation has been taken away because the asset has been disposed of.

The sixth heading of the cash flow statement must show receipts from selling fixed assets. This figure is the book value of the asset, plus any profit (or minus any loss). The book value of the asset is the amount that the asset cost (1c above), minus the cumulative depreciation on that asset (2b above).

Illustration 7.6

The Ham Company bought a special purpose vehicle three years ago for £20,000. They charged £5,000 a year depreciation. They then managed to sell it for £13,000, although the book value was only £5,000. The £8,000 profit on sale was classified as an 'exceptional item', and was separately identified and included in operating profit for the year.

Obviously a profit made on selling a fixed asset cannot be included twice in a cash flow statement. It is included in the sale proceeds, and so it must be taken out of the amount shown for operating profit.

A profit (or loss) arising on the sale of a fixed asset must be included as part of the sale proceeds in a cash flow statement. It must not be included in the operating profit shown in the first item on the cash flow statement (Illustration 7.6).

Preparing cash flow statements can help us to understand what they show, and how cash flow differs from profit. It can also be difficult, especially where the company's financial operations are complex. But the statements are usually already prepared for us by the company's accountants; our time is better spent trying to understand the significance of what they tell us, looking at trends over a number of years, and comparing with other companies.

International Accounting Standard 7 is at present less prescriptive than FRS 1 on which the above is based. It specifies only three categories of cash flows: (a) Operating; (b) Investing; and (c) Financing. It is useful to see (a) how much cash the business is generating from its normal operations; (b) how much is being invested in such things as additional fixed assets and other businesses; and (c) the extent to which this is financed by outside borrowing or the issue of additional share capital. IAS 7 has some flexibility on what should be included in each of the three headings. FRS 1 has more detailed and specific requirements.

7.3 Cash Budgets[15]

Most of us have some sort of cash budget in mind for our own personal receipts and payments. We like to know that, each month, there is enough

---

15 Sometimes the phrase 'cash flow statement' is used to mean a cash budget, particularly when business plans are prepared for banks. In normal accounting terminology a cash flow statement is prepared in accordance with financial reporting standards, as described in the previous section. Such statements are usually for the previous year(s), but a forecast cash flow statement could be prepared in the same form. A cash budget should show receipts and payments of cash in the form described in this section, and is typically prepared for the coming year.

coming in to meet the payments that we plan to make. Or we may plan it the other way around: we will spend no more than the cash that will be available to us. Failure to plan properly typically leads either to unexpected overdrafts and credit card borrowing – with crippling rates of interest; or we simply run out of money before the end of the month and cannot afford to eat or drink until our next salary comes in.

It is a similar story for companies. They need to plan their monthly receipts and payments for at least the next year.[16] It may be that a company is very profitable, and expanding rapidly, but they may not be producing enough cash to meet their monthly commitments. Some companies make substantial profits, but end the year with less cash than they started. Other companies may not be particularly profitable, but they generate lots of cash. Comparing a company's budgeted income statement with their cash budget for the coming year shows how their monthly cash flows differ from their monthly profits or losses, and why. The budgeted income statement gives a good indication of the viability of the business. The cash budget shows whether they are likely to have cash surpluses (which they may wish to invest); or whether there is going to be insufficient cash to get by. If a cash shortage problem is identified in advance, ways around the problem can be planned before it becomes a crisis. This can be seen by examining Illustration 7.7, the Holly Day Company.

A cash budget shows all of the (planned or expected future) receipts and payments of an organisation, typically on a monthly basis for the next year.

The receipts figure includes all cash that comes in directly from sales. It also includes receipts from debtors; they usually come in a month or two after the sales are made, so the figure is different from that shown on a profit and loss account. It includes any other receipts such as money that comes in from dividends, interest, rent, commission and royalties. The cash budget will show the money as a receipt in the month when the money is expected. A profit and loss account shows it in the month in which it is earned (or it 'accrues'), regardless of when the cash is received.

Some receipts do not appear on a profit and loss account at all. These include receipts from issuing shares or debentures; borrowing money; and sales of fixed assets.[17]

The payments figure includes all of the money that it is expected will be paid out. Payments for purchases are usually made a month or so after the purchases are made (and recorded for profit and loss account purposes). The cash budget also shows payments for expenses which will also appear on the profit and loss account. With most expenses the payment is made

16   Or weekly, or even daily; and, at least in broad outline, for more than the next year.

17   Only the profits or losses made on sales of fixed assets appears on a profit and loss account.

after the expense is incurred. Some expenses (such as rent, and perhaps advertising) are paid in advance. Again, in the cash budget, it is the period in which the payment is actually made that matters. In the profit and loss account it is when the expense is incurred that matters.

The cash budget also shows when tax and dividends are to be paid. These items also appear on the profit and loss account, but, again, the timing might be different. A company typically shows its tax charge on the profit and loss account of one year, but the cash is actually paid in the following year. Similarly a company typically decides on their final[18] dividend in one year (it appears on balance sheets as 'proposed dividend') and the cash is paid out in the following year.

Some payments do not appear at all on a profit and loss account. Cash has to be paid out to acquire fixed assets, and there may be payments to buy investments such as shares in other businesses, and to repay loans.

A cash budget shows the change in the cash balance each month. There is an opening balance at the beginning of the month. Total receipts and total payments are calculated to give a figure for net receipts (or payments) for the month. Net receipts are added to the balance at the beginning of the month to show the closing balance for the month. That then becomes the opening balance for the next month.

Figures can, of course, be the other way around. If the budget shows an overdraft at the beginning of the month, net receipts for the month will reduce the overdraft.

The budget should also show the total increase, or decrease, in cash expected during the year. This will be different from the budgeted profit figure, and it is useful to compare the two to see how, and why, the profit figure for the year differs from the cash flow figure. This is illustrated in this chapter with the Holly Day Company (Illustration 7.7) and with Rachel's business (Illustration 7.8).

Illustration 7.7

Question

The Holly Day Company manufactures seasonal goods for holiday makers and supplies them to retailers in many seaside resorts. There has been little change in their seasonal sales patterns in recent years. Sales start off at £15,000 a month in January, and increase by £15,000 a month until they peak at £120,000 a month in August; they fall to £90,000 a month in September; £30,000 a month in October, and then

---

18   Companies also pay interim dividends part way through the year.

Illustration 7.7 (continued)

to £15,000 a month in November and December. Customers pay for the goods, on average, 2 months after the sales are made.

The materials are bought and used in the month before sales take place; they are treated as an expense in the month that the finished goods to which they relate are sold;[19] and they are paid for one month later. The cost of materials for making the goods amounts to one-third of the selling price.

There is a basic labour force costing £4,000 a month in October–January each year. This increases to £6,000 a month in February, and £8,000 a month in March. The labour costs in the busy time of the year are £16,000 a month, from April to September inclusive.

The only other expense is depreciation[20] which amounts to £3,000 a month. One of the machines is getting towards the end of its life and will be replaced by a new one, costing £60,000, which will be paid for in June. Depreciation on the new machine will be charged at 20 per cent per annum on a straight line basis. The old machine will be sold for £15,000 (which is its net book value) at the end of the year (in December).

Taxation of £50,000 is payable in March, and dividends of £55,000 will be paid in May.

Required:

(a) Prepare the income statement for the coming year, showing sales, expenses and profit for each month, and in total.

(b) Prepare the cash budget for the coming year, showing receipts and payments for each month; the net cash surplus or deficit for the month; and the bank balance at the end of each month. Assume that the business starts the year with £50,000 in the bank.

(c) Explain why the company has generated more profit than cash during the year.

(d) From examining the cash budget, what changes in plan would you suggest to minimize the need for an overdraft?

▶

19   That is part of the accruals concept. In calculating gross profit it is the cost of the goods sold during the period that counts; not the cost of the goods that have been bought.

20   In practice there are bound to be other expenses. But we don't want to get into the complications of exactly when rent, rates, electricity and so on are paid, and when they are accrued.

Illustration 7.7 (continued)

Answer

HOLLY DAY

(b) **Cash Budget**

	£000 JAN	£000 FEB	£000 MAR	£000 APR	£000 MAY	£000 JUN	£000 JUL	£000 AUG	£000 SEP	£000 OCT	£000 NOV	£000 DEC	£000 TOTAL
RECEIPTS													
From Debtors	15	15	15	30	45	60	75	90	105	120	90	30	690
Sale of Machine	—	—	—	—	—	—	—	—	—	—	—	15	15
	15	15	15	30	45	60	75	90	105	120	90	45	705
PAYMENTS													
Materials	5	5	10	15	20	25	30	35	40	30	10	5	230
Wages	4	6	8	16	16	16	16	16	16	4	4	4	126
Fixed assets						60							60
Taxation			50										50
Dividends	—	—	—	—	55	—	—	—	—	—	—	—	55
	9	11	68	31	91	101	46	51	56	34	14	9	521
Net receipts or (Deficit)	6	4	(53)	(1)	(46)	(41)	29	39	49	86	76	36	184
Opening balance	50	56	60	7	6	(40)	(81)	(52)	(13)	36	122	198	
Closing balance	56	60	7	6	(40)	(81)	(52)	(13)	36	122	198	234	234

(a) **Budgeted Income Statement**

	JAN	FEB	MAR	APR	MAY	JUN	JUL	AUG	SEP	OCT	NOV	DEC	TOTAL
SALES	15	30	45	60	75	90	105	120	90	30	15	15	690
EXPENSES													
Materials	5	10	15	20	25	30	35	40	30	10	5	5	230
Wages	4	6	8	16	16	16	16	16	16	4	4	4	126
Depreciation	3	3	3	3	3	4	4	4	4	4	4	4	43
	12	19	26	39	44	50	55	60	50	18	13	13	399
Profit	3	11	29	21	31	40	50	60	40	12	2	2	291

The Budgeted Income Statement for the Holly Day Company shows a budgeted profit of £291,000 for the year; there are substantial profits in the busy summer months; more modest profits in the quieter months.

The cash budget shows net receipts during the year of £184,000. Looking at each month, there are significant timing differences.[21] But for the year as a whole the differences are more substantial: the business generated

---

21 This illustration may look complicated, but it is simplified in that, taking the year as a whole, there are no adjustments required for stocks, debtors and creditors. The level of business is assumed to be constant from year to year.

Illustration 7.8

Question

Rachel owns a specialist boring-digging machine which she hires out, together with an operator/driver to builders and farmers. A few years ago her accountant worked out that she should charge £500 a day and that should give her a comfortable living. In the last year demand has fallen, particularly in the winter months when the weather restricts the use of the machine, and in the summer months when many people are on holiday. In the coming year (Year 3) she estimates that she will have 10 days' work a month in January and February; 20 days' work a month in March, April and May and June. Then it will fall to 12 days a month in July and August. In September, October and November she expects 20 days work a month, and only 5 days in December.

At the end of Year 2 her debtors figure was £5,000, of which she expects to receive half in January and half in February.

On average customers pay 2 months after the work is done.

Operating expenses, including fuel and labour, amount to £100 per day.

Expenses are paid in the month that they are incurred.

Her fixed overheads, including depreciation, are £3,000 per month. The machine originally cost £140,000 and is expected to have a 5-year life, with a residual value of £20,000. She uses straight line depreciation.

At the end of last year she had only £1,000 in her business bank account.

Rachel would like to take £45,000 a year out of the business to cover her personal living expenses. But she does not want to have an overdraft; and she does not want to be living off capital.

Required:

(a) Prepare the income statement for the coming year, showing sales, expenses and profit for each month, and in total.

(b) Prepare the cash budget for the coming year, showing receipts and payments for each month; the net cash surplus or deficit for the month; and the bank balance at the end of each month. Assume that the business starts the year with £50,000 in the bank.

(c) Explain why the company has generated more cash than profit during the year.

(d) How much do you think that she can afford to take out of the business as drawings (or dividends if it is a company) during the year? Give your reasons.

Illustration 7.8 (continued)

Answer

RACHEL

(b) **Cash Budget**

	£ JAN	£ FEB	£ MAR	£ APR	£ MAY	£ JUN	£ JUL	£ AUG	£ SEP	£ OCT	£ NOV	£ DEC	£ TOTAL
RECEIPTS													
From Debtors	2,500	2,500	5,000	5,000	10,000	10,000	10,000	10,000	6,000	6,000	10,000	10,000	87,000
PAYMENTS													
Operating expenses	1,000	1,000	2,000	2,000	2,000	2,000	1,200	1,200	2,000	2,000	2,000	500	18,900
Fixed overheads	1,000	1,000	1,000	1,000	1,000	1,000	1,000	1,000	1,000	1,000	1,000	1,000	12,000
	2,000	2,000	3,000	3,000	3,000	3,000	2,200	2,200	3,000	3,000	3,000	1,500	30,900
Net receipts or Deficits	500	500	2,000	2,000	7,000	7,000	7,800	7,800	3,000	3,000	7,000	8,500	56,100
Opening balance	1,000	1,500	2,000	4,000	6,000	13,000	20,000	27,800	35,600	38,600	41,600	48,600	
Closing balance	1,500	2,000	4,000	6,000	13,000	20,000	27,800	35,600	38,600	41,600	48,600	56,100	

(a) **Budgeted Income Statement**

	JAN	FEB	MAR	APR	MAY	JUN	JUL	AUG	SEP	OCT	NOV	DEC	TOTAL
SALES	5,000	5,000	10,000	10,000	10,000	10,000	6,000	6,000	10,000	10,000	10,000	2,500	94,500
EXPENSES													
Operating expenses	1,000	1,000	2,000	2,000	2,000	2,000	1,200	1,200	2,000	2,000	2,000	500	18,900
Fixed overheads	3,000	3,000	3,000	3,000	3,000	3,000	3,000	3,000	3,000	3,000	3,000	3,000	36,000
	4,000	4,000	5,000	5,000	5,000	5,000	4,200	4,200	5,000	5,000	5,000	3,500	54,900
Profit	1,000	1,000	5,000	5,000	5,000	5,000	1,800	1,800	5,000	5,000	5,000	(1,000)	39,600

(c)

	£
Profit	39,600
Depreciation	24,000
	63,600
Increase in debtors (£12,500 – £5,000)	7,500
Increase in cash	56,100

(d) Drawings should not exceed profit of £39,600

£107,000 less cash than the amount of profit earned. The main reasons for the difference are:

(i)	profits are calculated before tax; but tax of £50,000 will be paid;	£50,000
(ii)	dividends of £55,000 will be paid out;	£55.000
(iii)	£60,000 is paid out for additional fixed assets.	£60,000
		£165,000

In calculating profits depreciation of £43,000 has been charged for the year, but this is not a cash payment.	(43,000)
There is also a cash receipt of £15,000 for the old machine; this does not count towards profits.	(15,000)
	£58,000
	£107,000

A brief examination of the Holly Day Company's cash budget shows that they are generating a cash surplus every month beginning in July.

By September they have money in the bank, and it builds up to £234,000 by the end of the year. But from May to August inclusive, there is an overdraft every month, peaking at £81,000 at the end of June. By preparing the cash budget well in advance the problem has been identified and can be dealt with. If the financial projections were shown to a bank, it would probably be very easy to borrow the money that is needed – but there would be interest to pay, and perhaps an arrangement fee. Careful planning could avoid the need for an overdraft and the costs involved.

It seems to be rather careless planning that taxation and dividends are paid in March and May respectively. These are months when the company is most short of cash. It would be more sensible to arrange to make these payments in the second half of the year when the funds are available without resorting to borrowing. This is worth doing even if it means changing the year end date for producing annual accounts.

Another possibility might be to plan the replacement of the machine differently. Paying for it in June hits the company's bank balance when they would be starting to generate good cash surpluses each month. It might be possible to arrange to buy the machine later in the year, or at least to pay for it a couple of months later. It may also be possible to get the money in for the old machine a little sooner.

7.4 Incomplete Records

Many small businesses do not bother to record fully all transactions using double entry bookkeeping. Sometimes they hand over a pile of papers, and their bank statements, to an accountant who is expected to construct a full set of accounts from these 'incomplete records'. It is usually straightforward to produce a summary of receipts and payments for the year, based on the business's bank statements. Whether or not all receipts really did go into the bank the accountant will not really know; reliance has to be placed on what the proprietor of the business remembers or says. The proprietor will probably remember any payments made for the business in cash, especially those that will reduce their tax liability. They may find it harder to remember any cash receipts that would increase it.

In the two examples in Illustration 7.9, a summary of the bank statement is provided, but this is insufficient information to be able to calculate profits.

Additional information also enables us to produce balance sheets. The balance sheet at the beginning of the year is fairly straightforward, as shown in Illustration 7.9, Answer part 2. After the profit for the year has been calculated we can produce the balance sheet at the end of the year. Depreciation has to be deducted from fixed assets; and the profit for the year has to be added to the balance shown for capital at the beginning of the year.

Illustration 7.9

The summarized bank accounts are available for Ahmed and Leong. Ahmed started the year with £20,000 in the bank; by the end of the year this had increased to £30,000, an increase of £10,000. Leong started the year with £15,000 in the bank; by the end of the year the bank balance had increased to £41,000, a much more substantial increase of £26,000. At first sight it seems that Leong is doing better than Ahmed because Leong has generated more cash.

In this instance, most of the big differences between cash flow and profit do not apply. Neither business has acquired fixed assets; there has been no borrowing or repayment of loans; and there has been no additional capital introduced, or withdrawn.[22] The differences between cash flow and profit are due to the application of the accruals concept – the normal way of measuring profit.

	Ahmed		Leong	
	£	£	£	£
Summarized Bank Statements				
Opening balance: cash at bank		20,000		15,000
Receipts from debtors	67,000		142,000	
Receipts from cash sales, banked	30,000		10,000	
	97,000		152,000	
Payments to trade creditors	77,000		91,000	
Payments for expenses	10,000		35,000	
	87,000		126,000	
Increase in cash balance during year		10,000		26,000
Closing balance: cash at bank		30,000		41,000

The cash figures alone do not give sufficient information about the performance of a business; they do not enable us to measure profit. Neither of the two businesses kept proper sets of double entry accounts, but they are able to produce a record of stocks, debtors and creditors at the beginning and end of the year, as follows:

	Ahmed		Leong	
	1 January	31 December	1 January	31 December
	£	£	£	£
Stocks	10,000	14,000	16,000	12,000
Debtors	8,000	11,000	9,000	7,000
Creditors	9,000	6,000	8,000	11,000

Additional information

Ahmed began the year with fixed assets of £30,000 on which depreciation of £5,000 is to be charged. Leong began the year with fixed assets of £50,000 on which depreciation of £10,000 is to be charged.

---

22 In a company there might be dividends paid, and the company could buy back its own shares; in an unincorporated business, drawings are the equivalent of dividends; and the owners are free to withdraw capital, or pay more in, as they wish.

Illustration 7.9 (continued)

As is clear from the summarized bank account there have been no purchases or sales of fixed assets, and neither of the owners have taken money out of the business as drawings. The owners state that all receipts from sales have been banked, and that there were no receipts or payments that did not go through the bank account.

There is now sufficient information to prepare the profit and loss accounts of the businesses. The sales figure includes the money received from cash sales, and money receivable from debtors.

Answer part 1: Ahmed

	£	£
Cash sales	30,000	
Receipts from debtors	67,000	
Deduct opening debtors	(8,000)	
Add closing debtors	11,000	
Sales		100,000
Opening stock		10,000
Payments to creditors	77,000	
Deduct opening creditors	(9,000)	
Add closing creditors	6,000	
Purchases	74,000	
		84,000
Deduct closing stock		(14,000)
Cost of goods sold		70,000
Gross profit		30,000
Expenses	10,000	
Depreciation	5,000	(15,000)
Net profit		15,000

In determining the correct sales figure for the year, the figures on the bank statement are inadequate. The figure for cash sales (receipts of money from sales paid directly into the bank) is probably[23] acceptable as it is. But some of the amount shown for receipts from debtors are for sales which took place in the previous year. At the beginning of the year, Ahmed was owed £8,000 by debtors. During the year he received £67,000 from debtors, but £8,000 of this was for the previous year. The figure of £59,000[24] is still not the correct figure for sales for this year. At the end of this year debtors owed Ahmed £11,000; this is for sales which have been made this year, but the money will not be received until next year. The correct figure for sales to debtors is therefore £67,000 − £8,000 + £11,000 = £70,000. Cash sales are added to credit sales to give the total sales figure for the year (£70,000 + £30,000 = £100,000).

23 The owner may have used some of the cash received from sales to pay expenses, or for personal drawings, without paying it into the bank. Records should be kept of this, otherwise it is a matter of memory and guesswork.

24 £67,000 minus £8,000.

Illustration 7.9 (continued)

It is a similar story in determining the correct purchases figure for the year. In this instance it seems that there are no purchases which have been paid for in cash. The total figure of cash paid to creditors includes payments for purchases which were made last year. At the beginning of this year Ahmed owed £9,000 to creditors. During the year he paid £77,000 to creditors, but £9,000 of this was for the previous year. But £68,000 is not the correct figure for purchases for this year. At the end of this year Ahmed owes £6,000 to creditors. The correct figure for purchases from creditors is therefore £77,000 − £9,000 + £6,000 = £74,000.

To arrive at gross profit we do not simply deduct purchases from sales; a stock adjustment is required and a summary of the bank statement does not provide the information required. Gross profit is the difference between sales, and the cost of goods sold. When we have arrived at the purchases figure, we need to add opening stocks to it, and deduct closing stocks from it to arrive at the cost of goods sold.

Net profit is arrived at after deducting all expenses. Most expenses are shown on the bank statement as payments; sometimes these have to be adjusted to allow for accruals and prepayments.[25] In some businesses there may be additional expenses which have been paid out of cash received from sales.[26] Depreciation has to be shown as an expense in calculating profit, but it is not a payment and so does not appear on the bank statement. Fixed assets and depreciation are part of the additional information that is essential to calculate profit from information from receipts and payments.

When all of this additional information is taken into account we can see how a 'receipts and payments' basis is converted into an accruals basis for profit. Ahmed's profit figure can be reconciled with his increase in cash as follows:

	£	£
Net profit		15,000
Add depreciation		5,000
		20,000
Deduct		
Increase in stocks	4,000	
Increase in debtors	3,000	
Decrease in creditors	3,000	10,000
Increase in cash		30,000

This reconciliation is, of course, just like a cash flow statement (but without all of the complications).

---

25 These are illustrated in the examples in the Appendix.

26 In which case the cash sales figure will be understated if it is no more than a record of the cash from sales that has been banked. The correct cash sales figure must include all of the money received for sales; this usually means adding back any expenses paid out of cash before it was banked.

Illustration 7.9 (continued)

Answer part 2

Balance Sheet at beginning of year	£	£	£	£
Fixed assets		30,000		50,000
Stocks		10,000		16,000
Debtors		8,000		9,000
Cash		20,000		15,000
(Creditors)		(9,000)		(8,000)
		59,000		82,000
Capital		59,000		82,000
Balance Sheet at end of year				
Fixed assets		25,000		40,000
Stocks		14,000		12,000
Debtors		11,000		7,000
Cash		30,000		41,000
Creditors		(6,000)		(11,000)
		74,000		89,000
Capital	59,000		82,000	
Profit for year	15,000	74,000	7,000	89,000

Companies are required by law to keep proper accounting records, but many small, unincorporated businesses do not bother. They manage by keeping a careful eye on their bank account and controlling their receipts and payments. But it is also important to be able to measure profit, and to appreciate how it differs from a 'receipts and payments' basis of accounting.

Summary

In many businesses generating profits and generating cash flows go hand-in-hand. Good profits are likely to result in healthy cash flows. But the two are unlikely to be identical. In many circumstances the profit (or loss) for the year can be very different from the increase (or decrease) in cash. The differences between the two show up well on a cash flow statement. Having cash available to meet liabilities as they fall due is essential for business survival, and healthy businesses should generate healthy cash flows. Businesses also need to generate profits if they are to survive and be healthy. If a business makes a profit, its wealth[27] increases. That increase in wealth is used in many different ways (such as paying dividends, and investing in more assets); it is unlikely to be matched by an exactly equal increase in cash.

We could debate whether cash flow or profit is more important to the survival and success of businesses. That would be a bit like debating whether eating or drinking is more important to the survival and success of people. Both are essential.

---

27 Or the amount of its net assets.

Review of Key Points

- Profit is not the same as cash flow. The accruals concept may be seen as being the theoretical justification and explanation of the difference

- A cash flow statement provides a reconciliation between operating profit for the year and the net increase or decrease in cash during the year

- A company's operating profit may be used to finance higher levels of stocks and debtors; to pay interest and taxation; and to buy additional fixed assets

- A detailed cash flow statement shows other differences between cash flow and profit in a standardized format

- A cash budget shows planned receipts and payments of cash, typically on a monthly basis for the next year

- The budgeted net receipts of cash are likely to be very different from the budgeted profit figure

- A small business may have only incomplete records showing receipts and payments of cash; with additional information these can be adjusted to produce balance sheets and profit and loss accounts

- Some differences between cash flow and profit are relatively minor, relating to the timing of receipts and payments compared with the timing of recognition of revenues and expenses

- Depreciation is an important expense in calculating profit; there is no equivalent payment[28] in cash terms

- Some of the biggest receipts and payments (such as issue of shares; purchase of fixed assets; paying back loans) have no direct effect on profit

- The availability of cash to meet liabilities as they fall due is essential to business survival. Making profits is essential if the business is to become 'better off'.

---

28 Except, of course, when the fixed asset is first bought.

Self-testing Questions

1 In what circumstances is a very profitable business likely to find that it has serious cash shortages?

2 Is it possible for a company to make losses year after year, but still to increase its cash balances? Explain.

3 Produce a cash flow statement for Pei Lun for the year ended 31 December Year 1.

Pei Lun

Summarized Balance Sheet as at 1 January Year 1

		£000
Fixed assets: net book value		
Machinery		20
Current assets		
Stocks	30	
Debtors	30	
Bank	10	
	70	
Creditors	20	50
		70
Capital		40
Retained profits		30
		70

Summarized Income Statement for the Year Ended 31 December Year 1

Sales		220
Cost of goods sold		
Opening stock	30	
Purchases	190	
	220	
Less closing stock	50	170
Gross Profit		50
Depreciation		5
Other expenses		13
Net profit for year		32

Summarized Balance Sheet as at 31 December Year 1

Fixed assets: net book value	
Machinery	15
Vehicles	45
	60

Self-testing Questions (continued)

Current assets			
Stocks		50	
Debtors		35	
Bank		–	
		85	
Creditors	18		
Overdraft	25	43	42
			102
Capital			40
Retained profits (30 + 32)			62
			102

The vehicles were bought on 31 December Year 1. No depreciation is to be charged on them for Year 1.

4 Produce a cash flow statement for Pressda for the year ended 31 December Year 1.

Pressda

Summarized Balance Sheet as at 1 January Year 1

		£000
Fixed assets: net book value		22
Current assets		
Stocks	30	
Debtors	28	
Bank	10	
	68	
Creditors	20	48
		70
Capital		40
Retained profits		30
		70

Summarized Income Statement for the Year Ended 31 December Year 1

Sales		200
Cost of goods sold		
Opening stock	30	
Purchases	150	
	180	
Less closing stock	10	170
Gross profit		30
Profit on sale of fixed asset		1
		31

Self-testing Questions (continued)

Depreciation		5
Other expenses	13	<u>18</u>
Net loss for year		13

Summarized Balance Sheet as at 31 December Year 1

Fixed assets		15
Current assets		
Stocks	10	
Debtors	15	
Bank	<u>45</u>	
	70	
Creditors	<u>28</u>	<u>42</u>
		<u>57</u>
Capital		40
Retained profits (30 – 13)		<u>17</u>
		<u>57</u>

A fixed asset which had originally cost £4,000 and on which depreciation of £2,000 had been charged, was sold during the year for £3,000. The profit had been included in profit for the year. No fixed assets were bought during the year.

5 You are required to prepare a cash flow statement for Penuham Ltd from the summarized financial statements below

Penuham

Summarized Balance Sheet as at 1 January Year 1

Fixed assets	Cost	Provision for depreciation	Net Book value
	£000	£000	£000
Buildings	100	10	90
Machinery	200	80	120
Vehicles	<u>120</u>	<u>40</u>	<u>80</u>
	<u>420</u>	<u>130</u>	290

Current assets			
Stocks		70	
Debtors		60	
Bank		<u>20</u>	
		150	

Creditors: amounts due within one year			
Trade creditors		50	
Proposed dividend		30	
Taxation		<u>40</u>	120	<u>30</u>
			320

Creditors: amounts due after more than one year

10% Debentures	100
	220

Share capital: Ordinary £1 shares	100
Retained profits	120
	220

Summarized Income Statement for the Year Ended 31 December Year 1

Sales		500
Cost of goods sold		
Opening stock	70	
Purchases	250	
	320	
Less closing stock	90	230
Gross profit		270
Depreciation		
Buildings	2	
Machinery	24	
Vehicles	25	51
Distribution costs		27
Administrative expenses		30
Profit on sale of vehicle		(8)
Operating profit		170
Interest		10
Profit before taxation		160
Taxation		44
Profit after taxation		116
Proposed dividends		35
Retained profit for year		81

Summarized Balance Sheet as at 31 December Year 1

Fixed assets	Cost	Provision for Depreciation	Net Book Value
	£000	£000	£000
Buildings	100	12	88
Machinery	240	104	136
Vehicles	100	50	50
	440	166	274

Current Assets	
Stocks	90
Debtors	84
Bank	10
	184

Self-testing Questions (continued)

Creditors: amounts due within one year

Trade creditors	58		
Proposed dividend	35		
Taxation	<u>44</u>	<u>137</u>	<u>47</u>
			321

Creditors: amounts due after more than one year

10% Debentures	<u>20</u>
	301

Share capital: Ordinary £1 shares	100
Retained profits	<u>201</u>
	301

6 Produce a statement showing the profit made by Leong in Illustration 7.9. The reconciliation should be in the same format as that shown for Ahmed on page 196

7 What is meant by 'free cash flow'? Estimate the free cash flow of Ted Baker and Tate and Lyle for the last two years, based on the cash flow statements provided on pages 178 and 180

8 From the following incomplete records supplied by Jack Kit, a clothes retailer, you are required to produce a profit and loss account for the year ended 31 December Year 3, and a balance sheet as at that date. In addition, as an arithmetic check on your work, you should produce a balance sheet as at the beginning of Year 3 and a Cash Flow Statement for the Year.

Summarized Bank Statement for Year 3

	£	£
Balance at bank on 1 January Year 3		20,000
Add *Receipts*		
Receipts from debtors	120,000	
Cash from sales paid in	60,000	
Loan from Mortgage Co	<u>170,000</u>	
	<u>350,000</u>	
Deduct *Payments*		
Payments to creditors for		
clothes purchased	125,000	
Wages	25,000	
General expenses	20,000	
Purchase of premises	<u>187,000</u>	
	<u>357,000</u>	
		(7,000)
Balance at bank on 31 December year 3		13,000

Additional information

Self-testing Questions (continued)

	At 1 Jan Year 3	At 31 Dec Year 3
Debtors	10,000	12,000
Creditors	15,000	17,000
Stocks	14,000	16,000
Fixtures and fittings	18,000	
Premises	–	187,000

It was agreed that £1,800 depreciation should be provided on fixtures and fittings. No depreciation would be provided on the premises as they were acquired immediately before the year end.

Assessment Questions

1 Judas has developed a plan for a rapidly expanding business selling and installing software for individuals using computers at home. He will operate on a 50 per cent mark up on the software that he sells, and will employ a team of highly paid technician/sales staff. He has piloted his business model on a number of customers and he knows that they are particularly afraid of computer viruses; he will provide a guarantee of 12 months free of viruses. But, somehow, after a year or so he knows that there will always be a return of viruses and most of his customers will request his services again. During the next twelve months he aims to build up his customer base, and make a small profit.

   He has discussed his business plan with his accountant, and the following seems to be soundly based.

(i)   Sales in January will be £220,000 and will then increase by £20,000 per month. Customers pay two months after the sale is made.

(ii)   Suppliers are paid one month after purchases are made. Stocks amounting to £100,000 will be bought in the first month and maintained at that level. Purchases will be made each month that are sufficient to supply sales for that month.

(iii) Wages and expenses will be £100,000 a month for the first 4 months of the year; then they will increase to £150,000 a month for the following 3 months; then they will be £200,000 a month for the next 5 months. They are paid during the month that they are incurred.

(iv)   At the beginning of the year he will spend £840,000 on fixed assets. All fixed assets are depreciated over 10 years. Depreciation is charged on a monthly basis. In June additional fixed assets of £360,000 will be bought.

His accountant advises him that although the business should make a modest profit, there will be substantial cash outflows to begin with. She prepared a monthly budgeted profit and loss

Assessment Questions (continued)

account, and a monthly cash budget. But Judas had £1 million available to finance the business and reckoned that there would be no problem. He refused to pay her fees and so she did not show him the monthly budgets.

You are required to:

(a) Prepare a monthly profit and loss account for the first year of the business, showing the profit or loss each month, and for the year in total.

(b) Prepare a cash budget for the year, showing the receipts and payments for each month, and the cash surplus or deficit each month.

(c) Explain and comment on the results.

2 You are given the following summarized balance sheets and profit and loss accounts for the Solverham Company for the past two years:

			Year 1 £000			Year 2 £000
Balance Sheet as at 31 December						
Fixed assets at cost			200			220
Provision for depreciation			60			82
Net book value			140			138
Current assets						
Stocks	95			70		
Debtors	80			50		
Cash	–			25		
	175			145		
Current liabilities						
Creditors	30			45		
Proposed dividends	10			15		
Overdraft	80			–		
	120	55		60	85	
		195			223	
Long-term liabilities						
12% Debentures		110			135	
		85			88	
Share capital			50			50
Retained profits			35			38
			85			88
Profit and Loss Account for the Year Ended 31 December						
Sales			520			500
Cost of sales			376			375
Gross profit			144			125
Administration expenses			35			36

Assessment Questions (continued)

Depreciation	20	22
Distribution costs	22	24
Operating profit	67	43
Interest paid	14	17
Net profit before tax	53	26
Taxation paid	16	8
Net profit after tax	37	18
Dividends proposed	10	15
Retained profit	27	3

Required:

(a) Prepare a cash flow statement in accordance with FRS 1 for the year ended 31 December Year 2.

(b) Explain how cash flow differs from profit.

(c) The company's Managing Director is pleased that the company has money in the bank having paid off a significant overdraft. He is particularly pleased that he ignored his Chief Accountant who said that the company could not afford to buy more fixed assets or to increase the dividend. Critically assess the Chief Accountant's advice.

3 Malcolm, the son of the founder of Solverham plc is aware that the Managing Director of the company believes that the company is strong, and is doing well, but the Chief Accountant says that the company's position is rapidly deteriorating. You are required to produce a report on the company's financial position and performance, based on the information given for Question 2. Your answer should include calculations of the ratios shown below for each year, and comments on them.

(a) Return on ordinary shareholders' funds

(b) Total return on long-term capital employed

(c) Capital gearing ratio

(d) Interest times cover

(e) Current ratio

(f) Liquidity ratio

(g) Debtors ratio

(h) Creditors ratio

(i) Stock turnover ratio

(j) Gross profit ratio

(k) Operating profit to sales

4 Mr Downund has been running a signwriting business for many years, and it continues to provide him with a high standard of living. The volume of business has declined in recent years, and he no longer employs any staff. But he maintains a healthy and increasing bank

Assessment Questions (continued)

balance, and is happy with his business. Then he employs an accountant, and provides her with the following information:

Summarized Bank Account for Year 13

Receipts	£	Payments	£
Opening balance	30,000	Trade creditors	40,000
Receipts from debtors	65,000	Materials	32,000
Cash sales	8,000	General expenses	18,000
Sale of surplus equipment	12,000	Personal drawings	29,000
Sale of premises	50,000	Balance carried down	46,000
	165,000		165,000

At the beginning of the year stocks of materials amounted to £8,000; by the end of the year this had reduced to £2,000. At the beginning of the year debtors amounted to £22,000; by the end of the year this had reduced to £7,000. At the beginning of the year creditors amounted to £16,000; by the end of the year this had increased to £24,000, but Mr Downund had taken to buying materials in a local cash and carry warehouse rather than using his traditional supplier. He was also doing a number of smaller jobs for cash and estimated that he had received about £8,000 for such work that he had not paid into the bank but had spent on his own living expenses.

The amount shown for general expenses included £5,000 paid for rent as Mr Downund has sold his premises because they were underutilized. A year ago he had total fixed assets of £75,000, including £40,000 which was the original cost of the premises; he sold half of his equipment. His accountant said that equipment should be depreciated at 10 per cent per annum on a straight line basis.

Mr Downund was happy with his lot, but his accountant made him unhappy. What did she do?

You are required to show the balance sheets at the beginning and end of the year, and the profit and loss account for the year, in as much detail as the above information permits.

Group Activities and Discussion Questions

1 A small business is more likely to prosper and to control its operations effectively by monitoring cash flows than by listening to its accountant. Discuss.

2 Analyse a number of companies' cash flow statements. Which figures seem to give the best indication of a company's performance? Can 'free cash flow' be assessed, and does it provide a useful indicator?

Group Activities and Discussion Questions (continued)

3 Analyse a number of companies' balance sheets, and calculate their current ratios, liquidity ratios and capital gearing ratios for the last two years. What do these ratios tell you about the companies' liquidity problems or strengths? What useful information do the companies' cash flow statements add to this?

4 In what ways, and to what extent, should cash budgeting avoid liquidity problems?

5 The financial statements of a small business are likely to reveal any liquidity problems; the financial statements of a major listed company are more likely to disguise them. Discuss.

6 It is useful for companies to have detailed analysis and control of all cash flows. Why would they want additional, accruals-based information?

References and Further Reading

Accounting Standards Board, FRS 1 Cash Flow Statements.

Elliott, B. and J. Elliott (2004) *Financial Accounting and Reporting*, 8th edn, Pearson Education.

Sutton, T. (2004) *Corporate Financial Accounting and Reporting*, Pearson Education.

Wood, F. and A. Sangster (2002), *Business Accounting Volume 1*, 9th edn, Pearson Education.

www.tateandlyle.co.uk (investor relations, annual reports)

www.tedbaker.co.uk (£m share info, investor relations)

8

Creative Accounting

Learning objectives

After studying this chapter you should be able to:

◆ Explain what is meant by *creative accounting* and understand that the term is sometimes applied to very different practices

◆ Explain why creative accounting practices have developed

◆ Give examples of a number of creative accounting practices

◆ Describe how existing accountancy arrangements are intended to restrict creative accounting

◆ Evaluate a variety of different approaches to deal with creative accounting

Introduction

This chapter examines what is meant by 'creative accounting', explains a number of different practices that have been described as creative accounting and then assesses a number of different ways in which the problem might be tackled.

8.1 What is Creative Accounting?

The term 'creative accounting' is used in relation to a variety of different accounting practices. At one extreme it is used to describe fraudulent and criminal activities. At the other extreme it might be viewed more benignly: as being no more than producing an honest presentation that emphasizes the favourable aspects of a company's performance. There is a natural desire for companies to put a positive spin on their financial position and performance.

It is unlikely that a company's annual report will say:

> The company has three divisions. Division A is the largest and is a complete disaster; losses continue to mount. Division B is going downhill and is now running at a loss. Division C is small, but it did make a tiny profit.

They are more likely to say:

> Division C has expanded rapidly and sales and profits are at record levels. Division B is coping well with difficult world economic conditions. Division A has made good progress in meeting its targets and is expected to show further progress in the coming year.

Investors and other users of annual reports and accounts can look at the published, audited figures to establish the relationship between management claims, and the 'real' financial performance and position. One of the functions of annual reports is to enable those who use them to assess the competence of the company's management. They can do this by comparing their fine words with the financial results that they go on to produce.

The Development of Creative Accounting

There have, no doubt, always been examples of directors, accountants and auditors who bend or breach the rules to show company performance in a more flattering light. Such abuses have been tackled by Companies Acts and by the accounting and auditing professions. As attention has been drawn to particular abuses, so action has been taken to try to stop them. The regulatory framework of accounting has steadily become more strict and detailed. But even 60 years ago there were relatively few accounting rules; they were very flexible; and enforcement was not strong.

In the late 1960s there were some serious and high profile accounting scandals from which it seemed that companies could choose almost any accounting principles they liked. What was a profit to one accountant would be a loss to another, and confidence in the accountancy profession was at a low ebb.

The accountancy profession set up the Accounting Standards Committee which, in the 1970s and 1980s, produced a series of Statements of Standard Accounting Practice (SSAPs) which were intended to raise standards of financial reporting, and to reduce the areas of difference and variety in accounting practice. They had some success in improving financial reporting, but it was in the 1980s that the term 'creative accounting' came to be widely used, even in the popular press.

Popular books on creative accounting by Griffiths (1986), followed by Jameson (1988), argued that companies had a wide choice of accounting principles, policies and practices, and could justify almost any profit figures that they wished. The reputation of the Accounting Standards Committee (ASC) was at a low ebb, and, following the recommendations of the Dearing Committee (1988) the accounting standards setting arrangements were revamped, and the Accounting Standards Board (ASB) was established.

The situation improved in the 1990s, but the scandals did not go away. In a new version of his book, Griffiths (1995) argued that some order had been brought to the chaos of the regulatory framework of accounting, and that the ASB had made tremendous progress in restoring the integrity and credibility of accounting standards. The more flagrant abuses had been banned, but an extensive range of techniques was still available which could be used to massage the figures. The Financial Reporting and Review Panel (FRRP) was demonstrating that it could be effective in enforcing the application of accounting standards. But, he argued, 'creative accounting still flourishes ... there is still tremendous scope for manipulation'. He concluded that his basic 1986 premise still held: companies were still fiddling their profits.

Other books popularized the idea that creative accounting was (and probably still is) widespread. Smith and Hannah (1991) highlighted a number of creative accounting practices. They produced a list of major companies, and put a number of 'blobs' against them, one blob for each of the questionable practices that the company adopted. Some companies came out with a clean bill of health, but serious questions were raised about the credibility of the financial statements of others. More recent versions by Smith show that the problems have not gone away. Other books in the 1990s (such as McBarnet and Whelan, 1999; Pijper, 1993) continued to highlight the problems of creative accounting in the UK.

But, in 2001–2002, the limelight was taken by US companies with a number of major accounting scandals that overshadowed what came to be seen as relatively minor problems in the UK.

In November 2001 Enron, one of the world's largest energy groups, admitted that between 1997 and 2000 various 'special purpose entities' should have been included in the group's accounts, which would have substantially reduced profits. In December 2001 they filed for bankruptcy. Arthur Andersen, Enron's auditors, admitted shredding or deleting thousands of relevant documents and were found guilty of obstructing the course of justice. Arthur Andersen, one of the world's largest accountancy firms, collapsed, and their business was split up and taken over by rival firms. Enron had paid Andersen $25 million in audit fees for 2001 and another $27 million for other non-audit services.

The next major scandal was WorldCom where the founder and chief executive, Bernie Ebbers, and the Chief Financial Officer, Scott Sullivan, resigned after admitting that the USA's Securities and Exchange Commission (SEC) was investigating the company's accounting practices. There were claims of frauds amounting to $3.8 billion in the company.

Soon it seemed that newspapers were making comments on almost every company's annual report suggesting problems of creative accounting: Xerox, Vivendi, Computacenter, Elan – the list went on and on. Many of the accounting policies that were criticized at the peak of the controversy had previously hardly been a matter for comment. Suddenly the climate changed and they were presented as scandals or abuses.

The Effects

The main and obvious intention and effect of creative accounting is to boost reported profits (or to reduce reported losses). When a company gets into financial difficulties, and a different team of accountants starts examining what has been going on, it sometimes comes to light that the company has been exaggerating profits in one way or another. A different team of accountants reinterprets the accounting data and comes up with very different profit (or loss) figures.

Exaggerated profits can have a number of effects. The share price is likely to be favourably affected – as long as the profits have credibility. When the credibility goes, the share price collapses.

An increasing proportion of the remuneration of chairpersons and chief executives (often the majority, and sometimes in millions of pounds) is performance-related pay. It is usually linked to the company's profits, and its share price. It is only to be expected that chief executives will do what they can to maximize profits and share price. That is what the shareholders put them there to do.

Sometimes creative accounting is more concerned with 'income smoothing' than with maximizing profits in a particular year. In a year when the company's performance is very good, there is a temptation to understate profits, and to keep something back to supplement profits in leaner years. Investors are probably more impressed by a company that manages to increase its profits every year, than by one which seems to swing from profits to losses. This is, of course, against all accounting rules, but it is likely that, at the margin, judgements in some companies are exercised in a more prudent way when the profits are very good, and in a less prudent way when profits have fallen.

Creative accounting is not only about reported profits. It can be used to manipulate key ratios that are used by analysts, and to produce more healthy looking balance sheets. If a company wants to demonstrate that they have a high return on capital employed they will want to maximize profits; but they will not want to see high figures for capital employed. Such companies may avoid increasing asset values, and find ways of reducing asset values that do not hit profits too hard, particularly in relatively lean years.

Other companies may have a need to borrow, and will want to emphasize the asset backing for such borrowings. Existing borrowings often come with covenants, to protect the position of existing lenders. Such covenants may require the company not to exceed specified gearing ratios, and other defined ratios. In these circumstances companies might seek to maximize assets and equity. If land and buildings are revalued (upwards), that automatically increases the figure for equity and may then make it easier for the company to borrow more money.

The use of creative accounting may be attractive to a new management team that has just taken over a company. The new team are likely to be under pressure to prove that they are more successful than their predecessors. The use of 'Provisions' may be a tempting way of doing this, as outlined in the section on page 217 below.

Judgement Becoming Creative

There is inevitably a need for judgement in many areas of accounting. There are no single, correct, objective figures, even in traditional, straightforward accounting – which operated successfully for many years, long before sophisticated creative accounting techniques were developed.

Depreciation is an area where there is a need for judgement. We can rarely be sure how long a fixed asset will be used, or what its residual value will be. If an airline changes its depreciation policy so that aircraft are depreciated over 25 years rather than 15 years, it will make a massive difference to profits. It should be reviewed every year; but it would not be amazing if, when profits are looking a little low, the company decides that fixed assets will be kept for longer than was previously the case.

We cannot be sure what the net realizable value of stocks of unsold goods will be.[1] When a company is doing well they probably have time to check that all stocks really are being written down to net realizable value. It would not be amazing, if, when profits are looking a little low, there are other priorities than estimating the latest net realizable value figures and ensuring that everything has been written down accordingly.

Perhaps provisions for bad debts are more prudent in some years than others. Similarly, in a year of low profits, there may be no harm if a few repairs and renewals get classified as capital expenditure. And it is only natural to delay doing repairs when times are hard. It can all start off fairly harmlessly and almost unconsciously: where there is a margin for error or judgement we understate profits a little in the good years, so that when the bad years come we can review our accounting policies to release something held back by our previous caution.

Gradually there can be more pressure to increase profits and accounting policies seem to be twisted in one direction only. At first this might all be legitimate, and within the rules. But it can go to dubious, illegal and criminal extremes.

A company might operate a number of hotels and be reasonably successful for many years. Then occupancy levels drop, perhaps because of the international situation. Keeping the hotels in a good state of repair, and maintaining their appearance is a major expense that hits profits. At first the company might decide to try to maintain profits by deferring all but essential repairs. Carpets are not replaced until they are threadbare and dangerous; rooms are not redecorated until the paper is peeling off the walls and the smart white paintwork has either turned to a gentle shade of puce, or gone mouldy; and the furniture is starting to fall apart. After a few years it is not repairs that are needed, but a total refurbishment. Fortunately refurbishment can be classified as capital expenditure, and does not hit profits. A new policy emerges: the expense for repairs virtually disappears; all hotels are refurbished every 4 or 5 years.

If there are still no profits from running the hotels, more extreme accounting policies are needed. Suppose that the company owns a hotel that originally cost £8 million, but now needs £2 million spending on it for refurbishment. It has a market value of £10 million. The company sells the hotel to a friendly building company for £10 million. The building company does the refurbishment, and sells the hotel back to the hotel company for £13 million. The building company is happy with the contract: they have made

---

1   Closing stock should be shown at the lower of cost and net realizable value; we have to know what the net realizable value will be in order to know which is the lower.

£1 million profit. The hotel company is happy with the arrangement: what might have been an expense for repairs, over the years, of £2 million has become a profit (on sale of the hotel) of £2 million. And their balance sheet looks better. Instead of having a tatty old hotel shown as £8 million, they have a newly refurbished one shown at £13 million. And they had to borrow only £3 million to achieve this.

It could get worse and more dubious, and illegal. Maybe the hotel is not really worth £10 million. But there may be ways of finding a building company willing to enter into a contract to buy it for £10 million, if there is a guaranteed profit of £1 million. Perhaps there is more profit to be made from specialized arrangements to buy and sell hotels than there is from actually running hotels.

Other strange contracts can be created. A hotel might find that it expects spare room capacity worth £1 million at quiet times of the year. They might be glad to sell that spare capacity to a Package Holiday Company for £500,000 – giving the hotel company £500,000 of revenues that they would not otherwise have had. The Package Holiday Company might then find that it has more capacity than it needs, and sell on half of what it has bought to a Conference Company for £600,000 (making £100,000 profit for doing almost nothing). Then the Conference Company sells part of what it has bought – and the Conference Company buys some surplus capacity on an airline's routes from London to one of the places where it has hotel capacity; the airline has bought that spare capacity from another airline, and they had bought it from a hotel who had bought it from another airline – or perhaps it was the original airline, or hotel or conference company. Okay, I am making this up about hotels and airlines (I think). But it did happen with telecommunications companies, making profits by selling spare capacity to each other.

Creative accounting can start with cautious use of judgement which varies a little from year to year, depending on the circumstances. It can end with serious fraud and criminal activity; and with the company going into liquidation – with lots of people losing their livelihood, their pensions and their savings. But some people probably manage to get out in time, after making a lot of money. Creative accounting can be a mechanism for redistributing wealth from the poor, weak and vulnerable to those who are strong, clever and ruthless. Financial accounting has an important role to play in trying to prevent and disclose such activities.

How Bad Are the Various Techniques?

Where there are suggestions or accusations that creative accounting has been used, we could ask, on a scale of 1 to 10, how bad is it? Number 1 would be almost nothing at all; number 10 would be the worst possible.

The following is not intended to be authoritative or definitive. But it does give an idea of the range of different activities that some might classify as being 'creative accounting'.

1 There is nothing questionable about the financial statements, but information has been presented to emphasize the more favourable aspects of financial position and performance, and to de-emphasize the least favourable.

2 The emphasis on the favourable aspects are so strong as to suggest more of a propaganda exercise than a balanced report.

3 All financial statements are properly drawn up, but somehow the rules seem to flatter the company's performance whereas a different selection of accounting policies and measurements would be less flattering.

4 All financial statements have been properly drawn up in accordance with the requirements of company law and accounting standards. Where the official accounting requirements allow choice or flexibility, the company selects those options which tend to flatter the financial statements.

5 There are departures from accounting standards, but these have been properly disclosed and explained, and the financial effects have been quantified.

6 There is just a suspicion that there are departures from accounting standards which have not been disclosed. Some of the figures seem to be a bit questionable.

7 Rules and definitions have been pushed to the limit, and perhaps a little beyond. Judgements have been exercised to come up with treatments that the auditors have been persuaded to accept, but on the face of it other accountants would find such treatments unacceptable.

8 Transactions and arrangements seem to have been deliberately designed to take advantage of, or to avoid, particular rules or accounting treatments.

9 Clear breaches of accounting standards without proper disclosure of departures or reasons for them.

10 Criminal activity, fraud and deception.

8.2 **Some Problem Areas**

One of the difficulties of describing the problem areas and neatest tricks of creative accounting, is that by the time they come to be described in books such as this, they have become so well known that the accounting standard setters have brought in measures to stop them.

There have always been the areas of judgement such as the amounts to be charged for depreciation, the amount to be shown for closing stock, provisions for bad debts, and with the difficult, grey area between capital expenditure and revenue expenditure. Other areas such as the following, are worth careful examination.

Exceptional and Extraordinary Items

In the 1970s one of the most controversial areas was extraordinary items and exceptional items, such as profits on sales of fixed assets, or losses on reorganizations and disposals. Sometimes companies would treat profits from such one-off transactions as an 'exceptional' item, which means that they were separately disclosed, and counted as part of earnings per share. But losses might be classified as 'extraordinary items'; these were shown 'below the line' – they were ignored in calculating earnings per share. This was all allowed by the old SSAP 6, although companies were expected to justify the treatment that they had adopted.

This problem was effectively tackled by FRS 3. Extraordinary items were virtually abolished. In the unlikely event that a company could defend something as being extraordinary, it still had to be counted in calculating earnings per share. FRS 3 also required specific disclosure of profits or losses on the sale or termination of an operation; costs of fundamental reorganizations; and profits or losses on the disposal of fixed assets. All of these have to be counted in calculating earnings per share.

But companies are still free to calculate two different earnings per share figures, one according to the official rules, and one dealing as they think appropriate with unusual (and not so unusual) items. They can give whatever interpretation and 'spin' they wish to the earnings per share figure that they have chosen for themselves. Some companies prefer to ignore non-routine bits of bad news (such as losses on a sale or reorganization of a business), or even fairly routine items (such as losses resulting from currency fluctuations, or write offs of goodwill). Unsophisticated investment analysts may even agree with the company's interpretation, and decide that the company's performance is better than is suggested by the figures resulting from strict adherence to the measurement rules in accounting standards.

Provisions

Strange things can happen when one company is taken over by another company. The 'victim' company may have been pottering along quite nicely with modest profits. Then along comes a new management, and what looked like last year's profits suddenly become substantial losses. The new management say that stocks and fixed assets are mostly obsolete and write them down to much lower values. There will have to be reorganizations and redundancies, and a provision must be made against the most recent profit figure to allow for this. Some of their customers look in poor shape, and might not pay up, so a large provision for bad debts is created. Any intangible assets that the 'victim' has paid for are likely to be virtually worthless, and so are written down to very low values, or written off completely. Last year's expected profits are suddenly converted into a substantial loss, and it is all blamed on the previous management.

The new management, perhaps they are company doctors,[2] are able to transform the company's performance. The dreadful losses which they inherited are suddenly turned into substantial profits the next year.

For some managements there may be a temptation to throw all sorts of dubious expenses and write offs into a 'big bath', or massive provision. All of the bad news can be got rid of in one year; future years can then only be better.

Illustration 8.1

The draft profit and loss account of Slowco for the year ended 31 December Year 5 showed a profit of £2 million for the year. The company was taken over by Fastgro on 31 January Year 6. Fastgro reviewed the accounting policies of Slowco, wrote down a number of assets, and created a provision for reorganization. As a result the draft profit of Slowco for Year 5 became a loss of £1 million.

Slowco had stocks of raw materials, components, work in progres and finished goods which were originally shown at cost of £800,000. Fastgro wrote these stocks down to £200,000 which they considered to be the net realizable value.

In Year 6 Fastgro managed to sell all of the stocks concerned for £500,000.

Stocks which had originally cost £800,000 had been sold for £500,000, and Fastgro showed this as a profit of £300,000. They had blamed the previous management for a loss of £600,000.

Twelve months later the new management were able to announce that Slowco had made record profits in Year 6. Not many people examined the underlying performance.

---

2 Perhaps even witch doctors who can create a massive improvement in a company's performance, as if by magic.

FRS 12 (Provisions, contingent liabilities and contingent assets) is intended to curtail such (ab)use of provisions. A provision is defined as a *liability* of uncertain timing or amount. It is not just an *intention* to do something, and it is certainly not somewhere to credit good profits in one year so that they can be taken out again[3] in a subsequent year. A provision should be recognized only where there is an *obligation* to make a payment. This might be a legal obligation, but a 'constructive obligation' is also an acceptable basis for a provision. This may be based on past practices, or published policies which lead to a valid expectation that a payment will be made; this is rather more subjective and may allow some scope for creative accounting.

There is also a problem in that we continue to use provisions for depreciation, and provisions for bad debts, although these are clearly not liabilities.

The ASB has produced stricter definitions of provisions than the Companies Act 1985, and requires additional disclosure. But they also positively encourage the regular review of asset valuations, and the possibility of these being used to push profits down in one year, and up in another year can never be eliminated entirely.

Goodwill

Goodwill arises in financial statements when one company buys another company, and pays more for it than its net asset value as shown on the balance sheet. This is normal practice. If a company has a net asset value of, say, £10 million, it is very unlikely that the owners of that company would be willing to sell it for £10 million, especially if the company has had a good profit record for a number of years. Assets are often undervalued on balance sheets, and when one company takes over another, the assets should be revalued to 'fair value'. A company might have net assets with a balance sheet value of £10 million, and a 'fair value' of, say, £12 million. But if the company is successful and profitable, anyone wanting to take it over should expect to pay more than £12 million. Perhaps they pay £15 million.

If we buy a business with net assets of £12 million, and we pay £15 million for that business, there should be no problem recording the payment of £15 million, or the net assets of £12 million that have been bought. But £3 million has been paid for goodwill. Is this to be recorded as an expense, or as an asset? Treating it as an expense would hit profits too hard. Showing it as an asset might be open to question: does the business really own something worth £3 million?

The old ASC preferred a treatment which avoided this stark choice. Goodwill was deducted from retained profits on the balance sheet. It did not

---

3   The bookkeeping would be debit Provision Account, credit Profit and Loss Account.

have to be written off as an expense on the profit and loss account. And it did not need to be shown on the balance sheet as a rather questionable asset. But if a company had reserves of only, say, £1 million, it was difficult to deduct £3 million from reserves without making the balance sheet look very weak indeed. With many 'modern' businesses, the main asset is often goodwill, and it is now not unusual, when buying a business, to pay more for goodwill than the retained profits available against which it could be written off.

FRS 10 introduced a new regime. Goodwill that has been purchased should be shown as a fixed asset on the balance sheet[4] and it should be amortized as an expense over its useful economic life. The life could be 5 years, or 10 years, or almost any period. Companies can argue that the useful economic life is more than 20 years, or that it is indefinite, provided they carry out an annual impairment review.

There can still be creative accounting with goodwill. It can be treated as a fixed asset with indefinite economic life, with no amortization required. Or it can be amortized, and an earnings per share figure can be reported which excludes amortization and so flatters the company's results.

If there is 'negative goodwill', there may be opportunities for those who like to be creative. Sometimes it is possible to buy a company for less than its net asset value, especially if the company is not doing very well. If a company has a net asset value of £10 million, and we are able to buy it for £8 million, then negative goodwill arises. It is shown on the balance sheet as a negative asset (a credit balance). Amortization is still required: it should be credited to the profit and loss account in the periods which benefit from it. Some companies may find it convenient to have a substantial balance available to be credited to the profit and loss account in appropriate periods.

There is nothing improper about this. A saving of £2 million has been made in acquiring a company; the profit and loss accounts will benefit from this as and when appropriate.

Choices Still Remain

There are a number of areas in accounting standards where choices still remain. Under SSAP 13, development expenditure, provided it meets certain conditions, may be capitalized and treated as a fixed asset. A company may, instead, choose to write it off immediately as an expense.

There are also areas where there is, at the time of writing, no accounting standard from the ASB.[5] When a company constructs its own fixed assets (perhaps building a hotel) most of the costs are capitalized and become part of the cost of the fixed assets. A company is likely to borrow money

---

4   And negative goodwill should be shown as a negative fixed asset.

5   Although International Accounting Standards do give guidance, and listed UK companies should be following them by 2005.

while building, and to incur interest costs. Most traditional accountants might say that interest costs should be written off in the period in which they are incurred. But some would choose to capitalize them and treat them as being part of the cost of the fixed asset.

It is not always clear exactly when a sale takes place, and when the revenues from sales should be recognized. For bookkeeping convenience, a sale may be recognized in an accounting system when the invoice is sent to the customer. But sometimes, companies who are not doing very well are tempted to bring forward the date on which sales are recognized; this will have the effect of increasing the sales in the current period.[6] They might, for example, choose to recognize the revenue when an order for goods or services is first received, and this is allowed.

The ASB and the IASB are steadily reducing the number of areas where there are still choices, and where no guidance exists. But there are also likely to be some clever accountants working in dark corners finding new ways of creating choices as fast as the standards setters curtail the old ones.

Fuzzy Rules

In some instances the ASB has tried to make it clear that companies do not have a choice in which accounting treatment to adopt. Most companies use the 'acquisition' (or purchase) method of producing consolidated accounts for groups of companies. In some circumstances the 'merger' (or pooling of interests) method is used. In theory companies have no choice: if particular conditions apply, they must use the merger method; if those conditions do not apply, they must use the acquisition method. Comparable approaches have been adopted with the treatment of associate companies, and with deferred tax. The rules appear to be clear; there appears to be no choice. But there is always some fuzziness in rules in marginal cases. And it is always possible that companies structure financial transactions in a particular way so as to be able to use the accounting treatment that shows their results in the best light.

When one company takes over another company, there are accounting advantages if it can be structured and presented as a merger rather than an acquisition.[7]

Off Balance Sheet Finance

Sometimes accountants are creative in producing profit figures which are not supported by the company's underlying performance. Perhaps people who work for the company know that it is going downhill; perhaps there

---

6   And reducing the sales in the next period.

7   Although merger accounting is likely to be banned within the next year or two.

are terrible delays in paying creditors. But still healthy looking profit figures are produced.

One way of detecting questionable accounting is to compare the amount of tax a company is paying with their reported profit figures. If a company is paying virtually no corporation tax they must be telling the Inland Revenue that they are making virtually no profits. But if at the same time they are declaring substantial profits in their annual reports, it is worth further investigation. It may be that the company has invested heavily in fixed assets, and so has generous writing down allowances for corporation tax purposes. Or it may be more suspicious.

A cash flow statement can also give indications of what is 'really' going on if profit figures seem questionable. It is easier to generate fictitious profit figures than to produce fictitious cash. Sooner or later a company is going to need more cash to keep going. A genuinely profitable company generates cash; and a healthy company can usually raise cash without much difficulty, typically by borrowing. But if a company keeps needing to borrow more, it may raise questions, and their balance sheet will start to look very weak if burdened by too much debt. The company may try to borrow in ways that do not appear on the balance sheet.

When a company wants more fixed assets they may:

(a) borrow the money and buy the fixed assets; or

(b) lease the fixed assets.

In the first instance there is clearly an asset and a liability; both appear on the balance sheet. In the second instance, the financial effects are very similar: the company has the use of the asset just as if they own it; and they have to make repayments, just as if they had borrowed the money. Leasing was seen as a way of, in effect, borrowing money, but keeping the borrowings off the balance sheets. Creditors would not know the extent of the company's commitments to make payments under leasing agreements, and might be misled into lending more money.

SSAP 21 put a stop to this. Some leases were defined as 'finance leases' and treated just as if the company owned the fixed asset that they had leased: both the asset, and the liability to pay for it, had to be shown on the balance sheet. One way of raising money 'off balance sheet' had been ended. But companies sought other methods.

FRS 5 requires companies to report the *substance* of transactions. Whatever the legal technicalities might be, if a company has incurred a financial commitment it must be shown as such. In the USA the rules appear to be stricter, but the more strict and clear the rules are, the easier it is to create financial arrangements that just fall within the letter of the rules, but are a breach of the spirit of them. The UK approach errs on the side of principle rather than strict rules, and the idea of 'economic reality' takes priority over 'legal form'. FRS 5 has now barred the practice of companies borrowing money and keeping it off the balance sheet, perhaps by using some legal nicety which puts the borrowings in the name of another friendly company.

The temptation to raise additional financing through dubious off balance sheet arrangements was a key feature of the major accounting scandal with Enron in 2002, and its subsequent collapse.

Share Options

If a company wants to minimize the amount of salaries that count as an expense, employees can be paid in share options instead of money. This became fairly common practice at the height of the dot com boom.

Illustration 8.2

Dorothy accepted a job with the e.vilwich company, selling potions on the internet. The job carried no salary or commission but she was given the option of buying 100,000 shares in the company for £1 each. When she joined the company the market price of the shares was only £0.50. But before she left the company the market price had gone up to £11.

Dorothy bought her 100,000 shares for £100,000, and then immediately sold them for £1,100,000. She had received no salary; she had cost the company nothing; and she had become a millionaire.

Share options appear to cost the company nothing, and are not recorded as an expense. But existing shareholders do lose out: when someone exercises their options to buy, existing shareholders suddenly own a smaller portion of the company, and the person who exercises the options has made a gain at their expense.

The Accounting Standards Board, and the International Accounting Standards Board are attempting to develop a standard which will require the issue of share options to be recorded as an expense.

Conclusion

Accounting standard setters are steadily becoming more strict; they are reducing and eliminating choices; and more effective enforcement mechanisms are being implemented. But it seems unlikely that the problem will ever be completely solved. Perhaps it is unrealistic to expect (m)any problems to be completely solved. The present trend is for a steady increase in the length and complexity of accounting standards. But as the rules get fuller and more detailed, so some practitioners find increasingly complex ways around them. This in turn leads to the need for even more detailed standards to close loopholes that have been found. When these become pressing there is an Urgent Issues Task Force to provide supplementary guidance. Finding ways around the additional guidance becomes more complex, and so it goes on. If present trends continue, by the time the average reader of this book reaches the present age of the writer, there will be more accounting and auditing standards, rules, principles and guidance than anyone could read in a lifetime.

In spite of the efforts of the accountancy profession and the standards setters, many would argue that creative accounting is still alive and well. A wide range of choices in the way that companies can measure and report their financial performance still remains. Perhaps we need different approaches to tackling the problems; and we may need to look at the problem in different ways.

8.3 How to Curtail Creative Accounting

Many different suggestions have been made for dealing with the problem of creative accounting. One group of suggestions builds on what is already happening. Work should continue on improving accounting standards, rules and principles; enforcement mechanisms should be improved. Problems with auditing arrangements should be sorted out. Offenders should be punished.

More radical proposals might take a right-wing approach (leave it all to the market), a left-wing approach (let the state take it over), or tackle the question from a different perspective, or try to beat everyone into submission by 'shock and awe' tactics.

Moderate Evolutionary Changes

Many assume that there is little wrong with the existing systems for accounting, auditing and the production and implementation of accounting standards. They acknowledge that there is a need for continuing reform and improvement. They also recognize that there are sometimes individual wrongdoers who either gently bend or sidestep the rules, or who are guilty of flagrant breaches of the rules. It is necessary to take action against such individuals. But the approach seems to assume that, generally speaking, the framework for accounting and auditing is proceeding in the right direction; and any serious threat to existing vested interests is inappropriate. The main suggestions within this approach are outlined below.

1 *The production of clearer accounting standards that reduce or eliminate choices.* There are still some accounting standards that specifically allow a

choice of accounting treatments. But the ASB and the IASB are continuing to work towards producing more clear-cut accounting standards, as was the old ASC. But there is the danger that companies may invent new, alternative treatments faster than the ASB manages to reduce existing variations. There are also pressures on the ASB to compromise to meet the needs of different interest groups. Although they have rather more power than the ASC to overrule special pleading, it is likely to be some years before the permitting of different treatments is phased out.

2 *The 'benchmark' argument.* This recognizes that there will never be 100 per cent agreement or standardization, and that as long as companies have the power to do so, some will continue to push variations in accounting treatment that make their own position look better. Standards should lay down a single recommended treatment which is a 'benchmark' against which all other treatments are measured. Where a company adopts a different treatment, the financial effects of doing this should be quantified and disclosed. This means that users of accounts should not be misled: reported figures can always be converted back to the preferred benchmark treatment.

3 *Stronger legal backing for accounting standards.* The position of the old ASC was weakened by the lack of legal backing for the enforcement of accounting standards, but the position has improved since 1989/90. The 1989 Companies Act gives legal recognition to the ASB's accounting standards, but falls short of requiring companies to adopt them. Directors have to state whether accounts have been prepared in compliance with these standards, and declare any departures from them; but such departures are allowed, and there is still the overriding requirement for accounts to show what the directors consider to be 'a true and fair view'.[8] Legal opinion suggests that accounting standards have, in effect, become a source of law, and it is difficult for companies to argue against the idea that following accounting standards is the most effective way of showing a true and fair view. But they can, and sometimes they do, and creative accounting still flourishes. The present accounting standards regime continues to work largely by consent, which means that standards have sometimes avoided difficult, clear-cut and controversial requirements. Firmer legal backing for standards has proved to be necessary and this has reduced the tendency to compromise with difficult issues.

4 *Relying on international standards.* In some respects International Financial Reporting Standards are more prescriptive than UK ones.[9]

---

8 A widely used phrase, the meaning of which is elusive. The use of the indefinite article indicates that there is no single true and fair view; many different 'views' of financial statements may be equally true and fair – that's the problem!

9 But in some respects they are less prescriptive!

The European Union requirement that listed companies should adhere to international standards from 2005 is likely to strengthen the authority of accounting standards.

5 *More effective monitoring and enforcement.* Current proposals mean strengthening the role of the existing Financial Reporting and Review Panel (FRRP) which operates under the auspices of the Financial Reporting Council. At present the FRRP works only in response to problems that are referred to it. It does not, on its own initiative, examine samples of company accounts to check that accounting standards, and other requirements, have been enforced.

Improved arrangements are being brought into force but UK regulatory and enforcement bodies are still under-funded compared with the equivalent bodies in the USA. But by 2004 it is most likely that the FRRP will be undertaking monitoring and enforcement of accounting standards under its own initiative.

6 *Principles rather than rules.* The fashionable defence of accounting in the UK, in the light of the US accounting scandals following Enron, is that UK accounting is based on principles rather than rules: difficulties arose in America because their approach depends on rules rather than principles. The argument is that simply following the rules can lead to creative presentations that do not represent 'economic reality'. The 'superior' British approach depends on 'substance', or 'economic reality' being more important than the rules or 'legal form'; and that the professional judgement of accountants and auditors about what is a true and fair view is more important than following the rules.

This is a curious argument in a number of respects. Some of the worst American problems seem to be due to people *not* following the rules. The fact that there were more serious accounting scandals in the USA than in the UK may be more a matter of chance than it is due to perceived differences in the emphasis on rules rather than principles. The idea that UK accounting is based on principles may be hard to defend: most accounting standards were produced before the ASB produced its *Statement of Principles* (1999); and our principles are not always very clear, and they seem to change almost as regularly as accounting standards change. As the ASB might have said: if you don't like our principles, we have others.

7 *Current cost accounting.* Those who advocate current cost accounting may hope that clear principles about asset valuation might reduce the amount of freedom to indulge in creative accounting. But moving away from historic cost, which is based on objective, verifiable transactions, is more likely to increase the scope for creativity than reduce it.

8 *Cash flow accounting.* If accounting was based simply on receipts and payments of cash, as opposed to the accruals basis[10] for measuring profit, most scope for creative accounting would be eliminated. There would, of course be a need to classify cash flows: the total figures alone would tell us little. We would probably want to separate payments for acquiring fixed assets from payments for normal operating expenses. Such classifications would be to some extent a matter for judgement, and the supposed objectivity of receipts-and-payments based accountancy would immediately disappear. More seriously, it would be, in effect, abolishing accounting as we know it: there would be no profit figure, and there would be nothing to show on the balance sheet apart from cash.

The term 'cash flow accounting' is sometimes used to mean something quite different. Some people advocate the production of balance sheets which use valuations based on the net present value of the future cash flows that an item is expected to generate. The amount of profit for a period would be based on the increase in the net asset value of the business between the two balance sheet dates. Given the amount of subjectivity involved in estimating future cash flows, this seems more like another way of encouraging creative accounting rather than a way of curbing it.

If the problems of creative accounting can be tackled effectively by improving accounting standards on an international basis, major steps forward have been taken in the last few years. Differences between European and British financial reporting are being hammered out, and by 2005 it is likely that there will be few significant differences. The approach in the USA differs significantly from Europe, but attempts are being made at convergence of accounting standards. In general this is likely to lead to better standards. The need for compromises might still leave options open and some areas of creative accounting might not be tackled effectively. But the strength of the movement towards clear and effective international financial reporting standards is such that enormous progress is likely to be made by 2005.

Improving Auditing Arrangements

Auditors are often seen as one of the main safeguards against creative accounting. Directors might favour a variety of weird and wonderful ways of calculating profit which serve to flatter their own management performance; auditors are expected to play a role in curbing such creative accounting. But if auditors are to be effective in this, they must be clearly independent of directors. If the auditors are in the directors' pocket, with

---

10   This distinction is examined in Chapter 7.

directors determining their appointment and remuneration, they are in a weak position if they need to stand up to directors. Areas where there are suggestions to increase the independence of auditors include the following.

1 *Rotating senior audit partners more often.* It is sometimes argued that auditors can become too close to directors and too easily influenced by them. The ICAEW has responded to recent criticisms by reducing the maximum period that a partner can be responsible for a particular audit from 7 years to 5 years.

2 *Audit fees being set by an independent body.* The idea that an auditor can be independent from directors, while at the same time negotiating their fees with the directors, strains credibility. In view of this, their fees are, in theory, decided by shareholders. But in practice it is the directors who decide. The moderate response to this problem is that auditors' fees should be approved by non-executive directors as part of a company's audit committee. A more extreme response would be that directors should not be involved at all: fees should be set by a completely independent body.

3 *Auditors being appointed by an independent body.* The arguments are much the same as with audit fees. The idea that auditors can be independent from directors while at the same time negotiating to be reappointed as auditors is questionable. In theory the appointment is made by shareholders; but in practice it is the directors who decide. It could be a matter for the audit committee, which should be independent from the executive directors.

4 *Prohibiting non-audit work.* Criticism of auditors' lack of independence because they are always looking for remunerative consultancy work is widespread. The European tradition is that auditors are restricted to auditing duties, and the USA has moved strongly in this direction since the WorldCom and Enron scandals. Following recent criticisms of auditing arrangements many of the large international accountancy firms have sold off their consultancy businesses. But they continue to offer a wide range of services to their audit clients. It seems only natural that when they are carrying out an audit they are able to make recommendations to improve a client's accounting and computing systems, and also to offer taxation advice. This can be very remunerative for the auditors.

It is now a requirement that a company's annual report shows not only the audit fee for the year, but also any other fees payable to their auditors for other services. Very often the fees paid for additional services is greater than the audit fee. Sometimes auditors have been accused of 'low-balling': deliberately quoting low audit fees in order to get other, more remunerative work from their audit clients. It is difficult to believe that auditors are really independent of directors when they seem to be on the look-out for additional lucrative work from those directors.

There are also criticisms when the individual accountants who audit a particular company subsequently leave their appointment with the auditing firm, and take up employment as a senior accountant with a former audit client. The idea of independent auditors seems to be compromised if we know that some of the auditors may be keen to impress the management of companies that they are auditing in the hope of a lucrative job offer.

The professional accountancy bodies have made progress in shoring up the reputation of auditors in relation to the problems of independence, and audit committees are expected to play an important part in this. But the professional accountancy bodies may be seen as acting primarily on behalf of their members, rather than on behalf of investors or the general public. Auditors are supposed to be there to act on behalf of shareholders, but sometimes seem to be more interested in supporting the directors – and protecting their own remuneration.

Punishing Offenders

It is sometimes convenient to blame individuals for problems that arise from creative accounting, and in some cases this is clearly appropriate. Individuals may be guilty of fraud, or deception, or breaches of relevant legislation, or of criminal offences. Sometimes the accounting and auditing systems should be given credit for bringing to light such offences. But sometimes there are serious questions about the adequacy of such systems where they have for long periods failed to detect problems.

Some might argue that, where accounting scandals have arisen because of wrongdoing by individuals, this is not a creative accounting issue. It is a matter for the criminal and civil law enforcement authorities.

But the line between wrongdoing and 'innocent' creative accounting is not always clear. The existence of creative accounting is due partly to weaknesses in the regulatory framework of accounting, and partly to the existence of a minority of individuals who are prepared to bend and break the rules in pursuit of their own advantage. In the USA the political response to the accounting scandals of 2002 sometimes seemed to be more concerned with blaming particular individuals than with challenging the vested interests of the accounting and auditing establishment. Although it is appropriate to take legal action against those who have clearly broken the law and abused their positions of trust, it is unrealistic to expect all accountants, auditors, regulators, chief executives, managers, executive directors and non-executive directors to behave like saints. Some need clearer and stronger rules to restrict the excesses of their bad behaviour. Others need clearer and stronger rules to support their attempts at good behaviour. Those who are trying to ensure that creative accounting is minimized, and that auditing and accounting requirements are properly implemented, can be severely hampered if close examination of accounting and auditing standards reveals that there are loopholes; if the rules that they are trying to enforce are not really clear; and there is still scope for those who are tempted by creative accounting practices.

Proposals for improving corporate governance and companies' auditing and accounting practices often rely heavily on the supposed role of non-executive directors. Even if there are enough competent people to carry out the functions expected of them, and there are more saints than sinners among them, it is difficult for anyone to be better than the system within which they operate.

Punishing a few wrong-doers does not solve the problems of the system within which they operate.

Radical Proposals

Right Wing

We could argue that the whole regulatory approach to accounting is a waste of time and money; it serves only to build up the bureaucratic empires of the regulators; it will always be unsatisfactory, and will always lead to demands for more resources for the regulators. Accounting and auditing is a matter for agreement between the shareholders and the directors.

A right-wing perspective could take a laissez faire approach, or it could rely on freedom of access to information.

1 *Laissez faire.* The market-based argument is that there is no need for legislation or public involvement in the ways in which companies do their accounting, or in the existence, role or operations of auditing firms. Companies have a vested interest in supplying credible information to capital markets, and auditing firms have a financial interest in maintaining their reputations. Companies that supply duff information will be punished in the capital markets; share prices will collapse; the companies will be taken over at bargain basement prices; and the directors will lose their jobs when their more credible competitors take over. Similarly, auditing firms that give their names to incredible accounting treatments will soon lose credibility, and be of no use to their clients. Eventually they will end up like Arthur Andersen.[11] The market takes care of everything. There is no need for public involvement.

---

11 The international accountancy firm that collapsed in the wake of the accounting scandals in the USA in 2002.

This argument is out of favour at present. As long as there are financial scandals, governments want to be seen to play a role in dealing with the problems. The UK approach tends to be gentle and consultative and the accountancy profession can usually talk governments around to their way of thinking. The US approach is to shock and awe.

2 *Freedom of access to information.* Financial statements provide summaries of transactions and of what can be a huge amount of financial data. In the early days of companies, when there were fewer shareholders and fewer financial transactions, it was practicable to open up the books of account to individuals[12] who could see all transactions for themselves. If someone chose to present 'creative' accounts of what had happened, it would be difficult to pull the wool over the eyes of shareholders who could inspect everything for themselves. Such an approach became impractical as the number of shareholders, and the number of financial transactions increased enormously. Shareholders became dependent on the version of events that was created for them by accountants, directors and auditors. But computerization may have changed all of that. When we read that schoolboys with computers in their bedrooms can penetrate the secrets of Pentagon defence systems, and fraudsters or pranksters can penetrate the security of banking systems – perhaps just for fun – we can no longer pretend that company accounting systems are inviolate. The public need no longer be dependent on accountants as intermediaries to present company financial stories in ways that suit company directors.

Such open access to information is potentially revolutionary, and could be associated with a dramatic shift of power in society. There could be no secrets in relation to creative accounting. But, unfortunately, very few people seem to be interested in the details of company transactions.

Accounting and auditing arrangements are no longer a matter just for directors and shareholders. When companies are listed on stock markets, the listing agreement requires appropriate arrangements to be in place. A stock exchange does not want its reputation undermined by companies which have chosen to opt out of accounting regulations. The most substantial shareholders are institutional investors, such as pension funds. They are unlikely to invest in companies which lack normal accountability mechanisms.

---

12 Something similar happens in local authorities today.

Left Wing

Many assume that that there is a legitimate public interest[13] in the numbers that purport to represent the profits, assets and liabilities of companies. If it can be demonstrated that the public interest is best served by competing power groups of 'experts', economists and vested interests, then there may be no need for public sector involvement. But when, as happens from time to time, there are accounting scandals, and financial reporting seems to be collapsing, there are increasing demands for more direct government/public control.

1 *Inland Revenue Rules OK*. Many Europeans are surprised to find that, in this country, profits for financial reporting purposes do not simply follow the rules laid down by the government for taxation (and other) purposes, and that this is deemed to be quite legitimate. The idea that companies can choose to depreciate ships, or aircraft over 10 or 20 or 30 years – or almost any period they like – seems quite fantastic. Perhaps it is central to the Anglo-American notion of 'freedom' – which includes freedom to be creative with accounting.

If we want to argue for clearer, more effective and enforceable accounting rules to curb creative accounting, we can argue that this should come from the government, and it can build on what the Inland Revenue already does. To someone from eastern Europe this would seem only natural. But the argument is rarely advanced in Anglo-American accounting cultures. It is argued that governments lack the necessary expertise in accounting, and that they would be too slow to respond to changing business and accounting circumstances and practices.

But if governments lack accounting expertise, they can easily buy it – as companies do. And if governments are slow to respond to changing circumstances they may be no worse than the accounting profession. The accountancy profession has still not produced a satisfactory response to the effects of inflation on accounts whereas the Inland Revenue produced workable solutions long ago. The Chancellor of the Exchequer is usually criticized for producing too many changes in the taxation system too quickly, not for slowness to respond.

2 *A State Auditing Board*. It may be too extreme to suggest nationalizing the whole of the auditing profession, but if auditing is seen as operating in defence of vested interest groups, rather than in the public interest, this must remain the ultimate solution. But a State Auditing Board, as advocated by Lyall and Perks (1976), could do much to shift the balance of

---

13 Which may be based on the allocation of resources in the economy, or the taxation paid by companies, or perhaps just in maintaining 'the system' and avoiding accounting scandals.

power without full nationalization. If there is a public interest in auditors being independent from directors[14] it is hard to defend a system where, in effect, the directors:

- decide which firm of auditors should be appointed, and how long they should serve

- decide what level of remuneration to pay to auditors

- allocate substantial contracts to auditors for non-audit work.

A public, or state auditing board could be responsible for appointing auditors to particular companies, determining the level of fees and the period of appointment, and deciding to whom non-audit work should be allocated.

Such a board would also have a vested interest in establishing and implementing clear-cut accounting rules that could be expected to minimize creative accounting.

Accountancy and Power

Anyone who believes that there is such a thing as 'correct' accountancy is likely to favour existing accountancy arrangements whereby accounting standards setters struggle with the problem of how particular items should be measured and reported. They then produce the best solution, and accountants and auditors have to ensure that these are properly applied.

But many accounting numbers and accounting standards are the result of negotiation, rather than being based on any underlying truth, principle or economic reality. Accounting standard setters have changed their conclusions and recommendations on issues such as the amortization of goodwill, providing for deferred taxation, and capitalization of development expenditure. A negotiated settlement is reached, but it may be changed a few years later. No new 'truth' is discovered. In negotiations the strongest usually get their way, and the way in which accountancy is applied is as a result of bargaining among powerful interest groups. Any serious attempt to change the way in which accountancy is applied in practice must involve a change in the balance of power between the different vested interest groups in society which influence accounting.

Shock and Awe

The accounting scandals in the USA in 2001–2002 called for a radical response from the American government. There was a serious loss of confidence in accountancy and auditing arrangements, and even in business itself. This crisis of confidence coincided with the beginnings of the Iraq war.

---

14   Which Companies Acts, and practice in many other countries, seem to require.

American military tactics were characterized as 'shock and awe': an overwhelming display of power which forced most of the Iraqi regime into submission. Only after the (very brief) war did it become clear that it was going to take much longer to sort out the problems of Iraq.

Parallels can be drawn with the problems in accountancy. The government used 'shock and awe' tactics – an overwhelming display of government might – to bully all of the participants in accountancy and business scandals into submission. This took the form of the Sarbanes–Oxley Act which was passed by the US Congress in July 2002. It came like a rapid reaction political bombshell with a variety of criminal and other penalties including prison, and reimbursement of any incentive payments deriving from misconduct. But it will probably take much longer to sort out the problems of creative accountancy.

Under the Sarbanes–Oxley Act the responsibility for financial statements is put on the shoulders of company chief executive officers, and chief financial officers. Each is required to certify financial information personally. Auditing firms are required to register with and report regularly to an Oversight Board. An audit committee becomes a requirement of listed companies and is to be responsible for the appointment, remuneration and oversight of the company's independent auditor who reports directly to the audit committee. The audit committee is required to deal with any disagreements between the auditors and management on accounting policies and to be involved in analysing any deficiencies in internal controls and any fraud.

The Act prohibits accounting firms from offering many non-audit services to audit clients, although the SEC may grant some exemptions. Other non-audit services, such as tax services, may only be provided if approved in advance by the company's audit committee and such approvals must be publicly disclosed.

In many ways the Sarbanes–Oxley approach is very much in line with the British approach. Most of it is one or two steps removed from direct government control. The UK still relies heavily on self regulation by the accounting profession, and reliance on audit committees is increasing. But it is unlikely that the UK will adopt a thoroughgoing 'shock and awe' approach comparable with Sarbanes–Oxley.

Summary

Many accounting and financial scandals arise because of illegal (sometimes criminal) activity by company directors and others. In many areas the laws and rules are clear, and it is often normal accounting and auditing routines and reports that uncover the problems.

Creative accounting also arises where the rules are not clear and so technically there is no wrong-doing. There will continue to be problems with creative accounting as long as directors have substantial control over the ways in which financial reports are presented. The problems of creative accounting can only be curbed, not cured; and the process may be slow, especially if reliance is placed on moderate, evolutionary changes. The UK is unlikely to implement radical right-wing or left-wing proposals, or to adopt the 'shock and awe' approach of the USA.

There may be potential for restricting creative accounting by requiring companies to use the Inland Revenue's taxation rules for measuring profit – as is (or was) the case in some European countries. But, somehow, the US–UK approach usually seems to win in any contest with European approaches. It may be unrealistic to expect a thorough, authoritative set of measurement rules to be developed and enforced which will close all of the creative accounting loopholes. Substantial improvement can come from fuller and more clear-cut disclosure requirements. The most effective curbs would come from the most significant shifts of power over the presentation of accounting information.

The most likely outcome is that we will continue with gentle reforms that largely preserve the status quo. More effective changes would come from statutory requirements for additional specific disclosures; and from removing the powers of directors over auditing and accounting. Those who have the power to do so create knowledge, accounting principles, and determine accounting practice. If creative accounting flourishes, it is because it is in the interest of those who have the power to allow it. Perhaps it can be effectively restricted only if there is a radical shift away from the existing power structures of the accountancy profession, standard setters, directors and auditors.

Review of Key Points

- The term 'creative accounting' is applied to a wide range of accounting practices

- The exercise of judgement is inevitable in some areas of accounting, and it may be tempting to exercise it in a creative way, and to extend this to other areas

- Some companies use questionable accounting practices to boost profits, to improve key ratios, to boost equity on the balance sheet, and to smooth out profits and losses from year to year

- Problem areas have included exceptional and extraordinary items, provisions, goodwill, and off balance sheet finance

- Accounting standards setters have reduced the scope for creative accounting, but there are some 'fuzzy' rules, and some areas of choice remain

- Moderate evolutionary changes are steadily reducing the scope for creative accounting

- Creative accounting is still a problem and more radical solutions may be considered

Self-testing Questions

1 In what areas of accountancy has there always been a need for subjective judgement, and scope for creative accounting?

2 Give examples of techniques that have been used in 'creative accounting'.

3 Is creative accounting illegal?

4 In what ways can accounting standards be improved to restrict creative accounting?

5 In what ways have auditors been criticized for lack of independence?

Assessment Questions

1 In what ways are the problems of creative accounting being tackled at present?

2 What more radical solutions do you think should be considered?

3 In what areas is it particularly difficult to restrict creative accounting?

Assessment Questions (continued)

4 Examine the case for more government involvement in the setting and enforcing of accounting standards, and in the regulation of auditors.

5 What is likely to happen to a company that overstates its profits year after year?

Group Activities and Discussion Questions

1 Obtain the annual reports of about four companies, two being major, well-known companies, and two being much smaller. Compare the reports in terms of the public relations material and 'spin' which they put on the results. Can the reports be ranked on a scale indicating the extent of 'spin'? Do some reports contain little or nothing more than the minimum required? Why do some companies provide a lot more information, comment and explanation than is strictly required?

2 Try to find a company whose accounting practices have been criticized. (Look for critical comments in the *Financial Times, Accountancy*, or *Accountancy Age* after the company has published its annual report and accounts.) Obtain a copy of the annual report and accounts (telephone the company if it is not one supplied by the *Financial Times* Annual Reports service on 020 8391 6000. http//ft.ar.wilink.com). Do you think that the company has been unduly 'creative'?

3 A company has a duty to maximize reported profits. If it uses creative accounting techniques to do so, it does not matter, as long as those profits have credibility. Discuss.

4 Examine a number of company accounts in detail. Express the taxation charge as a percentage of the profit before taxation, and compare the companies. Examine the cash flow statements of the companies. Do these comparisons reveal anything that causes you to question reported profit figures?

5 Produce a list of recent accounting standards, and select a few for detailed examination. Read the stated objectives in the standards, and try also to read between the lines. Can you suggest what 'creative accounting' techniques (if any) they are designed to address?

6 Should the rules for profit measurement be laid down by governments?

Financial Accounting in context

Discuss and comment on the following item taken from the press:
Fees 'pose risk to governance' by Jon Ashworth and Abigail Rayner
The Times, 8 September 2003

Britain's biggest companies are paying their auditors twice as much in non-audit fees than in audit fees, despite concerns about auditor independence in the wake of US accounting scandals.

Financial Accounting in context (continued)

FTSE 100 companies paid auditors £467 million in non-audit fees last year, compared with £247 million in statutory audit fees. Although non-audit fees have declined since 2001, the figures demonstrate the strength of the links between leading UK companies and the Big Four accountancy firms.

PricewaterhouseCoopers (PwC) is auditor to 44 companies in the FTSE 100 index. Last year it charged £217 million in non-audit fees and £102 million in audit fees. Chris Quick, editor of *Accountancy* magazine, which compiled the statistics, said: 'Despite FTSE 100 companies tightening up corporate governance rules in the wake of Enron, they are still paying their audit firms twice as much for consultancy work as for their statutory audits. A potential risk to audit independence still exists.'

Mr Quick said that the Big Four were braced for a big fall in overall fees from their FTSE 100 clients as new policies on non-audit work began to take effect. He said: 'The interesting question is whether companies will simply award their consultancy work to another Big Four firm, look to smaller firms or even outside the accountancy sector altogether.'

Moves to head off potential conflicts of interest follow developments in America, where the Sarbanes–Oxley Act continues to attract controversy. Firms involved in auditing US companies must sign up with a Public Company Accounting Oversight Board.

William Donaldson, chairman of the US Securities and Exchange Commission, appears before the Senate Banking Committee tomorrow to discuss the securities industry. He has described Sarbanes–Oxley as the most crucial securities legislation since the 1930s. Companies have complained about extra costs from the Act, which has also increased potential jail terms.

References and Further Reading

Accounting Standards Board (1999) *Statement of Principles.*

Dearing Committee (1988) *The Making of Accounting Standards,* ICAEW.

Griffiths, I. (1986) *Creative Accounting: How to Make Your Profits What You Want Them to Be,* Sidgwick and Jackson.

Griffiths, I. (1995) *New Creative Accounting,* Macmillan.

Jameson, M. (1998) *A Practical Guide to Creative Accounting,* Kogan Page.

Lyall, D. and R. Perks (1976) Create a State Auditing Board?, *Accountancy,* June.

McBarnet, D. and C. Whelan (1999) *Creative Accounting and the Cross Eyed Javelin Thrower,* Wiley.

Pijper, T. (1993) *Creative Accounting: The Effectiveness of Financial Reporting in the UK,* Macmillan.

Smith, T. and R. Hannah (1991) *Accounting for Growth,* UBS Phillips and Drew.

9

Advanced Interpretation of Financial Statements

Learning objectives

After studying this chapter you should be able to:

- Identify key information in published financial statements required to assess companies' solvency

- Undertake detailed investigation of companies' financial statements to find indications of their solvency using the accruals concept

- Explain how financial accounting information can be used to predict financial distress and understand the main elements included in Z scores

- Analyse the performance of companies using most of the detailed information included in published financial statements

- Describe segmental reporting and make use of the information disclosed to assess the performance of different segments

- Analyse the performance of investments made by companies

- Make use of financial information disclosed by companies in addition to that included in balance sheets, profit and loss accounts, and cash flow statements

Introduction

Financial statements provide useful information which can help in assessing the solvency and the performance of companies. These ideas were introduced in Chapters 1 and 2, and further developed in Chapter 4. This chapter examines additional information that is available for these assessments. Investors are also interested in the performance of their company's shares on the stock market; this is examined in Chapter 6.

9.1 Solvency: Predicting Financial Distress

The words 'financial distress' are widely used to cover a variety of different situations in which a company may find itself when it is unable to meet its liabilities as they fall due. Liquidations, receivership, bankruptcy and voluntary or compulsory winding up are all variations on a theme. Companies can negotiate arrangements with their bankers and other creditors. Recently Marconi plc arranged to give their creditors almost all of the company's share capital in exchange for the debts it owed them. The result was that previous shareholders were left with only a tiny proportion of the company: almost all of their investment had disappeared. In other situations a company may be the unwilling victim of a takeover bid; an agreed bid or merger may be sought; or parts of the business may be sold off to a variety of different companies, venture capitalists, and other investors and institutions. A management buy out (where managers buy a controlling interest in all or part of the company) is also a possibility.

If debt is excessive, the result is usually that the creditors' interest in the company is as well protected as circumstances allow; but some sort of capital reorganization and restructuring results in the ordinary shareholders, the owners of the business, losing out. If the shareholders have financed the bulk of the business, and creditors have financed only a small proportion, then the creditors are relatively well protected: the greater the shareholders' equity in relation to debt, the greater is the financial security – at least for the creditors. We saw in Chapters 1 and 4 that this relationship between debt and equity is a key indicator in assessing a company's financial strength and solvency.

In the end, a company gets into financial difficulties for one reason only: they are unable to pay their debts. All sorts of factors can lead to this situation: bad management, poor products, a weak economy, problems with exchange rates, government policies, poor industrial relations, changes in demand for products and services. There is usually no shortage of explanations for poor performance, and it can be difficult to identify these various factors – until it is too late. But it is not difficult to identify if the company is getting into too much debt. It is difficult to make a judgement about exactly how much debt is too much, and what is acceptable does vary from business to business – and from time to time. But it is not difficult to observe a trend of increasing debt. It is worth examining the figures over a period of 5 years or more.

When introducing the idea of assessing the solvency of a company it is convenient to separate short-term liabilities from long-term liabilities: that is the way in which a balance sheet is presented. But it is the overall level of debt that matters. It is not difficult for companies to reduce their short-term liabilities by long-term borrowing if their current ratio is starting to look too low. Similarly, it is not difficult to replace some long-term debt with current liabilities if the amount of gearing is looking too high. It makes more sense to look at the overall level of debt.

A straightforward calculation of capital gearing can be supplemented by a variety of calculations relating *all* liabilities to the amount of equity or shareholders' funds. There are different ways of doing this. For example, there might be some debate about whether or not some provisions such as deferred taxation should be included with liabilities. The important thing is to be consistent from year to year and from company to company in making comparisons. If the amount of liabilities as a percentage of equity is steadily increasing over a number of years, it is a cause for concern, and other information should be examined, as indicated below.

A high level of debt is not necessarily a cause for concern, especially if the company is well placed to meet all interest payments as they fall due. The repayment of the loan itself (the principal), is usually done by borrowing more money; it is worth keeping an eye on the creditworthiness of the company generally to see if this is likely to be problematic. Credit ratings are published for most major companies. If a company's rating weakens it usually means that they will have to pay higher interest rates.

Interest is payable on borrowings (but not on all liabilities). The total amount of interest payable by a company is shown on their profit and loss account, but it does not distinguish between interest on short-term borrowing and interest on long-term borrowing. It is worth calculating the average amount of borrowings a company has during the year; this can be estimated by taking the figure at the beginning of the year, adding it to the figure at the end of the year, and dividing by two. The total amount of interest paid during the year can then be expressed as a percentage of the average amount of borrowings. The rate can then be compared with interest rates payable in the market generally. If the company seems to be paying an interest rate that it too high, it may be that they are suffering from a poor credit rating; or it may mean that their actual level of borrowings during the year was higher than the balance sheets suggest. Such 'window dressing' at the year end is not unusual.

Profits

If the company has very healthy profits there should be no problem in paying interest, and avoiding financial difficulties. Earnings before interest and taxation for the year can be divided by the amount of interest payable; this gives the number of times interest is covered by earnings available to pay that interest. A company with an interest cover of 10 or more is obviously much safer in this respect than one where the cover is only 2 or 3 times.

It is worth trying to assess how 'healthy' the profits are by looking at the type of industry the company is in, and their record over a number of years. If they are in a cyclical industry which seems to have very good years followed by very bad years, or in a declining industry, a cover of 3 or 4 times may be a serious sign of weakness. If they are in an industry with very stable earnings (such as a property company, or a utility company), interest cover of 3 times may be quite satisfactory.

Assets

Solvency is often assessed by relating the amount of liabilities to the amount of equity or shareholders' funds. The amount of equity is determined by the amount of net assets owned by the company. It is worth looking at the kind of assets that a company owns, and how they have been valued. If a company's borrowings are starting to look high in relation to equity, they may be able to revalue some assets; an increase in assets will increase the amount of equity; as a result the relationship between liabilities and equity immediately looks healthier.

Some assets represent very good security for creditors. Cash is obviously most readily available to pay them, and there are often other investments which are easily turned into cash, and the balance sheet should show their current value. Debtors should become cash within a matter of months. Stocks are less liquid, but in most businesses they should be sold, and producing cash within a year. Fixed assets provide varying degrees of security to creditors. Freehold property is usually the asset which creditors prefer, and loans are often secured on such property. Properties held on short leases are more of a mixed bag: some may be very valuable; some may be very hard to dispose of (such as an unprofitable shop in a declining area): the company might be committed to continuing to pay rentals on properties which only produce losses. Plant and machinery and other tangible fixed assets offer reasonable security where there is a ready market for them.

Traditionally all assets should be prudently valued, but users of accounts may need to make their own estimates of how prudent the values are.

Goodwill is an asset that might be very difficult to dispose of; it is not really a 'separable' asset – it can be sold only as part of the business as a going concern. If the amount shown for goodwill is overstated, then the amount shown for equity is overstated, and the relationship between liabilities and equity may be misleading. Goodwill may be properly shown in accordance with all accounting standards and rules, but that does not mean that it has any value to creditors if the company gets into financial difficulties. It is not unusual for a company's main asset to be goodwill. In many companies, if goodwill were excluded from assets, there would be a negative net asset value; this would mean negative equity, and that assets provide little or no security for creditors.

The 20 June 2003 edition of the *Investors Chronicle* showed the following about a number of listed companies:

Wincanton (logistics)	Share price 199p	Net asset value 15p	Including intangibles 21p per share
Babcock International (defence contractors and support services)	Share price 109p	Net asset value 59p	Including intangibles 53p per share
Express Dairies (Milk processor)	Share price 35p	Net asset value 15p	Including intangibles 19p per share
Oasis Healthcare (Dentists)	Share price 22p	Net asset value 19p	Including intangibles 55p per share
Scipher (Electonic products developer)	Share price 10p	Net asset value 9p	Including intangibles 8p per share

In many cases the profits and cash flows offer greater security, and the market value of the company is very much in excess of the balance sheet value.

Cash Flows

Sometimes companies are successful in generating profits, but they never seem to show up as cash; the company continues to expand and pour money into additional assets. This may look good, but it does not pay the creditors. There are also sometimes suspicions about creative accounting: the company appears to be making profits, but somehow these are not backed up by cash being generated.

Lenders are interested in a company's business plans, particularly their cash budgets and how soon a company is likely to be able to repay their debts.

Published financial statements often include comments about this aspect of a company's financial situation, but cash budgets are not usually published.

Differences between cash flow and profit are explored in Chapter 7, and the use of published cash flow statements in explaining the differences between a company's cash flow and their profit is explained.

Z Scores

It is possible to find out which factors have been most closely associated with companies finding themselves in a situation of financial distress. A list of companies which have 'failed' in one way or another is compiled. The financial data for those companies is compiled for a number of years, including amounts of profit, equity, working capital, cash flows and so on. The data is then manipulated until a way of selecting it and arranging it is found which best predicts impending failure.

Altman (1983) found that the key data were:

◆ working capital

◆ total gross assets

◆ retained profits

◆ earnings before interest and tax

◆ market value of equity

◆ book value of debt

◆ sales.

By arranging these as five ratios, and giving a weighting to each, he calculated a Z score, which gave the best prediction of corporate failure.

Ratio	Weighting
1. Working capital ÷ Total gross assets	×0.012
2. Retained profits ÷ Total gross assets	×0.014
3. Earnings before interest and tax ÷ Total gross assets	×0.033
4. Market value of equity ÷ Book value of debt	×0.006
5. Sales ÷ Total gross assets	×0.010

Altman did not claim to be stating the causes of failure; it was a statistical calculation which, in his sample, gave the best results. Companies with a Z score of more than 2.99, using the above calculation, did not fail; companies with a Z score of less than 1.81 did fail. The outcome of companies with a score of between 1.81 and 2.99 was less predictable, but overall the prediction was accurate in 96 per cent of cases.

Their model suggests that the following are important in predicting failure:

1 The amount of working capital (in relation to total assets)

2 The amount of retained profits (in relation to total assets)

3 Some measure of return on capital employed

4 Some measure of gearing

5 Some measure of utilization of assets (or turnover of assets).

Their sample was based on manufacturing companies in the USA more than 40 years ago. But similar work has been done by Taffler (1983) and by Taffler and Tisshaw (1977) more recently in the UK. Taffler found that the key ratios included:

	Weighting
1. Profit before taxation ÷ Current liabilities	53%
2. Current assets ÷ Total liabilities	13%
3. Current liabilities ÷ Total assets	18%
4. (Immediate assets – Current liabilities) ÷ Operating costs excluding depreciation	16%

Taffler did not publish full details on the calculations but it is clear that the key information, manipulated in different ways, could give very good indications of corporate failure in a very different environment.

The message is clear: published financial statements, if interpreted with skill and care, can give very good indications of a company's solvency, or how safe it is from financial collapse.

9.2 **Performance**

At an introductory level, most interpretation of accounts concentrates on the performance of a company as a whole. Profitability is measured using return on capital employed, and this is analysed into its various components showing (a) costs and profits in relation to turnover; and (b) utilization of assets, relating sales or cost of sales to different categories of assets in varying degrees of detail. Cash flows are also analysed for the company as a whole.

There are good reasons for wanting to analyse the performance of different parts of the business.

If investors and analysts are interested in forecasting the future sales, profits and cash flows of a company, they are likely to assume different growth rates, different rates of profitability, and varying amounts of risk for different types of business – even if they are unable to do it correctly. At the end of the twentieth century it was assumed that there were great growth prospects in areas like telecommunications, pharmaceuticals and leisure. Many companies disappointed the investors, but investors do expect to know which sectors a company is involved in.

Investors are also concerned with assessing the competence of management. Many companies are becoming increasingly diversified, making money in one area where they have expertise and success, then investing it in other areas that need careful monitoring.

In many cases diversification is very successful. GUS made money in retailing, and now has a very successful credit rating business in Experian. As one area declined (home shopping), so another expanded, and it is an area which has very modest levels of capital employed. UK water companies operate in a tightly regulated market, and have diversified with varying degrees of success into other areas where they are freer to make more profits. The American GEC has expanded successfully from being an electrical manufacturer, into almost any kind of business that makes money, from vehicle hire to life assurance and perhaps even financing the underwear you are wearing at the moment.[1] Meanwhile the British GEC, which had been cautiously, carefully and very successfully built up by Arnold Weinstock over many years to make just about everything electrical – and a huge pile of cash – divested and diversified disastrously, and was destroyed almost as fast as an airline(r) can crash. They sold off boring electrical manufacturing too cheaply, and borrowed excessively, in order to buy more exciting, overpriced telecommunications manufacturers just as the market was collapsing. Their share price fell from over £12 to less than £0.02!

Unfortunately there are many other examples of unsuccessful diversification. Marks and Spencer expanded abroad, but when their results suffered, they changed their minds and began selling off their overseas operations. Abbey National was a very successful retail bank, and had all the expertise necessary; they then diversified into wholesale banking, where their expertise was limited, and ended up having to write off many hundreds of millions of pounds. United Utilities has done well as a water company, and has diversified successfully into electricity supply; but they have lost, and written off, tens of millions of pounds on their venture into telecommunications. Boots are a very successful pharmacy and retailer of a limited range of products; but their venture into Halfords was not successful, and their diversification into the Opticians business and other related health businesses have yet to succeed.

Many successes and failures of diversification are made public. We do not know how many attempts at diversification have failed and been

---

1   GE Finance provides credit cards for the Burton group, including Top Shop.

quietly brushed under the carpet. Fortunately there are official disclosure requirements that enable us to find out about different *segments* of a business, about *continuing and discontinued* operations, and about the results of investments in *associates* and *joint ventures*.

Reporting Financial Performance

The idea that the financial performance of a company can be distilled into a single figure is appealing, and the *earnings per share* (EPS) figure is the most suitable for this purpose. If earnings per share increases each year, that must be a good thing. If it falls, that must be a bad thing.

But a single measure of performance is likely to cover a multitude of sins. Investors who are trying to forecast future EPS figures need to consider whether or not this year's EPS figure has taken into account the following:

1 the results of parts of the business that have since been discontinued

2 the results of new acquisitions that have yet to come fully on stream

3 any exceptional items such as large, one-off profits on the sale of fixed assets or investments

4 exceptional write offs of goodwill or other assets

5 exceptional provisions for future reorganizations and redundancies

6 amortization of goodwill

7 depreciation

8 interest

9 unrealized profits on revaluation of assets

10 exchange rate gains or losses on translating the financial statements of overseas subsidiaries.

The requirements of IAS 33 and FRS 14 are clear on this: the EPS figure takes into account the first eight items, but not numbers 9 and 10. Items such as 9 and 10 have the effect of changing the total amount of equity shown on the balance sheet, but they are not reported in the income statement. They are separately disclosed, for example on a statement of total recognized gains and losses for the year.

Companies and investors may be unhappy about including all of items 1–8 in the EPS figure. What is the use of a EPS figure that includes all sorts of odd items that are unlikely to occur again?

One solution adopted by many companies is to produce two EPS figures: one fully in accordance with accounting standards, which takes into account items 1–8 above. They also produce a second EPS figure, which excludes some of these items. This may be done to give what they consider to be a true and fair view, or to provide a better basis for predicting future earnings. Sometimes it looks as though they try to exclude anything that would show lower earnings figures.

The solution adopted by the accounting standard setters is to require a lot of information to be disclosed so that users of accounts can produce their own earnings figure which meets their particular needs. All of the items listed above in 1–8 have to be disclosed separately unless they are too small to be of any significance.

Companies are required to disclose both turnover, and operating profit separately for:

(a) continuing operations;

(b) acquisitions; and

(c) discontinued operations.

Segments

A careful examination of the annual report and accounts of most large companies reveals information about the different segments of the business that enables us to assess the performance of the different parts.

For example, GUS plc show a breakdown of their turnover for 2002 including[2] the following:

	£million
Experian	1,092
Argos retail group	4,629
Reality	471
Burberry	499
South African retailing	123
Finance division	30

They also give a geographical analysis of their turnover, as follows:

UK and Ireland	4,783
Continental Europe	635
North America	800
Rest of World	238

These figures give an idea of the size and importance of the different parts of the business. More information is published that enables us to monitor

2   More detail is given in the GUS Annual Report and Accounts, and the published total of turnover by division is, of course, equal to the total of turnover analysed geographically.

the profitability and progress of the different segments of the business. For each segment we are also given the previous year's figure for turnover, and equivalent figures for profit before taxation, and for net assets.

There is sufficient information to undertake basic ratio analysis for each segment for each year, as follows:

1 Return on capital employed, measured as $\dfrac{\text{Profit before taxation}}{\text{Net assets}} \times \dfrac{100}{1}$

2 Profit/sales ratio, measured as $\dfrac{\text{Profit before taxation}}{\text{Turnover}} \times \dfrac{100}{1}$

3 Utilization of assets, measured as $\dfrac{\text{Turnover}}{\text{Net assets}}$

Official Requirements

Segmental Reporting

Companies are required to publish financial details of the various segments of their business both by IAS 14 *Segment Reporting* and by the UK SSAP 25 *Segmental Reporting*. The International Standard has more detailed requirements, but the two sets of requirements are broadly similar. Both require disclosures both for

(a) business segments which may be based on the nature of the product or service, the type of production, or the type of customer, distribution method, or regulatory environment; and for

(b) geographical segments.

The way in which segments are identified for external reporting purposes should be based on the way in which it is done for internal reporting and management. Any segment which accounts for more than 10 per cent of sales, profits or assets should be reported separately. Although management has considerable discretion in determining what is a segment, it would not be good enough to identify segments as follows:

UK and Europe	£100 million
Rest of the world	£200 million

It would be necessary to break this down separately for, say, UK, Germany, America, Asia and so on, so that any geographical segment accounting for more than 10 per cent of the total is separately identified. The following (if true!) would be acceptable:

UK	£500 million
Rest of the world	£40 million

In simple terms companies are required to disclose, for each segment:

(i)   the profit or loss (the segment 'result');

(ii)   the sales revenue; and

(iii)   the net assets.

IAS 14 has more detailed disclosure requirements. For their 'primary' category of segment (i.e. business segment or geographical segment) they are required to disclose both the assets and the liabilities rather than just net assets; they are also required to disclose the following separately for each segment: fixed assets, depreciation and amortization; and other provisions and amounts written off that are not cash expenses. For their 'secondary' category of segment (e.g. geographical) they are required to disclose total costs rather than operating profit; but costs can easily be deducted from sales to arrive at a profit figure. IAS 14 also encourages disclosure of exceptional items, and of cash flows for the various segments that have been identified.

Investments

It is possible to assess how successful management has been in making investments in other companies and other securities by comparing the dividends and interest receivable from those securities with the amount of shareholders' funds tied up in them. Investments are usually shown on balance sheets at cost, but some indication of current value should also be given. The income statements show dividends and interest receivable.

In most cases such 'normal' investments are relatively small. Companies are likely to make major investments either:

(a)   by taking a controlling interest in another company, which then becomes a subsidiary; its results are then 'consolidated' with those of the company which makes the investment and included in group accounts; or

(b)   by taking a significant shareholding in other companies, which then become joint ventures or associates.

With these major investments what matters is the profits or losses made by the company in which the investment has been made; dividends receivable are of much less significance. This is because profits are an indication of performance; dividends are a matter of choice, and increasing dividends are sometimes paid when performance is deteriorating.

Subsidiary Companies

Most large listed companies are in fact groups of companies: a listed company typically holds 50–100 per cent of a number of subsidiary[3] companies. It is possible to get separate information about each of the separate companies in the group but for most purposes this is not really necessary. They produce 'group accounts' which include figures for all of the subsidiary companies. These figures are included in the holding company's figures: separate figures for each subsidiary are not provided in group accounts.

Group balance sheets include all of the assets and liabilities controlled by the group, even where the holding company owns only, say, 75 per cent of the subsidiary; the net assets of the subsidiary which are owned by the 25 per cent of the shareholders outside the group are shown, next to shareholders' funds, as 'minority interest'.

The first parts of a group income statement, or profit and loss account, includes 100 per cent of the results of all subsidiary companies. Each item from turnover down to profit after taxation includes the figures for the subsidiary companies. But then it is recognized that part of the profit after taxation belongs to subsidiary company shareholders who are outside the group. Their 'minority interest' in the profits is then deducted to arrive at the profit attributable to group shareholders; dividends are deducted from this figure to arrive at the profits for the year that are retained in the group.

Joint Ventures and Associate Companies

Joint ventures and associates are special categories of investments in other companies where we are less concerned about any dividends receivable than we are about the profits and losses earned by those companies with which there is a special relationship that is defined as a joint venture or associate.

IAS 31 defines a joint venture as a contractual arrangement whereby two or more parties undertake an economic activity which is subject to joint control. The FRS 9 definition of a joint venture is very similar. Two or more companies might decide to set up a new operation jointly to share the expenses and benefits.

IAS 28 defines an associate as being an enterprise in which the investor has significant influence but which is neither a subsidiary nor a joint venture. If the investor has 20 per cent or more of the voting power, then 'significant influence' is assumed.[4] The FRS 9 definition of an associate is very similar.

---

3 There are other ways of controlling a subsidiary, even if over 50 per cent of the shares is not owned.

4 Unless it can be proved otherwise, for example if another investor has more than 50 per cent of the voting power, and there is no evidence of significant influence being exercised by the 20 per cent investor.

One company may buy a substantial shareholding in another company; that company remains separate and independent from the investing company, but the investing company exercises significant influence over it.

There are technical differences between the way accounting is done for joint ventures, and the way it is done for associates, and between UK requirements and International requirements. Rather more information may be disclosed for joint ventures than for associates. With joint ventures the amount of assets and liabilities is shown separately; with associates they are combined. With joint ventures the amount of turnover is disclosed; with associates this is not required.

The investing company's share of the profit or loss of joint ventures and associates is clearly disclosed. The amount of the investing company's share of the net assets of the associates and joint ventures is also easily identified. This includes any amounts paid for goodwill.[5] It is based on the original cost of the investment, including any amounts paid for goodwill; each year the amount will be reduced to reflect amortization of goodwill, and increased to bring into account retained profits for the year (or reduced by any losses).

The fact that there is a figure for capital employed, and a figure for profit, means that it is possible to compare the return on capital employed in associates and joint ventures with the return on capital employed for the company as a whole.

The information[6] to assess the success of joint ventures and associates is found in the group (or 'consolidated') financial statements. Different companies present the information in different ways, and there is some variation in the amount of detail disclosed. It is usually the operating profit figure which is shown for joint ventures and associates, which is calculated after depreciation charges and amortization of goodwill (which may not be separately identified), but before deducting interest, any exceptional items, and taxation (which are usually separately identified). Care must be taken to ensure that calculations of return on capital employed are made on as comparable basis as is possible, given limited information.

It is possible to calculate return on capital employed using the operating profit figure (comparable with EBIT), which is taken before deducting interest. Normally this would be expressed as a percentage of total long-term capital employed, which includes borrowings. But as the borrowings of joint ventures and associates is not usually separately shown, the figure for capital employed would include only shareholders' funds. In calculating return on capital employed it is therefore preferable to take the results of

---

5 Which is usually reduced by amortization over a number of years.

6 In each case it is the investing company's proportion of these figures (e.g. 25 per cent) which is shown, not the total figures for the joint venture or associate company as a whole.

joint venture's associate company, and then deduct interest and taxation (if this information is available) after interest and taxation and express them as a percentage of the shareholders' funds invested in that associate.

There is no requirement to disclose the sales revenue of associated companies, although some companies with investments in associates do so. Companies are expected to publish the names of significant associates, and the proportion that they own; by obtaining the financial statements of the associate company separately it is possible to obtain the sales figure and further additional information.

Where the sales figure is available, the performance of associates can be measured using the same three ratios used in assessing segmental performance.

An Example of More Detailed Analysis: Bristol Water

It is useful to assess the profitability of different parts of a business by calculating the return on capital employed for each. Bristol Water discloses two segments: (1) water supply and related activities; and (2) contracting. Comparing 2002 results with 2001 results, the company showed little progress with water supply and related activities. The increase in turnover was only 4.8 per cent; the increase in operating profit was a meagre 0.6 per cent.[7] Return on capital employed fell from 25 per cent to 24 per cent.

Bristol Water has moved rapidly to diversify into contracting. The turnover of contracting has expanded rapidly (by 57.8 per cent) so that it is now greater than that for water supply activities. But the profits from contracting are, so far, meagre. Contracting has a lower return on capital employed, and a lower profit/sales ratio than water supply. But the capital employed for contracting is much lower than what is required for water supply, and it may have good prospects to increase the profitability of the group. In 2001 contracting produced a loss of £3.5 million; in 2002 this was converted to a profit of £1.25 million. Further progress in this direction would improve the profitability of the group, but there is a long way to go: even if the capital employed in contracting can be maintained at its present level, operating profit would have to more than double before it achieved the same return on capital employed as water supply activities.[8] This may well be achievable, but even at this level profits from contracting would still be only 13 per cent of total profits.[9]

---

7   2001's results were flattered by a £600,000 exceptional item; if this is excluded, operating profits increased by 4.2 per cent.

8   $24\% \times 11,117 = £2,680,000$.

9   $£2,680,000 \div (2,680,000 + 17,741,000) = 13\%$.

The return on contracting is still meagre. A profit/sales ratio of only 1.8 per cent is very low. Contracting now accounts for the majority of turnover but the amount of profit it contributes is less than 7 per cent of total profits. In the short term the company appears to be seeking additional work which produces very little profit. But, if there is as much improvement in future years as there was in 2002, it could be very successful. It is worth monitoring the group's success with contracting.

The story with joint ventures is similar: very high sales; low profits in relation to sales; a very small contribution to the profits of the group as a whole; but a very high return on capital employed.

A suspicious accountant might wonder why profits in joint ventures are so high in relation to the net assets involved. It is always worth checking if there have previously been any significant amounts written off from joint ventures. If a company can reduce the capital employed, by significant write downs, then it should not be surprising that operating profits look good in relation to the written down figure. In 2001 Bristol Water wrote off a significant amount in relation to a wholly owned subsidiary, but there is no evidence of such write offs in relation to joint ventures.

Bristol Water is doing well in investing in diversified activities that produce substantial profits in relation to the amounts invested. But they are still a very small proportion of total profits, and the substantial sales revenue produces little profit.

	2002	2001
Operating profit/Net assets		
Water supply	$\dfrac{17{,}741}{73{,}946}$	$\dfrac{17{,}629}{70{,}272}$
	24%	25%
Contracting	$\dfrac{1{,}282}{11{,}117}$	$\dfrac{(3{,}534)}{8{,}455}$
	11%	(42%)
Operating profit/Turnover		
Water supply	$\dfrac{17{,}741}{68{,}013}$	$\dfrac{17{,}629}{64{,}887}$
	26%	27%
Contracting	$\dfrac{1{,}282}{70{,}005}$	$\dfrac{(3{,}534)}{44{,}345}$
	1.8%	(8%)
Turnover/Net assets		
Water supply	$\dfrac{68{,}013}{73{,}946}$	$\dfrac{64{,}887}{70{,}272}$
	0.920	0.923
Contracting	$\dfrac{70{,}005}{11{,}117}$	$\dfrac{44{,}345}{8{,}455}$
	6.30	5.24

Joint ventures		
Sales	6,897	4,572
Operating profit	157	200
Net assets	332	205

The analysis provided of Bristol Water indicates how published information can be used to assess the performance of different parts of a business.

9.3 Other Information from Annual Reports

Users of financial statements may be concerned with more than solvency and profitability. They may be concerned with other aspects of a company's activities and performance. They may be seeking more detailed explanation of what is revealed by the balance sheet, the profit and loss account and the cash flow statement, and they may be looking for information about future performance. Companies may choose to disclose all sorts of things in their annual reports and there is often a Chairman's Statement full of fine sounding information in the style of advertising and public relations. But there is also quite a lot of useful additional information that is required by law, and which is presented by companies in a fairly standard way.

Directors' Report

Companies are also required to produce a Directors' Report which contains a great deal of fairly standardized formal information, including the following:

♦ *Principal Activities* of the company, and any changes

♦ *Business Review* of the activities during the year and of the position at the year end

♦ *Future Developments*

♦ *Research and Development* activities

♦ *Post Balance Sheet Events*: any important changes since the balance sheet date

♦ *Value of Land and Buildings*: significant differences between balance sheet values and market value of land and buildings

♦ *Statement about employee involvement*: policies on providing information to employees, consulting them, any schemes for employees' shares, and increasing understanding of shared ideas about factors affecting the company's success (in companies with over 250 employees)

- *Number of disabled employees* and employment policies regarding disabled employees (in companies with over 250 employees)

- *Donations* to charities and to political parties are each disclosed separately

- *Purchase of own shares*: number of shares purchased, amount paid, and reasons for doing it

- *Information about Directors:* their names and the number of shares held by each at the beginning and end of the year

- *Creditor payment:* the company's policy should be disclosed and a calculation of the average number of days taken to pay creditors.

Operating and Financial Review

The ASB has, since 1993, recommended that an *Operating and Financial Review* should be published by companies. It is only a recommendation, and it is rather less specific than a Directors' Report. The ASB (unsurprisingly) recommend that it should be fair (balanced and objective), showing both favourable and unfavourable aspects; focused on significant items; and be designed to be helpful to users who want to understand the financial circumstances of the business.

The operating section of the Review should discuss the results for the year, indicating what factors are likely to be most influential in the future, and how the business is investing to meet future needs.

The financial review should deal with financing, borrowing and gearing; cash flow and current liquidity; and any restrictions on transferring funds from overseas.

The information specified for the Directors' Report is all required by law and is fairly specific. The Operating Review is only a recommendation, and is set out in general terms only, leaving it to directors to decide exactly what should be shown and how.

Smaller Companies

Disclosure requirements are significantly reduced for small and medium-sized companies. It is not difficult to get the annual report and accounts for any company (if necessary via Companies House); but the amount of information disclosed for smaller companies is very disappointing compared with that for a public company that is listed on the Stock Exchange.

Social and Environmental Reporting

Most financial accounting requirements are based on providing information for actual and potential shareholders and creditors. It is sometimes argued that companies have much wider responsibilities and should be accountable to many other groups in society, and to society as a whole. This book is intended to help readers to understand financial accounting as it is, not to argue a political case for or against particular disclosures to various groups in society.

The ASB's *Statement of Principles* considers a number of different users of accounts: investors, lenders, suppliers and trade creditors, employees, customers, governments and their agencies, and the public. But they come to the conclusion[10] 'that financial statements that focus on the interest that investors have in the reporting entity's financial performance and financial position will, in effect, also be focusing on the common interest that all users have in the entity's financial performance and financial position'. This comes close to saying that all users are interested in balance sheets and profit and loss accounts, and so the production of these statements will meet the common interest of all users of accounts. The possibility that other users of accounts might want different information is brushed aside.

But from the information required in Directors' Reports we can see that there are concerns to make companies accountable more widely in some senses. There are concerns about employees: their numbers, their remuneration and policies for consultation and involvement. There are similar concerns about disabled employees. Although the overwhelming concern is with investors, there are also concerns about trade creditors, and whether or not companies are taking too long to pay them. The requirement to disclose political and charitable donations may be seen as a concern with companies' social involvement more generally. But the amount of disclosures intended primarily for employees, customers, environmentalists, idealists and so on is very small indeed.

There is an argument that a requirement to disclose information can change the ways in which companies behave. Much of the case for corporate social reporting rests on this idea. It does appear that the requirement to disclose how long companies take to pay their creditors is associated with improvements in this aspect of companies' behaviour. Even the requirement to disclose fees to auditors for non-audit work is at last having some effect; but large companies still typically pay consultancy fees to their auditors in excess of the amount of the audit fee, apparently compromising their independence.

Many companies voluntarily provide substantial additional information on various aspects of their performance including their practices regarding social and environmental issues.

---

10   Or, in their words, the 'rebuttable assumption'.

Summary

It is not very difficult to learn to calculate a dozen or so standard accounting ratios based on the simplified versions of company accounts that are usually presented in textbooks – and examinations. But when examining the complexities of real companies' financial statements it is easy to be overwhelmed. Relatively straightforward real company financial statements were introduced early in the book. More complicated financial statements should be seen as a challenge and as an opportunity: a challenge to answer the same basic questions about solvency and profitability that have already been introduced; and an opportunity to make use of more detailed information that is available to produce a fuller analysis.

Review of Key Points

◆ More sophisticated assessments can be made of a company's solvency than the main ratios shown in Chapters 1 and 4

◆ Companies disclose key information that enables us to analyse the performance of the different business and geographical segments in which the business operates

◆ Companies also disclose important information that enables us to assess the performance of investments that they have made in different other companies

◆ The Directors' Report and Operating and Financial Review provide additional information that can help us to assess companies' performance

◆ Most information that is disclosed is in relation to companies' financial performance, financial position, and cash flows; some information is provided on other aspects of companies' activities

Self-testing Questions

1 What information is most useful in assessing a company's solvency?

2 What key information is disclosed to assess the profitability of the various segments of a company?

3 You are given the following information about the Goodwynne Company:

	Year 2	Year 3
	£000	£000
Sales	1,000	1,100
Operating profit	100	115
Operating assets[11]	700	800

Making use of appropriate ratios, assess the view that the company should concentrate on reducing its operating assets.

11 Fixed assets plus current assets, minus current liabilities. This should be equal to shareholders' funds plus long-term liabilities.

Self-testing Questions (continued)

4 You are given the following information about Gobbiediggan International plc.

Segment	UK		Africa		South America	
	Year 1	Year 2	Year 1	Year 2	Year 1	Year 2
	£000	£000	£000	£000	£000	£000
Sales	800	860	300	270	100	180
Operating profit	80	78	40	44	20	21
Operating assets	900	760	200	175	40	60

Making use of appropriate ratios, comment on the performance of each of the geographic segments.

One of the directors of the company considers that the UK market should be abandoned because profits are declining. A second director considers that the Africa market should be abandoned because sales are declining. A third director considers that the South America market should be abandoned because it keeps needing additional investment. Critically assess each of these views.

Assessment Questions

1 Select one or two companies' annual report and accounts and assess the financial position and performance of its various segments and investments in as much detail as the information permits.

2 If a company analyses the return on capital employed (ROCE) of every division, branch, investment or segment that it operates, and closes down all of those with a below average ROCE, then the average ROCE for the company as a whole is bound to increase. Assess this approach to managing a large business.

3 You are given the following segmental information about the Willaston Company:

Segment	Men's things		Women's things		Children's things	
	Year 1	Year 2	Year 1	Year 2	Year 1	Year 2
	£000	£000	£000	£000	£000	£000
Sales	400	405	800	820	60	130
Operating profit	80	95	90	92	(20)	(4)
Operating assets	200	180	250	260	10	11

Making use of appropriate ratios, comment on the performance of each of the segments.

Group Activities and Discussion Questions

1 What information would you like to see disclosed in company annual reports and accounts in addition to that which is at present required? Examine the annual report of a few companies that provide a lot more information than the minimum required. To what extent does that information provide you with what you want?

2 Think of a number of companies, or types of company, that have gone bankrupt or have found themselves in serious financial difficulties recently (perhaps airlines, telecommunications companies, Polaroid). What do you think led to their financial difficulties? Try to identify some comparable companies, and examine their annual report and accounts. Is there evidence of impending financial difficulties?

3 To what extent do you consider that financial reporting is, or should be, involved in reporting on the social and environmental performance of companies.

4 It is unrealistic to assess the performance of a company on the basis of one figure, such as earnings per share. But, following FRS 3, profit and loss accounts are now so complicated that it is difficult to know what figures to use. Discuss these statements.

5 Companies that generate cash surpluses can afford to diversify, but they should return the money to the shareholders, and it is for shareholders to decide the extent to which they wish to diversify their investments. Companies that cannot afford to diversify often borrow money that they cannot afford and make their shareholders' investments more risky; it is for shareholders to decide whether or not they want more risk. Critically assess these statements.

6 Try to find two very different annual reports: one which is full of additional information about the company, and one which discloses little or nothing more than the minimum required. How 'useful' is the additional information which the first company supplies?

7 Z scores are only the beginning. Sophisticated statistical models which produce accurate predictions of share prices are becoming available. Discuss the practicability, limitations and implications of these statements.

Financial Accounting in context

Discuss and comment on the following item taken from the press:
Bristol Water to pay £50m to shareholders by Andrew Taylor
Financial Times, 24 September 2003

Bristol Water, which supplies 1m customers in south-west England, plans to create a new holding company as part of financial restructuring that will return £50m to shareholders. The company said it would pay about £1.35 a share – totalling almost half the stock market value of the company – if the scheme is approved by the courts and shareholders. The shares closed up $9\frac{1}{2}$p to 288p.

Financial Accounting in context (continued)

The cash return, announced earlier this summer, followed pressure from Ecofin, a specialist investor in utilities, which bought a 24.5 per cent stake in Bristol last year from Vivendi.

Ecofin and Axa Investment Managers, which together own 38.9 per cent of the group, have said they will vote in favour of the creation of the new holding company, Bristol said. It said current trading remained in line with the board's expectations, although trading at Lawrence, the contracting division, was below expectations because of poor performance on two contracts.

It had 'received a number of preliminary offers for Lawrence' which the board was evaluating.

The restructuring would involve more debt, and Ofwat, the industry regulator, has indicated it will seek licence modifications.

Bristol said these were likely to be 'broadly similar to those agreed by other companies in the sector which have substantially increased their gearing'. The company said that the main changes were likely to involve 'a financial ring fencing' of its regulated water business.

References and Further Reading

Altman, E.I. (1983) *Corporate Financial Distress*, Wiley.

Gray, R., D. Owen and C. Adams (1996) *Accounting and Accountability*, Pearson Education.

Owen, D. (1992) *Green Reporting: Accountancy and the Challenge of the Nineties*, 1st edn, Thomson Learning

Pendlebury, M. and R. Groves (2003) *Company Accounts: Analysis, Interpretation and Understanding*, 6th edn, Thomson Learning.

Rees, B. (2005) *Financial Analysis*, 3rd edn, Pearson Education.

Reid, W. and D.R. Myddelton (2000) *The Meaning of Company Accounts*, 7th edn, Gower Publishing.

Taffler, R.J. (1983) The assessment of company solvency and performance using a statistical model – a comparative UK-based study, *Accounting and Business Research*, Autumn.

Taffler R.J. and H. Tisshaw (1977) Going, going, gone – four factors which predict, *Accountancy*, March.

Walton, P. (2000) *Financial Statement Analysis: An International Perspective*, 1st edn, Thomson Learning.

www.asb.org.uk

www.bristolwater.co.uk (pdf documents)

www.experian.com

www.gusplc.com (annual report)

www.investorschronicle.co.uk

10

Assets and Liabilities

Learning objectives

After studying this chapter you should be able to:

- Define assets and liabilities

- Explain a number of reasons for measuring and disclosing assets

- Outline the historical development of approaches to asset valuation

- Assess a number of different bases for asset valuation

- Describe and understand the main categories of assets and liabilities shown on balance sheets

- Discuss and analyse various types of provision

- Understand all of the main items shown on balance sheets

Introduction

Assets and liabilities were introduced in Chapter 1 (The Balance Sheet). Their importance in relation to profit measurement was explored in Chapter 5 where it was explained that profits can be measured either in relation to an increase in net assets, or as being the difference between revenues and expenses. It is important to understand what is included under each of these headings, and how it is measured, in order to understand and interpret financial statements, as seen in Chapters 4 and 9, and throughout financial accounting. This chapter provides further explanation of these two key elements of financial statements.

10.1 **Assets**

The first part of this section traces the development of the various functions of, and approaches to, asset valuation. The second part defines what is meant by the term 'asset' and explores what is and what is not included as an asset on the balance sheet.

The third part examines each category of asset in turn and explains how each is shown on a balance sheet.

The ASB's *Statement of Principles* defines assets as 'rights or other access to future economic benefits controlled by an entity as a result of past transactions or events'.

It is tempting to think of assets as being things that the company owns but it is now clear that control is the key, not ownership. If a company owns the lease on a building, it has always been shown as an asset, although the company does not own the building itself. If a company leases a vehicle or piece of equipment, under a finance lease, for perhaps 5 years, then the vehicle or equipment is shown on the balance sheet as an asset because the company controls it (under a finance lease). If Company H owns 60 per cent of the share capital of Company S, the consolidated balance sheet will show all of S's assets as group assets, even though they are only 60 per cent owned; the key is that 60 per cent ownership is 100 per cent control.

Developing Approaches to Asset Valuation

If there was one, simple, clear reason for wanting to know the amount that should be shown for assets on company balance sheets it might be easy to specify exactly what should be included, to define what we mean by an asset, and to decide the basis on which asset should be valued. But there are many different reasons for wanting to know the amount of assets, which, in turn, means that there are different ways of defining exactly what should be included as an asset, and ways of valuing or measuring assets.

Reasons for Showing Assets

When double entry bookkeeping first evolved the idea of listing assets and liabilities was of little importance. What mattered was to record transactions, and to know who owed what and to whom. The accuracy of the recording system was (and is still!) important, and producing a listing of debit and credit balances that had not been written off was a useful check in the double entry bookkeeping system. For many years no-one pretended that such listings of balances in the form of a balance sheet were of any particular use – unless such a listing was needed because the old ledger was full, and the balances needed to be transferred into a new ledger.

Major changes came with the development of companies in the middle of the nineteenth century. Industrialization led to many businesses needing much more machinery and other assets, which, in turn, meant that they needed more money to finance their activities. Potential investors were attracted to the idea of investing in companies where their liability for potential losses was limited to the amount of capital they had invested. A company would have many different shareholders who could not manage the investment themselves: they elected directors to look after it for them. The idea was (and should still be) that directors manage companies on behalf of the shareholders who own the company, and the directors are accountable to the shareholders. The origins of modern accountancy are in the requirement for companies to provide accounts of their activities to shareholders.

Today shareholders want steady growth in company profits, year after year, and to see this reflected in the value of their shares steadily increasing. In the nineteenth century they were more concerned to see that the directors had not run away with their money. A balance sheet shows how much money the shareholders have put into the business, and what has happened to that money: it should still be there either in the form of cash, or other assets such as buildings, machinery, stocks and debtors. If the company is successful, that equity interest should increase each year, unless the company opts to pay out all profits as dividends. The important thing was to maintain the amount of the original capital invested; any dividends must be paid out of profits, and there could be no profit unless the amount of capital originally invested had been maintained. As fixed assets became worn out and used up, so a depreciation charge had to be made, and there were no profits available to be paid out as dividends unless the capital (now invested in assets) had been maintained.

Although at first it might seem an obscure point, asset values are important in determining how much a company can pay out as dividends. Unless a company has maintained the value of its shareholders' funds (by ensuring that the amount of net assets in which they are invested is not less than the shareholders invested in the company), then it cannot pay dividends. Dividends must come out of profits that the company has earned, not out of the capital which the shareholders invested in the company.

Companies have access to more funds than those supplied by shareholders. On a short-term basis they can finance assets such as stocks through normal trade credit. Although shareholders' funds may be used mainly to finance fixed assets, companies may still want or need more long-term funding as they expand and invest in more fixed (and current) assets. They may borrow money by issuing debentures, or by persuading others such as banks to lend money to them.

Companies generally have a variety of creditors, short-term and long-term; and creditors are likely to know that a company's liability is 'limited' to the amount of funds that shareholders have in the company – these funds are, of course, tied up in fixed and current assets – and, if the company does not have, or cannot generate enough to meet liabilities as they fall due, then creditors are likely to face losses. Neither the directors nor the shareholders are required to put more money into the business to enable it to meet its liabilities. The position of creditors in relation to a company is much weaker than it is in relation to individuals or a partnership: individuals and partners have unlimited personal liability to their creditors. The fact that companies have limited liability may be seen as a privilege; and in return for that privilege companies are required to make their financial statements public. Creditors, and potential creditors, can scrutinize a company's balance sheet, and see what assets they have, and how much equity they have in relation to liabilities.[1] If they are concerned that a company has too many liabilities in relation to equity, they can decide not to become creditors of the company. If the company has ample assets in relation to its liabilities, then creditors are more likely to see this as making their position more secure, and so be happier about the company owing money to them.

Balance sheets can provide reassurance to actual and potential creditors, and they have an interest in seeing that balance sheets are prudently prepared: that the company's assets are worth *at least* as much as the balance sheet states. If a building is shown at cost, £1 million, but, after a number of years, it is really worth £2 million, then the creditors are happy: their security has increased. Where businesses are particularly dependent on banks to finance their activities, such a prudent approach is welcomed by the banks.

At least until the middle of the twentieth century, most of the reasons for valuing assets pointed towards conservative or prudent valuations. The assumption was that assets are worth at least as much as the balance sheet showed.

---

1   Equity = Assets − Liabilities.

Prudence was even seen as being a fundamental accounting concept and was incorporated into the old Accounting Standards Steering Committee's second Statement of Standard Accounting Practice as a fundamental accounting concept. Assets were shown at historic cost,[2] unless such a figure was more than the company was likely to get out of the asset in the normal course of business. When historic cost was too high it was necessary to estimate how much the asset was worth to the business, and write it down to that value. The seeds of the debate on what we mean by 'value to the business' were sown long ago.

The effects of inflation, particularly in the 1970s, led to pressures to move away from historic cost. This was partly to do with profit measurement, and partly to do with the asset values shown on the balance sheet.

Profit is measured after charging all costs incurred in earning the revenue of a particular period. The two costs most affected by price changes are cost of sales, and depreciation. If cost of sales is based on the *historic cost* of the goods sold, then we might say that costs are understated; that replacement cost would be higher, and that reported profits should be lower. Similarly, if depreciation is based on the historic cost of the fixed assets, then we might say that depreciation is understated (in relation to the current cost of the fixed assets) and so profits are overstated. Both directors and shareholders might be happy with this: overstated profit makes their company look good. But if taxation is based on overstated profits, then taxation may be seen as excessive. Because of the effects of changing prices, companies pressed governments for more generous allowances in calculating profits for taxation purposes.

Although companies were happy to seek taxation advantages, there was less enthusiasm for restating asset values to reflect changing prices. Whichever of the various systems was adopted, the effect was to reduce profits: as fixed asset values increases, so depreciation charges increased; the cost of sales figure also increased. If asset values were restated upwards, the balance sheet figures for net assets and for equity would increase accordingly. Whatever way return on capital employed was measured, the reduction in profits, and the increase in capital employed, worked together to reduce return on capital employed, one of the key measures of company performance.

There were other pressures to revalue assets upwards. In many companies the current market value of assets was much higher than the balance sheet indicated, and asset stripping became an art form. If a company was not doing particularly well it was often possible to buy a whole company for less than what the total of all of its separate assets was worth. A company

---

2 Although revaluations were permitted.

might have a net asset value – according to its balance sheet – of, say, £10 million. If they were making only £1 million a year, it might be possible to buy the whole company for, say, something between £12 million and £15 million. But if someone managed to estimate the current value of all of the various parts of the business, and it came to £20 million, they were well placed to make a killing. If it is possible to buy a company for less than £15 million and sell it for £20 million, that is quite a good profit.

The best defence against such takeovers is to have a good profits record, and a high share price – so that it would cost a lot more than the net asset value to buy the company. Revaluing assets on the balance sheet to give more realistic, up-to-date figures is no guarantee against unwelcome takeover bids. But the values are there for all to see, and it is less likely that someone will succeed in buying up a company for less than its net asset value. But, even when assets are shown at current values, if a company is doing badly, the value of the company as a whole can still be less than the value of its separate assets.

The desire or need for companies to borrow increasing amounts of money encourages them to adopt current values for assets, particularly property. Lenders are concerned that a company's borrowings should not be excessive in relation to the company's own money, or equity. Low asset values result in low figures for equity, which in turn can restrict the amount of money that a company can borrow. Property companies generally revalue their properties every year; with other companies there is little consistency – some revalue frequently, while others revalue infrequently or not at all.

Although most practitioners seem to be happy enough to continue with a wide variety of different asset valuation bases, the Accounting Standard Board's *Statement of Principles* (December 1999) appears to offer some sort of theoretical justification for what happens. It may even be attempting to bring together the different strands of valuation practice and to create an image of consistency. But it accepts historic cost with all of its many modifications, and also seems to encourage the 'value to the business' approach.

From the point of view of those who try to get useful information from balance sheets, the only redeeming feature of the current hotchpotch of valuation bases is that companies do disclose what basis they have used for each category of asset. Users of accounts have to read the notes to the accounts carefully, and assess the information about asset values in the light of the information disclosed.

The reasons for showing assets on the balance sheet have changed over the years. Until the last few decades of the twentieth century, prudence was the order of the day. Creditors wanted reassurance that companies had adequate assets to meet their liabilities. When companies wanted to increase their borrowings, it became important for companies to show higher asset figures. Asset valuation is also important in profit measurement, and, today, increasing importance is given to 'value to the business' as the basis for balance sheets and profit measurement.

Different Bases of Asset Valuation

The story of developing asset valuation is a story of steadily developing modifications to historic cost.

Financial statements are based on the idea that assets are shown at their original cost price. Even the idea of putting a 'value' on assets, as opposed to simply stating what they cost, is a relatively recent development. Financial accounting, and financial statements, are the product of a bookkeeping system, and a bookkeeping system records transactions. If you pay £1 million for a building, it is recorded as a £1 million transaction, and it will continue to be shown in the accounts, and on the balance sheet, as being a £1 million building until someone decides to change the figure.

The advantage of showing assets at cost price is that it is objective, clear and verifiable. It was the market price at the time of the transaction. But, as time goes by, it may be worth a lot more (buildings, for example), or a lot less (cars, for example). We cannot even be sure that all buildings are worth more as time goes by: some sorts of specialist building may be worth less if they no longer have a valuable use, and/or are now falling down.

Modified Historic Cost

Originally, balance sheets were simply a list of left-over balances from a bookkeeping system. But gradually people came to see it as being useful to have an idea of what assets and liabilities a business has, and even to start relying on balance sheets as an indication of how creditworthy a business is. As balance sheets are increasingly relied upon, so simple listings of assets at cost price become inadequate.

Things like machinery, vehicles, and furniture obviously have limited lives, and wear out over a period of years. A company estimates the useful life of an asset, and depreciates the asset over that life. So balance sheets traditionally show three figures for each fixed asset: its original cost; the amount of depreciation that has been charged so far; and the net book value. Even conventional 'historic cost' balance sheets are not pure historic cost: they are modified by the fact that most fixed assets are depreciated.

Stocks of raw materials, work in progress and finished good that have not yet been sold are usually shown at cost price. It would be wrong to show them at selling price – that would be anticipating profits that have not yet been made. But sometimes even the cost price is unrealistic. Sometimes stocks of goods have to be sold for less than their cost price – such things as out-of-date books, magazines, software, and fashion goods; components and raw materials that have gone rusty, or have been damaged, or for which there is now little demand.

It is not much use showing stocks of goods at a cost price of £100 if really the business would be lucky to sell them for £50. If £50 is the 'realizable value', they should be shown on the balance sheet at £50, not at £100. The rule is that stocks should be shown at the lower of cost and net realizable value.

We cannot be sure that all debtors will pay the amount that they are due to pay. Most companies have some experience of bad debts, and it is usual to create a provision for bad debts. Debtors are usually shown on balance sheets after deducting the provision for bad debts to give a better assessment of how much is really likely to be received from debtors.

Although traditional accounting is based on historic cost, it is generally modified. Fixed assets are shown after deducting a provision for depreciation. Debtors are shown after deducting a provision for bad debts. Stocks are written down to 'net realizable value' if the price at which they can be sold is lower than cost price. Each of these adjustments is on the cautious, or conservative, or prudent side. The idea is that assets should be worth at least as much as shown on the balance sheet; and many assets are worth much more than the amounts shown on the balance sheet. Traditionally, asset values tended to be understated; and if the net asset value of a company is understated, then the 'equity', or shareholders' funds, are understated. Whatever amount is shown for reserves or retained profits was understated – at least in terms of current values of assets.

Although there are requirements to 'write down' asset values when the cost figure is higher than what they are really worth, there is no requirement to revalue assets upwards. But companies are allowed to revalue assets upwards, and often have good reasons for doing so, especially when there are assets such as land and buildings which were bought many years ago, and which are now worth far more than their historic cost.

The inflation accounting debate of the 1970s encouraged the idea that assets should be revalued to reflect price changes.

Asset Values and Price Changes

During the 1970s pressure to move away from historic cost increased as, with inflation rocketing up to 27 per cent per annum, historic cost values for assets became increasingly irrelevant.

The easiest way to adjust accounts for inflation is simply to multiply every item in the financial statements by the rate of inflation since the transaction was first recorded. If there has been 10 per cent inflation since goods were bought for £100, all you do is multiply the 100 by 1.1 and the goods are restated, after adjusting for inflation, at £110. This inflation accounting system is known as current[3] purchasing power (CPP) accounting and was recommended by the Accounting Standards Committee for general adoption in 1973.[4]

With fixed assets such as buildings, where prices have increased steadily over many years, the use of CPP accounting is likely to give much more realistic values than showing historic cost figures. CPP is based on inflation, as measured by the Retail Price Index; it therefore shows the effects of changes in the general price level which is based on the price of food, housing, clothes, leisure and all of the usual things which domestic households spend their money on. It is unlikely that any specific type of business asset will increase in value precisely in line with the Retail Price Index, but it is likely to produce more realistic figures than historic cost – in most cases.

But in the 1970s *prudence* was still of great importance. And in some cases particular assets do not increase in line with inflation. Computers and electronic equipment have increased much less than inflation; and the value of stocks of oil depends on world oil prices, not on the UK Retail Price Index. To multiply *all* assets up in line with inflation would lead to the value of some assets being seriously overstated. Prudence reasserted its head, and CPP accounting included the rule that assets should be restated in line with inflation; but if the figure that was produced was in excess of the asset's value to the business, then the asset had to be written down to that figure.

Although CPP accounting is the only pure form of inflation accounting, it was never really established in the UK. In response to the accountancy profession's recommendations the government set up the Sandilands Committee, which recommended a system of current cost accounting (CCA). This is based on the idea of assets being shown at replacement cost.[5] Historic cost goes out of the window. It does not matter how much you did pay for the asset in the past; what matters is how much you would have to pay, now, to replace it. Sometimes it is easy to establish replacement cost – just by looking at the current price lists of suppliers. Sometimes the best way is to use price indices, not the Retail Price Index, but special indices for the type of asset concerned. The whole thing becomes much more subjective, and is harder to verify, and makes the auditor's job more difficult.

Replacement cost accounting has been around for many years, and has long been used by some major Dutch companies. But CCA is not a pure form

---

3   Or constant purchasing power.

4   ED 8. PSSAP 7 was published in 1974.

5   Current cost accounting is a *modified* version of replacement cost accounting, using 'value to the business', which is not always replacement cost.

of replacement cost accounting. In some circumstances the replacement cost of an asset may be too high – so high that the business would not want to replace it. A business should not buy an asset unless it is going to get more out of that asset than it paid for it. Retailers will buy something for £10 if they believe they can sell it for £15. But they would not pay £16 to replace such an asset – it is worth, at most, £15 to them; if the replacement cost were £16 the rational businessperson would not replace the asset. What counts is what they can sell the asset for – its net realizable value.

Similar arguments apply with fixed assets. A business might pay £100,000 for a machine which will generate cash flows[6] of £30,000 a year for 5 years. If we know the company's cost of capital, it is easy to work out the net present value of future cash flows. If the net present value of £30,000 a year for 5 years is £113,700[7] it is worthwhile for the company to pay more than £100,000 to replace such an asset, but it would not be worth paying more than £113,700. If the replacement cost of that asset rose to £120,000, then the replacement cost is an irrelevant figure: the business would not replace the asset. The value to the business of that asset is £113,700.

Current cost accounting is based on the idea that assets should be shown at their 'value to the business', which is their 'deprival value'. It is based on the replacement cost of the asset. But if the replacement cost is higher than what the business expects to get out of the asset, then the asset is shown either at net realizable value (for example, in relation to stocks), or at the net present value of the future cash flows that the asset is expected to produce (this is also known as the economic value). If replacement cost is too high, then the choice is between (i) net realizable value and (ii) net present value; the rules of current cost accounting state that value to the business is the higher of these two values.

A Variety of Asset Values

There are many different ways of valuing assets, and the number of possible combinations of possible asset valuations on a single balance sheet is almost infinite.

The main approaches are

1 *Historic cost.* This is objective, verifiable, and the true market value at the time of the transaction. It appears increasingly irrelevant as time goes by.

---

6   Cash flows, not profit. If an asset cost £100,000 and had a 5-year life with zero scrap value, then the average annual depreciation charge would be £20,000. If such an asset generated annual profits (after depreciation) of £10,000 per annum, its net present value at 10 per cent would be about £113,000 (£30,000 × 3.7908 = £113,724).

7   Which it is, assuming a cost of capital of 10 per cent per annum.

2 *Historic cost less depreciation.* This allows for the fact that fixed assets wear out, or are used up over a period of a year. There are many different ways of estimating depreciation.

3 *Net realizable value.* This means the amount for which the asset could be sold, after deducting any necessary costs of getting it into a condition and location that enable it to be sold. Net realizable value could be estimated on the basis of an asset being sold in the normal course of business, or in the event of a forced sale.

4 *Economic value, or net present value.* This is based on the future cash flows that an asset is expected to generate, discounted at an appropriate discount rate. This is easy to apply where there are long-term debtors, and the dates on which they will pay are known; similarly, with investments in gilts and debentures where amounts and dates of interest receivable are known, and the redemption date is fixed. It is much more difficult to estimate with most other assets.

5 *Replacement cost.* This can be based on list prices for equivalent assets, or it can be estimated using appropriate price indices and applying them to historic cost. Where technology is changing rapidly, a company would not replace an existing asset with an identical one. Instead they may try to identify an equivalent alternative asset, perhaps equivalent in productive capacity or operating capability.

6 *Face value.* Notes and coins are usually shown at face value. Debtors and some investments may also be shown at face value.

7 *Face value less a provision.* Debtors are usually shown at face value, less a provision for bad debts.

8 *Market price.* The market price for an asset is likely to be very different, depending on whether you are buying or selling, as anyone selling or buying a second-hand car knows. Market price, when we are buying, is replacement cost; market price when we are selling is net realizable value. The difference could be very extreme, for example with a railway line. If it is uneconomic and closed down, the net realizable value of a narrow strip of land in a rural area could be very small, or even negative if it was accompanied by obligations to maintain fences, ditches, bridges and rights of way. But the replacement cost, or the cost of building a new railway line, for example Crossrail between Paddington and Liverpool Street, is likely to be many millions of pounds.

Market price is most easily used in relation to listed investments such as shares, debentures and government gilt edged securities.

9 *Directors' estimate of market value.* With investments that are not listed, the easiest alternative to historic cost is to have an estimate of market value

made by the directors. Stocks are sometimes valued on this basis, perhaps where there are unsatisfactory records.

10 *Valuer's report.* Land and buildings, especially investment properties, are sometimes revalued regularly on the basis of valuers' reports produced by specialist valuers, who provide a report, for a fee, which can be verified by the company's auditors. Valuers are, of course, like auditors: they are independent professional experts, and their opinions are objective and neutral, and not influenced by what directors want or their need to earn fees.[8]

11 *Insurance values.* Assets are insured on the basis of the valuation that insurance companies put on them. As insurance premiums are usually based on the asset value, they are likely to be overstated rather than understated. If a company is desperate, and can think of nothing better, they might use insurance values.

12 *Historic cost adjusted for inflation.* The basis of inflation accounting (current purchasing power) is to adjust all non-monetary items in the financial statements by the amount of inflation since the transaction was recorded. This gives very unrealistic asset values where price changes for specific types of assets are very different from the average change in retail prices recorded by the Retail Price Index.

13 *Various combinations.* Most balance sheets are a combination of various different approaches to asset value. Where historic cost adjusted for inflation gives unrealistically high asset values, for example where retail prices have increased, but the cost of electronic equipment has decreased, the inflation adjusted asset values should be written down to something such as value to the business. The approach used in current cost accounting is based on replacement cost, but where this is higher than economic value or net realizable value, the higher of these two is shown.

As the methods of valuation for the various groups of assets vary considerably, it is difficult to be sure exactly what, if anything, the total amount for assets shown on the balance sheet means. In the days before creative accounting, and current cost accounting, it used to mean the total amount that the company has spent on assets that are still around, less any amounts written off because they are no longer 'worth' as much as they cost. We could be reasonably sure that the assets were 'worth' at least as much as was stated on the balance sheet. But what an asset is worth to a business that is using it might be very different from what it could be sold for, and that might be very different from what it would cost to buy an equivalent replacement for the asset.

---

8 And you will probably believe in Father Christmas too, if it is in your interest to (appear to) do so.

Current thinking with accounting standards is based on showing what assets are worth to the business. What they are worth is the net present values of the future cash flows that they will generate. This is, of course, hopelessly futuristic. We know that the price of oil can quadruple in a matter of months; that steady growth in demand for flying can be shattered by an act of terrorism; and that growth forecasts for telecommunication have been so hopelessly over-optimistic that share prices and companies have collapsed. In such a world it seems quite unrealistic to base asset values on forecasts of future revenues and costs.

Even if we could produce reliable asset values based on the net present value of future cash flows, we should be wary of the idea that a total of such asset values has much meaning or much use. It does not show what the assets could be sold for. And it does not show what the business as a whole is worth. Most successful businesses should be worth a lot more than the amount shown for its separate assets on the balance sheet. This is because, in a successful business, there is 'internally generated' goodwill that has not been recorded. If the accounting standards setters are moving towards a world when even internally generated goodwill is shown on a balance sheet, based on estimates of its net present value, then perhaps the total of the net asset value of a company will be equal to its market capitalization on the stock market. We will then have moved to a world where accountancy, based as it is on recording transactions, is superseded by predictions, fictions, and economic theory, and fantasy.

Definition of Assets

At first sight it seems easy to define what an asset is in a set of company accounts: an asset is something of value which the company owns. But the emphasis has now moved from ownership to control.

If something has no value, or a negative value, it is not an asset. When a piece of equipment comes to the end of its life, it may still be an asset if it has a scrap value. But if the cost of disposing of it is greater than its scrap value,[9] then it becomes a liability, not an asset.

There are few problems with such a straightforward definition of an asset; the main problems are deciding how to value an asset. Even if the asset is simply shown at cost, there are problems in deciding exactly which costs should be included. There are some difficulties in deciding whether an asset has been created, because the distinction between capital and revenue expenditure is not always clear: capital expenditure creates or adds to a fixed asset; revenue expenditure is written off as an expense. Repairs

9 Old cars, fridges and mobile phones come to mind as examples of assets that are difficult/expensive to dispose of.

and maintenance are revenue expenditure, but additions and improvements are capital expenditure. If rotting, draughty wooden window frames are replaced with modern, plastic, double glazed windows, it is partly an improvement, adding to the value of an asset, and partly ordinary maintenance or revenue expenditure. It is clear that the building is an asset, and it is just a question of determining what expenditure adds to the asset, and what simply maintains it as it should be. There are always going to be difficult lines to be drawn, but, in general, to a person with common sense, it is not difficult to decide what is an asset and what is not.

But accountancy has become too sophisticated for common sense and straightforward definitions. A number of problems have arisen which have steadily moved official recommendations away from common sense to more controversial bases for determining what is, and what is not, an asset. The story of asset definition is a story of steady movement into a fantasy world as 'events' have pushed accounting standards setters towards defending the increasingly dubious propositions to try to maintain the façade of their Statement of Principles.

Common sense suggests that an asset must be 'separable' – capable of being sold without disposing of the business as a whole. Double glazing is not really 'separable' from the building: the building as a whole is the asset, not the double glazing. Almost all tangible assets are separable, in the sense that a business can sell all of its land and buildings, plant, machinery, fixtures and vehicles separately, without selling the business as a whole. The same is true of many intangible assets: it is possible to sell licences, copyrights and patents separately. But goodwill is not separable. It is the value of a business as a whole, over and above the value of the separable assets.

Traditionally goodwill was always seen as being a rather questionable asset on the balance sheet. Bankers and other creditors are not very interested in assets that do not represent security because they cannot be sold. It is inevitable that goodwill arises when one business buys another, and pays more for it than the book value of its assets. The extra that they have paid has to be shown, and either it is an asset on the balance sheet, or an expense on the profit and loss account – or some compromise solution has to be found. Until the 1990s companies usually allowed goodwill to disappear by deducting it from retained profits: it did not go through the income statement as an expense, and it was not shown as an asset on the balance sheet. But now the standard setters require that it is shown as a fixed asset on the balance sheet, and that it is amortized, or depreciated, in much the same way as any other fixed asset. This means that assets are not necessarily tangible, or separable.

Another problem in deciding exactly what an asset is arises with research and development costs. In the good old/bad old days before Rolls-Royce collapsed, a company could spend a lot of money on research and development, in developing a new aero engine for example, and there were no rules on whether this should be regarded as normal revenue expenditure, or whether the expenditure could be regarded as creating an additional asset to be shown on the balance sheet. Eventually accounting standards were produced (IAS 38 and SSAP 13) which said that all research expenditure was revenue expenditure; but development expenditure, if it met specified conditions, could be treated as capital expenditure, or it could be treated as revenue expenditure. The company can decide. There is still no definition of an asset which makes it clear whether it includes such development expenditure; and there is no definition of development expenditure that specifies when it becomes an asset. If the strict conditions for recognition as an asset are met, it is for the company to decide whether or not it is an asset.

The biggest departure from a common-sense definition of an asset came with finance leases. If a company needs a vehicle, or a piece of specialist equipment for a couple of days, the item concerned remains an asset of its owner, and does not immediately become an asset in the books of the company which is using it for a short period. But if a company buys the lease of a building for, say 99 years (or even just for a few years), then the cost of buying that lease becomes a fixed asset on the balance sheet. The problem arises with leases which are for a period of years. (Where there is an initial premium, this is treated as capital expenditure and amortized over the life of the lease.)

A company may decide to lease an asset, perhaps for 5 or 10 years. The 'economic reality', or the 'substance' of such a transaction is much the same as if they had bought it, and borrowed the money for 5 years. They have the use of the asset as if they own it, and they have a commitment to make the lease payments which would be seen as a liability. It was always clear that if a company *buys* an asset, and *borrows* the money, both the asset and the liability are shown on the balance sheet. But accounting standards (IAS 17, SSAP 21) now require both the asset and the liability to be shown on the balance sheet if it is a 'finance lease'. A finance lease is one which transfers substantially all of the risks and rewards of ownership, which usually means a lease for a number of years, depending on the life of the asset. Any other lease is an 'operating lease', which usually means a shorter term; there is no asset or liability shown on the balance sheet for operating leases.

This leads us to the position that an asset is no longer something that the company 'owns', and results in tortuous definitions of assets ...

An asset on a company's balance sheet can be something that is not tangible; something that is not separable; and something that the company does not even own. It must be something of value; and something that the company has bought or created.

The IASC's *Framework for the Preparation and Presentation of Financial Statements* (1989) defines an asset as 'a resource controlled by the enterprise as a result of past events and from which future economic benefits are expected to flow to the enterprise'. The ASB's *Statement of Principles* (1999) defines assets as 'rights or other access to future economic benefits controlled by an entity as a result of past transactions or events'. Both definitions emphasize control rather than ownership, and so an asset held under a finance lease is included. Neither require separability, and so do not exclude goodwill. Both also require that the asset is 'controlled', which may make it difficult to apply to goodwill. A company cannot 'control' goodwill in the way that it can control most other assets. Both include the idea that assets can arise because of past 'events', not just transactions, which presumably means that an organization can create assets; they do not have to buy them.

The IASC's definition sees the asset as the thing itself which gives rise to future economic benefits. The ASB's *Statement of Principles* is clear that the asset is not the item of property itself; the asset is the right to future economic benefits. With most assets, the future economic benefits are net cash inflows. But cash itself is not an asset; it is the right it gives to acquire future economic benefits that is the asset. In Ernst and Young's 'UK and International GAAP' it is stated that:

> In fact it is an inescapable logical consequence of this definition of assets that 'future economic benefits' cannot be items of property or cash – which obviously they are. This logical bind, and the absence of any other meaning being given to the phrase 'future economic benefits' has the inescapable consequence that the ASB has a flawed definition at the heart of the *Statement of Principles*. If the definition of assets is flawed the entire logical structure derived from it is too, including all the remaining definitions of the elements of financial statements the SoP contains.

Traditionally, the definition of assets was easy: assets are something a business owns. There are difficulties in drawing an exact line between revenue expenditure (which does not create a fixed asset) and capital expenditure. There are difficulties in specifying exactly which costs should be included, for example in stocks of goods that a business has made. There is room for subjectivity in creating provisions for depreciation and provision for bad debts. Where assets are not 'material', there is no need to include them – a bucket used in cleaning is technically a fixed asset, but its cost is so small that it is usually immediately written off as an expense. But there was no difficulty in deciding whether or not something is an asset, in most cases.

There are particularly difficult areas in defining and measuring assets such as goodwill, research and development, human assets, and leased assets.

Categories of Assets

A balance sheet usually starts by listing asset, with fixed (or long-term) assets being shown separately from current (short-term) assets. International accounting standards lay down no particular format for this although IAS 1 (Presentation of financial statements) does specify the main items which should be disclosed. The European Union's Fourth Directive has more detailed guidance. It allows a 'horizontal' or 'two-sided' balance sheet with assets shown on the left, and liabilities on the right. But it also allows the 'vertical' version more commonly used in the UK. In simple terms this starts with assets, then deducts liabilities, to give equity. It begins with fixed assets; then current assets are shown; current liabilities[10] are then deducted from current assets to give a figure for net current assets/liabilities.[11] This is then added to fixed assets to give a figure for total assets less current liabilities. Long-term liabilities are then deducted, with three different types of deduction specified. The final total equals capital and reserves.

The main headings and usual format are as follows:

Fixed assets		200
Current assets	300	
Prepayments and accrued income	10	
	310	
Creditors: amounts becoming due and payable within one year	210	
Net current assets		100
Total assets less current liabilities		300
Creditors: amounts becoming due and payable after more than one year	50	
Provisions for liabilities and charges	20	
Accruals and deferred income	10	80
		220

This total is equal to capital and reserves. But as capital may include preference share capital, which is not part of equity, the total may be different from the figure for equity. Preference share capital must be deducted from the total of shareholders' funds to give the figure for ordinary shareholders' funds, which is equity.

10 Current liabilities are referred to as 'Creditors: amounts becoming due and payable within one year'.

11 Net current assets are also known as working capital.

More detail is required for each category of assets. Fixed assets are shown under three headings: (1) Intangible assets, (2) Tangible assets, and (3) Financial assets.[12] Current assets are shown under four headings: (1) Stocks, (2) Debtors, (3) Investments, and (4) Cash at bank and in hand.

All of these headings should be shown in the order given. Additional categories and sub-headings may be combined, and are often shown in the notes to the financial statements.

There is also provision for two categories of doubtful assets: subscribed capital unpaid and formation expenses.

Each of the main categories is examined in turn below. The general rules are that fixed assets are originally recognized at cost; that an annual depreciation or amortization charge is applied; that fixed assets may be revalued from time to time; that in some circumstances directors are required to show the market value of particular fixed assets; and that an 'impairment review' is sometimes required.

Fixed Assets (1) Intangible Assets

The main item is the *cost of research and development*. The cost of research should not appear on a balance sheet; it is an expense to be charged as it is incurred. Companies may choose to show the cost of development expenditure as a fixed asset on the balance sheet if it meets strict conditions. The company must be able to demonstrate all of the following: that it is technically feasible, and when completed it will produce something that is available for use or sale; that the company intends to, and is able to complete it and sell it; how it will generate future economic benefits – that there is a market for it, or how they will use it; that there are adequate technical, financial and other resources available to complete it, and sell it or use it; and that the expenditure on developing it can be measured reliably.

There are inevitably grey areas where it is not clear whether or not development expenditure is allowed to be capitalized. An obvious example is the development of software. The Accounting Standards Board has issued more detailed guidance on when the costs of developing a website may be capitalized.

Other categories of intangible fixed assets are: *concessions, patents, licences, trade marks* and similar rights and assets; *goodwill*, to the extent that it was acquired for valuable consideration; and *payments on account*.

Fixed Assets (2) Tangible Assets

The main items are: *land and buildings; plant and machinery; other fixtures and fittings, tools and equipment;* and *payments on account and tangible assets in the course of construction.*

12   These are long-term investments.

Fixed Assets (3) Financial Assets

The third category of fixed assets is for investments.

Current Assets (1) Stocks

The main items are: *raw materials and consumables*; *work in progress*; *finished goods and goods for resale*; and *payments on account*.

Current Assets (2) Debtors

(Amounts becoming due and payable after more than one year must be shown separately for each item.)

The main items are: *trade debtors*; *amounts owed by affiliated undertakings*; *amounts owed by undertakings with which the company is linked by virtue of participating interests*; *other debtors*; *subscribed capital called but not paid*; and *prepayments and accrued income*.

Current Assets (3) Investments

The main items are: *shares in affiliated undertakings*; *own shares*; and *other investments*

Current Assets (4) Cash at Bank and in Hand

Summary and Conclusion

The debate on asset valuation sometimes seems to proceed as if there is a 'correct' answer, as if accountants have been at fault for years for failing to show 'true' values. But we never really know the value of an asset until it is sold and the price is agreed; historic cost was a 'true' value when it was first recorded. We can produce more asset valuations which are more up to date, and accept some loss of reliability; but we must remember that even if we are able to value all assets on an acceptable and consistent current basis, the total of the values is of limited meaning. We need to deduct liabilities to arrive at a net asset value. But the resulting figure tells us neither what the individual separable assets could be sold for, nor what the value of the business as a whole is. The value of a business depends on investors' expectation of the future cash flows that the business will generate.

10.2 Liabilities

Definitions

The ASB's *Statement of Principles* defines liabilities as 'obligations of an entity to transfer economic benefits as a result of past transactions or events'.

It is tempting to think of liabilities as being amounts of money that a company owes. It is easy to think of a straightforward balance sheet as showing 'current liabilities' (such as trade creditors, accruals, taxation, proposed dividends, overdraft), and 'long-term liabilities' (such as debentures and other loans). Most figures for liabilities are straightforward and provide a valuable indication of a company's solvency. There is usually little debate about the figures to be shown: the amount you owe is simply a matter of fact.

If the amount is not due to be paid for some years it may be appropriate to 'discount' it.[13] That means applying a discount factor (or interest rate) to it to allow for the number of years. But there are a few items on balance sheets that are more difficult to interpret.

Current Liabilities

The term 'current liabilities' has been replaced on published balance sheets by 'Creditors: amounts falling due within one year'. Most of the figures are fairly straightforward.

Companies usually have trade creditors for the usual purchases and expenses that a company has bought or incurred during the year which has just ended, and payment is made for them a few weeks later. The term 'accruals' is just an extension of this. At the year end estimates have to be made of all expenses that have been incurred during the year although no bookkeeping entries have yet been made for them. At the balance sheet date there will always be some expenses such as electricity and gas, and perhaps interest, which have to be 'accrued'.

In addition most companies are likely to have current liabilities for taxation, and proposed dividends. During the year the company may have paid an interim dividend, which has been fully accounted for. At the year end a dividend is proposed, but as it has not been paid at the balance sheet date, it is shown as a current liability.

Companies often also have overdrafts and other short-term borrowings from banks and other institutions which are shown as current liabilities.

There can also be odd current liabilities which are harder to understand – particularly items that were shown under the heading for 'Creditors: amounts falling due after more than one year', under a sub-heading such as 'Provisions for liabilities and charges'. Longer-term liabilities that eventually are paid (and not all are – as explained below) become current liabilities during the last 12 months before they are paid. Most of the items that are shown as long-term liabilities eventually become current liabilities as the date for payment approaches.

---

13   Discounted cash flow is explained more fully in Chapter 14.

Creditors: Amounts Falling Due After More Than One Year

The most substantial long-term liability is usually in the form of debentures or other borrowing where the amount is due to be repaid more than a year after the balance sheet date. There are also various 'Provisions for liabilities and charges' which are described below.

When a company acquires fixed assets under a finance lease, the interest accrues annually, and is shown as an expense in the profit and loss account; if it is unpaid at the year end, it is shown as a current liability. The main part of the liability – the capital element, or the principal – is shown as a long-term liability under the heading 'Obligations under finance leases'. If there are any amounts due after more than 5 years, they have to be shown separately. Each year part of the long-term liability becomes a current liability as it falls due. As a result we usually see part of the obligations under finance leases as a current liability, and part as a long-term liability.

'Negative Assets'

A balance sheet starts with fixed assets and current assets; then short-term and long-term liabilities are deducted. The resulting figure is variously labelled as net assets, or shareholders' funds, or equity. The basis is therefore: Assets minus Liabilities equals Equity. But not every item is easily classified as assets or liabilities (or equity).

Depreciation is deducted from assets. The assets figures on balance sheets show the cumulative depreciation over the years as a deduction from the amount shown for assets to give a net book value. This cumulative depreciation is not a liability. It is perhaps best thought of as being a negative asset.

When one company buys another company, it typically pays more for it than the net asset value. The extra is labelled as goodwill. But there can also be negative goodwill, which is shown as a deduction from other assets. Negative goodwill is a negative asset, not a liability.

The figure for debtors on a balance sheet is often shown net of a provision for bad debts. If a company has debtors of, say, £100,000, they may show it on the balance sheet as being a net figure of £90,000, if their experience suggests that about 10 per cent of debtors do not pay up. It is usually the net figure that is shown on a published balance sheet. But the provision for bad debts is not a liability; there is no obligation to pay anything or to transfer any sort of economic benefits. It is a negative asset.

Where there are 'negative assets' they are best deducted from other assets; the net figure should be considered in interpreting financial statements.

'Provisions'

Provisions are created as a result of a charge against profits. If a provision of £100,000 is created, the profits are reduced by £100,000. If the provision is increased in the following year by £50,000, the charge against profits is £50,000, and the total provision shown on the balance sheet is £150,000. In a later year, when the provision is reduced, profits are increased by the amount of the reduction. Provisions have been used in 'creative accounting',[14] particularly in 'income smoothing': to reduce the profits in booming years, and to boost them in lean years.

The Companies Act 1985 defines provisions as 'amounts retained as reasonably necessary to cover any liability of loss which is either likely or certain to be incurred'. This gives companies a fair amount of freedom in deciding how much to make use of provisions. They are typically labelled as being for reorganizations, redundancies, disposals, legal liabilities, decommissioning costs, and future losses and costs of various sorts.

FRS 12 created a stricter definition: a provision is a liability of uncertain timing or amount. It is therefore a liability, and there must be an obligation to transfer economic benefits. It is supposed to be much like any other liability; the difference is the uncertainty of the timing or amount. Provisions have sometimes been established where there is no real obligation to transfer economic benefits, and even today FRS 12 allows provisions where there is no legal obligation, but only a 'constructive' obligation.

According to FRS 12, provisions should be recognized only where there is a (constructive or legal) obligation to transfer economic benefits as at the balance sheet date; and it is probable that the transfer will be required; and that a reliable estimate can be made of the amount of the obligation. It is difficult to eliminate an element of subjectivity in deciding whether to create provisions, and the amounts to be shown.

The ASB is in a difficult position. If they allow too much freedom in creating, increasing and reducing provisions, they leave the door open to creative accounting. But if they are too strict in not allowing provisions, there would often be cases where companies knew of some likely bad news, and kept quiet about it. A prudent set of financial statements would disclose all potential liabilities – including 'contingent liabilities'.

Warranties

Companies may make specific provisions for the cost of guarantees or warranties and other after sales service that they are expected to provide. This may appear on a balance sheet as a provision, or it may not be separately

---

14   This is explored more fully in Chapter 8.

disclosed. Sometimes companies deduct appropriate provisions from the figure for sales; sometimes it is included in a more general provision.

Contingent Liabilities

Contingent liabilities can arise as a result of legal action. Maybe the company will have to pay out a lot of money as a result of losing a case; but the result has not yet been determined. A contingent liability is a possible obligation whose existence will be confirmed only by the occurrence of an uncertain future event; or it can be where a transfer of economic benefits is not probable, or the amount cannot yet be measured reliably. Contingent liabilities should not be shown on a balance sheet. They should be disclosed as a note to the accounts (unless it is only a remote possibility).

In assessing the solvency or creditworthiness of a company it is worth looking not only at the actual liabilities shown on the balance sheet, but also at the contingent liabilities; there may a risk of substantial payments having to be made.

Deferred Taxation

Deferred taxation arises because the rules for calculating profit for inclusion in annual reports and accounts are different from the rules for taxation purposes. Depreciation allowances for taxation purposes ('writing down allowances') are typically quite high in the early years of a fixed asset's life; these high allowances reduce taxable profits, which means that the amount of corporation tax payable is much reduced in the first years after substantial acquisitions of fixed assets. Profits for tax purposes are much lower than the profits reported in the annual accounts – which would make the tax charge look peculiarly low, and might mislead shareholders by exaggerating the after tax profits available for dividends.

A few years later this reverses. As the fixed assets get towards the end of their lives (and if there have been few additional purchases of fixed assets) the position reverses: allowances for tax purposes are smaller; the amount of tax payable is larger; and this might mislead shareholders by showing low after tax profit being available for dividends.

Deferred taxation is a bit like a taxation equalization account. In the early years after acquisitions of fixed assets, the tax actually payable is low; but a higher charge against profits is made; this extra 'deferred taxation' is not yet payable but is shown as if it is a liability. After a few years it may reverse: the tax actually payable is higher, but only a modest 'equalized' charge is made against profits; the extra is charged against the balance for deferred taxation which was built up for that purpose in the early years of the fixed asset's life.

In many cases the amount shown as a long-term liability for deferred taxation will never actually be paid. If a company continues to invest in additional fixed assets it is likely that the writing down allowances on the new fixed assets will have the effect of building up the credit balance on the deferred taxation account faster than it is used up by the smaller writing down allowances on the older fixed assets. The old Accounting Standards Committee experimented with a 'partial provision' for deferred taxation, based on the idea that provisions should be made only for amounts that it was reasonably probable would become payable. But this was rather subjective and not consistent with international practice.

FRS 19 requires full provision for deferred taxation for all timing differences. The effect can be to build up a substantial provision on the balance sheet which never actually becomes a liability.[15] This makes interpretation of financial statements, and the calculation of accounting ratios, rather difficult. Some people simply ignore it: they exclude it from capital employed, and from liabilities, but this can lead to inconsistent ratios that never properly add up or reconcile. Essentially the choice is between treating it as a liability (which it is not, yet; and may never be), or treating it as part of equity (which it is very close to being at present, but may not be in the future).

Deferred taxation is normally shown as a liability under the heading 'Creditors: amounts falling due after more than one year', and the sub-heading 'Provisions for liabilities and charges'. Sometimes there is a negative provision for deferred taxation; this is shown as a current asset along with debtors.

As in so many areas of interpretation of financial statements there can be no definitive, 'right' answer. The important thing is to treat it in a consistent way in comparing one company with another, and comparing one year with another.

Deferred Income and Deferred Credits

Most items of revenues and income are credited to the profit and loss account and contribute towards profit immediately. Sometimes revenues are received in advance of the company providing the goods or services required, and these should not (yet) be credited to the profit and loss account. They may be shown as payments in advance,[16] or deferred income, or deferred credits.

---

15 Companies are allowed to estimate when it is likely to become payable and to apply an appropriate discount factor for a number of years into the future.

16 Payments *received* in advance are shown under a heading for creditors, which may be short term or long term. Payments *made* in advance are shown as an asset, usually a current asset.

When a company receives a government grant towards the cost of acquiring fixed assets, this should not be credited to the profit and loss account immediately. The income should be spread over the life of the asset. This is done by showing it as a deferred credit on the balance sheet; each year part of this is credited to the profit and loss account – in line with depreciation.

We may think of liabilities as simply being amounts that a company owes. But the ASB's definition is more careful. It refers to an obligation to transfer economic benefits. It is, however, difficult to see that all of the items shown on a balance sheet as liabilities, or credit balances, involve an obligation to transfer economic benefits. Some appear to be more like negative assets, or balances left over in transferring income or expenditure from one period to another.

Pension Funds

Companies with pension funds have usually built up assets to meet the need to pay future pensions. Each year, companies and their employees put money into a fund, and the money is invested in shares, debentures, government bonds, property and, occasionally, in less conventional assets such as works of art. As the company expands, so there are more employees; more money is put into the fund; and the investments increase in value; and, with a bit of luck, the income from the investments is more than enough to pay the pensions as they fall due.

There used to be cases where companies took a 'pensions holiday', and made no contribution to the pension fund because its value was more than enough to meet all expected liabilities. Such 'holidays' helped to boost companies' profits.

In some cases there are no serious problems with pension funds. The scheme may be one where the amount that has to be contributed each year is defined; but there is no definition of the amount of pensions that has to be paid. If the pension fund turns out to be very valuable, pensions may be generous. If the fund turns out to be rather poor, then pensions are rather poor.

Most employees prefer a 'defined benefit' or 'final salary' scheme where the amount of pension they will receive depends on the level of salary they are earning before retiring. If they have been in the pension scheme for, say, 30 years, their pension may be 30 sixtieths, or 30 eightieths of their final salary.[17] Each year when companies prepare their annual accounts they have to estimate what their future liability for pensions will be, and disclose any shortfalls.

17 In the public sector the less generous eightieths is more common; but it is more generous in that it is usually increased in line with inflation.

Where the number of employees in a company is declining, the level of contributions to the pension scheme is also declining. More seriously, pension funds have typically depended heavily on investments in equities, and the value of these has declined substantially between the beginning of the year 2000 and the middle of 2003. As a result many pension schemes are in deficit; in some cases the deficits are enormous. This information has to be disclosed in the annual reports of companies.

Categories of Liabilities

The usual format for balance sheets, following the 1985 Companies Act, provides for four categories of liabilities, provisions and the like, details of which are as follows:

1 Creditors: amounts falling due within one year. The main items are: *debenture loans; bank loans and overdrafts; payments received on account; trade creditors; bills of exchange payable; amounts owed to group companies; amounts owed to related companies; other creditors including taxation and social security;* and *accruals and deferred income.*

2 Creditors: amounts falling due after more than one year. The main items are the same as with short-term creditors; the only difference is that they are payable after more than one year.

3 Provisions for liabilities and charges. The main items are: *pensions and similar obligations; taxation, including deferred taxation;* and *other provisions.*

4 Accruals and deferred income.

Summary

It is easy to criticize variations in practice and uncertainties in definitions and rules produced by accounting standards setters. It is much more difficult to come up with clear-cut and consistent definitions, and measurement bases, which are both reliable, and relevant to the needs of those who use accounts. Increasingly, sophisticated accounting standards have led to a situation where a wealth of information about companies' assets and liabilities is published, and – with care, and some reservations – the information is available to meet a wide range of users' needs.

Review of Key Points

- Assets include all of the things that a company owns, but the official definition includes all rights or other access to future economic benefits that are controlled by the company

- The emphasis in asset valuation has changed over the years from more 'prudent' approaches to more 'relevant' approaches

- There was never a 'pure' historic cost system for reporting assets

- Measuring and reporting assets has a useful role in assessing solvency, measuring profits and providing other important information to those who use companies' financial statements

- Liabilities are obligations to transfer economic benefits resulting from past transactions or events

- Provisions are included in the liabilities section of the balance sheet, but there are often provisions which do not seem much like liabilities

- Definition and measurement of liabilities is generally more straightforward than it is with assets, but there are problems with provisions

Self-testing Questions

1 Define assets and liabilities.

2 What purposes are served by measuring and reporting a company's assets?

3 List at least 12 different methods of asset valuation.

4 Why do we not have 'pure' historic cost accounting?

5 List the main categories of asset and give examples of each.

6 List the main categories of liability and give examples of each.

7 Which liabilities do not seem to be like other liabilities? Give your reasons.

Assessment Questions

1 Is an asset simply something that a company owns?

2 Discuss the role of 'prudence' in accounting.

Assessment Questions (continued)

3 Produce a list of different approaches to asset measurement or valuation. Give each a mark out of ten for (a) relevance and (b) reliability, and provide a brief justification for each of the marks given. You might choose to do this in respect of typical assets for which that approach could be used. Alternatively, you could select two or three particular assets and give a score for the relevance and reliability of each approach to asset management in respect of those particular assets.

4 Discuss the view that it is a reasonable generalization to say that liabilities are more easily defined and measured than assets.

Group Activities and Discussion Questions

1 Assess the case for including key employees on the balance sheet (presumably as assets).

2 The balance sheet is said to show assets less liabilities as being equal to equity. Is it over-simplistic to assume that all items that should be included on balance sheets may legitimately be included under one of these three headings?

3 Have a competition to describe the asset that it is most difficult on which to put a value. Each member of the group should describe one such asset, and explain why a meaningful valuation is (almost) impossible. Other members of the group should suggest ways in which the asset could realistically be valued.

   The assets chosen must be ones that the group agree exist, and are of a type that is likely to be owned or controlled by a business. The group would probably not agree to trying to value ghosts, Uranus, a marriage, or someone's soul.

   Does the group agree that it is possible to put a meaningful value on anything which could legitimately be described as a business asset?

4 Should a Tobacco Company include on its balance sheet a liability for damage done to its customers' health by smoking? When and how would such a liability be recognized?

Financial Accounting in context

Discuss and comment on the following item taken from the press:
Pension crisis? What crisis? by Florian Gimbel
Financial Times, 28 July 2003

Companies with retirement problems are outperforming the FTSE 100
   Top fund managers are building up their stakes in UK companies with the worst pension problems, after dramatically reassessing the corporate impact of the retirement crisis.

Financial Accounting in context (continued)

Rolls-Royce, the UK aerospace group, and Royal & Sun Alliance, the insurance house, have seen their share price more than double since March, when the FTSE 100 reached its eight-year low.

British Airways, whose pension fund is nearly five times its market capitalisation, also saw its share price double – before its public row with check-in staff dented its international reputation.

In all, seven of the 10 most exposed FTSE 100 companies – plus BA – have significantly out-performed the FTSE 100 index.

The other five were BAE Systems, the defence company, GKN, the engineering firm, BT Group, the telecommunications giant, Whitbread, the leisure group, and Allied Domecq, the drinks company. It represents a sharp reversal of sentiment, amid signs that fund managers over-reacted to the avalanche of brokers' notes that warned of pension 'black holes' and 'leaking vats'.

Some fund managers think companies with major pension problems – where the fund's assets are insufficient to meet its 'liabilities' or commitments to pay the pensions of all its contributors – can perform well in rising markets.

This is because the companies' funds, which are heavily invested in equities, will be able to rely on the rising value of the equity markets rather than new contributions from the company in order to close the gap between assets and liabilities. Sacha Sadan, a senior UK equities fund manager at Gartmore, the US-owned investment house, said: 'It is more than a coincidence that so many companies outperformed. During the downturn, these stocks became detached from their fundamentals, because their pension funds were geared to the stock market. The same thing that pushed them down is now giving them an extra boost.'

Robert Talbut, chief investment officer at ISIS Asset Management, said: 'The market is saying: "these pension problems are not as serious as we thought six months ago".' David Cummings, head of UK equities at Standard Life Investments, one of the top 10 shareholders in several of the companies with the worst pension problems, said: 'We are well aware of the pension issue and the concerns have diminished since the first quarter.'

A £10,000 investment in an equally-weighted portfolio of the most exposed FTSE 100 stocks – ranked by their pension fund deficits as a proportion of market capitalisation – would have generated a return of £5,693 in less than five months.

Rolls-Royce has a pension fund deficit as a percentage of market cap of 91 per cent, according to figures compiled by UBS, the Swiss bank. Yet its share price rose by more than 117 per cent between the March trough of the bear market and the end of last week.

British Airways, which has been mocked as 'a large hedge fund with a few wings attached' and whose deficit accounts for 67 per cent of its market cap, saw its shares jump by 95 per cent over the same period.

In March, BA reported a FRS17 pension deficit of £1.2bn, up from £340m a year ago. Last month, Standard & Poor's cut BA's credit rating to 'junk status', thereby raising the company's cost of borrowing.

But the companies insist that their revival has little to do with the pension problems and every-thing to do with executive's management skill. 'The pension fund may have been one factor,'

Financial Accounting in context (continued)

according to a Rolls-Royce spokesperson, 'but most of the share price increase has come in response to our profit guidance [earlier this year].'

BA said: 'The rise in our share price can be completely explained by the change in expectations about the profitability of the company. We are in no way constrained in what we can do because of our pension fund.'

References and Further Reading

Accounting Standards Board (1997) FRS 10 Goodwill and Intangible Assets.

Accounting Standards Board (1998) FRS 11 Impairment of Fixed Assets and Goodwill.

Accounting Standards Board (1999) FRS 15 Tangible Fixed Assets.

Accounting Standards Board (1999) *Statement of Principles for Financial Reporting.*

Lewis, R. and D. Pendrill (2004) *Advanced Financial Accounting*, 7th edn, Pearson Education.

11

Revenues and Expenses

Learning objectives

After studying this chapter you should be able to:

◆ Define revenues and expenses

◆ Understand and describe the main items included under these headings in financial statements

◆ Appreciate the problems in defining when revenues are recognized

◆ Explain items that are credited to a profit and loss account but which do not look much like revenues

◆ Explain items that are charged to a profit and loss account but which do not look much like expenses

◆ Know which expenses can be found in a company's annual report

◆ Explain how the accruals concept affects the recognition of revenues and expenses

Introduction

Revenues and expenses were introduced in Chapter 2. Their significance in relation to profit measurement was followed up in Chapter 5 where it was explained that profits can be measured either in relation to an increase in net assets, or as being the difference between revenues and expenses. It is important to understand what is included under each of these headings, and how they are measured, in order to understand and interpret financial statements, as seen in Chapters 4 and 9, and throughout financial accounting. This chapter provides further explanation of these two key elements of financial statements.

11.1 Definitions

There is no formal, generally agreed definition of revenues and expenses. In this chapter the word 'revenues' will be used to include turnover, or sales, and any other income[1] that is credited to the profit and loss account and during a period. The word 'expenses' will be used to mean the costs incurred in earning the revenues of a period, and any other charges made to the profit and loss account. Revenues should be 'realized', which usually means that something has been sold, and a transaction has taken place.

The ASB's *Statement of Principles* refers to gains and losses rather than revenues and expenses, which does not fit comfortably with traditional accounting practice. The ASB specify that 'The terms "gains" and "losses" therefore include items that are often referred to as "revenue" and "expenses", as well as gains and losses arising from, for example, the disposal of fixed assets and the remeasurement of assets and liabilities'.

Gains are defined as 'increases in ownership interest not resulting from contributions from owners'. This includes anything that adds to the net asset value of a business, other than additional capital paid in by shareholders. It includes revaluations of fixed assets, and any other unrealized gains.

Losses are defined as 'decreases in ownership interest not resulting from distributions to owners'. This includes anything that reduces the net asset value of a business, other than the payment of dividends, or reductions in share capital, such as those resulting from a company buying back its own shares. It includes any reductions in the value of assets.

There is room for debate on the extent to which reductions in the value of assets should be recognized in the profit and loss account. When such

---

1   Terminology in financial accounting is often confusing. Some people use the word 'income' as if it is the same as 'revenue'. And the word 'income' is often used as if it means the same as profit. In this chapter the word 'revenue' is used to include any items that are credited to a profit and loss account.

reductions are recognized, the profit for that period is reduced. The 'historic cost' convention of accounting might seem to permit continuing to show assets at cost, even if their value has declined. But historic cost has always been moderated by 'prudence'. Stocks are shown at the lower of cost and net realizable value; provisions are made for bad debts; and fixed assets are depreciated. Where there has been an additional reduction in the value of assets, or 'impairment', most accountants would probably say that this should be recognized as an expense in the profit and loss account for the year, perhaps separately disclosed as an 'exceptional item'. But, generally, companies can choose whether to show assets at cost, or at current value.

There is less room for debate on unrealized gains on holding assets – at least in the eyes of a traditional, prudent accountant. The ASB talks about 'the remeasurement of assets and liabilities', which really means 'revaluation'; and this may result in a decrease or an increase in the value. The idea that it may be necessary from time to time to 'write down' assets is certainly normal accounting practice, and such write downs may be regarded as an expense. They certainly reduce the earnings per share figure. But revaluing (or 'remeasuring') assets upwards is a different matter. If assets increase in value then that is, on paper, a 'gain' to the owners (the shareholders); but it is certainly not a 'realized' profit until the asset is sold. The Companies Act permits the payment of dividends from profits which have been realized, not from unrealized profits. It is inappropriate to include unrealized gains on a profit and loss account because one of its main purposes is to provide a basis for dividend decisions.

A separate *Statement of Total Recognized Gains and Losses* is included in published financial statements. This shows gains and losses that it is not appropriate to include on the profit and loss account and which are not recognized as being part of profit for the year. The main examples of such gains or losses are on revaluing fixed assets, and because of differences in exchange rates on translating the financial statements of overseas investments into the home currency. The Statement is necessary to reconcile profit for the year with the amount by which total retained profits on the balance sheet have increased or decreased during the year. Most analysis of published accounts concentrates on the profit and loss account. But it is worth keeping an eye on the total amount of net assets. It could be that a company' s profit and loss account shows reasonable profits, but too much is being lost as a result of asset values falling, or because of currency fluctuations.

In theory it may be only the total of gains less losses that matters. But for those who want a full and detailed analysis of a company's performance, it is important that all of the various elements are separately disclosed.

There is room for disagreement on whether or not profits on sales of fixed assets are 'revenues'. They are clearly 'gains', and they are gains that have been 'realized': a sale has taken place, some payment is receivable, and the amount realized is usually very clear. They should be disclosed as separate items on a profit and loss account; and they should be included in the earnings per share figure. The reason for separate disclosure is to enable users of accounts to separate out any exceptional gains if they wish to do so, perhaps to provide a better basis for predicting future years.

The ASB's emphasis on gains and losses rather than revenues and expenses suggests a preference for an 'all inclusive' measure of profit, based on the balance sheet, rather than refining profit and loss accounts. But they are not suggesting that there should be a single figure for profit, in which 'remeasurement' gains and losses are hidden. The emphasis in recent developments is on increasingly detailed disclosures of the various items that make up the overall gain or loss during a period.

11.2 A Fully Detailed Profit and Loss Account

The usual[2] form for a profit and loss in accordance with the Companies Act 1985 is shown below.

1. Turnover
2. Cost of sales
3. Gross profit or loss
4. Distribution costs
5. Administrative expenses
6. Other operating income
7. Income from shares in group undertakings
8. Income from participating interests
9. Income from other fixed asset investment
10. Other interest receivable and similar income
11. Amounts written off investments
12. Interest payable and similar charges
13. Tax on profit or loss on ordinary activities
14. Profit or loss on ordinary activities after taxation
15. Extraordinary income
16. Extraordinary charges
17. Extraordinary profit or loss
18. Tax on extraordinary profit or loss
19. Other taxes not shown under the above items
20. Profit or loss for the financial year

----

2   An alternative format 2 is permitted but is not widely used; it provides a little more information on the face of the profit and loss account, most of which would otherwise be provided in the notes to the accounts.

A published profit and loss account for a large and complex group of companies, and the above format which they follow, can look formidable. But many of the items are already familiar, and some are so rare that they need not trouble us.

The familiar items are: 1, 2, 3, 4, 5, 10 and 12 (interest receivable and payable), 13, 14 and 20. The items that are too rare to bother with are: 15, 16, 17, 18 and 19. Other items that need to be considered in interpreting financial statements are: 6, 7, 8, 9 and 11.

Published accounts look more complicated, include additional items, and do not use the numbering shown above. But they do follow the same order, sometimes using different words, and sometimes including additional items, which companies are free to do.

Companies also disclose 'exceptional items' separately, sometimes partly as 'operating' under heading number 6, or an earlier expense heading; and sometimes as 'non-operating' before number 10, or as number 11.

There is not usually much detail about what, if anything, has been included under item number 6, and items which might seem like 'other operating income' may have been included in earlier headings, and not be separately disclosed.

The words shown above for items 7, 8, and 9 do not often appear in published accounts. But we often see such items more helpfully disclosed as being a proportion[3] of the profits or losses of associate companies and joint ventures.

Published financial statements follow the requirements of accounting standards which are usually consistent with the Companies Act 1985, but require more detailed disclosures.

11.3 Revenues

It is important to be clear about what is included in a profit and loss account as if it is a revenue; it is also important to be clear at what point an item of revenue is said to be realized.

The main item of revenue for most companies is sales or turnover. This is may be shown in varying degrees of detail where the business is involved in a number of different types of business, and in a number of different parts of the world.[4]

Companies' profit and loss accounts are also credited with various income from investments such as interest receivable, dividends receivable,

---

3   The word 'share' is usually used, but this is easily confused with the word 'share capital'.

4   Segmental reporting is explained in Chapter 9.

and a proportion of the profits from investments in associated companies and joint ventures. These are clearly 'gains', but whether or not they should be called 'revenues' is a matter which can be debated. Many of these items can, of course, be negative. A company may pay more interest than it receives; and interest payable is clearly an expense. If a company has invested in an associate company,[5] and the associate makes a loss, then the profit and loss account of the company that made the investment must include their share of that loss; the loss would look very much like an expense, but somehow the word 'loss' seems more appropriate.

Additional revenues can come from such things as rents receivable, and from patents, licences, copyrights, all of which are disclosed in varying degrees of detail in published financial statements. The main difficulties in interpreting these published figures is to realize that:

1 Not all items of revenue are separately identified and published. Modest amounts of rents receivable would not be shown separately.

2 Revenues are accounted for on an accruals basis.[6] This means that credit is taken for them as they are earned, not as and when the money for them is received.

3 Some items are credited to the profit and loss account as if they are revenues, although they may seem more like accounting adjustments than revenue.

A profit and loss account is sometimes credited with items that do not look much like revenues. Examples include discount receivable, exceptional items, reversals of provisions, and amortization of negative goodwill.

Discount Received

Companies which buy goods on credit, and pay for them reasonably promptly, often 'receive' a discount for so doing. If a company owes £200, and the discount receivable is 2.5 per cent, they pay only £195. This is recorded as an expense of £200 (typically as part of cost of sales), and 'revenue' of £5 is recorded. This is a sensible way of recording it if the intention is to measure the relationship between sales and cost of goods sold (the gross profit ratio) without it being distorted by an item that is more to do with financing decisions than to do with the cost of the goods that are being sold. In the financial accounts that businesses produce for internal purposes, discount received is added to gross profit. It is not usually shown at all in published accounts.

---

5 Or in a joint venture, as explained in Chapter 9.

6 Explained in Chapter 7.

Exceptional Items[7]

Exceptional items can be gains or losses; or a company may have both. Some have to be disclosed (under FRS 3); companies decide to disclose some others. Most companies buy fixed assets fairly frequently, and dispose of old ones. When a fixed asset is sold it is unlikely that it will be sold for exactly its book value; the actual sale proceeds usually lead to a profit or loss on disposal being recognized. Gains on sales of fixed assets are shown on the profit and loss account as exceptional items: special attention is drawn to them as if they are not normal items of revenue.

Reversal of a Provision

Exceptional items can also be reductions in provisions. A substantial provision for reorganization may no longer be required and so part or all is credited back to the profit and loss account. This is not revenue: it is a reversal of a previous over-provision for expenses. The ASB's FRS 12 has tried to put a stop to misuse of provisions: they should be created only where there is a genuine liability, not as an exercise in 'income smoothing'.

Given the traditional accounting emphasis on prudence it is not surprising that it sometimes turns out that expenses were over-provided, or assets had been written down excessively. The reversal of excessive prudence is a credit to the profit and loss account. But it looks more like an accounting adjustment than an item of revenue.

Illustration 11.1

A publishing company has 5,000 rather boring history of art books in stock. They originally cost £4 per unit to produce, and were intended to sell for £20 per unit. But after a year they were remaindered, and the company was able to realize only £2 per unit when selling them. The books were therefore written down to the net realizable value of £2 per unit.

The company added a new cover to the book which featured some erotic art and cost £1 per book. There was also a revival in interest in history of art. The books began to sell at £8 per unit.

As stocks should be shown at the lower of cost and net realizable value, the books were then written up to (£4 original cost + £1 for the cover) £5 per unit. This was a credit to the profit and loss account.

---

7 Exceptional items are discussed more fully in Chapter 8.

Companies routinely make provisions for bad debts. Experience might suggest that normally a proportion of debtors will not pay up, and the company might show a provision for bad debts of, say, 5 per cent of debtors. On the balance sheet, if the company has debtors of £100,000, the net figure, £95,000 is shown. In most years the provision is likely to increase,[8] and that increase is treated as an expense. Sometimes a company decides to reduce the provision, perhaps because of more reliable customers, better credit control procedures, or because they have been too prudent in the past. Such reductions are credited to the profit and loss account as if they are income. But there is usually no separate disclosure of modest changes in provisions for bad debts.

Substantial, or 'exceptional', changes in provisions should be separately disclosed.

Amortization of Negative Goodwill

This is a particularly strange item that is credited to the profit and loss account as if it is revenue. It seems more like a negative expense, or a negative loss. It is perhaps best understood after considering amortization of positive goodwill, as explained in the section below.

11.4 Revenue Recognition

One of the main problems with revenues is determining the date on which they should be recognized, and there is considerable variation in practice, and little official guidance. In practice it is probably easiest to say that revenues are recognized when the customer is invoiced: the act of raising the invoice introduces the transaction into the bookkeeping system. But when should the invoice be raised?

A sale may go through various stages such as those shown below, and there is the possibility of recognizing it as a sale at any of these stages.

27 February	Customer telephones with order for special purpose machine to be manufactured
1 March	Raw materials and components are ordered so that the machine can be manufactured
2 March	Written confirmation of order received from customer
10 March	Manufacture of machine is completed
11 March	Machine is despatched to customer
12 March	Customer receives the machine
13 March	Written confirmation arrives showing that customer has received the goods

8 If sales are increasing.

14 March	Invoice is sent to customer
16 April	Customer receives free after sales service for machine
18 April	Cheque received from customer in full payment
24 April	Cheque is cleared by bank

There is a case for recognizing revenue at almost any of these points in the process. It is tempting to say that the exact date does not really matter: the sale took place in March. But it would matter if the company's year end happened to be 28 February, or 10 March, or 31 March – or any of the dates between 7 February and 24 April. Is it going to count as a sale in the year just ending, or not?

In most cases it probably does not really matter at what stage the revenue is recognized, provided there is consistent practice from one year to the next. But it can be a fertile ground for creative accounting practices. Most listed companies are under pressure to increase profits year after year. If, as the year is coming to an end, it is clear that sales and profits are lower than planned, various ways may be found to boost sales in the last month of the year. Sales staff, who may be incentivized by special bonuses to increase sales just before the year end, could encourage customers to buy extra goods and increase their stocks by offering special discounts, or offering goods on a sale or return basis. Orders could be received just before the year end, and recognized as sales, only to be cancelled a week or two later.

Accounting staff may find ways of speeding up their procedures – especially if it means recognizing the sales at an earlier stage, and so increasing sales in the current year. In the above listing of stages the invoice was sent to the customer on 14 March. This could be brought forward to 11 March when the goods are despatched; or perhaps to 2 March when the written order is received; or perhaps to 27 February when the order is received by telephone. The effect of bringing forward the date in one year is to increase the sales (and profits[9]) for that year. It is even possible to bring the date forward a little each year for several years, although this could not continue indefinitely. There have been some well-publicized cases of companies bringing forward revenues and profits by changing the date on which sales are recognized.

Unfortunately there is no clear rule as to when sales should be recognized, nor any standard practice. There is little problem with most retailers: a sale is recognized when the cash is received – or when the customer signs the credit card slip.[10] There is wide variation from one type of industry to another.

---

9 Assuming the sales are profitable.

10 But the retailer may need to make provision for warranties and after-sales service. It might not be prudent to recognize 100 per cent of the sales revenue immediately.

In some industries, such as gold or diamond mining, revenues are sometimes recognized as soon as the materials are obtained. There is an immediate and ready market for the products, and it is getting the gold or diamonds out of the mine that is the most critical event. The sale easily follows. But the practice of recognizing revenues when the materials are obtained is unusual.

In some industries, for example where there are long-term building contracts, revenues are recognized during the production process. If a company has a contract for a major civil engineering project (to build a new road, or railway, or tunnel, or pipeline for example) which will take several years, there are usually established procedures to take credit for revenues and profits on a regular basis as parts of the job are completed, and probably in line with progress payments receivable. It should, of course, be done on a prudent basis; but it is generally accepted that it is more realistic to recognize the revenues in stages – and to show realized profits which can justify dividends – than to wait until the contract is finally completed.

If the business already has the goods in stock (or perhaps if it is very easy to obtain them immediately) it may be justifiable to recognize the revenue immediately that the order is received. But this is not normal practice.

It is more usual to recognize the revenue when the goods are delivered to the customer. But even here there may be some flexibility on whether it is the date of despatch, the date of delivery, or the date on which confirmation of delivery is received. Although delivery may be seen as the 'normal' event which justifies revenue recognition, there may be good reasons for not recognizing 100 per cent of the revenue. Some or all of the goods may be returned by the customers as being unsatisfactory, or not exactly what they thought they had ordered; the customer may not pay for them, or may not pay the full amount; and there may be future liabilities under warranty.

When goods are sold on a 'sale or return' basis – with the option to return the goods within, say, one month, it might be prudent not to recognize the revenue until that period has expired. But if a company's experience suggests that such returns are unusual they would probably justify recognizing the sale when the goods are delivered or first accepted by the customer.

In some types of business the 'accretion' approach to recognizing revenues is normal. Where a business has rents receivable, it is appropriate to recognize the rental income as it accrues, on a daily basis. With the production of crops, or timber, or livestock it is common practice to recognize revenues as they grow and mature. The balance sheets show stocks at valuation (costs[11] of growing crops and animals may be difficult to measure, or irrelevant), which has the effect of recognizing the revenue before anything is sold.

---

11 Such as the provision of sun and rain to make things grow.

Problems of revenue recognition also arise with the provision of services. A solicitor or an architect or an accountant, whose clients know that the charge is £x per hour, could justify recognizing the revenue as soon as some work is done. It is more usual to recognize it when an invoice is sent to the client. It might be more prudent, especially in some types of professional practice, to wait until the client has actually paid. When a professional practice is going to be sold, or when the practitioners' personal remuneration depends on revenues generated, there may be a temptation to bring forward the recognition of revenues as much as possible.

Official guidance on how and when revenues should be recognized is likely to be established in the near future. It is likely to adopt a 'critical event' approach which means that revenues should be recognized when the most critical event in the cycle has taken place. In most cases this will still be delivery, but other practices will probably be allowed to continue.

11.5 Expenses

Expenses are usually seen as being the costs incurred in earning the revenues that are recognized during that period. This is the basis of the accruals concept: costs are matched against the revenues earned.

The ASB's *Statement of Principles* seems to prefer the term 'losses', which can include all sorts of debits to the profit and loss account.

As with revenues there are the problems that:

1   Not all items of expense are separately identified and published. There is usually no separate disclosure of most expenses such as lighting and heating, postage, stationery and telephones, rates, insurance, repairs and maintenance. But, as shown below, a surprising amount of detail about expenses is available for those who bother to hunt around in the notes to the accounts and the Directors' Report.

2   Expenses are accounted for on an accruals basis.[12] This means that they are charged as they are incurred, not as and when the money for them is paid. The big differences are that:

   (a)   Purchases are not charged as an expense: it is the cost of the goods that are sold that is the expense.

   (b)   Depreciation is an expense; the amount incurred to buy fixed assets is not (yet) an expense.

3   Some items are debited to the profit and loss account as if they are expenses, although they may seem more like accounting adjustments than revenue. Examples include losses on sale of fixed assets, discount allowed, and increases in provisions.

12   Explained in Chapter 7.

The profit and loss account shows separately any debits or charges (that are, in effect, expenses) for interest payable, and for losses incurred by companies where investments have been made in businesses which are associates or joint ventures. Other kinds of investments may result in losses, but companies do not necessarily show these in the profit and loss account (treating them as expenses). With relatively modest investments (less than about 20 per cent of the shares of another company) credit is taken for dividends receivable, not for a proportion of the profits earned. If the company in which such an investment is made makes losses, there is no requirement for investors to charge a proportion of those losses in their profit and loss accounts.

Companies which own properties, shares in other companies and other forms of investment usually show them on the balance sheet at the price they originally paid for them – at least in the early years. They are also required to show the market value of those investments, or if they differ significantly from the value shown on the balance sheet. If the market value goes down, there is no requirement to show this immediately. But, if the reduction in value looks as though it is long lasting, the company will probably write down the asset. This is rather like depreciation. It reduces the amount shown for the asset on the balance sheet, and the amount of the reduction is shown as an expense, or a loss, on the balance sheet. It is usually separately disclosed as an 'exceptional item', and companies choose labels such as 'adjustment' or 'impairment' to describe it.

On the face of a published profit and loss account little detail about expenses is disclosed. There are usually just a few headings: cost of sales, distribution costs, administrative expenses and interest payable. But companies are required to disclose much more, and a little digging around in the notes to the financial statements and the Directors' Report reveals a lot of additional detail about expenses.

The following additional information about expenses should be available in notes to the accounts:

1 Segmental information, including the operating expenses of the different business segments in which the company operates.

2 Directors' remuneration, in total, and giving details of gains made from exercising share options, amounts receivable under incentive schemes, and company contributions to pension schemes.

3 Depreciation. On the face of the profit and loss account depreciation is not shown as a separate expense; it is included in cost of sales, distribution costs and administration expenses, as appropriate. Depreciation of machinery that is used to make the goods is included in cost of sales; depreciation of vehicles that are used to distribute the company's products is included in distribution costs; and depreciation of office furniture

and equipment is included in administration expenses. But there is no requirement to disclose the amount of depreciation included under each of these headings. The year's depreciation charge for each category of fixed asset (e.g. buildings, plant and machinery) is separately shown.

4 Amortization of goodwill is separately shown.

5 Where development costs have been capitalized (and treated as an intangible fixed asset) they must be amortized, and the amount of amortization is disclosed.

6 Auditors' remuneration is disclosed, showing separately the amount paid for audit work, and the amount for non-audit work.

7 Staff costs are disclosed, showing separately: wages and salaries; social security costs; and other pension costs. In addition, the average number of people employed is shown for the UK and other areas. This enables average levels of remuneration to be calculated.

11.6 Depreciation of Tangible Fixed Assets

It is tempting to think of depreciation as being the reduction in value of a fixed asset over time. The reduction may be due to the asset becoming worn out, or used up, or obsolete. But depreciation is not an attempt at valuing an asset. It is usually seen as being an allocation of the cost of the fixed asset, so that it is treated as an expense over a number of years.

FRS 12 defines depreciation as being the measure of the economic benefits of tangible fixed assets that have been consumed during the period. It is usually based on the original cost of the asset, as shown in Illustration 11.2. But if the asset is revalued, then depreciation is based on the revalued amount. It may seem strange that an asset can be revalued upwards, but it is still depreciated: there seem to be two contradictory processes going on at the same time.

Fixed assets normally have a limited life, and so they must be written off over the length of that life. Some assets such as freehold land are assumed to last forever, and so depreciation is not required. It is sometimes argued that as buildings often increase in value, it seems pointless to depreciate them. If the buildings are held as investments, and not for use, this argument is accepted: special accounting rules apply to investment properties.[13] If the buildings are used as fixed assets, then the principle that they have a limited life must apply. Companies can argue that the life of a building may

---

13   SSAP 19 Accounting for investment properties.

be 100 years or more, and that as they keep it in good condition, then the depreciation is negligible. They therefore choose not to make a charge for depreciation because the amount involved is so small. But, if they choose not to charge depreciation, they are required to carry out an annual impairment review. For companies which own a lot of properties (such as retailers with shops; or breweries with pubs) this is a small price to pay if the alternative is to have to reduce profits with a substantial depreciation charge.

In Illustration 11.2 'straight line' was used: the company charged the same amount of depreciation each year. FRS 12 requires that the depreciation method used should reflect as fairly as possible the pattern in which the asset's economic benefits are consumed by the entity. If a fixed asset is 'used up' more in its early years than its later years, a depreciation method can be chosen which reflects this. The 'reducing balance'[14] method is widely used; its calculation is shown in Illustration 11.3.

Illustration 11.2

The Adle Company buys a new machine for £256,000 and intends to use it for 5 years, after which it is expected to have a trade-in value of £36,000.

The company decides to use straight line depreciation. The amount of depreciation charged as an expense each year for 5 years is therefore £44,000.

Illustration 11.3

The Adle Company buys a new machine for £256,000 and decides to use the reducing balance method of depreciation, charging 25 per cent per annum. The amount of depreciation charged as an expense each year is as follows:

	Depreciation charge for year	Remaining balance
Cost of machine £256,000		
Year 1	£64,000	£192,000
Year 2	£48,000	£144,000
Year 3	£36,000	£108,000
Year 4	£27,000	£ 81,000
Year 5	£20,250	£ 60,750

14   Or 'diminishing balance'.

As can be seen from Illustration 11.3 the reducing balance method charges much more for depreciation in the early years; much less in the later years; and it would take almost forever to get down to zero.

Companies have a wide measure of freedom in determining what method of depreciation to use. All sorts of weird and wonderful methods of depreciation can be devised but, in practice, most companies use the straight line or the diminishing balance methods.

There is inevitably an element of subjectivity in deciding the period over which a fixed asset is to be depreciated, the method of depreciation, and what value, if any, the asset will have when it comes to the end of its economic life. Whatever assumptions are originally made when the asset is first acquired, what actually happens is likely to be different: the asset may have a shorter or longer life; depreciation may be revised; the asset may be revalued; and when it is finally disposed of the sale proceeds are usually different from the book value. These changes to the original assumptions may be regarded as 'exceptional items', but there is nothing exceptional about normal depreciation, and it should always be regarded as an expense and charged as such in the calculation of earnings per share.

11.7 Amortization of Goodwill

Most large, listed companies are really groups of companies with a number of subsidiaries. When a subsidiary company is first acquired it is usually the case that the price paid to acquire the business is higher than the balance sheet value of the net assets acquired. If the balance sheet of a successful company shows a net asset value of £2 million, the owners of the company are unlikely to be willing to sell it for as little as £2 million. They will expect an extra payment for the goodwill of the company. Perhaps the agreed price will be £3 million, of which £1 million is paid for goodwill. Goodwill is an intangible fixed asset, and, like other fixed assets, it should be amortized[15] over its useful economic life. Perhaps the goodwill is expected to last for ten years, and £100,000 a year is charged for amortization. There should be nothing exceptional about normal amortization, and it should always be regarded as an expense and charged as such in the calculation of earnings per share.

But many companies are as unhappy about charging amortization as they are about depreciating buildings. They can argue that goodwill will last indefinitely – because they will keep spending to maintain it – and so no amortization is required. This is acceptable under FRS 10, provided there is an annual impairment review.

---

15 Amortization is the same as depreciation. The word is used for writing off intangible assets.

Some companies also choose to show two versions of their earnings per share: one after charging amortization of goodwill, and one before charging it. There can be circumstances where there are abnormal write offs of goodwill, and such 'impairment' may be exceptional. But it is becoming commonplace to ignore routine write offs of goodwill, and to use earnings per share figures which ignore it.

Sometimes negative goodwill arises. A company might buy a business which is not doing very well. They might manage to buy assets with a book value[16] of £2 million, and pay only £1.5 million for them. There is then negative goodwill of £500,000. This is shown on the balance sheet as a negative asset, and it must be amortized over the periods which benefit from it. But the amortization is negative: it is credited to the profit and loss account – as if it is revenue. But it is more like a negative expense.

11.8 Capital Expenditure, Revenue Expenditure, Deferred Expenditure

This chapter is concerned with expenses that are charged in the profit and loss account in calculating profit for the year. Capital expenditure – buying or adding to fixed assets – is not an expense in calculating profit. It is the annual depreciation that is an expense.

There are sometimes problems in drawing an exact line between capital expenditure and expenses which are to be charged in the current year. Problem areas include repairs to buildings that are more like improvements; or improvements to buildings that also include an element of repairs. There is no doubt that creating a new fixed asset is capital expenditure, even if the company creates their own new fixed assets. But whether or not a company should 'capitalize' any interest on money borrowed to construct the new asset is more controversial.

Sometimes expenditure incurred in one year is 'deferred' and charged as an expense in future years. There are rules about when development expenditure can be deferred, or capitalized; at present these are set out in SSAP 13. Sometimes other expenditure may be deferred. The cost of advertising which is expected to benefit future periods may be deferred, even if this does not seem very prudent. There can be conflicts between the accounting concepts of prudence (write it off immediately) and accruals (match it against the revenues it is expected to generate). In any such conflicts today, the ASB would probably decide on the basis of whether or not an asset exists: if, at the balance sheet date, the expenditure represents an asset,

---

16 Which should also be their 'fair value': assets should be revalued to 'fair value' on acquisition.

then it should be carried forward to future periods. If there is no asset, it should be written off.

The prudent accountant might argue that this approach leaves a door wide open: many expenses (such as advertising, publicity, staff recruitment, training, the provision of medical, counselling and welfare services to staff, investor relations departments) add to the goodwill of a company. There could be a case for deferring all such expenditure which would significantly boost most companies' profits. But the ASB is clear. When a company buys goodwill, it must be treated as an asset. But internally generated goodwill must not be treated as an asset.[17]

11.9 Share Options

Some companies have chosen to give part or all of their employees' remuneration in the form of options to buy shares rather than in cash. This became particularly common in the 'dot com' boom, where companies were not generating much cash, and so wanted to minimize the payments that they made. Their share prices were going up and up, and employees found the idea of being paid in share options was very attractive. When the company's shares were trading at £2 each, they might be given the option to buy 100,000 shares at £2.50 each. That seemed like giving them nothing; and no expense was recorded. But when the company's share price increased to, say, £4.50 each, the employee could make £200,000 (100,000 × [£4.50 − £2.50]), apparently at no cost to the company.

But such an arrangement does have a cost to the original shareholders: suddenly they own a smaller proportion of the company. In 2003 Microsoft set the trend by treating the issue of stock options as an expense. The accounting standards setters are attempting to find a way of recording such an 'expense' that will command general acceptance.

11.10 Interpreting Revenues and Expenses

As the amount of information disclosed about revenues and expenses has steadily increased it can be difficult to select and interpret the information that is provided. The use of appropriate ratios can help, especially if information is

---

17 There is a slight contradiction here. A company can argue that goodwill need not be depreciated because it will last indefinitely. But if goodwill does last indefinitely it is because it is constantly being maintained: new employees replace the ones that leave; new advertising campaigns attract new customers as old ones fade away; and new, improved products wash whiter than ever. In other words, internally generated goodwill gradually replaces the goodwill that has been purchased – and internally generated goodwill is accepted as an asset.

provided over a number of years, as is shown in Illustration 11.4 with Ottakar's.

In more complex companies it is more difficult to pick one's way through a detailed published profit and loss account, as is shown in Illustration 11.7 with GUS.

Ottakar's

When interpreting profit and loss accounts it is useful to compare one year with another; and better still, if trends can be monitored over a number of years. Many companies provide 5- or 10-year summaries of their results, and they are free to present such summaries as they wish. In Illustration 11.4, Ottakar's (the bookshops) provides a summarized profit and loss account, including all of the main items, with just one balance sheet figure. The only ratio provided is for earnings per share. Some companies choose to provide a variety of balance sheet figures, profit and loss account figures, and ratios; other companies provide no such summaries at all.

Illustration 11.4					
Ottakar's					
Five Year Summary					
	1999 £000 (1)	2000 £000 (1)	2001 £000	2002 £000	2003 £000
Turnover	57,316	72,643	86,287	98,049	114,839
Gross profit	22,343	28,092	33,532	38,897	47,729
Operating profit	3,312	1,650	3,516	4,616	5,625
(Loss)/profit on sale of fixed assets	–	(336)	4	(53)	–
Net interest	(257)	(560)	(724)	(560)	(525)
Profit before tax	3,055	754	2,796	4,003	5,100
Tax	(775)	(319)	(925)	(1,417)	(1,822)
Profit after tax	2,280	435	1,871	2,586	3,278
Dividends	(494)	(302)	(503)	(640)	(800)
Retained profit	1,786	133	1,368	1,946	2,478
Basic earnings per share (pence)	12.36	2.17	9.3	12.88	16.41
Diluted earnings per share (pence)	11.69	2.15	9.28	12.70	16.18
Net asset value	12,304	12,540	13,279	15,268	17,796

(1) The results for 1999 and 2000 have not been restated to reflect the adoption of FRS 19 'Deferred Tax' and UITF 24 'Accounting for Start Up Costs'. Turnover for 1999 and 2000 excludes concession income.

Examination of Ottakar's results shows steadily increasing turnover and increasing gross profits in each of the five years. There was a set back in the year 2000, but otherwise the profit and loss account figures generally show increases each year, with steadily increasing dividends and earnings per share. This looks quite good, but more sophisticated analysis is possible. We could measure the rate of increase in each item in the profit and loss account, and we would see that there is 'double digit' growth in sales each year; but profits do not seem to have kept up, and expenses may have increased more quickly. A useful analysis is to express each item on the profit and loss account as a percentage of sales, and this is done in Illustration 11.5.

The published summary does not provide the figures for operating expenses, but these must be the difference between gross profit and operating profit.

Dividends have increased substantially each year since 2000, and we can see the extent to which such dividends are justified by profits; this is done by calculating how many times dividends are covered by profits after tax.

We can also assess the profitability of the company by expressing profit after tax as a percentage of net asset value.

Illustration 11.5 provides useful additional analysis, but is perhaps too full to show the picture very clearly.

It is always the case that information has to be edited: it is never possible to show everything. And all editing is 'partial', both in the sense that it is incomplete, and that someone has decided what to include, and what to exclude. The edited version of Ottakar's results shown in Illustration 11.6 can be defended as being easier to understand. It has also been edited to show the profit and loss figures as a percentage of sales; to show the dividends times cover, and the return on capital employed. Profits and losses on sales of assets have been excluded, as have retained profits for the year.

A clearer picture now emerges. In most respects 1999 was the best year, and 2000 was the worst. The recovery since 2000 has been remarkable with a steady increase[18] in operating profit, profit before tax, profit after tax, and in dividend cover. This has been achieved in spite of an increasing tax burden. It has been helped by a reduction in the burden of interest payable. But the picture with operating expenses is mixed: they hover around 33–37 per cent of sales, and there is no clear pattern of reduction. The improvement in profits has been due mainly to a steady increase in the gross profit ratio of nearly 3 percentage points (from 38.67 per cent to 41.56 per cent). This may be due to increasing 'buying power' as the company gets larger and is able to negotiate more favourable prices with suppliers.

---

18 Measured as a percentage of turnover; but as turnover has also steadily increased, so have the absolute figures.

Illustration 11.5

Ottakar's

	1999	%	2000	%	2001	%	2002	%	2003	%
Turnover	57,317	100	72,643	100	86,287	100	98,049	100	114,839	100
Gross profit	22,343	38.98	28,092	38.67	33,532	38.86	38,987	39.76	47,729	41.56
Operating expenses		33.20		36.40		34.79		35.05		36.66
Operating profit	3,312	5.78	1,650	2.27	3,516	4.07	4,616	4.71	5,626	4.90
(Loss)/profit on sale of fixed assets	–		(336)		4		(53)		–	
Net interest	(257)	0.448	(560)	0.771	(724)	0.839	(560)	0.571	(525)	0.457
Profit before tax	3,055	5.33	754	1.04	2,796	3.24	4,003	4.08	5,100	4.44
Tax	(775)	1.35	(319)	0.44	(925)	1.07	(1,417)	1.45	(1,822)	1.59
Profits after tax	2,280	3.98	435	0.60	1,871	2.17	2,586	2.64	3,278	2.85
Dividends	(494)		(302)		(503)		(640)		(800)	
Dividend cover	4.6 times		1.4 times		3.7 times		4.0 times		4.1 times	
Retained profit	1,786		133		1,368		1,946		2,478	
Basic earnings per share (pence)	12.36		2.17		9.3		12.88		16.41	
Net asset value	12,304		12,540		13,279		15,268		17,796	
Profit after tax/Net asset value	18.5%		3.47%		14.1%		16.9%		18.4%	

Illustration 11.6

Ottakar's

	1999	2000	2001	2002	2003
Turnover	100%	100%	100%	100%	100
Gross profit	38.98	38.67	38.86	39.76	41.56
Operating expenses	33.20	36.40	34.79	35.05	36.66
Operating profit	5.78	2.27	4.07	4.71	4.90
Net interest	0.448	0.771	0.839	0.571	0.457
Profit before tax	5.33	1.04	3.24	4.08	4.44
Tax	1.35	0.44	1.07	1.45	1.59
Profits after tax	3.98	0.60	2.17	2.64	2.85
Dividend cover	4.6 times	1.4 times	3.7 times	4.0 times	4.1 times
Basic earnings per share (pence)	12.36	2.17	9.3	12.88	16.41
Profit after tax/Net asset value	18.5%	3.47%	14.1%	16.9%	18.4%

Some retailers succeed in achieving growth at the expense of margins. Ottakar's has achieved growth, and improved margins. Still further improvement in profits could be achieved by controlling operating expenses so that they are nearer to 34 per cent of sales than the current level of nearly 37 per cent.

GUS

Many different questions could be asked about the performance of GUS, but even a simple question is difficult to answer. Did GUS make more profit in 2003 than in 2002?

From the point of view of the ordinary shareholders of GUS, the 'Profit for the year', from which dividends are payable, fell from £257 million to £251 million, and this was reflected in the basic earnings per share figure falling from 25.7 pence to 25.1 pence.

But the group profit and loss account (Illustration 11.7) also shows a different earnings per share figure which increased from 41.7 pence to 47.8 pence. If profit is taken before amortization of goodwill and exceptional items, then profits have increased.

It seems that the group made more profits in 2003 than in 2002, but the amount of that profit which is attributable to their own shareholders, has fallen. Their 'Profit on ordinary activities after taxation', increased from

Illustration 11.7

**Group profit and loss account
for the year ended 31 March 2003**

	Notes	2003 Before Exceptional Items £m	2003 Exceptional Items (Note 5) £m	2003 Total £m	2002 £m
Turnover		7,146	–	7,146	6,457
Continuing operations		5,473	–	5,473	4,678
Discontinued operations		1,673	–	1,673	1,779
Cost of sales	4	(4,130)	–	(4,130)	(3,869)
Gross profit		3,016	–	3,016	2,588
Net operating expenses before goodwill charge		(2,386)	(22)	(2,408)	(2,064)
Goodwill charge		(143)	(19)	(162)	(127)
Net operating expenses	4	(2,529)	(41)	(2,570)	(2,191)
Operating profit		487	(41)	446	397
Continuing operations		452	(22)	430	381
Discontinued operations		35	(19)	16	16
Share of operating profit of BL Universal PLC (joint venture)		26	–	26	25
Share of operating profit of associated undertakings		44	–	44	33
Loss on sale of fixed asset investments in continuing operations		–	–	–	(2)
Trading profit		557	(41)	516	453
Profit on Initial Public Offering of Burberry – continuing operations		–	161	161	–
Provision for loss on disposal of Home Shopping and Reality businesses – discontinued operations		–	(210)	(210)	–
Loss on sale of other businesses – continuing operations		–	–	–	(6)
Profit on ordinary activities before interest		557	(90)	467	447
Net interest	6			(58)	(67)
Profit on ordinary activities before taxation	7			409	380
Tax on profit on ordinary activities	8			(141)	(122)
Profit on ordinary activities after taxation	9			268	258
Equity minority interests				(17)	(1)
Profit for the year				251	257
Dividends	10			(232)	(217)
Retained profit for the year				19	40
Earnings per share	11				
– Basic				25.1p	25.7p
– Diluted				25.0p	25.5p
Earnings per share before amortisation of goodwill and exceptional items	11				
– Basic				47.8p	41.7p
– Diluted				47.5p	41.4p

£258 million to £268 million. But the amount of this attributable to 'Equity minority interests'[19] increased from £1 million to £17 million. This means that the amount left for GUS shareholders fell from £257 million to £251 million. The group made more profit, but it was distributed differently.[20]

But if we are to measure profits on a basis that will be comparable with next year, a more optimistic picture can emerge. If we take 'Profit on ordinary activities before interest', the figure has increased from £447 million to £467 million, but that was not much help to GUS shareholders. If, however, we exclude 'Exceptional items' – which will presumably not recur in 2004 – the 'Profit on ordinary activities before interest' has increased much more substantially: from £447 million to £557 million. It looks as though shareholders can expect a significant increase in 2004.

But how 'exceptional' are the 'exceptional items'? The profit on the Initial Public Offering of Burberry is presumably a one-off. The company still has substantial goodwill, and the amortization in the profit and loss account is shown in two ways: most is treated as a normal charge (£143 million); only £19 million is deemed to be exceptional. But we need to be wary of the earnings per share figure: one charges the whole of the goodwill write off; the other charges none.

With a large group of companies and shops it may be seen as 'normal' that, each year, the weaker parts are disposed of, and/or 'exceptional' costs are incurred to deal with them. But the GUS provision for losses on discontinuing operations (£210 million) does seem exceptionally large, and unlikely to be repeated next year. There do not appear to be other parts of the business which are substantially underperforming, but we do not know what will be disclosed next year, and what new 'exceptional items' there may be.

Although we may be reasonably confident that 'Profit for the year' will increase in 2004, it is clear that £35 million of operating profit that was made in 2003 will not be made in 2004; £35 million was the operating profit of operations that have been discontinued.

If we are to predict the profit for 2004 we might start with the operating profit from continuing operations which increased from £397 million in 2002 to £446 million in 2003. A reasonable guess for 2004 might be £500 million. To this we could add something for the joint ventures and associates which seem to be increasing nicely – say, £80 million; this would make a total 'Profit on ordinary activities before interest' of £580 million. A detailed calculation of the likely cost of interest is possible; borrowings have increased substantially, and rates of interest seem more likely to increase

19 Outside shareholders in subsidiary companies of the group.

20 Because there were more outside shareholdings.

than decrease. The cost of interest could easily increase from £58 million in 2003 to £120 million in 2004. This would leave profit before tax of £460 million. Taxation, and the amount attributable to equity minority interests could amount to about £180 million. This would leave profit for the financial year of £280 million. That would be an increase of about 11 per cent on the figure (£251 million) for 2003.

This is, of course, rather simplistic and subjective. Professional investment analysts would make use of a wider range of information and produce more sophisticated forecasts.

Summary

Revenues and expenses may be seen as being all of the items which are credited and debited to the profit and loss account and which, in turn, affect the earnings per share figure. Too much emphasis has been given to finding principles and rules for determining a single, correct figure which is expected to summarize a company's performance. The detailed items which make up revenues and expenses, and the assumptions which underlie them are more important. Those who make use of profit and loss accounts want to be able to find the exact information that they need, not a summary figure based on someone else's assumptions, and the trend towards requiring increasingly detailed disclosures is likely to continue, at least for large, listed companies.

Review of Key Points

- A profit and loss account includes revenues and expenses which are recognized on an accruals basis

- Revenues arise from a number of different sources

- Expenses appear in summary form on a profit and loss account, but more detail is available in the notes

- Gains and losses are more widely defined than revenues and expenses

- Profit and loss accounts include some accounting adjustments that do not look much like revenues and expenses

- Expenses include some debits to the profit and loss account which may seem more like accounting adjustments

Self-testing Questions

1 Explain how 'increases in ownership interest' differ from revenues.

2 Explain how 'decreases in ownership interest' differ from expenses.

3 How does the accruals concept affect what is recognized as expenses?

4 What are the main categories of expense shown on the face of a profit and loss account?

5 What are 'exceptional items'?

6 How could companies avoid charging depreciation on land and buildings, and amortization on goodwill?

Assessment Questions

1 Give examples of gains that do not seem like revenues.

2 Give examples of losses that do not seem like expenses.

3 Why is depreciation of fixed assets not normally disclosed as a separate expense in the profit and loss account?

4 What is the importance of 'exceptional items'?

Group Activities and Discussion Questions

1 Depreciation of fixed assets reduces earnings per share; appreciation does not increase earnings per share. How is this practice justified?

2 What additional detail about expenses would you like to see published in company financial statements?

3 Revenue recognition should not be a problem. A sale should be recognized when the goods or services have been delivered or provided to the customer, and when a legal contract for the sale exists. Discuss these statements, and explain why revenue recognition is a problem area in accountancy.

4 Definition and measurement of revenues and expenses is no more reliable than the definition and measurement of assets and liabilities. Discuss.

5 In the light of question 4, is it therefore essential that profit is measured in two different ways (balance sheet and profit and loss account) and that the two are made to agree?

6 What was the 'Profit for the year' of GUS for the year ended 31 March 2004? How does that compare with the forecast of £280 million made in this chapter? What are the main reasons for the difference? Is the amount that the company has borrowed,[21] and the cost of interest a lot lower than predicted? Have sales and operating profits increased more than predicted? What exceptional items are there?

Financial Accounting in context

Discuss and comment on the following item taken from the press:

Telecoms – activation fees

accountancymagazine.com

September 2003

A telecoms entity charges its customers a one-time activation fee to enable them to get a number and access to the telephone line. How should the activation fees be accounted for in the financial statements?

Revenue, states that if the activation fee entitles the customers to services that will be provided during a membership period, it is recognised on a basis that reflects the timing, nature and value of the benefits provided.

By analogy, the entity provides its customers with the access to the telephone line in exchange for the activation fee. The entity continues to incur certain expenditure in order to support the line. The activation fees should be recognised over the length of the customer contract. If this is not specified, the expected life of the relationship should be estimated.

---

21 Including finance leases.

References and Further Reading

Accounting Standards Board (1999) *Statement of Principles for Financial Reporting*.

Accounting Standards Board (1992) FRS 3 Reporting Financial Performance.

Lewis, R. and D. Pendrill (2004) *Advanced Financial Accounting*, 7th edn, Pearson Education.

12

Sources of Finance

Learning objectives

After studying this chapter you should be able to:

◆ Describe the main sources of finance used by companies

◆ Appreciate the differences between the various sources, and evaluate the appropriateness of each in different circumstances

◆ Understand the advantages and disadvantages of high gearing

◆ Evaluate different dividend policies

◆ Understand how published accounts indicate companies' financing needs and policies

Introduction

The main sources of finance for a business are (a) the capital subscribed by the owners of the business, which could be a few, or thousands of shareholders; (b) borrowings, which may be short term, such as overdrafts; or long term, such as debentures; and (c) retained profits: most companies 'plough back' part of their profits to finance expansion rather than paying all profits out as dividends. This chapter considers the balance between these different sources, and how they affect the company. It therefore considers gearing and dividend policy. It also considers a number of other approaches to financing a business.

Starting a Business

If you are thinking of starting a business there are two main sources of finance:

1 Your own money or 'capital'. If you do not have enough of your own money to finance the business you might decide to go into partnership with a number of individuals; each is expected to put in some money. Or you might decide to set up a company with a number of shareholders, each of whom invests some money as 'share capital'.

2 Borrowing. If the owners of businesses do not have enough money to pay for everything themselves they will probably borrow some money. Partners and shareholders are all part owners of the business. The business may borrow short term or long term, from a bank, friends, relatives, or anyone who is willing.

If the business is successful, and profitable, it will generate profits and cash flows which provide the third main source of finance for businesses:

3 Retained profits. As shown in Chapter 7 profits do generate cash flows. Some of the profits may be paid out to the owners of the business (as drawings; or as dividends if it is a company). As the business generates profit and cash, so they are used from day to day to finance stocks, debtors, and whatever else the business may need.

   Retained profits are shown under a heading such as 'Reserves' on the balance sheet.

The same main sources of finance apply to all businesses, large or small. They are considered below in Section 12.1, finance from the owners of the business; 12.2, from borrowing; and 12.3, from retained profits. But there are other ingenious ways of financing a business – or of avoiding the need to finance a business. You may decide, for example, to lease premises or other assets rather than having to find the money to buy them. Each of the

Illustration 12.1

The three main sources of finance are shown in the following simplified company balance sheet:

		£
Fixed assets		
Machinery and furniture		2,600
Current assets		
Stocks, debtors and cash	1,200	
Current liabilities		
Creditors	(800)	400
		3,000
Long-term liabilities		
Debentures		(1,000)
		2,000
Financed by		
Share capital		1,000
Retained profits		1,000
		2,000

In this instance the three long-term sources of finance are each £1,000, making a total of £3,000 long-term funding. With this £3,000, the company has managed to finance assets of (2,600 + 1,200=) £3,800. They have been able to do this because they have short-term liabilities of £800. Perhaps their stocks of goods have been financed by the company's creditors.

three main sources of finance is considered in turn in the following sections. A fourth section examines 'Other' ways of financing a business.

12.1 Share Capital

Share capital is perhaps the most important source of finance for companies, and it is mostly 'ordinary' share capital. There are other types of shares, including a variety of preference shares.

Ordinary Shares

If you start your own company you will probably own most of the shares yourself. If you make profits, you can pay yourself dividends out of those profits. But there is no requirement to pay a dividend if you do not want to. It is the same with a very large company: there is no requirement to pay dividends on ordinary shares. From time to time, especially when the company is doing badly, even very large companies decide to pay no dividend.

In 2003 British Energy, British Airways, Marconi, and a number of telecommunications companies did not pay dividends. Many companies do not pay dividends in their early years when they are still developing their products and services, even if they are profitable.

Ordinary share capital appears to be an attractive source of finance for companies: if there is no requirement to pay a dividend, it appears to be a cost-free source of finance. But the shareholders are the people who own the company, and ultimately it is their decision how much dividend is paid. An odd individual may be happy with no dividends. But most share-holders, particularly institutional investors who need a regular flow of income from their shares (to pay pensions for example), expect regular dividends. They probably expect their dividends to increase each year, and company directors are under pressure to increase profits each year so that they can afford to pay increasing dividends.

It is important for companies not to disappoint shareholders. If share-holders are not happy with the performance of their directors, sooner or later the directors are likely to find themselves out of office.[1] Most directors want to keep their jobs – especially if they are well paid and have lots of additional benefits.[2] It is difficult to vote directors out of office. But if their performance (particularly in profits and dividends) disappoints share-holders, then the shares become less popular. As demand for the shares falls, so the share price falls; and it can keep falling until it is so low that another company comes along and makes a takeover bid. If one bunch of directors is not doing well enough, they may be pushed out by another bunch who (think that they) can do better.

Companies need to earn enough profits to keep the shareholders happy, and to keep the share price buoyant. Ordinary share capital does therefore have a cost. It cannot really be calculated as precisely as many theoreticians pretend. But it is worth looking at the profit and dividend record of the company, and of other companies, to get some indication of what share-holders expect. If they can get a return of 5 per cent per annum in a risk free investment, they expect more than that if they are taking the risk of investing in shares. They may be content with modest dividends in the short term; but they expect dividends and profits to increase each year; and they expect the value of their shares to increase as time goes by. Ordinary share capital should not therefore be regarded as being cheap, or cost free. Satisfying expectations can be expensive. Many people who start their own

---

1   In many small companies there may be only two or three shareholders (e.g. a husband and wife, or a mother and daughter) who are also the directors. In large companies that are listed on a stock market there are likely to be many thousands of shareholders, and only a handful of directors.

2   Such as bonuses, share options, an expense account, a Mercedes: 'Mercs and Perks'.

businesses know that they expect a high return on their capital. Failure to satisfy expectations can be particularly costly if it results in a low share price and an unwelcome takeover bid.

Most share capital consists of ordinary shares. They may be called £1 shares, or 20 pence shares or 5 pence shares, or any amount that the company chooses. But these 'par' or 'nominal' values of shares are of little importance. Investors are much more interested in the market value of the shares, which should be much higher than the nominal value – unless the company is doing badly.

Even if a company has shares with a nominal value of £1, that does not mean that they were originally issued at £1, or that their market price was ever £1. When a company is first incorporated the proprietors are likely to issue themselves with a number of shares in exchange for whatever assets the business may have. The company may start with two shareholders, each being given 1,000 £1 shares. If the company is successful and expands, and needs more capital, new shareholders may be invited to invest in the company. The company is then likely to be worth much more than £1 per share, and any new shareholders will be expected to pay a premium. They may be invited to buy £1 shares for £2.50 each.

Share Premium

Most shares are issued at a 'premium'. This means that £1 shares might be issued for, say, £2.50. In analysing a company's balance sheet 'share premium' is, in effect, just like share capital. The share premium is the amount over and above the nominal value of the shares which investors paid for those shares. In the above example the investors paid £2.50 per share; £1.00 was share capital and £1.50 was share premium.

When a company is first established, shares may be issued in exchange for assets other than cash (see Illustration 12.2). The same can happen with a long established company.

Illustration 12.2

Big Company agrees to pay £2,500,000 to take over Little Company. Big Company's shares are highly regarded by investors and their market value is £2.50. The £2,500,000 is paid not in cash, but by the issue of one million £1 shares.

The effect of this transaction is that the Big Company's balance sheet will show £1,000,000 of additional share capital, and £1,500,000 of share premium. The total, £2,500,000, was issued in exchange for assets (the Little Company).

Shares may be issued in exchange for cash or any assets.

A company may grow and develop in three stages. It might start as a private limited company, with perhaps just two shareholders, typically two family members. Each might put £1,000 into the company and have 1,000 £1 shares. After a number of years of successful trading the company might want to finance significant expansion by issuing more shares. They could convert to a public limited company, and they might choose to issue shares to a wider group of people. The original shares in the company might then be worth a lot more money, and the original shareholders (the owners of the company) would not want new investors to be able to buy a fresh issue of shares at the bargain price of £1 each. If they wanted to raise an additional £100,000, they might choose to issue 40,000 £1 shares, but to issue them at a premium of £1.50. They would then raise £100,000 cash, which would appear on the balance sheet as £40,000 additional share capital, and £60,000 share premium.

A third stage of development would be when a public limited company obtains a listing on the Stock Exchange. This would usually be after further successful trading for a number of years. The new issue of shares would probably be at a price very much higher than the par value of the shares.

Growing companies might not seek a full listing on the stock exchange to begin with. They may first invite a financial institution or venture capitalist to buy some shares. Companies such as 3i invest in growing companies that are not yet large enough for a stock market listing. The formalities, administrative burden and costs of a full stock market listing may be too much for companies of modest size and they are likely to seek a listing on the Alternative Investment Market (AIM). AIM is regulated by the London Stock Exchange (LSE) but has less demanding rules, and a listing is less costly, than being on the LSE's Official List.

Companies often increase their share capital a little each year, especially when there is some sort of incentive scheme for directors and other staff which provides them with shares. But any significant increase in funding through the issue of shares is a major event for a company, and does not happen very often. Similarly, a company may, from time to time, buy back some of its own shares and so reduce share capital.[3] For most companies this would not happen very often. Companies do not keep a supply of shares for investors to buy and sell: investors buy and sell shares from each other, usually via a Stock Exchange. Investors cannot go to Marks and Spencer and buy a few shares along with their new underwear and microwave dinner! They have to go via some sort of stockbroker, and there

3 The success of companies is often judged on their ability to increase their earnings per share figure, year after year. If a company reduces the number of shares that it has, the earnings per share figure will increase, even if there is no increase in total earnings.

are lots of easy and flexible ways of buying and selling shares via a range of banks and other financial institutions, and on the internet.

Rights Issue

When a company wants to raise substantial additional funds by issuing shares they often make a *rights issue* to existing shareholders. This usually means that they offer new shares at a price lower than the current market price (see Illustration 12.3).

A *rights issue* is the normal way in which established companies raise additional funds and it is intended to be attractive to existing shareholders. If the current market price of a company's shares is £2.50, the right to buy more shares at £1.50 each sounds attractive. After the rights issue the total value of the company[4] will, in theory, be worth the amount it was worth before the rights issue, plus the amount of money raised from the rights issue. In practice, if investors believe that the additional funds will be invested sufficiently profitably, the total value of the company will increase by more than the amount of cash raised. If investors believe that the additional funds will not be invested profitably enough, the total value of the company will not increase by as much as the amount of cash raised. Only time will tell.

Illustration 12.3

The Right Company has one million ordinary shares with a nominal value of 50 pence each, and a market value of £2.00 each. The company decides to make a rights issue, offering existing shareholders one share for every five that they already hold, at a price of £1.50 per share.

Shareholders might choose to exercise their rights (by buying the additional shares), or to sell them.

After the rights issue the theoretical value of the company will be:

Existing one million shares at £2.00 each	£2,000,000
Cash raised from rights issue	
200,000 at £1.50	300,000
	£2,300,000
Number of shares after issue	1,200,000
Theoretical share price after rights issue	

$$\frac{£2,300,000}{1,200,000} \quad £1.92$$

---

4 Its 'market capitalization'.

If shareholders take up all the rights to which they are entitled, they will continue to own the same proportion of the company. Shareholders may, instead, choose to sell their rights.

The right to buy shares cheaply may look attractive, but the record of rights issues is mixed. Sometimes it seems that companies make rights issues because they are a bit desperate to get hold of more money to finance activities that do not earn their keep. Sometimes they provide a good investment opportunity. In a recent article in the *Daily Telegraph*[5] Alison Steed examined the rights issue proposed by United Utilities in 2003. At the time of writing it is too soon to know how this will fare, but she provided evidence on a number of other recent rights issues, as shown in Illustration 12.4.

The results are rather mixed; some modest gains, some large losses. We should be careful of generalizing from a sample taken at a time when some companies were doing badly, as was the stock market generally.

Bonus Issue

A bonus issue (or a scrip issue) is quite different: it raises no additional funds – and so should not really be included in a chapter on sources of finance!

Many shareholders seem to like receiving a bonus issue, although they really receive nothing. Most people would probably rather have two pieces of cake than one. But if the second piece of cake is created just by cutting

Illustration 12.4

Company	Rights Price	Deal	Theoretical ex-rights price	Price this week	Gain/Loss
L&G	60p	13 per 50	89.8p	98.7p	+8.9p
BT	300p	3 per 10	458p	198p	−260p
Kingfisher	155p	1 per 1	223p	281p	+58p
Imperial Tobacco	480p	2 per 5	959p	985p	+26p
Pearson	1,000p	3 per 11	1,712p	586p	−1,126p
ICI	180p	7 per 11	267p	160p	−107p
easyJet	265p	4 per 11	389p	235p	−154p

Source: Barclays Private Clients.

5   Saturday 2 August 2003, p. B5.

the original piece of cake in half, there is no gain. In effect that is what a bonus issue does. A one-for-one bonus issue means that everyone has twice as many shares, but nothing has changed; each still owns the same proportion of the same total.

In practice a bonus issue is more likely to be one new share for every three, or four, or five shares already held. Shareholders may think that they will still receive the same amount of dividend per share, and so they will be better off. Bonus issues are often associated with good performance, and optimism, which could lead to an increase in demand for the shares, and so an increase in share price and in the total value of the company. It is often said that share prices higher than about £8 or £10 become less 'marketable': shareholders would rather buy 5 shares at £2 each than one share for £10. In 2003 Bristol Water made such a share split, like a bonus issue, so that the shares started to trade at around £2.70 each rather than around £11 each. But companies like AstraZeneca continue happily with shares trading at around £25. On the whole most attempts to justify bonus issues need to be taken with a pinch of salt, and awareness that there is a lot of conventional 'wisdom' around.

There is no *requirement* for companies to pay dividends on ordinary shares, and companies may therefore see them as being a low cost and low risk source of finance. But ordinary shareholders bear most of the risk of companies, and have high expectations; and companies have to perform well to meet those expectations and to maintain and increase their share price, and to survive.

Preference Shares

Preference shareholders take less risk, and can expect less reward than ordinary shareholders. Preference shares have a fixed rate of dividend, perhaps 7 per cent. This means that for each £1[6] preference share, investors receive 7 pence dividend each year. Sometimes a company might decide not to pay the preference dividend (for example in a year when performance is very poor). But if no preference dividend is paid, then no ordinary dividend can be paid either. The preference shareholders have preference over ordinary shareholders with payment of dividends.[7]

Preference shares are usually *cumulative*, which means that if the preference dividend is not paid in some years, all arrears of preference dividends must be paid before any ordinary dividends can be paid. Preference shareholders are usually reasonably secure in receiving their set amount of

---

6　The nominal value of the share is assumed to be £1 in this instance. The market value is likely to be rather higher or lower.

7　They do not necessarily have preference if a company winds up.

dividend each year.[8] But preference shares are not very popular for a number of reasons. Ordinary shareholders always have the prospect that the company might do really well, and there could be a substantial increase in profits, dividends and share price: they might make loads of money! Preference shareholders are more secure, but their level of dividend is fixed – whether the company does well or badly.

Preference shares can be made more attractive if they are *participating* and/or if they are *convertible*. Participating preference shares can participate in higher levels of dividend when the company does well, and ordinary dividends rise above some predetermined level. Convertible preference shares can be more attractive: they can be converted to ordinary shares, at a predetermined rate (see Illustration 12.5).

The prospect of a substantial capital gain if the company is successful can make convertible preference shares seem very attractive to investors; they get a decent dividend in the short term, with reasonable security. But the dividend is likely to be very expensive to the company – mainly because dividends (unlike interest) are not allowable as an expense to be charged against taxation. If we assume a corporation tax rate of 30 per cent, then a company needs to earn £10 profit[9] to pay £7 dividend. It is cheaper for the company to borrow money: a company earning £10 profit[10] could pay £7 in interest and still have £3 (pre-tax) profit left for shareholders.

Illustration 12.5

The Fastgro company issues £1 ordinary shares at a premium of 50 pence per share. On the same date it issues 6 per cent convertible £1 preference shares giving the shareholders the right to convert 3 preference shares into one ordinary share at any date they choose.

In the early years preference shareholders are unlikely to give up 3 preference shares, worth about £3, for one ordinary share, worth £1.50. But if the company is successful the market price of the ordinary shares might increase steadily to, say, £10 per share. An investor with 900,000 preference shares, worth about £900,000, could then convert them to 300,000 ordinary shares worth £3 million; this would give a profit of over £2 million!

---

8   Although any company can get into difficulties, and there is a risk with all shares.

9   Earnings before interest and taxation.

10 Earnings before interest and taxation.

Interpretation of Balance Sheets

When interpreting the last part of a balance sheet, for most purposes the total figure for 'equity' is used. Equity (or ordinary shareholders' funds) includes all of shareholders' funds (share capital, share premium and all reserves/retained profits) except preference share capital. This figure is used in calculating gearing, and in calculating the net assets per share. It is also used in calculating the profitability of ordinary shareholders' funds: net profit after tax (and after deducting any preference share dividends) is expressed as a percentage of equity.[11] It is usually a mistake (often made by students) to use the share capital figure instead of including all of shareholders' funds.

The nominal value of shares is of little or no importance except perhaps in calculating the number of shares which make up share capital. Calculations of earnings per share, dividend per share, and net assets per share are based on the number of ordinary shares.

12.2 **Borrowing**

Some very prudent individuals and businesses may think that it dangerous to borrow: the business may not be able to meet the interest and repayments, and there is always the risk of insolvency if the business gets into difficulties. Those who want to minimize risk probably want to minimize borrowing. But if they are so risk averse, they should probably not go into business, and will probably never make much money.

It is safest and easiest to put your money in a bank, and earn a steady, low rate of interest, with little or no risk. But people invest in businesses because they think that it is worth the risk in order to earn more money. If banks are paying, say, 5 per cent interest, investors hope to earn more than that by investing in companies. Perhaps they expect a return on capital employed of 10 per cent or more. A business could argue that if the cost of borrowing is less than the return on capital employed that they can earn, then the more they borrow, the more profit they will make. If you can borrow money at 7 per cent per annum, and invest it to earn 10 per cent per annum, then the more money you borrow, the more profit you will make – as shown in Illustration 12.6.

Borrowing can increase the return to shareholders, as is demonstrated in Illustration 12.7. Borrowing can also be relatively cheap, and is a cheaper source of finance than issuing ordinary shares because the interest is allowable

---

11   If there are preference shares it is also possible to calculate the profitability of *all* shareholders' funds: net profit after tax (including any preference dividends) is expressed as a percentage of the total shareholders' funds (including preference share capital). But in most analyses, consideration is given only to the ordinary shareholders.

Illustration 12.6

Two companies in the same industry each have a return on capital employed of 10 per cent, and they are each able to borrow money at an interest rate of 7 per cent.

The Lowgear Company borrows an extra £1 million	
Cost of borrowing £1 million at 7 per cent	£ 70,000 per annum
Additional earnings, 10 per cent of £1 million	£100,000 per annum
Net additional earnings	£ 30,000 per annum
The Highgear Company borrows an extra £100 million	
Cost of borrowing £100 million at 7 per cent	£ 7,000,000 per annum
Additional earnings, 10 per cent of £100 million	£10,000,000 per annum
Net additional earnings	£ 3,000,000 per annum

Illustration 12.7

Low geared company	Capital structure		Equity	£100 million
			10% Debentures	£ 10 million
				£110 million

	Year 1	Year 2		
	£ million	£ million		
EBIT	10	12	+20%	
Interest	1	1		
Pre-tax profit	9	11		
Tax (say) 30%	2.7	3.3		
Profit after tax	6.3	7.7	+22.2%	

High geared company	Capital structure		Equity	£ 50 million
			10% Debentures	£ 60 million
				£110 million

EBIT	10	12	+20%	
Interest	6	6		
Pre-tax profit	4	6		
Tax (say) 30%	1.2	1.8		
Profit after tax	2.8	4.2	+50%	

In both cases EBIT (earnings before interest and taxation) increased by 20 per cent between Years 1 and 2, but the effect of gearing was a larger increase in the profit after tax earned for the ordinary shareholders. In the low geared company the return earned for ordinary shareholders increased by 22.2 per cent. In the high geared company it increased by 50 per cent.

as an expense for tax purposes; and because shareholders expect a higher return as they are taking more risk than lenders. But what they expect, and what they get can be very different.

There are other good reasons for borrowing rather than issuing more shares. In a family-controlled company the existing shareholders and directors might not want to risk issuing more shares if it would result in new and different people being shareholders and controlling the company. In spite of what some textbooks say, directors do not always make rational economic decisions: many like to keep their positions of power and influence, even if (by not issuing more shares) they restrict the growth and profitability of the company.

The costs involved in issuing shares also tend to be higher than the costs in obtaining loans.

Another advantage of borrowing is that it comes in many forms, and can be very flexible. It may be short term or long term. The most flexible way of borrowing is through an overdraft. Interest rates are negotiable, and are usually a number of percentage points above base rate. Individuals with unauthorized overdrafts may find that they are charged with ridiculously high interest rates – perhaps even 10 or 15 points above base rate. A company ought to be able to negotiate an overdraft interest rate at just a few points[12] above base rate. Some businesses are seasonal and need to borrow at particular times of the year. A business such as a seaside hotel is likely to be flush with cash in October, after the holiday season; but by March they need short-term borrowings until the money starts coming in for the next holiday season. Many businesses have plenty of money in the middle of the month, but need to borrow at the end of the month, when wages and salaries are paid. Overdrafts are most appropriate for such short-term financing because interest is payable only for the actual days that the overdraft facility is used. There is no point in having a fixed loan throughout the year, and paying interest throughout the year, if the money is needed only for a few days each month, or for a few months each year.

Although overdrafts are supposed to be a short-term source of finance,[13] many individuals and companies seem to have significant (and increasing!) overdrafts that go on for years. Banks are interested in converting overdrafts into fixed loans for a few years, especially if they can earn more interest by so doing. Businesses need to work out carefully how much it is appropriate to borrow with fixed-term loans and fixed interest rates, and how much it is appropriate to use overdraft facilities for.

12   Typically between 1 and 5.

13   And are, in theory, repayable on demand.

Debentures are a form of long-term borrowing (typically 5–10 years), usually with a fixed rate of interest, which can be listed on a stock market. Investors can therefore sell them when they wish, and the company can choose to buy them back on the market, if they have nothing better to do with their money. Debentures are usually 'secured' on some assets of the company; perhaps on land and buildings; perhaps a floating charge on most of the assets of the company. The effect is a bit like taking out a mortgage: if the company does not meet its payments as they fall due, the debenture holders can eventually get their money back by selling off the company's assets.

Debentures are sometimes 'convertible' into ordinary shares – which can make them very attractive to investors if it is expected that the company's shares will do very well in the future. Investors in a new or expanding business may be attracted by the security of a debenture with a reasonable interest rate to begin with, together with the possibility of conversion to ordinary shares (and increases in the share price, and increasing dividends) once the venture has proved to be successful.

The main attraction of borrowing is the idea that the more you borrow, the more profit you can make. It may be an attractive idea, but there are a number of problems with ever increasing borrowings:

1 Borrowing may be no problem as long as the company can be sure of always having earnings[14] above the required level of interest payments. But businesses tend to have good years and bad years; the economy tends to run in cycles; some industries are particularly cyclical; some industries run into bad patches, with bad luck and/or bad management. If in some years the company does not earn enough to make the necessary interest payments, lenders may repossess vital assets and force the business to curtail its activities or close down.

2 The more you get into debt, the more difficult it is to borrow more money. There is probably always someone, or some bank, that will lend to you, but as you get more into debt, the higher the interest rates become to compensate the lender for additional risk.

3 Lenders usually look for some sort of security. It is easy to borrow money secured on land and buildings. Lenders may be happy to take some sort of 'floating charge' on whatever other assets the company has. But when all assets have already been used as security, it is increasingly difficult to borrow more money.

4 Those who have already lent money to the company often lay down conditions to restrict the ability of the company to borrow more.

---

14 Earnings Before Interest and Tax

These 'restrictive covenants' may specify that a company's total borrowing must not exceed some (small, e.g. 1 or 1.5) multiple of the amount of equity.

5 Companies that are heavily in debt may get a reputation as being 'high risk', and other businesses may be reluctant to do business with them. Sometimes investors steer clear because the risk is too great.

A good, old-fashioned view might be that a company should keep increasing its borrowing, as long as it can get away with it. Theory suggests that eventually lenders will see that the company has borrowed too much (gearing is too high), and they will start to charge higher interest rates. As borrowing increases, interest rates increase until eventually the cost of borrowing is higher than the return that the company can generate from the borrowings. High levels of borrowing are also associated with high risk, and this can affect the share price, especially if it starts to look as if the company is so heavily in debt that it might be forced into liquidation. There is thus, in this traditional view, an optimal level of borrowing (although it is difficult to establish what this level is).

A more modern view, following Modigliani and Miller (1958), is that the level of gearing has no effect on share price. Even if the amount of borrowing changes, it is still the same business, with the same earnings stream and the same business risk. Modigliani and Miller's presentation is sophisticated, but it depends on a number of unrealistic assumptions; and it is often misinterpreted. Their emphasis is on the value of the company, which depends on the investments that they have, and the cash flows that they will generate; how the company is financed is a secondary issue.

In practice, many companies seem to borrow as much as they can get away with. Some companies constantly need additional funds because of expansion and development. But some companies (like some individuals!) do not seem to be able to live within their means, and borrow until they go bust.

In Illustration 12.1 at the beginning of this chapter the company had total long-term funds of £3,000, of which £1,000 was borrowed. In other words, one-third of their long-term funding was borrowed, or their gearing ratio was $33\frac{1}{3}$ per cent. There is of course no 'correct' or 'best' level of borrowing; nor is there a single correct way of measuring gearing.[15] Companies that are able to borrow extensively are likely to have a steady, secure income stream so that they can be confident about being able to pay the necessary interest every year. They are also likely to have lots of good quality assets (particularly land and buildings) to offer as security to lenders.

---

15 Various approaches to measuring gearing are dealt with in Chapter 4.

Companies in very cyclical industries (they tend to have a few very good years, and then a few very bad years!) should avoid high gearing – but many do not, and they get into financial difficulties. The airline industry is noticeably susceptible to epidemics of war, terrorism and disease; many airlines are highly geared; and many found themselves in serious financial difficulties in 2002–2003.[16]

When the telecommunications industry was expanding and share prices were booming at the end of the twentieth century, many companies got away with very high levels of borrowing – for a while. Then the business climate turned against them, and many share prices collapsed. British Telecommunications plc had a debt mountain of £30 billion,[17] which did not look too bad in relation to the market value of their equity – when share prices were high. But in comparison with the balance sheet value of equity it looked terrible. And when telecommunications share prices took a nose dive, the amount of debt looked unsustainable in relation to the market value of equity. BT took decisive action, and halved the amount of debt in just a few years.

12.3 Retained Profits

A successful company makes profits which materialize in the form of additional cash or other net assets. The company may choose to pay out all of its profits as dividends, in which case profits will not be a source of funds. Most companies choose to pay out a proportion (perhaps 60–70 per cent) of their profits as dividends, and so a proportion of their profits are retained and used to finance the business. Obviously the more profit a company makes, the greater is the potential for using retained profits as a source of finance. Raising finance through retained profits depends on how profitable the business is. It also depends on the company's dividend policy.

Dividend Policy

In deciding how much dividend to pay, or what proportion of profits are to be paid out as dividends, companies need to consider some important matters. Dividend policy usually requires striking a balance between (a) paying out *all* profits as dividends, and (b) paying *no* dividends at all.

16 Air travel tends to be a cyclical business; the businesses, like the aircraft, go up and down, and can easily crash.

17 Equivalent to about £1,000 for every household in the UK.

Pay Out All Profits as Dividends

There is a good case for paying out all profits as dividends. The profits belong to the shareholders, not the directors. The directors might see retained profits as being too easy a source of finance, and not bother to ensure that they are reinvested in the company properly and profitably. As profits are earned, they may simply disappear into higher levels of stocks and debtors – or even cars and 'conference centres'[18] for the comfort of directors.

Many companies find themselves with surplus funds which they invest in disastrous diversification (ad)ventures or waste on more or less (un)successful takeover bids and mergers. Abbey National lost millions of pounds attempting to move from its secure base in retail banking into areas of wholesale banking where they had no experience. Marks and Spencer lost millions of pounds in spreading its operations overseas, and then withdrawing. Marconi wasted millions of pounds investing in overpriced telecommunications companies just before they collapsed. Some companies have a history of merging with others, and then de-merging, or selling off the bits they no longer want (e.g. Kingfisher, Hays). The evidence so far suggests that a takeover is more likely to destroy shareholder value than to create it.

There are of course plenty of exceptions: well-managed companies that succeed in re-investing retained profits year after year and which have a good record in increasing profits and dividends; some even succeed in increasing their return on capital employed, and, with a bit of luck, the company's share price. There are also many companies where the directors know that they are unable to do this. Arnold Weinstock of GEC[19] sat on mountains of cash rather than risk wasting it on ill-advised investments. Other companies, knowing that there are limited opportunities for successful investment of surplus funds, simply return them to shareholders as special dividends; or they use the money to buy their own shares on the market and cancel them.[20]

Many companies, or their directors, cannot be trusted to invest retained profits successfully. But there are good reasons for not expecting companies to pay out all of their profits as dividends.

1 Rising prices, or inflation, usually mean that companies need to retain some of their profits, not for expansion, but merely to maintain the

18 Are directors going to admit having fine country houses primarily for entertaining their 'friends'?

19 Before it was mayonnaised into Marconi.

20 Reducing the number of shares will increase the earnings per share – even if profits do not increase.

existing level of operations. More funds are required to finance debtors (as selling prices increase); to finance stocks of goods (as replacement costs increase) and to replace fixed assets as the cost of these increases. Inflation in the UK in recent years has been very low, and the cost of replacing many items (e.g. computers and electronic equipment) has actually fallen. But few businesses can afford to finance even their existing level of operations without retaining some profits.

2　Investors, particularly financial institutions, generally want to see dividends increasing steadily each year,[21] preferably by rather more than the rate of inflation. Illustration 12.8 shows how company profits can fluctuate, but attempts are made to keep dividends steady.

3　Many companies boast that they have succeeded in increasing dividends every year since anyone can remember.[22] Early in 2003 Prudential cut back its dividend by 40 per cent after a record of steady or increasing dividends for 89 years. It was widely expected that Lloyds TSB would also cut its dividend – apparently for the first time in its 138 years. In the event the dividend was maintained at the interim stage; but the company's low share price, and high dividend yield, suggest that many investors are not confident about future dividends being maintained at the existing level.

Illustration 12.8

The earnings per share and the dividend per share of the Cycle Company for the last few years are shown below (in pence).

Year	1	2	3	4	5	6	7
EPS	100	134	60	116	180	10	191
Div	50	53	56	59	63	64	70
Cover	2	2.5	1.1	2.0	2.9	0.2	2.7

Compared with dividend expectations, profits are less predictable, less controllable, more cyclical, and more affected by one-off 'exceptional' items. Companies usually prefer to increase dividends only modestly in the very good years so that there is more scope for maintaining or increasing dividends in the lean years.

In mid 2003 BAT announced a 25 per cent drop in first half profits, but kept many investors happy with a 10 per cent increase in the interim dividend.

21　Pension funds want this to be able to pay the constantly increasing pensions to which they are committed.

22　Although memories can be short.

Pay Out No Dividends

There is a case for paying no dividends at all, even in successful companies. When a company is making serious losses, or when they have massive borrowings, scrapping the dividend for a year or two makes good sense. Companies at an early stage of their development need all of the money that they can get hold of and so are not inclined to pay dividends. In the great dot com and TMT[23] bubble of the late 1990s many companies did not pay dividends. A quick look at the *Financial Times* today will show which companies are not paying dividends;[24] usually there are plenty of mining companies and pharmaceuticals and biotechnology companies that have not yet found their pot of gold or wonder drug, and are burning up cash in their efforts; there is unlikely to be a dividend until a worthwhile discovery has been developed. The story is different with many information technology hardware companies: they probably thought that they had found their pot of gold, but it disappeared over the horizon as demand collapsed.

If a company can invest the shareholders' money and earn a better rate of return than the shareholders can themselves, then there is a case for the company to keep the money, and not pay dividends. If shareholders receive dividends they will only waste the money. If the money stays within the company, the value of their shares should increase. If shareholders need some income, they can sell a few shares; and (they hope!) the value of their shares will increase because of all of the retained profits being reinvested. If they sell a few shares they may have to pay capital gains tax; but for many shareholders the taxation of capital gains is lower than the taxation on income from dividends. Paying no dividends at all may suit some companies and some shareholders – sometimes.

Dividend Policy in Practice

Most companies do not opt for the extremes of no dividends, or 100 per cent distribution. Usually a proportion of profits is distributed. Listed companies typically pay out rather more than half of their profits as dividends. Recent figures for the FTSE 100 index and a number of companies are shown in Illustration 12.9.

Company profits tend to fluctuate from year to year, not least because of 'exceptional' items such as profits or losses arising from the sale of fixed assets, or closing down part of the business. As shown in Illustration 12.8 it makes more sense to try to maintain a record of steady and increasing dividends, rather than to pay out the same proportion of profits each year.

23   Technology, Media and Telecommunications.

24   Look for companies where the 'Yld' (dividend yield) is shown as '–'.

Illustration 12.9							
	FTSE100	Compass	HSBC	United Utilities	Granada	Shell	BT
Dividend cover	1.7	2.9	1.5	0.9	2.8	2.0	2.3
Proportion of profits distributed[25]	59%	34%	67%	111%	36%	50%	43%

Some companies pay an extra 'special' dividend in a particularly good year. But most try to keep an upward trend, even when profits fall. And many seem to increase their dividends more than the underlying profits justify; this results in the dividend cover declining over a number of years, and the dividend begins to look less safe.

In making dividend decisions, companies need to consider what 'signal' any change in dividends gives to investors. A sudden reduction in dividends suggests that directors are not confident about future years. Companies also need to consider what cash is available to pay dividends and their plans for expansion, investment and borrowing.

12.4 **Other Sources of Finance**

Companies are assumed to need funds to finance the purchase of fixed assets and stocks; and to pay expenses until the profits come rolling in, in the form of cash. The need to find additional funding can arise when a business is first established; when it is going through a period of rapid development and expansion; and when it is in financial difficulties, perhaps with excessive borrowing after a period of making losses. The main sources of such financing are usually the owners' capital, plus borrowing, plus, in due course, profits. But there are various ways of avoiding the need to raise finance.

1 Fixed assets can be leased instead of buying them. Obviously this applies to premises, but most machinery, equipment and furniture can be leased if necessary. It is sometimes possible to arrange for an initial rent free period to minimize initial funding requirements. But most lessors will not rent out equipment to any Tom, Dick or Harry: the lessee usually needs to produce evidence that they are creditworthy.

2 Sale and leaseback. A business can raise finance by selling assets that it owns and wants to continue using to a finance company (such as a bank

---

25 The proportion can be calculated by dividing 1 by the times cover and converting to a percentage: $1 \div 1.7 \times 100 = 58.82\%$.

or insurance company), and then leasing the asset back from that company. This is often done with premises, and it is sometime surprising to find that many chains of retail shops no longer own the freehold of their premises: they made a sale and leaseback arrangement. This can make sense both for the finance company and for the retailer. The finance company gets a guaranteed return in rental income at the going rate (say 6 or 7 per cent per annum); the retailer continues to use the premises and raises additional funds at a reasonable cost.

Cautious proprietors may prefer the security of continuing to own their premises. But creative accountants will record a profit on the sale of the premises (which boosts earnings per share), and make sure that the cash which is raised is used by the business to earn more than the cost of the lease payment. The cautious proprietor may argue that there is more money to be made by holding on to the property on a long-term basis. Such proprietors are free to decide that they prefer to invest in property rather than manufacturing goods, retailing, providing a service, or whatever else they may be doing.

Cautious proprietors can retain the ownership of their premises, and raise loans or mortgages secured on them – but it is difficult for businesses to borrow 100 per cent of the value of the property; and creative accountants probably have more tricks up their sleeves!

3 Businesses often find that they have more fixed assets than they need, especially when they find themselves in financial difficulties. Warehouses can be 'rationalized': the company may find that it can manage with two instead of six, and raise the odd few million pounds by selling off any spare premises that it owns. Sometimes, when really pushed, the directors may find that they can manage without the country house that was supposed to be used as a training centre; the expensive central London Head Office; the sports and social facilities that are little used; the executive jet. They might even reduce the number of company cars – and perhaps travel by taxi, or even bus![26]

4 Outsourcing or subcontracting some activities (e.g. computing, accounting, catering, manufacture, cleaning, transport – indeed, almost anything) may free up surplus assets that can be sold to raise funds.

5 Careful management of working capital (e.g. reducing stocks and debtors; delaying paying creditors) can also free up funds to be used for other purposes. Management of working capital is dealt with more fully in Chapter 13. If customers can be persuaded to pay in advance for the

---

26   Unless they believe the old aristocratic saying that anyone over the age of thirty who is seen on a bus has been a failure in life. (Don't tell Ken Livingstone – he wants us all to travel by bus!)

company's goods and services, all of the money tied up in debtors can be freed up for other purposes. If the company can persuade suppliers to deliver directly to customers when an order is received, then the money tied up in stocks can be freed. It is sometimes possible to negotiate with customers for part or all of the payment to be made in advance. Where selling on credit is unavoidable, factoring debtors or invoice discounting are ways of using the amount tied up in debtors to raise funds.

6   Increasing profits also generates additional funds. This can be done both by reducing costs (e.g. eliminating a layer of management, or transferring production to Morocco or China), or by increasing sales (the volume of sales, and/or selling prices).

7   Reducing dividends, or even not paying dividends for a year or two is another way of making more funds available.

8   Careful cash budgeting can also make more funds available when needed by delaying major payments at times when there is a particular shortage of cash. Sometimes the easiest way to deal with a cash shortage is to delay capital expenditure programmes.

Businesses rely mostly on funds contributed by their owners (sole proprietors, partners, or shareholders); on borrowing money; and on generating profits that are ploughed back into the business. But there are more creative ways of financing businesses.

Summary

The safest way of financing a company is to issue more shares, but this can be an expensive business, and there is no guarantee that existing shareholders will approve such a course of action. Borrowing is in many ways easier and cheaper, but excessive gearing can lead to excessive risk which can adversely affect share prices, and increase the cost of borrowing. Retained profits are also an attractive source of funds, and companies need to have dividend policies which strike a balance between keeping shareholders happy, and retaining profits to finance expansion – where such reinvestment is justified. There are other ways of financing a business, and there are no 'correct' solutions. A company's dividend, retention and gearing policies may change from time to time, and companies' funding policies tend to vary as circumstances change.

Review of Key Points

◆ The three main sources of funds for companies are share capital, borrowing and retained profits

◆ There is no requirement to pay dividends to ordinary shareholders; they bear most of the risk of the business, and, if the business does well, will get substantial rewards

◆ Borrowing can 'gear up' the return to the owners of the business, but excessive gearing is risky

◆ Profits may be paid out to shareholders as dividends, or reinvested in the business as they are earned

◆ Dividend policy strikes a balance between retaining funds within the business that are needed, and maintaining a payment record to satisfy shareholders

◆ Much of business activity can be financed without using share capital, borrowing or retained profits

Self-testing Questions

1 What are the three main sources of finance for businesses?

2 What are the main differences between preference shares and ordinary shares?

3 Explain the advantages and disadvantages of a company increasing its gearing.

4 You are given the following information about two companies:

Summarized Balance Sheets as at 31 December	TimeBall Company		DownsPier Company	
	Year 6 £000	Year 7 £000	Year 6 £000	Year 7 £000
Fixed assets plus Current assets less Current liabilities	300	342.2	300	284.1
9% Debentures	100	140	100	50
	200	202.2	200	234.1
Share capital	100	100	100	115
Share premium	–	–	–	15
Retained profits	100	102.2	100	104.1
	200	202.2	200	234.1

Self-testing Questions (continued)

Summarized Income Statements for year ended 31 December				
Sales	100	110	100	95
Gross profit	40	44	40	41
Operating profit	20	21.6	20	17.5
Interest	9	12.6	9	4.5
Pre-tax profit	11	9	11	13
Taxation	3.3	2.7	3.3	3.9
Profit after tax	7.7	6.3	7.7	9.1
Dividends	4	4.1	4	5
Retained profit	3.7	2.2	3.7	4.1

(a) You are required to calculate for each company for each year:

(i)   Capital gearing ratio
(ii) Interest cover
(iii) Dividend cover
(iv) Proportion of profits paid out as dividends.

(b) Explain what each shows.
(c) Comment on the financial performance and position of the two companies making use of appropriate ratios.

Assessment Questions

1 Why might a company issue convertible preference shares rather than debentures?

2 The capital structure of two companies is as follows:

	Loborough plc £ million	Hiborough plc £million
Equity	180	50
11% Debentures	20	150
	200	200

The EBIT of both companies was as follows:

Year 1	£19 million
Year 2	£22.8 million
Year 3	£15.2 million

Assessment Questions (continued)

The rate of corporation tax on profits is 25 per cent.

(a) Calculate the net profit after tax earned for ordinary shareholders for each year and for each company.

(b) Comment on the effect that gearing has had on the results.

3 The directors of the Palazine Company are seeking funding of £50 million to finance an expansion programme. The summarized financial statements for the most recent year are set out below:

Income Statement for the year ended 31 December Year 6

		£000
Sales		120,000
Cost of sales		90,000
Gross profit		30,000
Distribution costs	8,000	
Administration expenses	12,000	(20,000)
Operating profit		10,000
Debenture interest		(5,000)
Net profit before taxation		5,000
Taxation		(3,000)
Net profit after taxation		2,000
Dividends		(1,000)
Retained profit for year		1,000

Balance Sheet as at 31 December Year 6

				£000
Fixed assets	Land and buildings at cost			45,000
	(Market value £55 million)			
	Plant and machinery			18,000
	Investments at cost			45,000
	(Market value £30 million)			108,000
Current assets	Stocks		8,000	
	Debtors		5,000	
	Bank		1,000	
			14,000	
Current liabilities	Creditors	23,000		
	Proposed dividend	1,000	24,000	
				(10,000)
10% Debentures (secured)				(50,000)
				48,000
Share capital				30,000
Reserves				18,000
				48,000

Assessment Questions (continued)

The following suggestions have been made for raising the additional finance. You are required to explain the effects of each of the suggestions and to comment on their practicability.

The company could:

(i)   issue more debentures

(ii)   make a sale and leaseback arrangement on their premises

(iii)   sell their investments (although some directors object to this as it would involve a loss of £15 million)

(iv)   reduce stock levels by one half

(v)   halve the period that debtors are allowed to pay (all sales are on credit)

(vi)   extend the period for paying creditors by 50 per cent

(vii)   cancel the proposed dividend

(viii) use the reserves

(ix)   issue more ordinary shares

(x)   obtain a bank overdraft.

4 The earnings per share and the dividend per share of Uppen Down plc for the last few years are shown below (in pence):

Year	1	2	3	4	5	6	7
EPS	20	25	18	30	10	13	24
Div	10	10.4	10.8	11.2	11.7	12.2	12.7
Share price	300	400	200	270	250	270	300

(a) You are required to calculate the dividend cover for each year; the proportion of profits that was distributed as dividends; and the dividend yield based on the share price at the year end given above.

(b) Comment on the company's dividend policy.

(c) Since the end of year 7 the dividend yield, as shown in the *Financial Times* has increased to 10 per cent. What is this likely to indicate?

Group Activities and Discussion Questions

1 What is the minimum amount of funding with which it is possible to start a business? Could a business be started with zero funds? What sort of business could each member of the group start, with little or no funding? Prepare a (very brief) business plan. Would it be necessary to raise substantial funding to develop the business so that it becomes large scale? How would you define 'large scale' (big enough to provide you with a suitable life style; big enough for a stock market listing)?

2 Prepare a list of companies that are not currently paying dividends. (Look for shares with a zero yield in the *Financial Times*'s listing.) Why are these companies not paying dividends?

Group Activities and Discussion Questions (continued)

Each member of the group could research a number of companies. Can the companies be classified into groups each with similar reasons for not paying dividends (e.g. developing new products/services; recent losses)?

3 Why do some companies always seem to be needing to raise more finance, while others generate huge cash piles that they do not seem to know how to use? Some companies seem always to be borrowing more, and sometimes making rights issues. Other companies have piles of cash that they sometimes return to shareholders, and sometimes use (or waste) in acquiring other businesses. Try to find examples of each, and identify the factors which seem to be associated with each. Are expanding, high-tech companies always running out of money? Are 'mature' companies generating surplus funds?

4 Why are some companies high geared, and others low geared? Each member of the group should examine the balance sheets of a number of companies, probably in different sectors. It may be easiest to do this using the companies' websites. The group should agree the way in which gearing should be measured (for example, is short-term borrowing to be included with long-term borrowing?). Are utility companies more highly geared than retailers? Are breweries more highly geared than oil companies? Can you identify what factors seem to be associated with high gearing and with low gearing?

5 What is the effective rate of interest paid by particular companies? Examine the annual reports and accounts of a number of companies. The amount of interest payable each year is easy to find on the profit and loss account or income statement. The amount of borrowings at the beginning and at the end of the year can be found on the balance sheets; remember to include overdrafts and long-term and short-term borrowing. Calculate the average amount of borrowings (the amount at the beginning plus the amount at the end, divided by two). Express the year's interest charge as a percentage of the average amount borrowed. Why do some companies appear to be paying a much higher interest rate than others? Could it be that their real borrowings are much higher than the year end figures suggest? (Is that 'creative accounting', or 'window dressing'?). Are they paying interest for other reasons than straightforward borrowing? Is some of the interest payable for assets that the company has obtained on finance leases?

Financial Accounting in context

Discuss and comment on the following items taken from the press:
Potter launch events a bonus for Ottakar's by Sharlene Goff
Financial Times, 26 September 2003

Ottakar's, the bookseller, yesterday said sales had risen 37 per cent in the first half of the year, driven by the spectacular launch events for the release of the fifth Harry Potter book and the acquisition of 24 Hammicks Bookshops.

Financial Accounting in context (continued)

The group also announced a 38 per cent increase in the interim dividend, in spite of a widening of its pre-tax losses from £2.33m in 2002 to £2.95m this time.

The group sold 80,000 copies of *Harry Potter and the Order of the Phoenix* on its release day in June.

It said the transformation of its stores – which opened at midnight – into 'Harry Potter grottos', with live owls and snakes, had helped achieve a 'notable performance against other book retailers'.

Phillip Dunne, chairman, said: 'The events brought people into our stores and reminded them what they were about and then they came back for other books.'

The BBC's 'The Big Read' promotion, which has highlighted the top 100 books of all time, also lifted sales.

'The promotion has provided great publicity for books on television and encouraged people to try them for the first time,' said Mr Dunne.

The group said the integration of 24 stores from Hammicks Bookshops, which it acquired in April, was going well, with 17 of the stores already rebranded as Ottakar's.

The new stores added £6.6m of turnover and an operating loss of £135,000 for the period. 'There is still some work to do but we are pleased with the progress of the integration,' said Mr Dunne.

The increased pre-tax loss resulted from a £420,000 cost for the closure of the group's East Kilbride store and a further £400,000 in rationalisation costs relating to the new stores.

Mr Dunne said the second half would not benefit from 'one huge bestseller', but flagged releases such as David Beckham's autobiography, *My Side*, and Robert Harris's new novel, *Pompeii*, as strong Christmas titles.

Group sales increased from £41.9m to £57.5m. The interim dividend was 2p (1.45p).

Losses per share were 9.33p (7.77p). The shares closed down $5\frac{1}{2}$p yesterday at 321p.

Kodak to target digital market by Amy Yee and Scott Morrison

Financial Times, 26 September 2003

Eastman Kodak yesterday announced ambitious plans to shift from its traditional film and camera business to digital technology, challenging established rivals such as Fuji Film, Canon, Hewlett-Packard and Epson.

The company said it would slash its dividend by 72 per cent to 50 cents to fund the expansion in digital printers, cameras and medical imaging.

Daniel Carp, chief executive, said: 'We are acting with the knowledge that demand for traditional products is declining, especially in developed markets.' But the move met a sceptical reaction from investors, who questioned Kodak's ability to catch up with entrenched competitors. The shares fell almost 18 per cent during the day to close at a 20-year low of $12.15.

Financial Accounting in context (continued)

Kodak said it planned to spend up to $3bn (£1.8bn) on investments and acquisitions to boost annual revenues from $12.8bn to $16bn by 2006. The consumer film and paper businesses would receive no further significant investment and Kodak would seek to increase market share by cutting prices.

The printer market has shifted dramatically in the past two years, with HP driving the push toward digital photography.

Peter Grant, printer analyst at consultants Gartner, said Kodak had little alternative but to adopt the new strategy. 'It's something they have to do. But they are late and I'm not sure they have the capability to compete with HP, Epson and Lexmark,' he said.

Standard & Poor's immediately lowered its credit ratings on Kodak's debts. The downgrades reflected 'doubts about the profit potential of digital imaging relative to conventional photography' and the need to reduce debt given Kodak's rising business risk, said Steve Wilkinson, S&P credit analyst.

Kodak already spends about two-thirds of its research budget on digital technology and will increase that figure to 78 per cent by 2006, the company said.

References and Further Reading

Brealey, R.A., S.C. Myers and A.J. Marcus (2003) *Fundamentals of Corporate Finance*, 4th edn, McGraw-Hill.

Modigliani, F. and M.H. Miller (1958) The Cost of Capital, Corporation Finance and the Theory of Investment, *American Economic Review*, 38, 261–96.

Samuels, J.M., F.M. Wilkes and R.E. Brayshaw (1996) *Management of Company Finance*, 6th edn, Thomson Learning.

Investors Chronicle (weekly) Published by the *Financial Times*.

13

Management of Working Capital

Learning objectives

After studying this chapter you should be able to:

- Define working capital and explain its importance in relation to solvency, overtrading and profitability

- Explain how to manage debtors and calculate the financial implications of different policies for managing debtors

- Discuss stock control and apply the Economic Order Quantity model

- Explain how to plan, control and manage cash, and how to manage and avoid cash crises

- Understand the role of control and management of creditors

Chapter contents

Introduction

A company needs managers who can bring together all of the resources of the company, financial, physical, human and a variety of less tangible factors to achieve success. The management of working capital should not be regarded as being separate and distinct from the overall management of a company and its resources: it is a vital part.

13.1 **Working Capital**

Definition and Importance of Working Capital

A large part of a company's capital is usually tied up in assets such as buildings and machinery for a period of years. But companies also need some capital to finance short-term assets such as stocks and debtors, and there is a need for some cash for day-to-day operations. A company's long-term funds consist of share capital, retained profits, and long-term borrowing; much of this is used to finance fixed assets. The amount of long-term capital available after financing fixed assets is known as 'working capital'. A simple definition of working capital is:

Long-term funds – Fixed assets = Working capital

From the balance sheet in Illustration 13.1 we can see that working capital in Year 1 was:

Year 1   85,000 + 110,000 – 140,000 = £55,000
Year 2   88,000 + 135,000 – 138,000 = £85,000

The more usual definition of working capital is:

Current assets – Current liabilities = Working capital

From the balance sheet above we can see that working capital is:

Year 1   175,000 – 120,000 = £55,000
Year 2   145,000 – 60,000 = £85,000

The two definitions appear to be different, but provided all items on the balance sheet are classified under the same five headings, the two approaches will produce the same figure.

   Although most businesses finance their stocks and debtors partly from their long-term funds, current assets are also partly financed from short-term funds (creditors). On the above balance sheet we can see that in Year 2 the figure for stocks is £70,000, and the figure for creditors is £45,000. We can say that stocks are mainly financed by creditors. In some companies, particularly retailers, stocks are wholly financed by short-term creditors.

Illustration 13.1

Solverham Company Ltd		Year 1		Year 2	
		£000		£000	
Balance Sheets as at 31 December					
Fixed assets at cost		200		220	
Provision for depreciation		(60)		(82)	
Net book value		140		138	
Current assets					
Stocks	95		70		
Debtors	80		50		
Cash	–		25		
	175		145		
Current liabilities					
Creditors	30		45		
Proposed dividends	10		15		
Overdraft	80		–		
	120	55	60	85	
		195		223	
Long-term liabilities					
12% Debentures		110		135	
		85		88	
Share capital		50		50	
Retained profits		35		38	
		85		88	

How Much Working Capital Should a Business Have?

There is usually a relationship between a company's turnover, and the amount of working capital they have. As turnover increases we can expect working capital to increase in proportion – although many business people forget this. If turnover goes up by 25 per cent, it does not mean that the amount of cash coming into the business immediately goes up by 25 per cent. An increase in turnover usually necessitates an increase in stocks and debtors, although this may be partly[1] financed by an increase in creditors.

But companies must plan and control their working capital. It is not good enough simply to watch it drift upwards, apparently out of control, as sales increase. There is, however, no ideal level for working capital. It is a question of balancing (a) *solvency* against (b) *profitability*.

A company that is very safe in terms of solvency will have lots more current assets than current liabilities. There will always be more than

1 Or wholly, or more than wholly. The increase in creditors could be more than the increase in stocks and debtors.

enough current assets, either in the form of cash or of debtors (and even stocks) that will soon become cash, to meet short-term liabilities as they fall due. This short-term financial strength can be expressed in the form of *current ratios* and *liquidity ratios*. In Illustration 13.2, the first of the four companies (Alice Ltd) has most working capital, the strongest current ratio (3 : 1), and the strongest liquidity ratio (2 : 1). The fourth company (Dora Ltd) has the least working capital: a negative amount! Dora also has a very low current ratio (0.17 : 1) and a very low liquidity ratio (0.1 : 1).

A company that is more concerned with profitability than with appearing to be solvent will concentrate on keeping down the amount of working capital. Profitability is best expressed as return on capital employed. In order to maximize return on capital employed companies need not only to maximize profits or returns, but also to minimize capital employed in relation to profits. Other things being equal, companies which manage with the least working capital are likely to be the ones which are most profitable.

Each of the four companies in Illustration 13.2 has the same amount of fixed assets, and the same amount of profit. The only differences between the companies are the amounts of working capital. As working capital decreases, so the return on capital employed increases. The company with the lowest amount of working capital (Dora Ltd has £50,000 *negative* working capital) has the highest return on capital employed.

In terms of solvency or liquidity, however, Dora looks very weak. There are creditors of £60,000, but current assets amount to only £10,000. There are not many businesses which would be likely to have such a pattern of working capital, but it might be possible with a business such as a florist's shop. Fresh flowers do not keep for long and so stocks would be low – perhaps especially so if the year end is 31 December. Retailers tend to sell mostly on a cash basis, and so a low debtors figure is to be expected. And retailers buy mostly on credit and so a significant creditors figure is normal.

We should not say that any particular level of working capital is normal, or optimal, or best. It very much depends on the type of business. We can see, however, that higher working capital is associated with higher levels of solvency; and lowering levels of working capital can increase profitability.

Overtrading

Having too little working capital is associated with 'overtrading'. This occurs when a company is trying to do too much business with too little long-term capital. If a company is generating lots of cash, and manages its working capital carefully, they may survive and prosper in a situation which many would regard as overtrading. But having insufficient liquid resources (or access to them) to meet liabilities as they fall due is fatal for businesses.

Illustration 13.2

	Alice Ltd £000	Bertha Ltd £000	Colin Ltd £000	Dora Ltd £000
Fixed assets	150	150	150	150
Current assets				
Stocks	100	50	100	4
Debtors	150	80	150	2
Bank/Cash	50	10	–	4
	300	140	250	10
Current liabilities				
Creditors	100	80	200	60
Overdraft	–	–	50	–
	100	80	250	60
Working capital	200	60	–	(50)
Net assets = Capital employed	350	210	150	100
Profit	35	35	35	35
Return on capital employed	10%	16.7%	23.3%	35%

The problem can start with a major outflow of cash, perhaps to buy additional fixed assets or another business; to repay a loan; or paying too much out as dividends. It is sometimes the result of success: rapid expansion can lead to a rapid outflow of cash (stocks, debtors and fixed assets increase) before the cash comes in from customers. High levels of inflation make the problem worse: the amounts of cash required to replace assets increases in line with inflation.

Overtrading can also be the result of failure. A company which makes substantial losses is likely to find that cash is haemorrhaging out of the business.

A mild case of overtrading is easily treated with various tactics to bring in cash more quickly. Debtors can be chased and pressed to pay more quickly. Stock levels can be reduced by careful monitoring of new purchases, and by 'special offers' to bring in some cash from existing stocks. And there can be some delay in paying creditors.

A cash shortage, and the effects of reducing stocks and debtors, and of increasing creditors, soon show up in reducing a company's current ratio. There is no such thing as an optimal current ratio, but the trend can be important; and reductions in current ratios are a matter for concern.

In a serious case of overtrading the symptoms get worse, and attempts to deal with it can lead to further deterioration. The overdraft limit can often be increased, but if an increased limit is breached, the bank soon loses patience with a business that seems unable to manage its cash. If a company reduces its stock levels too much they will soon find that they are losing business because they are not able to supply what the customers want. Customers are easily upset, and go elsewhere, if they are pushed too hard, or too often, to pay their bills too quickly. Creditors will usually put up with a little delay in making payments, but most will not tolerate repeated or increased delays in making payments. If a company cannot pay its bills without excessive delay they soon find that they are unable to obtain supplies on credit. If they are to continue in business they have to find cash to buy supplies – which makes the original problem worse.

Many of us have been in shops where the signs of overtrading are obvious. There is very little on the shelves because suppliers are no longer willing to sell to them on credit. Each day they hope to bring in a few hundred pounds from customers so that they can go to their local cash and carry suppliers to replace what they have sold; they cannot buy very much because they have to use some of the cash to pay off some of the amounts due to whichever creditors are pressing hardest.

Often it is a wages bill that precipitates the crisis, especially at the stage when the bank is no longer willing to honour cheques because the business has already exceeded its overdraft limit – which has probably already been increased several times. At this stage desperate measures are needed. When difficulties first arise, surplus assets are sold off to raise cash. Towards the end they even have to sell essential assets, and sell off stocks at ridiculously low prices, just to bring in some cash to survive another day. At this stage the business has little chance of survival.

It is not difficult to spot the early symptoms of overtrading, and good financial planning and management can avoid a crisis. The usual problem is trying to do too much with too little money, especially where there is too little long-term finance. Solutions include raising more long-term capital, and careful management of working capital and of profitability, with a particular emphasis on cash budgeting so that crises can be identified and averted before they become critical to survival.

13.2 **Managing Debtors**

From the point of view of profitability, the ideal level of debtors is zero, or even less than zero. Many retailers sell on a cash only basis and avoid having money tied up in debtors. Some businesses in effect have negative debtors by requiring their customers to pay in advance. Most mail order businesses require payment in advance, as do many service organizations:

some hotels require customers to pay a deposit in advance, and to pay in full on arrival – before the service has been provided. When buying a house, the bank or building society usually requires the customer to pay the survey fee in advance.

There are good reasons for a business preferring to receive money in advance. All capital has a cost. Perhaps the business is paying 10 per cent per annum on an overdraft, or shareholders expect a 10 per cent return on the funds they have invested in the business. If a business has an average of £100,000 of debtors during the year, the cost of that, just in terms of the cost of capital, is £10,000 a year.

There are also administrative costs in having debtors. It is necessary to send out invoices and statements, and to record what payments are received, and what is still owed. Even if all customers pay the correct amounts on time there is a significant administrative cost. But costs are even higher when there are customers who delay making payments, and come up with a whole series of excuses for not paying the correct amount on time. Additional costs include the costs of chasing up slow payers. And most businesses have some experience of bad debts – customers who do not pay at all.

Much can be done to encourage customers to pay on time, and to minimize losses through bad debts. The following steps should be considered in implementing an effective 'credit control' policy.

Selling on Credit

Most business-to-business transactions are on a credit, not a cash basis. But for many businesses it is worth asking the question: should we sell on credit at all? Sometimes customers can be required to pay in advance, if only part of the amount due. Many suppliers now operate on a 'cash and carry' basis with very few, if any, credit customers. Accepting credit card sales can eliminate most of the work and risk of selling on credit. There are, however, some businesses where it is essential to be able to sell on credit, if only because of competition: there are other suppliers willing to sell on credit.

Who Should Be Accepted as Credit Customers

If it is necessary to sell on credit, the next question is: To whom should we sell on credit? It would be foolish to sell on credit to every Tom, Dick and Harry. There are always a few dodgy customers who will not pay up, and attempts have to be made to determine who is likely to be creditworthy. There are various ways of tackling this.

1 Traditionally it depended very much on personal judgement: whether or not someone was accepted as a credit customer depended on the

impression that they gave, and their apparent status in life. There is still something to be said for this, and no amount of investigation or calculation can eliminate the need for personal judgement. Sometimes even the most reputable businesses and customers go into receivership and are unable to pay their debts, and some countries and governments also prove not to be creditworthy. But we should not rely on a smart suit and a flashy car being the guarantee of financial strength – they can be financed by excessive borrowing. A visit to a customer's premises can be revealing: many businesses with impressive internet sites and publicity are operated from a backroom above a shop, or a teenager's bedroom.

2 Bankers' references are another traditional piece of evidence in judging whether or not a customer is creditworthy. But they usually say very little that is of any use. On the other hand, with current regulations about banking and money laundering, the mere fact that someone has a bank account is some indication that they exist, and have an address – or they did when they opened the account.

3 Accountants like to think that company annual reports and accounts are there to guide potential creditors on the financial strength of a company. In theory, before accepting a credit customer, the supplier should check their annual report and accounts to see what other liabilities they have, whether or not they look strong enough to survive and pay their liabilities, and how long they seem to take to pay existing creditors. Most companies probably think that it is not worth the effort to go through this exercise, even if they have the expertise to do so. It is easier to rely on a credit rating agency to do the work.

4 One of the easiest ways to find out how long a company takes to pay its creditors is to ask other creditors. This can be done formally, by taking up trade references. It is likely to be more revealing if done informally, through business contacts, simply asking other people in the business about a particular company, and its record for making payments. Often it becomes widely known when a particular company becomes a slow payer.

5 Credit rating agencies such as Experian, Moodies, and Standard and Poor provide information on the creditworthiness of individuals and firms. For a fee such information can be provided instantly by telephone or via the internet.

How Much Credit to Allow

Having decided to accept a particular business or individual as a credit customer, the next question is, how much credit to allow. This should be tackled in four parts.

1 How much *time* to allow. It is important that both the buyer and the seller are clear about the period of credit allowed, and it is wise to sign a contract with the agreed terms for payment. Problems will obviously arise if the customer assumes that it is okay to pay 2 months later whereas the seller expects payment within 2 weeks.

2 How much *money* to allow each individual debtor to owe. It is important to set a credit limit for each customer, based on their size, and on the assessment of their creditworthiness. Obviously some customers (e.g. the UK government) can be trusted for millions of pounds, but it is unwise to allow some customers to owe as little as £100.

3 How much the business can afford to be owed by one individual debtor. If the business is owed a substantial sum by a particular debtor who goes bankrupt, and pays nothing, it can, in turn, bring down the company to whom the money is owed. Most companies expect, and plan for some small amounts of bad debts. But one substantial default can mean disaster. Some companies drift into relying too heavily on one customer, and do not know what to do when that customer turns out to be a very slow payer.

4 How much money in total the business can afford to be owed. It may be prudent to estimate the maximum total debtors figure that the business can afford to finance. Profitable expansion usually looks attractive, but if it involves additional working capital that the business cannot afford, it could be very risky.

Collecting in the Money

The first step in collecting in the money from debtors is to send out the paperwork promptly, and correctly, and for it to be clear when payment is due. Small businesses are sometimes very slow at this. Businesses are often set up by individuals who are keen on making a particular product, or offering a particular service. They are usually less keen on sorting out the bills and sending out the invoices. Larger businesses usually have fairly tight – sometimes aggressive – credit control systems.

When payments come in it is necessary to check carefully the amounts received – some customers are good at disputing invoices and taking discounts to which they are not entitled.

Offering cash discounts for prompt payment can be an effective way of encouraging customers to pay within, say, 14 days. But the cost of offering such discounts needs to be carefully calculated. A 10 per cent discount is likely to be attractive to customers, and may encourage them to pay up, say, one month early. But a 10 per cent discount for one month is very expensive – equivalent to 120 per cent per annum! Even offering 2 or $2\frac{1}{2}$ per cent is expensive when converted to an annual rate. But offering much less than that is not likely to do much to encourage early payment.

Offering a 4 per cent discount is very expensive, as shown in Illustration 13.3, and even if it was successful in encouraging customers to pay in 6 weeks instead of 3 months, it would still not be worthwhile. It might be more cost-effective to employ a competent credit controller to encourage debtors to pay up more quickly.

Illustration 13.3

Last year the Vinelia Building Company's turnover was £12 million. All sales were made on credit. Their debtors figure was £3 million at the balance sheet date and that figure was typical of the figure throughout the year.

The company usually has a large overdraft and their cost of capital is 15 per cent per annum. The Sales Director recommends offering customers a 4 per cent discount for prompt payment and estimates that this would halve the debtors figure.

The costs and benefits of this proposal would be as follows:

Annual cost of discount: 4% × £12 million	£480,000
Reduction in debtors: £1.5 million	
Annual interest savings on reduction 15% × £1.5 million	£225,000

The cost of offering the discount is more than the saving in interest.

Instead of offering discounts for early payment some businesses charge extra for late payment, with a predetermined (and profitable) amount of interest being added for each week that payment is delayed beyond the date specified in the original agreement to do business on credit.

It is important to have a credit control system that carefully monitors the payment record of customers, and what has been done about late payers. It is usual to produce an 'age analysis' of debtors, showing little detail where the sale took place only a month or two previously. But where amounts have been outstanding for more than 2 or 3 months the amounts and dates should be carefully detailed for each customer, together with what action had been taken, and what promises and payments have been received.

When payments do not come in at, or immediately after the date that they are due, the next step is a prompt and polite reminder. Problems arise when customers have still not paid a few weeks after the due date. There are three main approaches to get customers to pay up:

1 Phoning them, following up promises to pay, and visiting them. Sales staff often have good relationships with customers, but they are not

Illustration 13.4

The Vinelia Building Company (as in Illustration 13.3) is considering employing a credit controller and instituting more effective procedures for collecting money from debtors. The annual cost of doing this is expected to be £40,000. If the average period taken by debtors to pay their bills is reduced from 3 months to $2\frac{1}{2}$ months, would this expense be justified?

Reduction in debtors: half of one month's sales =	£500,000
Annual saving in interest £500,000 × 15% =	£ 75,000

Additional expenditure of £40,000 a year is justified if it has the effect of reducing the average level of debtors by £500,000, and reducing interest costs by £75,000 a year.

usually keen on spoiling those relationships with the sordid business of asking them for money. But sales staff who make sales for which the customer does not pay are not very useful.

2 Threatening the customer that they will receive no further supplies, and then implementing the threats if necessary. It is relatively easy for suppliers who are in a near monopoly position to persuade/force their customers to pay. Few of us want to have our telephones, gas or electricity cut off. It is much more difficult with a 'good' customer when we do not want to lose their business. But, sooner or later, the supplier has to make the difficult decision. If they continue to supply a customer who is not paying, they just get deeper and deeper into trouble. It is usually possible to negotiate some compromise: supplies will continue if the customer pays for them on delivery, *and* begins to pay off some of the amounts due for previous supplies.

3 Threatening legal action. In most cases the threat of legal action should be enough to frighten customers into paying pretty promptly. Legal action can be very expensive. There may be a few who are determined not to pay, or who are unable to do so, and businesses need to consider whether or not it is worth the effort of pursuing a non-payer through the courts. Some companies have a very inexpensive way of (nearly) starting legal action by writing to customers to say that they will refer the matter to their solicitors if payment is not received within seven days, and that the customer will be incurring legal expenses thereafter. Even a routine letter (that appears to come) from solicitors may be cost effective.

Businesses have to face the fact that some customers will never pay up, or that the cost of pursuing them is not worth it. When negotiations and promises have failed to get the customer to reduce the amount owed, it is better to make the difficult decision to cut off supplies to a customer than to carry on until the debt becomes so large as to threaten the viability of the company.

The Costs and Benefits of Different Approaches

The costs of having debtors include:

1 Cost of capital

2 Administration

3 Bad debts

4 Discount allowed.

Companies need to evaluate the costs and benefits involved in different strategies. Sometimes they may be concerned mainly with reducing costs, and perhaps reducing the amount of money tied up in debtors, perhaps by factoring or invoice discounting. At other times they may be more concerned with increasing sales, and recognize that this is likely to necessitate an increase in debtors. Offering attractive credit terms can be an effective way of increasing sales. It is sometimes possible to offer more generous credit periods to customers in some markets without slowing down payments by existing customers.

If we know the contribution/sales ratio of a company[2] we can estimate the additional profits that will be brought in by an increase in sales. We can also estimate how much additional debtors there will be, including any increases as a result of offering more attractive credit terms. If we also know the company's cost of capital, we can estimate the annual cost of an increase in debtors. We can then calculate if it appears to be worthwhile to offer a more generous credit terms to customers, as shown in Illustration 13.5.

Factoring and Discounting of Debtors

A business can outsource, or subcontract, almost any activity, and the management of debtors is an obvious candidate. With factoring, most of the money tied up in debtors (typically 75–80 per cent) can be turned into

---

2 In marginal costing a distinction is made between fixed costs and variable costs. 'Contribution' is what is left after deducting variable costs from sales; it is a 'contribution' to fixed overheads. When the volume of sales produces enough contribution to cover fixed costs, any additional contribution is profit. It is convenient to assume that contribution represents a constant proportion of sales: as sales increases, so the amount of contribution increases in proportion.

Illustration 13.5

The Tightar Company specializes in surfacing driveways and minor roads. They have a strict credit control policy because they are short of funds, and depend on an overdraft which has an interest rate of 18 per cent per annum.

They do not undertake work for public institutions or building contractors because such customers are slow to pay, taking on average 10 weeks.

The Company's annual turnover is £520,000, and their average debtors figure at any one time is £30,000.

The direct costs of surfacing a driveway amounts to 40 per cent of the selling price.

Would it be worth extending their average credit period to 10 weeks if they could double turnover?

Direct costs as a proportion of turnover	40%		
Contribution[3] as a proportion of turnover	60%		
Proposed additional sales	£520,000		
Additional contribution (60%)			£312,000
Existing debtors figure			£ 30,000
New debtors figure	$\dfrac{10 \text{ weeks}}{52 \text{ weeks}} \times £1,040,000$	=	£200,000
Increase in debtors			170,000
Annual cost of increase in debtors			
	18% × £170,000	=	£ 30,600

It is worthwhile to pay interest on the necessary additional borrowings because the cost of the interest is substantially lower than the additional contribution generated.

cash immediately. The factoring company provides the money, and charges interest for so doing. The factoring company also takes over the administration of the client's sales accounting, invoicing and credit control – for which they also charge a fee, typically of between 0.75 per cent and 2 per cent of debtors. This is a significant cost to the business using the factor, but it may be more than offset by savings in the business's own administration, and advantages in getting the money in more quickly so that it can be used for other, more profitable purposes. Factoring is likely to be

---

3   Contribution to fixed costs and profit. If we assume that fixed costs will be covered regardless of any expansion, the 60 per cent is all profit.

particularly appropriate in small, rapidly growing businesses, where the business has relatively little expertise in credit control and the factor is likely to be more efficient and effective, with economies of scale in carrying out their specialist activity. Using a factor can mean that cash from debtors becomes readily available as the business expands; otherwise, the need to finance working capital can be a significant constraint on growth: increased sales usually require increases in stocks and debtors which are only partly financed by creditors. Factoring can be a way of financing growth.

Factoring can also result in significant savings in management time, particularly in dealing with difficult and dodgy customers who do not want to pay, and with an area of business in which management has no particular expertise. Effective management of debtors can minimize bad debts. And the factor usually takes responsibility for losses through bad debts. From management's perspective, factoring makes an uncertain world more predictable and manageable, at least in some respects.

Sometimes a business may be concerned about their customers' reaction to the use of factors to collect in the money, and the possible effect on the image and reputation of the business. But most factoring is done confidentially: the customer does not even know that a factor is being used – it is all done using the client's name and stationery. A business should be careful to calculate the costs and benefits of using a factor: it may seem to be more expensive, but if it is more effective in the long run, it may prove to be more economical. It usually has to be a long-term arrangement: once a business becomes reliant on getting the cash in quickly by using a factor, it is difficult to go back and establish a replacement source of finance, and to set up a credit control function again. Another disadvantage of factoring is that, sometimes, the factor may be unwilling to take on particular types of customer where they anticipate problems.

Invoice discounting is usually a short-term way of using debtors to make cash available quickly. In effect the debtors are 'sold' to a financial institution who provides around 75 per cent of the amount immediately. The client (not the financial institution) continues with the administration of debtors and continues to bear any risks of bad debts. This usually applies only to selected debtors, and can be a useful source of short-term finance.

13.3 **Managing Stocks**

It is always handy to have lots of stuff in stock – just in case it might be needed. But holding stocks is a very expensive business. There are all of the costs involved in providing storage space (there is often a more profitable use for the space), including rent, rates, lighting, heating, insurance, security and administration. But the most substantial costs of holding stocks are:

1 The cost of capital. A company's cost of capital might typically be between 10 per cent and 15 per cent per annum. This means that, just in terms of the cost of capital, it costs between £10,000 and £15,000 a year to have average stocks of £100,000.

2 Obsolescence. Clothes go out of fashion; publications go out of date; and technological items are soon superseded. Stocks of computers, software or mobile phones that are only a year or two old are worth very little. Technology constantly advances and becomes cheaper, and companies seem to have a vested interest in always promoting the latest version of any product. They should not be surprised that most of their stocks of goods for sale, and even of raw materials and components, rapidly become out of date.

3 Physical deterioration. Stocks of goods physically deteriorate – or even disappear – in various ways. Some things are eaten by rats and other creatures; some things evaporate, go mouldy, or become unusable in a variety of ways. And some things are stolen – or apparently just disappear!

It is clear that holding stocks of any kind is an expensive business and might typically cost, on average, about 25 per cent per annum when all the costs of holding stocks are considered. A company which on average holds stocks of £100,000 is likely to incur costs of about £25,000 a year. If a company wants to maximize profitability there is an obvious pressure to reduce stock levels. Various approaches are used to achieve this.

It is important to analyse stocks into different categories as a different approach is likely to be appropriate for each. Where stocks of raw materials appear to be excessive it is worth concentrating on the production budget, and ensuring that actual purchases are in accordance with planned production, and that economic ordering quantities are used. Where work-in-progress appears to be excessive it is worth concentrating on production planning, and chasing progress to ensure that products are completed rapidly, and that too many different items of production are not left around, incomplete, because of some temporary problem, such as delay in obtaining a component.

It is also worth concentrating only on the most valuable items in stock. Sometimes as much as 90 per cent of the value of stocks may be in only 10 per cent of the items. It may not be worth bothering too much about lots of small items of little value.

Where stocks of finished goods appear to be excessive, there has presumably been a mismatch between the sales budget and the production budget: too much has been bought or produced, and/or not enough has been sold. Ways need to be found to reduce this problem in the future (perhaps by using appropriate control information more quickly). Consideration also has to be given to what special offers might be appropriate to clear excessive stocks.

Economic Order Quantity

Various quantitative techniques are available for effective management of inventories (or stocks). If the aim is to keep stocks at as low a level as practicable, there is a need to order small quantities at frequent intervals. But every time an order is placed there are significant administrative costs: placing the order, checking what has been received, and checking and paying invoices. The administrative costs of ordering suggest that it would be better to order larger quantities less frequently. It is possible to balance these two factors, as shown in Illustration 13.6.

Just in Time

Not many of us are interested in buying stale bread, and supermarkets do not plan to stock stale bread. They aim to have enough bread delivered each day to meet expected demand for that day. The idea is that stocks of bread arrive 'just in time' to meet the demand from customers; they do not plan to have 'buffer stocks' of bread to tide them over for a few weeks in case demand increases, or supplies become difficult to obtain. A sophisticated supermarket can plan demand for most of the things that it sells, and avoid having unnecessary stocks. The effectiveness of such arrangements depends partly on their forecasting abilities and partly on the quality of relationships with suppliers. A business that keeps making excuses for delaying payments to suppliers is less likely to be able to negotiate a quality service from them than a business which prioritizes the quality of relationships with suppliers, and ensures that they are paid on time.

This 'just in time' approach can also be applied to manufacturing, and many different organizations. If demand and production are properly planned, and good relationships are established with suppliers, it may be possible to have almost no stocks of raw materials and components at all. Everything arrives on the day that it is needed, and it is used straight away.

It may be more difficult to plan finished goods stocks in the same way, to minimize stocks, and to arrange that they are made 'just in time' for immediate sale. This is achievable where companies produce only those goods which have already been ordered.

A 'just in time' approach to stock levels is likely to keep stock levels to a minimum, and so to increase profitability. It is very different from a more traditional approach, keeping lots of items in stock 'just in case' suppliers prove not to be reliable. If the company does not care much about the

Illustration 13.6

The Chemvee company uses 10,000 special purpose disks each year, and pays 50 pence each for them. The administration cost associated with each order is £200, and annual stock holding costs are estimated at 25 per cent per annum. Calculate the Economic Order Quantity.

$$\text{EOQ} \quad \sqrt{\frac{2 \times \text{annual demand} \times \text{ordering cost}}{\text{Price per unit} \times \text{stockholding cost}}}$$

$$\sqrt{(2 \times 10{,}000 \times 200) \div (50\text{p} \times 0.25)}$$

$$\sqrt{4{,}000{,}000 \div 0.125} = 5{,}657$$

If the company orders 5,657 units at a time they will have to order $(10{,}000 \div 5{,}657 = 1.77)$ just less than twice a year: about once in 29 weeks. The average annual ordering cost will be $1.77 \times £200 = £354$ per annum.

When they receive each new order they will have 5,657 units in stock which will be gradually whittled down to zero units. On average they will have half of 5,657 units in stock ($2{,}828\frac{1}{2}$ each costing 50 pence) amounting to £1,414. Annual stockholding costs amount to 25 per cent of the amount of stock ($0.25 \times £1{,}414=$) £354.

We can see that the economic order quantity is the quantity at which the annual stock holding cost is equal to the annual ordering cost. If the company ordered more often, the annual cost of ordering would increase. If they ordered larger amounts, the annual stock holding cost would increase.

A formula such as this is useful in drawing attention to two of the key variables in determining stock levels, and providing rough guidelines. In practice it might be difficult to determine ordering costs and stock holding costs with the accuracy inherent in the use of the formula. Even annual demand may not be so predictable. A more serious weakness of the EOQ formula is that it ignores quantity discounts. It is often possible to negotiate price reductions in return for more substantial order quantities.

quality of its relationships with suppliers, and concentrates on buying the cheapest, and does not pay its suppliers on time, then a just in time approach is less likely to succeed.

13.4 **Managing Cash**

Sometimes companies choose to hold very substantial, and increasing amounts in the bank, as Lord Weinstock's GEC famously did. This may be a strategy to build up resources to buy another business; or it may be that the company generates lots of cash, and does not know what to do with it. Keeping money in the bank pays a very modest amount of interest, but it is stable and risk free, and a useful boost to cyclical earnings. Lord Weinstock's successors soon spent all of his cash pile on what turned out to be risky investments, and they destroyed almost all of the value of the company. It may seem pathetic if a company can think of nothing better to do with the shareholders' money than to put it in the bank to earn interest; but it is better than losing it all!

Other companies may have very substantial overdrafts for months or years. Overdrafts are a very flexible source of finance, and are particularly appropriate for financing seasonal variations, or short-term needs. Interest rates on overdrafts are generally higher than on borrowing for a period of years; but it may be worth paying a higher interest rate for the flexibility it can give. Interest is payable only for the exact amounts of money used, and only for the exact number of days it is used. A company might need an overdraft of £100,000 for only two months a year in the build up to Christmas. It is better to pay 12 per cent interest for the two months that the money is needed (=£2,000) than to take out a long-term loan at 6 per cent interest, and have to pay £6,000 a year interest.

Most of the time, however, companies plan their cash (or 'treasury' activities) carefully to ensure that they have enough in the bank to meet their regular needs. They do not want too much in the bank because it does not earn its keep – rates of interest are very modest. Companies *ought* to be able to invest surplus funds more profitably than simply leaving it in the bank. Sometimes the most sensible thing is to return surplus cash to shareholders, either as special, extra dividends, or by buying up shares on the market and cancelling them. Most of the time, companies also want to avoid excessive overdrafts, because borrowing money on overdraft for any extensive period tends to be more expensive than fixed rate/fixed term loans.

Careful planning, or cash budgeting, is required to avoid excessive overdrafts, and excessive surplus cash. Companies typically produce a detailed cash budget for a year in advance. The first draft of such a budget will reveal whether or not the company is likely to encounter serious cash shortages – perhaps in the month when they are due to pay dividends, or taxation, or buy additional fixed assets. By identifying the problem in advance they are likely to be able to find a planned way around it instead of being hit by a crisis. The preparation of cash budgets is illustrated in Chapter 7.

Planning and Control of Cash

Accountants often confuse us by sometimes using the word 'cash' to mean petty cash (i.e. coins and notes), and sometimes to mean money in the bank.

Some small businesses are very much 'petty cash' based, especially if they are avoiding keeping proper records and paying taxes. In most of this book the word 'cash' is used mainly in relation to money in the bank. A business generally has better control of bank-based transactions; special care is needed where there are a lot of transactions using coins and notes – especially in the retailing and hospitality industries. Coins and notes easily disappear; some staff can easily be tempted to 'borrow' cash; and many organizations not only use sophisticated electronic tills, but also arrange for access to them to be monitored by security cameras. Most of it probably ends up in the bank, and most of this chapter is concerned with money in the bank.

Sensible control of cash is likely to include the following:

1 Prompt banking of all cheques and surplus coins and notes. It is too easy to leave them sitting around in a safe or drawer for a week or more when the money could be in the bank earning interest, or reducing an overdraft. It is sensible to lay down a limit, such as £25,000, requiring any such sums to be banked on the day that they are received. Sometimes it is worth collecting large cheques from debtors and paying them into the bank immediately. Interest of 5 per cent per annum on £250,000 amounts to about £50 per working day. By collecting and banking a cheque today, instead of waiting to receive it, and then leaving it until a weekly visit to the bank, there can be a substantial gain in interest. It is worth devoting some staff time to prompt collection and banking of cheques; and even more worthwhile if the company is paying overdraft interest rates.

2 Centralized banking. Many businesses have a number of different branches or subsidiaries, some of which have plenty of cash while others need to borrow. It does not make sense for one part of an organization to be paying interest on an overdraft when another part of the same organization has surplus cash that is earning very little.

3 Making payments by cheque rather than cash. This is sensible from the point of view of security and control. As cheques take a number of days to clear, the company also has the benefit that the amounts involved remain in their bank account for a few days longer.

4 Receiving payments as cash, by direct debit or electronic transfer, rather than by cheque wherever possible. Customers can also be encouraged to make payments directly into a bank, by including a bank giro credit slip on the invoice; this means that the company's bank account is credited more quickly than waiting to receive a cheque and then putting it in the bank.

A neat way of summarizing the advantage to companies of receiving money quickly and paying it slowly is to say that first-class post should be used for sending invoices and reminders to debtors; second-class post should be used to send cheques to creditors!

5 Planning to make payments when most funds are available. Dividends should be paid out at times of the year when most funds are available – probably not in the month when most taxation is payable. Routine payments to creditors should be made at a time in the month when the company is likely to be most flush with cash – probably not at the end of the month when the salaries are paid. Payments for major acquisitions of fixed assets should be planned similarly, perhaps negotiating timing for payments which best suit the company buying the assets.

Most large companies have reasonably sophisticated treasury operations. Many small businesses can gain considerable benefit from devoting effort and planning to these activities.

Emergency Measures

Careful planning and control can avoid the need for 'emergency measures'. Banks are more helpful to businesses that can show that they know what they are doing, and are planning and anticipating periods when they will need additional borrowing, than they are to businesses that seem to have no effective planning, and suddenly hit an unexpected crisis.

1 The first port of call when a business has a 'liquidity crisis' is usually the bank, looking for an (increased) overdraft. It is worth cultivating a good relationship with a bank in the hope that they will be helpful when the need arises. Some people criticize banks for their caution in lending: they will lend only to those who do not really need to borrow! In deciding whether or not to lend, banks are concerned with security (what assets can a business offer as security for borrowing?). They are also concerned with profitability and cash flow (how much, and how soon will the business be able to pay back any borrowing?). They are, perhaps more than anything, concerned with the competence of management: if a business can show that they are in control, and can anticipate and solve problems, they are more likely to be supported than if they are suddenly hit by a crisis which should have been evident some months previously. Banks are also looking for realism. Businesses sometimes ask for too little money (when it seems to the bank that they are likely to need more), and they ask too late (the bank thinks that the problem could easily have been anticipated).

If a company has a good record with its bank, and can take advantage of additional overdraft facilities every time there is a problem, it may become a bad habit, and inappropriate. They should consider longer-term finance, investigate what the underlying problem seems to be, and consider alternative financing strategies. But, in an emergency, they may be driven to a number of expedients.

2 Delaying payments to creditors is an obvious short-term measure.

3 Pressing debtors to pay up more quickly may be sensible. But if severe problems lead to excessive pressure to encourage debtors to pay too quickly, this can lead to a serious loss of goodwill among customers.

4 Raising cash by reducing stocks can be useful. Many businesses have special clearance sales, and almost anything can be sold off for cash if the price is low enough.

5 Capital expenditure can be postponed, or special payment terms negotiated.

6 Surplus assets can be sold. Businesses often have more premises, or machinery, or vehicles than they really need, and they can raise cash by selling them. Some large companies, in times of crisis, suddenly appear to discover that they have expensive head office buildings in the centre of London, or country houses, or sports grounds (or even executive jets) that they do not really need. Smaller businesses can consider transferring their main administrative office to the spare bedroom at home! Sometimes companies deliberately maintain surplus capacity in case demand for their products increases. An alternative strategy, which frees up assets, is to plan to subcontract work at times of peak demand. Machinery can be rented on a short-term basis when required. And businesses can free up cash by selling off company cars and using taxis or bicycles instead – especially when the only realistic alternative is bankruptcy.

7 Deferring the payment of taxes can be negotiated with the Inland Revenue, although, of course, interest will be payable.

8 Dividends can be delayed, or reduced, or cancelled, although it looks better if this is planned in advance.

Some short-term crisis measures can do more harm than good, especially if there is an underlying problem, such as overtrading. But tackling a problem promptly and harshly is better than undue optimism – a key cause of business failure.[4]

13.5 **Managing Creditors**

To some extent stocks and debtors are financed by creditors, and such trade credit is an attractive source of finance. It is cost free, and the amount

---

4 Readers may think that accountants are unduly pessimistic, and that the optimists are the ones who are most likely to succeed in business. Optimism is fine – but don't get carried away. Make a friend of an accountant. The optimists may be the biggest successes in business, but they are also probably the biggest failures!

of creditors tends to increase in line with increases in sales, stocks and debtors. When a company has short-term liquidity problems, the easiest thing to do is to delay paying creditors. This does not cause much of a problem if it is only for a week or two, especially if, after a short-term blip, the company goes back to paying their creditors on time. But there is a danger that a company may be unable to resume normal payment periods, and that further delays will occur if they become too heavily dependent on creditors as a source of short-term funding.

Excessive delay in paying creditors is not cost free. Creditors soon lose patience with slow payers and are likely to cut off supplies, take legal action, or add interest to the amount due. If supplies are cut off because of slow (or no) payment, it may be difficult to get supplies on credit elsewhere – especially if a company gets a reputation as being a poor payer.

There is much to be said for cultivating good relationships with suppliers, keeping to the terms of the contract, and concentrating on the quality of the relationship including payment. A company that delays making payments is in a weak position when it comes to negotiating improvements in the quality of goods or services received from suppliers.

To some extent stocks and debtors are financed by creditors. It may even be that the amount owing to creditors is greater than the total of current assets; in this case short-term creditors are, in effect, financing some of the company's fixed assets. But a 'normal' working capital cycle would show that stocks represent a number of days sales; debtors represent a number of days sales; and this is only partly offset by the number of day sales represented by creditors.

Summary

In learning to interpret financial statements, working capital is one of the first things assessed; when the ratio of current assets to current liabilities (the current ratio) is calculated, it gives an indication of short-term solvency. In more advanced interpretation of accounts, working capital plays a key role in calculating Z scores and predicting financial distress. High levels of working capital are associated with financial strength. But excessive working capital reduces a company's profitability. Much of working capital management is concerned with ensuring that excessive funds are not tied up unprofitably in stocks, debtors and cash.

It may be convenient for managers and students to deal with working capital separately from fixed assets. But they should work together to generate successful returns for the company; both need to be financed and to earn their keep; and in most appraisals of new investment projects you can't have one without the other.

Review of Key Points

◆ Working capital is usually measured as current assets minus current liabilities

◆ Insufficient working capital is likely to be associated with liquidity problems

◆ Excessive working capital restricts profitability

◆ Debtors should be managed to minimize bad debts and to encourage debtors to pay up quickly

◆ The cost-effectiveness of different ways of managing debtors should be assessed

◆ Carrying excessive stocks is expensive for companies

◆ Careful planning and control of cash is essential

◆ Creditors should be paid in accordance with agreed terms; some companies prefer the short-term financial advantage of delaying paying their creditors

◆ Financial accounts indicate whether working capital and its constituent parts appear to be relatively high or relatively low

◆ Calculations and estimates can be made of the costs and benefits of different policies for managing each element of working capital

Self-testing Questions

1 Why might a company want high levels of working capital?

2 Can a company operate with zero or negative levels of working capital?

3 How would you detect overtrading, and why does it matter?

4 What steps can be taken to speed up the collection of debtors? Why might a company deliberately allow an increase in the time taken for debtors to pay?

5 What factors are taken into consideration in the conventional model for calculating Economic Order Quantities?

6 How can a company avoid having liquidity crises?

7 The Congle Company uses 40,000 wongles a year. Each wongle costs £1.25 to buy; stock holding costs are estimated to be 32 per cent per annum of the cost of the stocks held;

each order costs £20 to place. What ordering quantity will minimize costs? How many orders will be placed each year? How often will goods be delivered, and what is the average stock level? What is the annual stock holding cost?

8 Fleshwick Traders has a large overdraft on which interest of 17 per cent per annum is being charged. The directors are considering offering cash discounts to customers to encourage prompt payment. Annual sales, all on credit, amount to £365,000, and the debtors figure at present is £90,000. The sales director considers that a discount of 2.5 per cent for settlement in 10 days would be taken up by about one-third of their customers. The finance director thinks that a larger discount would be required to achieve this result. Assuming that the sales level remained constant:

(a) Would it be worth offering the discount if the sales director is right?

(b) What is the largest discount the company could offer without a reduction in profits?

(c) Assume that each £1 of sales contributes 20 pence to fixed costs and profits. If the company decided to offer a 5 per cent cash discount for payment in 10 days, and it is taken up by one-third of their customers, how large an increase in sales would be required to maintain profits?

9 Stokeypokey Wholesalers Limited are proposing to set up a branch in Northern Ireland. Experience elsewhere suggests that sales will start off at £100,000 a month in January, and then increase by £100,000 a month until reaching £400,000 in April. Then sales will increase by £80,000 a month until they reach £640,000 in July. In August sales are expected to reach £700,000 a month and remain at that level until the end of the year. Customers are expected to pay 2 months after the sales are made.

The cost of purchases is 80 per cent of the sales figure, and they are paid for in the month following the purchase. In January purchases will amount to £240,000; then, each month they purchase the amount of goods required for the following month.

Rent of £100,000 per quarter is payable at the beginning of January, and then in March, June, September and December. Other expenses, payable in the month that they are incurred, are expected to amount to £10,000 per month for the first 4 months; they will increase to £15,000 a month in May, and then to £16,000 a month in August–December.

The only capital expenditure is for purchase of fittings with £50,000 payable in January and £50,000 in September. Depreciation is at 10 per cent per annum with a full year's depreciation being charged in the first year.

The Northern Ireland branch starts business with an interest free loan of £1 million from Stokeypokey Wholesalers, which is put into a separate bank account.

(i) Prepare a summarized income statement (profit and loss account) for the first year of business.

(ii) Prepare a balance sheet as at the end of the first year.

(iii) Prepare a cash budget showing receipts and payments for each month for the year.

(iv) Comment on the results highlighting key learning points.

Assessment Questions

1 How can a company operate with minimum levels of working capital?

2 Working capital should be managed to maximize profitability. Explain and comment.

3 What steps can be taken to minimize bad debts?

4 What are the main limitations of the EOQ model?

5 The Scottish Cake Company has annual sales of £1,200,000. Annual fixed costs are £150,000 and last year's profit was £50,000. At the year end the debtors figure was £100,000.

   The company has been offered a contract for supplying cakes to the Swaysco Supermarket Group in England. Sales would be £300,000 in a year, and Swaysco would require 3 months' credit. The Scottish Cake Company's cost of capital is estimated at 15 per cent per annum. Is the proposed expansion worthwhile if all customers are given 3 months' credit? Is the proposed expansion worthwhile if only Swaysco is given 3 months' credit?

6 The summarized balance sheet of the Warmel Trading Company at 31 December last year was as follows:

	£	£
Fixed assets		3,000,000
Current assets		
Stocks	500,000	
Debtors	600,000	
Cash	10,000	
	1,110,000	
Creditors	110,000	1,000,000
		4,000,000
Share capital and reserves		4,000,000

Last year sales amounted to £3,600,000 and net profit before tax was £600,000. The company's target return on capital employed is 15 per cent. It is estimated that variable costs amount to 50 per cent of sales, and that fixed costs amount to £1,200,000 per annum.

   The purchasing manager is concerned about the very small amount of cash available and that the company may be unable to meet its current liabilities as they fall due.

   The financial accountant says that the level of debtors is too high, and proposes to appoint a credit controller at an annual cost of £25,000. He reckons that by doing this the amount of debtors could be halved.

   The sales manager believes that many customers are put off by the strict credit control policies, and would like to allow 3 months' credit to customers. If this policy was adopted he reckons that sales would increase by at least 10 per cent. The finance director estimates that such a policy would result in debtors taking, on average, 4 months to pay, that stocks and creditors would each increase by 10 per cent, and that bad debts would increase by £18,000 per annum.

Assessment Questions (continued)

Required:

(a) Evaluate the comments made by:

    (i)   the purchasing manager

    (ii) the financial accountant

    (iii) the sales manager and finance director.

(b) What would be your recommendation and why?

7 The following information has been extracted from the most recent annual report and accounts of Greyhound Leather Manufacturers Ltd:

	Year 1	Year 2
	£000	£000
Sales	20,000	22,000
Cost of sales	16,000	17,800
Gross profit	4,000	4,200
Operating profit	2,000	2,050
Net profit after tax	1,500	1,300
Shareholders' funds	15,000	16,000
Fixed assets	6,200	12,680
Stocks		
Raw materials	1,600	2,000
Work in progress	400	420
Finished goods	2,000	2,500
Debtors	5,000	3,200
Bank	2,000	(2,000)
Creditors	(2,200)	(2,800)
Net current assets	8,800	3,320

(a) The finance director is pleased with the management of working capital, but the chairman is more concerned about profitability. Making use of appropriate calculations you are required to analyse the financial management of the company and comment on the two points of view expressed.

(b) What is meant by the working capital cycle? Illustrate your answer with appropriate calculations for Greyhound Leather Manufacturers Ltd.

(c) What steps can a company take to improve stock turnover?

(d) The company uses one million hides of leather a year which they buy for £16 each. Stockholding costs are estimated to be 25 per cent per annum of the cost of the items in stock. Administration costs for placing and receiving an order are estimated to be £50. How many hides should the company order at a time? (i.e. calculate the Economic Order Quantity.)

(e) Illustrate the financial effects of implementing the EOQ in practice and suggest its limitations.

Assessment Questions (continued)

8 The directors of Woebun Standard Components plc have been very successful in persuading their customers to pay, on average, in one month. However, they believe that this policy is restricting sales and that sales would increase by 15 per cent if the average collection period for debtors was allowed to increase from one month to two months.

 The selling price of the component is £40 per unit and variable costs per unit are £30. Annual sales revenue is £6 million. A sales increase of 15 per cent would lead to an increase in stocks of £400,000 and an increase in trade creditors of £100,000.

 Woebun expects a return on capital employed of 27 per cent per annum.

(a) On purely financial grounds, should the company allow its customers to enjoy the extended credit period of 2 months?

(b) Assess the practicability and financial viability of restricting the 2 months' credit to new customers only.

(c) What are the main causes and symptoms of *overtrading*? To what extent and in what ways, can effective management of debtors avoid the problems of overtrading?

9 The Bonjarron Decorating Company uses 14,400 large size cans of white gloss paint in a year. They use different suppliers and, on average, pay £20 per can. They have limited storage space and reckon that the annual stock holding costs amount to 20 per cent of the cost of the stocks held. Administration costs amount to £50 per order placed.

(a) Calculate the EOQ.

(b) For what reasons might the company use (i) a much higher, or (ii) a much lower ordering quantity?

Group Activities and Discussion Questions

1 Many small businesses may be seen as 'overtrading'. Accountants are too conservative about such things. To be successful, a rapidly expanding small business needs to sail close to the wind. Discuss these views.

2 Large businesses should not have working capital problems. It is easy for them to borrow large sums on a long-term basis. The problem for large businesses is not working capital; it is excessive gearing.

3 Would you rather be a salesperson or a credit controller? Why?

4 Discuss the effects on just in time of increasing proportions of manufacturing (for the UK) taking placed in eastern Europe, Africa and Asia.

Group Activities and Discussion Questions (continued)

5 Can working capital, like manufacturing, be 'outsourced'? Could a company operate with zero or negative capital employed, make some profits, and therefore have a ROCE of infinity?

6 Large companies can bully small customers to pay up promptly, while they need not bother paying their own bills on time. Small companies have to pay up promptly if they are to continue to receive supplies, but they cannot force large customers to pay them promptly if they are to continue to make sales. Discuss these views.

7 How does cash budgeting for a business differ from the way in which you do your own, personal cash budgeting. Should it differ? (Other than the amounts of money being very different!)

Financial Accounting in context

Discuss and comment on the following item taken from the press:

How to defeat the Perkins principle of late payment by Jonathan Guthrie

Financial Times, 23 September 2003

I have found a name for the pain afflicting many small businesses, and it is Mr Perkins. He is the company accountant who is 'talking on another line' when you call about a three-month-old invoice. Alternatively he is 'travelling', or 'attending a meeting'.

Mr Perkins is doing none of these things. He is shaking his head at his secretary so she will dishonestly fob you off. This lets him return to his favourite pastime: gazing fondly out of the window at his shiny new Mondeo, paid for with the interest his company earns on balances rightfully belonging to its suppliers.

The fictional Mr Perkins is not a bad man. He loves his kids and pays at least some of his taxes. But when you put down the receiver you feel – quite wrongly from a legal viewpoint – that cutting off his Bugs Bunny tie with a big pair of scissors and making him eat it would be entirely justifiable.

The European Commission says that one in four business failures across the community results from bad debts. In the UK alone, the net trade debt that big companies owe small ones is estimated at £20bn. Then there is the cost of chasing late payment. Professor Nick Wilson of Leeds University Business School, who has studied the problem, says 'Firefighting late payment ties up a lot of effort which could otherwise be used making sales.'

In 1998 the government introduced a law allowing small companies to charge big customers interest on overdue money. The overall effect, according to recent research by Experian, the business information group, has been a big fat zero. The period that UK companies take to pay their bills is now 57.9 days, the same as six years ago.

Worse, figures compiled by Prof Wilson show the number of days companies with turnover of less than £5m have to wait for payment beyond agreed credit periods has doubled. The figure was in the mid-teens in 1999. Now it is about 30 days, against 11 days for larger companies.

Financial Accounting in context (continued)

The disparity shows that late payment reflects power relationships, not concepts of fairness or access to legal remedies. Stephen Alambritis, president of the Federation of Small Businesses, says: 'The fundamental problem is that our members are loath to use their power to charge interest for fear of souring relations with large customers. But experts believe big businesses have begun using their right to charge interest, gained a year ago, with the gusto that smaller peers have so conspicuously lacked. They must meanwhile be fuming at the abandonment of plans for a postal strike which would have given extra vim to the excuse "the cheque's in the post".'

The terrible reality for small business owners is that to get paid they sometimes have to reclassify Mr Perkins – a man they might normally view with the disfavour accorded a used surgical plaster – as a kind of secondary sales target. Would-be entrepreneurs freshly freed from the shackles of corporate wage slavery learn the hard way that 'a sale isn't a sale until you have collected the money and it has registered in your bank account,' as John Thorpe, a Lancashire businessman, puts it.

Mr Thorpe's company, Arras Services, a project management consultancy and recruitment agency, felt the pinch recently when a client let payment of a £30,000 invoice drift past the three-month mark. That created a cashflow problem for a business with annual turnover of just £300,000.

Mr Thorpe says extracting the money came down to understanding his customer's payment process and 'getting to know' accounts staff.

'There is a disconnect in most organisations between the people you do the work for and back-office people for whom your invoice is just another piece of paper,' he says. Clive Lewis, chairman of the Better Payment Practice Group, a campaigning body funded by the Department of Trade and Industry (www.payontime.co.uk), advocates agreeing clear payment terms with customers from the outset. 'People are often embarrassed to discuss these. It is a bit like talking about sex,' he says.

Openness is fine if your counter-parts are halfway honest. But there are plenty of chancers in business, who, as one jaded contact puts it, 'think delaying payment until they get a solicitor's letter is a way of proving their virility'. And there will always be well-intentioned companies whose perilously irregular cashflows means they cannot honour payment schedules.

The counsel of perfection that flows from this is to never let one customer represent a chunk of your sales larger than you can survive without. That gives you the option of 'sacking' a payments slowpoke and extracting the money in ways otherwise off-limits – through the courts or debt collectors.

I met two of these gentlemen a few years ago when they visited a struggling business where I worked. They wore leather jackets and radiated that special serenity that comes from being far too big to argue with. They departed clutching one of the few cheques written on those premises not predestined to bounce higher than a kangaroo on a pogo stick.

John Kelly, manager of the Direct Collections agency, says: 'It's simple. If a company has 15 creditors, it pays the one which sends a debt collector to visit first.' Do clients ever want him to get heavy with debtors? 'We have been asked to do many things,' he replies, 'but we are not thugs. We collect debts through discussion, not violence.' So I refrain from mentioning Mr Perkins, his Bugs Bunny tie, and the use a big pair of scissors might be put to.

References and Further Reading

Brealey, R.A., S.C. Myers and A.J. Marcus (2003) *Fundamentals of Corporate Finance*, 4th edn, McGraw-Hill.

Samuels, J.M., F.M. Wilkes and R. Brayshaw (1996) *Management of Company Finance*, 6th edn, Thomson Learning.

14

Investment Appraisal

Learning objectives

After studying this chapter you should be able to:

- ◆ Understand the difference between using cash flow and profit in making investment appraisals
- ◆ Calculate and interpret the return on investment (ROI), or return on capital employed of a project and appreciate its uses and limitations
- ◆ Calculate and interpret the payback period of a project and appreciate its uses and limitations
- ◆ Understand the principles of discounting and calculate a project's net present value and internal rate of return
- ◆ Evaluate the strengths and weaknesses of discounted cash flow (DCF) approaches to investment appraisal
- ◆ Understand which cash flows are relevant and should be included in a DCF calculation, and which are not
- ◆ Appreciate the importance of cost of capital in investment appraisal, and evaluate the relevance of cost of capital calculations
- ◆ Understand that there is always uncertainty and risk in investment appraisal and appreciate various ways of dealing with this

Introduction

Financial accounting is concerned with reporting to shareholders on the success of management in achieving what shareholders want. It may be assumed that the objective is to maximize 'shareholder value', and this value depends on the future profits and cash flows that a company is expected to generate. Actual results are reported regularly and can be compared with expectations. There is always the risk that expectations are exaggerated; that actual results will disappoint; and that companies' share prices will reflect this. A company's share price will suffer if they are known to produce fine sounding plans which fail to deliver the promised results. Companies which plan effectively how their shareholders' funds are to be utilized in financing fixed assets and current assets – and their actual results reflect their plans – are most likely to maximize shareholder value. To achieve this they should use proper investment appraisal techniques to ensure that shareholders' funds are used only to finance activities which will produce an adequate return. They must allow for risk and uncertainty; strike a balance between high risk projects which seem to promise a high return, and safer projects producing a lower return; and they should try to manage investors' expectations. They should also be aware of a company's cost of capital. A company with a low cost of capital should be able to find many investment opportunities which will generate substantial returns. A company with a cost of capital of 10 per cent per annum will find that projects yielding 12 per cent per annum are attractive. A company with a higher cost of capital (e.g. 15 per cent) will find that fewer projects are attractive, and it is more difficult to generate good returns for shareholders.

14.1 **Investment**

Individuals and companies invest money in the short term with the idea of getting back more, in the longer term, than the initial cost of the investment. This is a straightforward enough idea, but there are a number of issues that have to be addressed if we are to 'appraise' our investments properly.

1 How much do you need to get back to justify the amount invested?

2 How quickly does the money need to come back? If you can invest £1 today, and get back £10 after 50 years, the return might look brilliant, but the timing is terrible!

3 Risk. How sure are you that we will get back the amount suggested? There are various ways of allowing for risk and uncertainty in investment appraisal, but there is still a need for judgement, and to recognize that some uncertainty is inevitable in most businesses and projects.

Illustration 14.1

Elizabeth was made redundant recently and was given a severance payment of £55,000 which she uses to buy a special purpose delivery vehicle, and she employs a driver. Each year she receives money from customers for delivering goods; each year she pays all of her expenses in cash (wages, petrol, repairs, insurance etc.); and each year she pockets what is left: this amounts to £15,500 a year, which she reckons is a pretty good return on her initial capital of £55,000.

Unfortunately, Elizabeth forgot to allow for depreciation. After five years the vehicle is worn out, and she manages to sell it for £5,000. She should have allowed £10,000 a year for depreciation.

In terms of cash flow, Elizabeth made £15,500 a year. In terms of profit she made only £5,500 a year.

In this simple business we can see that

Profit	+ Depreciation	= Cash flow
£5,500	+ £10,000	= £15,500

Before considering the various approaches that are used in investment appraisal, it is necessary to be clear whether the returns that we expect an investment to make will be measured as

(a) profit; or
(b) cash flow.

Profit and Cash Flow

Profits are measured in accordance with all the usual rules that apply to income statements. Profit, by definition, should always mean after depreciation has been charged as an expense. But as depreciation is not 'paid' (no cash goes out of the business), the annual *cash flows* from a project are usually much higher than the annual *profits*. This is clearly illustrated by Elizabeth's proposed project in Illustration 14.1.

14.2 Methods of Investment Appraisal

Return on Capital Employed

One way of appraising an investment is to calculate its return on capital employed, also known as its *return on investment* (ROI). This assesses a project on the basis of future *profits*, which means that depreciation is charged as an expense (or deducted from cash flows), before calculating the return.

It can be expressed as follows:

$$\frac{\text{Average annual profits}}{\text{Amount initially invested}} \times \frac{100}{1}$$

The calculation of Elizabeth's return may be calculated as follows

$$\frac{5,500}{55,000} \times \frac{100}{1} = 10\%$$

Using ROI is an appealing approach to investment appraisal in a number of ways. It is in many ways consistent with conventional financial accounting. If the performance of a company as a whole is judged on the basis of profitability, using return on capital employed, then it makes sense to judge the performance of each part of the business using a return on capital employed. If a company wants to achieve a return on capital employed of, say 15 per cent per annum, they can be sure of achieving this if every part of the business, and every project achieves this return.

But calculating the return on the *initial* amount invested is likely to understate the returns that a company subsequently achieves. If a project has no scrap value, that is, the capital employed at the end of its life is zero, then the average capital employed is exactly half of the initial capital employed. The return on average capital employed will be double the return on initial capital employed.

If we think of Elizabeth's project, the amount of capital invested in the project will reduce each year as depreciation is charged. The amount invested is £55,000, initially. After one year's depreciation the amount of the investment will be reduced to £45,000. After 2 years it will be £35,000. After 3 years it will be £25,000. After 4 years it will be £15,000. At the end of 5 years it will be down to £5,000. We can say that the *average* amount invested in the project is the amount half way through its life, that is, after $2\frac{1}{2}$ years. The average amount invested is £30,000, and is calculated as follows:

$$\text{Average capital employed} = \frac{\text{Initial capital employed} + \text{Value at end}}{2}$$

$$£30,000 = \frac{£55,000 + £5,000}{2}$$

$$\text{Return on average capital employed} = \frac{5,500}{30,000} = 18.3\%$$

Elizabeth
Return on initial capital employed   10%
Return on average capital employed   18.3%

In deciding whether or not a proposed project is acceptable it is probably better to use the *average* amount invested, rather than the *initial* amount

Illustration 14.2

The Trudo machine will cost £50,000, and will have a 4-year life with zero scrap value at the end of 5 years. It will generate cash flows as follows:

Year 1	10,000
Year 2	16,000
Year 3	20,000
Year 4	20,000
Total	66,000

To calculate average annual profit it is necessary to calculate average annual depreciation charges.

There is no need to know what method or rate of depreciation will be used. The total amount to be written off, whatever method is used, is £50,000. The total cash flows are £66,000. The total profits must therefore be £16,000. Averaged over 4 years, the profits are £4,000 a year.

We could work out average annual profits as follows

Average annual cash flows	£66,000 ÷ 4 = £16,500
Average annual depreciation	£50,000 ÷ 4 = £12,500
	£ 4,000

The return on initial amount of capital employed is:

$$\frac{£4,000}{£50,000} = 8\%$$

The return on the average capital employed is:

$$\frac{£4,000}{£25,000} = 16\%$$

invested. This is a less prudent approach: as we saw above, using the average amount invested shows a higher return. The Trudo Machine should not be rejected on the grounds that its ROI is 'only' 8 per cent. And Elizabeth should not reject what might be a perfectly good project on the basis that it achieves a return on initial investment of only 10 per cent.

It is difficult to relate the ROI of a project to the company's cost of capital. It would be appealing to say that if a company's cost of capital is, say, 12 per cent, any project with a ROI of greater than 12 per cent should be accepted because it would increase the company's average return on capital employed, and so increase the value of the company. There are several important reasons why such a neat rule of thumb could lead to some very bad decisions.

1 There are many different ways of calculating ROI. As we have seen, choosing to use the average amount of capital employed in a project produces a very different answer from using the initial amount of capital employed. If the ROI achieved by a project is to be compared with the company's cost of capital, then it is incorrect to treat interest as an expense in calculating the ROI. But some users and advocates of ROI do strange things with interest; some revalue assets and do strange things with depreciation. Great care is needed in using ROI, to ensure that like is compared with like.

2 ROI ignores the timing of future cash flows and profits. It simply averages profits over the life of the project. It assumes that making £10,000 profit next year is the same as making £10,000 profit after 2 years, or any number of years. Shareholders want to see results within a relatively short period of time. The problem can be illustrated by comparing two projects, one of which generates cash flows and profits more quickly, and one which generates more profit and cash flow, but over a longer period.

In Illustration 14.3 the Jaggie project makes only £40 profit, but the Lardie project makes £45 profit. The ROI is therefore higher for the Lardie project than it is for the Jaggie project. But the Jaggie project makes the money much more quickly, and might be a better project.

3 Use of ROI can also be criticized because it depends on all of the usual assumptions in financial accounting. ROI, and attempts to make consistent and comparable decisions, are limited by the extent to which there are variations in accounting policies, the use of 'creative accounting', and any questionable assumptions in measuring profits or capital employed.

Return on investment, or return on capital employed, is the only method of investment appraisal which uses profit figures as opposed to cash flow figures. The 'return' means profit, and in calculating profit, depreciation has to be deducted.

Other methods of investment appraisal are based on cash flows, not profit. Depreciation is not deducted from cash flows when calculating payback period, or discounted cash flow.

Payback Period

The easiest way to deal with the timing of future returns is to ask the simple question: how quickly do we get our money back? A project which gives you your money back in 3 years is likely to be better than one which takes 5 years to give you your money back.

Illustration 14.3

Year	Jaggie Project Cash Flow	Depreciation	Profit	Lardie Project Cash Flow	Depreciation	Profit
0	(100)			(100)		
1	45	20	25	10	20	(10)
2	40	20	20	20	20	–
3	35	20	15	30	20	10
4	10	20	(10)	40	20	20
5	10	20	(10)	45	20	25
Total	140	100	40	145	100	45

	Jaggie	Lardie
Average annual profits	$40 \div 5 = 8$	$45 \div 5 = 9$
Average capital employed	50	50
Return on average investment	16%	18%

In deciding between Jaggie and Lardie we need a method of investment appraisal which takes into account not just the amounts of cash flows or profits that a project generates, but also the timing of them. It is better to get our money back quickly than slowly.

In both of these projects there are years when no profit is being made. But as long as a project is generating positive net cash flows it is usually worth continuing with it, even if it makes no profit after depreciation has been charged.

A quick look at Jaggie and Lardie shows that both require an initial investment of £100, but Jaggie pays it back much more quickly. After only 2 years Jaggie has already produced cash flows of £95, and will have paid back the full £100 just a couple of months into the third year. But Lardie is much slower: it has not repaid the full £100 until the end of the fourth year.

As a method of investment appraisal payback period has a number of clear advantages:

1 It is easy to calculate, easy to understand, and easy to present.

2 It is based on cash flow, not profit, and so is seen as being more objective with less dependence on questionable accounting assumptions.

3 It emphasizes the need for projects to repay quickly, which is important, especially if we take into account the cost of the funds invested in a project.

4 Projects with shorter payback periods are likely to be less risky than projects which take longer to pay back the initial investment. In forecasting the results of a project we can be much more certain about costs and revenues in the first few years than we can be about what might happen 5 or 10 years into the future.

If we combine ROI with payback period we might make reasonable investment decisions. ROI takes into account all the profits that a project makes throughout its life; it ignores timing. Payback period considers only the length of time it takes for cash flows to amount to the amount of the original investment; it ignores cash flows after the payback period.

Using only the payback period as a method of investment appraisal could lead to really silly decisions, as Illustration 14.4 shows.

Illustration 14.4

Rudi pays £100,000 for a 3-year lease on an office building that will generate cash flows of £50,000 a year for 3 years, and then have no residual value.

Duri pays £100,000 for the freehold of some shop premises which will bring him cash flows of £12,500 a year for many years into the future.

Rudi's payback period is 2 years.
Duri's payback period is 8 years.

If the two investments were compared solely on the basis of payback period, Rudi's is clearly the better investment. But in this case it is worth waiting longer to get a lot more money back. It is clear that Duri's project is the better one (unless the cost of capital is very high).

The disadvantages of using the payback period are:

1 It ignores cash flows after the initial amount has been paid back.

2 It does not consider the timing of cash flows in a systematic way.

Looking at the payback period may be a convenient way of screening out projects that take far too long to pay back, but it does not indicate whether or not a project is worthwhile. A project must produce enough total cash flows, as well as doing so within a reasonable period.

It is also necessary to consider the timing of cash flows more precisely. This is done by allowing for the fact that any delay in receiving money has a cost, which is like the cost of interest for the period of the delay.

Methods of investment appraisal should take into account the amounts and timing of future cash flows. This is best done using discounted cash flow.

Discounted Cash Flow: Net Present Value

It is obviously better to receive £100 today than to receive £100 in one year's time. We might prefer to receive the £100 today because we fear that it might not be on offer in a year's time – there is always an element of risk. We might prefer to receive the £100 today because we fear that inflation will erode its value: in one year's time it might be able to buy less than today. But even if we assume that there is no risk, and that there is no inflation, we would still prefer to receive £100 today rather than wait a year for it. If we receive £100 today we can invest it, and after a year it might be worth £104, or more, depending how successful the investment is. In waiting for the money we lose the opportunity of using it to generate a return – even if the return is only 4 per cent interest.

We could say that if we have to wait to receive money, we need to receive more to compensate for the waiting, and the fact that we were unable to make use of the money while waiting. Companies ought to be able to invest money more profitably than putting it in a bank to earn 4 per cent. People invest in companies for that very reason: companies should have better investment opportunities than individuals.

If we have the choice of receiving £100 today, or £120 in a year's time, the decision is a little more difficult, but it is always worth waiting to receive money, *if* we are going to receive extra money to compensate for the delay. Indeed, that is the whole nature of investment: we pay out money in the short term in order to receive more back in the future. If a company's cost of capital[1] is 10 per cent, it is well worth waiting a year to receive £120 than having only £100 today.

If we assume that a company's cost of capital is 10 per cent per annum, then we can calculate the cost of waiting to receive money. If we know the cost of an investment, and we know what cash flows it will generate in the future, and when, then it is a matter of arithmetic to determine whether or not an investment is worthwhile. We apply a 10 per cent interest rate to 'discount' future cash flows. If we have to wait one year to receive £100, that is the equivalent of receiving £90.91 today. This is because, if we received £90.91 today, we could invest it at 10 per cent for a year, and then it would give us exactly £100 in a year's time. If we have to wait 2 years for it, then the 'present value' is £82.64. If we have to wait 3 years for it, then the net present value is £75.13. If we have to wait 4 years for it, then the net present value is £68.30 and so on.

It is easy to check this. If we had £68.30 today, and it earned 10 per cent a year interest, at the end of 4 years it would amount to £68.30 × 1.1 × 1.1 × 1.1 × 1.1, which comes to £100.

----

1   There are problems in determining what a company's cost of capital is, and that will be dealt with in Section 14.3 below.

A company's 'opportunity cost' of capital might be 10 per cent because they have opportunities to invest in projects which give a positive net present value when discounted at 10 per cent. If they have £100 today, they expect it to become £110 after one year. If this is the case, we can make the following statements:

1 Receiving £100 today is equivalent to receiving £110 after one year.

2 Waiting one year to receive £110 is equivalent to receiving £100 today.

3 Waiting one year to receive £100 is equivalent to receiving £90.91 today. This is because if we have £90.91 today, and we invest it at 10 per cent, we will make £9.09 interest in one year which will give us (£90.91 + £9.09 =) £100 after one year.

4 Waiting 2 years to receive £100 is equivalent to receiving £82.64 today. This is because if we have £82.64 today, and we invest it at 10 per cent, we will make £8.26 interest in the first year, giving us (£82.64 + £8.26 =) about £90.90,[2] which, after another year at 10 per cent will give us £100.

5 We can look at any future cash flows and discount them in this way.

This is all very important in investment appraisal. The nature of investment is that we pay out money now, and expect to get returns in the future. To start with we need to work out what those future returns are likely to be, and to assess the timing of them. Then we need to 'discount' the future cash flows to take into account the cost of having to wait for them. We will continue to assume that the cost is 10 per cent per annum, but equivalent calculations can be made for any 'discount rate'.

We have already established that receiving £100 after

| 1 year | is equivalent to receiving | £90.91 today |
| 2 years | is equivalent to receiving | £82.64 today |

We can continue as follows:

| 3 years | £75.13 |
| 4 years | £68.30 and so on |

The easiest way of finding these 'discount factors' is to look them up in a present value table, as shown in Illustration 14.5.

We can then apply these discount factors to the cash flows of a particular project to find the 'present value' of the future cash flows, assuming a cost of capital of 10 per cent. This is applied to Jaggie and Lardie as shown in Illustration 14.6.

---

2   There are usually some 'rounding' errors with discounting, so the figures may not be exact.

Illustration 14.5

Present value table

	5%	10%	15%	20%	25%	30%
1	0.952	0.909	0.870	0.833	0.800	0.769
2	0.907	0.826	0.756	0.694	0.640	0.592
3	0.864	0.751	0.658	0.579	0.512	0.455
4	0.823	0.683	0.572	0.482	0.410	0.350
5	0.784	0.621	0.497	0.402	0.328	0.269
6	0.746	0.564	0.432	0.335	0.262	0.207
7	0.711	0.513	0.376	0.279	0.210	0.159
8	0.677	0.467	0.327	0.233	0.168	0.123
9	0.645	0.424	0.284	0.194	0.134	0.094
10	0.614	0.386	0.247	0.162	0.107	0.073

Illustration 14.6

Year	Jaggie Project Cash flow	Jaggie Project Discount factor	Jaggie Project Net present value	Lardie Project Cash flow	Lardie Project Discount factor	Lardie Project Net present value
0	(100)			(100)		
1	45	0.9091	40.91	10	0.9091	9.09
2	40	0.8264	33.06	20	0.8264	16.53
3	35	0.7513	26.30	30	0.7513	22.54
4	10	0.6830	6.83	40	0.6830	27.32
5	10	0.6209	6.21	45	0.6209	27.94
Total	140	100	113.31	145		103.42

After reducing all future cash flows using a 10 per cent discount factor, we can see that the total net present value for each of the projects is as follows:

Jaggie	(£113.31 − £100 =)	£13.31
Lardie	(£103.62 − £100 =)	£3.42

Although Lardie brings in more money than Jaggie, it is not worth waiting for. Jaggie earns enough to cover the cost of capital, and an extra £13.31.

Illustration 14.7

Year 1   Divide the cash flow by 1 + the discount rate
Divide the cash flow by 1.1 for a 10 per cent discount rate

Cash flow $\dfrac{45}{1.1} = £40.91$

Year 2   Divide the cash flow by 1.1 × 1.1 to allow for 2 years (i.e. 1.1 squared)

Cash flow $\dfrac{40}{1.1 \times 1.1} = £33.06$

or $\dfrac{40}{(1.1)^2}$

Year 3   Divide the cash flow by 1.1 × 1.1 × 1.1 to allow for 3 years (i.e. 1.1 cubed, or 1.1^3)

Cash flow $\dfrac{35}{(1.1) \times (1.1) \times (1.1)} = £26.30$

Year 4   Divide the cash flow by 1.1 × 1.1 × 1.1 × 1.1 to allow for 4 years (i.e. 1.1^4)

Cash flow $\dfrac{10}{(1.1) \times (1.1) \times (1.1) \times (1.1)} = £6.83$

Year 5   Divide the cash flow by 1.1 multiplied by itself 5 times to allow for five years (i.e. 1.1^5)

$\dfrac{10}{(1.1)^5} = £6.21$

Lardie does cover its cost of capital, and has a positive net present value. But Jaggie has a greater net present value, and so is the better investment.

Discount rates can be applied in this way to most projects. Once the discount rate, or cost of capital[3] has been decided, the best project is the one that produces the highest net present value.

If discount tables are not available, it is possible to work out the figures for Jaggie as shown in Illustration 14.7.

For those who are not particularly good at mathematics it is probably easier to use discount tables. But if you want to do it without tables, here are the three easy steps:

(a) Decide on the discount rate, and add it to 1, as follows:

3 Or opportunity cost of capital.

5%	becomes	1.05
10%	becomes	1.1
15%	becomes	1.15

(b) Multiply the figure given in (a) by itself once for year 1; twice for year 2; three times for year 3; four times for year 4 and so on.

(c) Divide the cash flow for each year by the figure given in (b) above to 'discount' it to give the 'present value'.

When we have identified all of the future cash flows, and then allowed for the delay in receiving them by 'discounting' them, we know the net present value of the future cash inflows. This can be compared with the amount of the initial outflow to see if the project has earned us the 10 per cent which we specified as the cost of capital. Investment decisions should be based on choosing those projects which give the maximum cash flows, after applying the appropriate discount rate. This is called the net present value.

Discounted Cash Flow: Internal Rate of Return

With the net present value (NPV) approach to investment appraisal we need to select a discount rate; then the net present value of the project is calculated. With Jaggie, the NPV was £13.31. With Lardie the NPV was £3.42. The answer will always be a sum of money (it could happen to be zero).

If we do not know what discount rate to use, we could put the question the other way around: what discount rate would make future cash flows exactly equal to the amount of the initial investment? In other words, at what discount rate does the project break even, or give a zero net present value?

With the internal rate of return (IRR) we do not assume a discount rate. Instead we try to find a discount rate at which the net present value of the project is zero. The answer will always be a percentage. A quick glance at Jaggie and Lardie suggests that the IRR of Jaggie is well above 10 per cent. As Lardie has a much smaller NPV its IRR is likely to be not much above 10 per cent. In the calculations in Illustration 14.8 20 per cent is chosen as a guess for Jaggie, and 15 per cent for Lardie.

When the cash flows of Jaggie and Lardie are discounted using higher discount rates we can see that the totals amount to less than the £100 originally invested. Comparing these results with those shown using a 10 per cent discount rate we can say that:

Jaggie earns more than 10 per cent: it has a positive NPV of £13.31 when discounted at 10 per cent

Jaggie earns less than 20 per cent: it has a negative NPV of (£100 − £94.37 =) £5.63 when discounted at 20 per cent

Illustration 14.8

	Jaggie Project			Lardie Project		
Year	Cash flow	Discount factor 20%	Net present value	Cash flow	Discount factor 15%	Net present value
0	(100)			(100)		
1	45	0.8333	37.50	10	0.8696	8.70
2	40	0.6944	27.78	20	0.7561	15.12
3	35	0.5787	20.25	30	0.6575	19.72
4	10	0.4823	4.82	40	0.5718	22.87
5	10	0.4019	4.02	45	0.4972	22.37
Total	140		94.37	145		88.78

Jaggie's IRR is between 10 per cent and 20 per cent; but it is closer to 20 per cent

Lardie earns more than 10 per cent: it has a positive NPV of £3.62 when discounted at 10 per cent

Lardie earns less than 15 per cent: it has a negative NPV of (£100 − £88.78 =) £11.22 when discounted at 15 per cent

Lardie's IRR is between 10 per cent and 15 per cent; but it is closer to 10 per cent

A better estimate of IRR can be made using interpolation.

We know that Jaggie's IRR is between 10 per cent and 20 per cent. It is 10 per cent plus a part of 10 per cent.

$$\text{IRR} = 10\% + \frac{13.31}{(13.31 + 5.63)} \times 10\%$$

$$= 10\% + 0.7 \times 10\%$$

$$= 17\%$$

We know that Lardie's IRR is between 10 per cent and 15 per cent. It is 10 per cent plus a part of 5 per cent

$$\text{IRR} = 10\% + \frac{3.62}{(3.62 + 11.12)} \times 5\%$$

$$= 10\% + 0.24 \times 5\%$$

$$= 11.2\%$$

We can now compare the two investments, Jaggie and Lardie, using different approaches to investment appraisal.

	Jaggie	Lardie
Return on average investment	16%	18%
Payback period	2.14 years	4 years
Net present value at 10%	£13.31	£3.62
Internal rate of return	17%	11.2%

Jaggie is clearly the better project. Lardie showed a better return on investment because it produces slightly more profits. But because Jaggie produces cash flows more quickly it shows a shorter payback period, and it is better using discounted cash flow (DCF).

Advantages of using internal rate of return are:

1 It deals properly with the timing of all cash flows

2 Seeing an answer as a percentage appears to be easy to understand and can be compared with a company's cost of capital

3 It is difficult to know what a company's cost of capital is, and so what discount rate should be used to calculate NPV. Using IRR sidesteps this. A company could simply rank all projects according to the IRR that each achieves; it would select the projects with the highest IRRs, and reject those with the lowest. Assuming that the company has only limited funds for investment, those funds would be allocated to the projects which have the highest IRR.

The main disadvantages of using internal rate of return are:

1 It involves more calculations than other methods

2 It is technically flawed and can lead to incorrect decisions. This is particularly true where there are irregular patterns of cash flows (perhaps with inflows coming before outflows), and high discount rates.

A variety of different techniques for investment appraisal may be used. Sometimes the use of one technique rather than another can lead to a different, and perhaps a poor, investment decision. The best approach is to use DCF to calculate the NPV. In order to do this it is necessary to know what discount rate to use, or the 'cost of capital'.

Which Cash Flows to Include

It is easy to get lost in the technicalities and complications of DCF and overlook the fact that the calculations can be no better than the basic data on which they are based. Estimates have to be made of the cost of the project, of the future cash inflows and outflows that it will generate, and of the cost of capital, and there is always an element of risk and uncertainty.

The appraisal should take into account all cash flows that would result from the project being undertaken, and exclude all cash flows that would arise whether or not the project is undertaken. There are a number of problem areas, including those shown below. It is important not only to have the best estimates of the amounts of the cash flows, but also to be clear about the timing of them.

1   Working capital. Where a project involves expansion, there is usually a requirement for additional working capital (financing stocks and debtors) at the beginning, which is treated as a cash outflow. It is usually assumed that at the end of the project's life the additional working capital will no longer be required, and so becomes a cash inflow.

2   Installation. Where a new piece of equipment is being bought, the cash outflow for it should include any payments for installation and setting it up.

3   Scrap values. If a new machine is being bought there is often a cash inflow from the sale of the old machine. If this scrapping is a direct result of buying the new machine, then the cash inflow from the scrap value should be included in the appraisal. When the new machine comes to the end of its life, perhaps after 5 or 10 years, we usually assume that there will be a cash inflow from selling it.

4   Taxation. If a new project is going to make more money for the company (that is usually the intention), more corporation tax will be payable on the profits, and the appraisal should include these additional payments. They usually take place in the year after the profit has been earned. The tax computations can be rather complicated. The Inland Revenue allows profits to be reduced for tax purposes by substantial allowances for depreciation (usually more generous than the amounts that the company charges in their financial accounts). There may also be additional payments in respect of any profit on sale of the old machinery; or a reduction in payments if there is a loss.

5   Relevant costs. Some costs will be incurred, and the payments made, whether or not the project is undertaken. A project may be charged its share of fixed overheads (such as the costs of providing a factory and its administration), but as those costs will be incurred whether or not the project is undertaken, the cash flows for fixed overheads are usually excluded.

6   Sunk costs. There are often significant payments for market research and feasibility studies which are undertaken before a decision is made on

whether or not to go ahead. As those costs have already been incurred or paid (they are 'sunk'), they are irrelevant in deciding whether or not to go ahead, and should not be included in the appraisal.

7 Opportunity costs. The cost of using an asset for a particular project is often the 'opportunity cost' and the best alternative use.

Illustration 14.9

A company owns a machine which they originally bought for £100,000 and on which depreciation of £80,000 has been charged. They could sell for scrap for £10,000; alternatively they could hire it out to another manufacturer, and the net present value rentals receivable for doing this would be £15,000.

The net book value of £20,000 is irrelevant. The opportunity cost of using for another purpose is £15,000.

14.3 Cost of Capital

Some organizations establish a 'cut off' cost of capital figure almost arbitrarily. Any project which gives a positive net present value when discounted at, say, 10 per cent is acceptable. One advantage of this is that everyone knows where they are, and which projects are going to be acceptable, and which are not. In the unlikely event that a company has unlimited funds available at a cost of 10 per cent, then the more projects they take on, provided they clear the hurdle rate of 10 per cent, the better.

If the amount of finance available is limited, the company chooses those projects which give the greatest net present value when discounted at 10 per cent.

One way of establishing the cost of capital is to look at the 'opportunity cost of capital'. If there are limited funds available, and more than enough projects that show a net present value when discounted at, say, 14 per cent, then the cut off rate for projects should be 14 per cent. No projects should be undertaken unless they show a positive net present value when discounted at 14 per cent. If there are plenty of projects that can do better than 17 per cent, then the company should undertake only those projects which show a positive net present value at 17 per cent. There is no point in tying up limited funds on projects that achieve only, say 11 per cent, if there is the opportunity to invest in projects that achieve 14 per cent or more. Shareholders are not likely to be impressed when companies start investing in projects that have lower returns than previously. If management are trying to maximize shareholder wealth, they must aim to increase profitability and cash flows, and so (hopefully) share prices. They should not undertake projects which are likely to lower the company's returns, and share price. When companies cannot find sufficiently profitable opportunities for investing funds that they have available, they should return those funds to shareholders as dividends, or use them to buy up the company's shares. There are plenty of examples of companies that have invested surplus funds unwisely, and so have reduced the value of the company.

Most companies have some idea of a 'hurdle rate' which an investment should achieve, otherwise the investment will be rejected. The hurdle rate should also be the company's opportunity cost of capital: they should not invest in a Lardie if that would mean losing the opportunity to invest in a Jaggie.[4]

In practice it is usually difficult to know for sure what cash flows an investment will produce, how many years the return will continue for, and what its value will be, if any, at the end – if indeed the proposal has an end in mind. Given these uncertainties, any sophisticated attempts to calculate a company's cost of capital may be a waste of time and effort. It is probably better to put the effort into forecasting the project itself, and evaluating alternative scenarios, than trying to pretend that we can guess what discount rate is required to meet shareholders' expectations.

Most companies prepare some sort of business plan, perhaps looking 5–10 years into the future. Often, particularly with smaller businesses, these are prepared mainly for their bankers, or others who supply funds. If the bank is going to charge, say, 10 per cent per annum interest, this is probably a reasonable approximation of a company's cost of capital. If budding entrepreneurs decide to accept all projects with a positive net present value when discounted at 10 per cent, and reject those that do not, they probably won't go far wrong. Their hurdle rate would be the rate of interest to be charged.[5]

It is important that a company has a sensible hurdle discount rate for investment appraisal. If it is set too low, perhaps at 7 per cent, then the company is likely to invest in projects that barely earn their keep; that disappoint the owners of the business; and that result in the value of the business falling.

If the hurdle rate is set too high, perhaps at 22 per cent, then the company is likely to reject projects that more than earn their keep. If projects which earn a good return are rejected, then the business loses opportunities to increase its value.

---

4   Based on the figures in Illustration 14.6 where a 10 per cent cost of capital has been assumed.

5   After allowing for taxation, the cost of interest would be less; but the cost of shareholders' funds would be more; so 10 per cent would be a reasonable approximation. A higher discount rate, up to say 15 per cent, could be used for more risky projects.

Companies are usually financed partly by borrowing, and partly by shareholders' funds. At first sight it is not difficult to establish the cost of borrowing: the interest rate on borrowings is usually specified. The cost of shareholders' funds is more difficult. As there is no requirement for companies to pay dividends on ordinary shares, we might be tempted to think that shareholders' funds have no real cost. They are 'free', and provided the company makes *some* profit, that is OK. But directors who do not meet shareholders' expectations in terms of profit will probably soon find themselves out of a job. Low profits lead to low share prices; low share prices invite takeover bids; and when another company acquires a company that is seen to be failing, they will soon get rid of the previous managers.

The cost of ordinary shareholders' funds depends on market expectations. The company should aim to invest in ways which increase the value of the company, not in ways which reduce the value of the company. Attempts to identify a company's cost of capital are attempts to identify the discount rate that projects must achieve in order to at least maintain the value of the company. There are widely used methods of indicating the cost of capital for a company that is listed on the stock market. For unlisted companies, comparisons can be made with listed companies, and common sense suggests a discount rate of between 10 per cent and 15 per cent would usually be a reasonable approximation.

Weighted Average Cost of Capital

A company might be half financed by borrowing, which costs 8 per cent per annum; and half financed by shareholders' funds, which cost 14 per cent per annum. In this case the company's average cost of capital is 11 per cent

Another company might be 25 per cent financed by borrowing, which costs 8 per cent per annum; and 75 per cent financed by shareholders' funds, which cost 14 per cent per annum. In this case the company's weighted average cost of capital is 12.5 per cent.

$$
\begin{aligned}
25\% \times 8\% &= 2\% \\
75\% \times 14\% &= \underline{10\%} \\
& \underline{12.5\%}
\end{aligned}
$$

In calculating the weighting of the different types of capital (e.g. shareholders' funds 75 per cent; loan capital 25 per cent), it is probably better to use the *market* value of shareholders' funds, and the *market* value of borrowings rather than the amounts shown on the balance sheet.

Cost of Borrowing

A company might have issued £1 million of 10 per cent debentures, but that does not necessarily mean that the cost of those debentures is 10 per cent per annum. If the market value of debentures falls below the balance sheet value, the amount of interest payable remains the same; but the *effective* rate (interest payable as a percentage of market value) will be higher. Similarly, if the market value of debentures increases, the effective interest rate declines. A number of other factors have to be taken into consideration:

1   Interest is an allowable expense for corporation tax purposes. If the company's effective rate of corporation tax is 25 per cent, then the effective cost of 10 per cent interest to the company immediately falls to 7.5 per cent.

2   Most debentures are redeemable at some future date, perhaps 5 or 10 years into the future. They may be redeemable at par (or book value, or face value); they may be redeemable at a discount (e.g. £100 debentures redeemable for £95); or they may be redeemable at a premium (e.g. £100 debentures redeemable at £110).

The calculation of the cost of debentures can look like doing a DCF calculation to arrive at the internal rate of return as shown in Illustration 14.10.

Cost of Equity (Cost of Ordinary Shareholders' Funds)

Establishing the cost of equity is more difficult: there is no requirement to pay dividends, and it might be tempting to think that there is no cost attached to shareholders' funds. Shareholders have money invested in the business, and if they are lucky they will receive dividends, and the value of their shareholdings will increase. If they are unlucky there will be no dividends, and the value of their shareholdings will decline.

In a small company, perhaps where all of the equity is owned by one or two directors, they can do what they like. If they choose to regard shareholders' funds as having zero cost, and to invest in duff projects, that is their own business.

If a listed company decided that shareholders' funds are cost free, they would soon find themselves in trouble. If a company does not produce enough profits, dividends and whatever else shareholders might expect, the share price will soon fall.

In order to determine a company's cost of ordinary shareholders' funds (or the cost of equity capital) we need to know what rate of return the company needs to maintain, or increase, the value of the company. This really depends on shareholders' expectations. If they are expecting a return of 10 per cent, and the company generates 15 per cent, then the value of the company should increase. If they are expecting 15 per cent, and the company generates only 10 per cent, then we can expect the value of the company to decrease.

We assume that the cost of equity depends on investors' expectations about the future. But it is not clear how these expectations can be quantified.

Illustration 14.10

The market value today of Air UK's 6% Debentures is £80 for £100 par value. The debentures are redeemable at £105 four years from today. The company is profitable and their effective rate of taxation is 30 per cent.

The cost of interest each year is 70 per cent of £6 which is £4.20. At first sight the cost of the loan capital looks like 70 per cent of £6 per annum, which is 4.2 per cent. But the effective cost is increased by the premium which is payable on redemption, and by the fact that the current market value of the debentures is well below the £100 par value.

The cash flows associated with it are shown in the second column below. As the cost of the debentures is likely to be more than 6 per cent, as a first guess we try discounting the cash flows at 10 per cent.

Year	Cash Flow	Discount factor 10%	Net present value	Discount factor 15%	Net present value
0	(80)	1.0	(80)	1.0	(80)
1	4.2	0.9091	3.81	0.8696	3.65
2	4.2	0.8264	3.47	0.7561	3.18
3	4.2	0.7513	3.15	0.6575	2.76
4	109.2	0.6830	74.59	0.5718	62.44
			85.02		72.03

When discounted at 10 per cent, the future cash flows associated with the debenture are more than the price of the debenture now. The cost of the debentures to the company (in relation to the current market value) is therefore more than 10 per cent per annum.

When discounted at 15 per cent, the future cash flows associated with the debenture are less than the price of the debenture now. The cost of the debentures to the company (in relation to the current market value) is therefore less than 15 per cent per annum.

$$\text{Interpolation suggests a cost of} \qquad 10\% + \frac{5.01}{(5.01 + 7.97)} \times 5$$

$$= 11.9\%$$

If the company has nothing better to do with its money it should consider buying up the debentures on the stock market. But if the company's opportunity cost of capital is 12 per cent or more, it should be able to find a more profitable use of funds.

Even if we could find out what it is that determines future share prices, by the time we have found out, the picture would have changed; any model that predicts share prices, based on historic data, needs to be constantly updated to maintain credibility.[6] Sometimes companies seem to promise a lot, and their share price goes up and up. But if they then disappoint, the share price will collapse. It seems sensible to manage expectations: to plan and promise only what can be delivered with reasonable certainty.

In assessing shareholders' expectations, as in so many areas of accounting, we need to consider whether what shareholders expect should be expressed in terms of profit, or cash flow. Return on capital employed and price/earnings ratio are two ways of quantifying shareholders' expectations which are based on earnings. The dividend growth model is based on dividends. The capital asset pricing model (CAPM) can also be used to assess a company's cost of capital.

Return on capital employed

If a company has a return on capital employed of, say, 15 per cent, then we can assume that shareholders expect that this rate of return will continue in the future; and if the company fails to achieve this, the share price is likely to fall. This does not, however, mean that the company's cost of capital for DCF purposes is 15 per cent. If the company rejected all projects that did not show a net present value when discounted at 15 per cent, they might be rejecting good projects that would increase the value of the company. Return on capital employed (or return on investment) is based on profits, not cash flows; and the calculation ignores timing. There are also different ways of calculating return on capital employed. If we are going to compare ROCE for the company as a whole with ROI for particular projects, we should look at the return on the *average* amount of capital employed over a project's life, not the return on the *initial* amount of capital invested in the project.[7]

A company which accepts all projects that show a positive net present value when discounted at 12 per cent, might achieve a return on capital employed of 15 per cent. It would be a mistake to assume a 15 per cent cost of capital for DCF purposes; and it would be a mistake to reject all projects which failed to show positive net present value when discounted at 15 per cent.

It could also be the other way round, particularly with projects that are very profitable, but which take a long time to earn the profits. A company might be tempted to invest in projects which show a return on average capital employed

---

6 Don't expect truth. Credibility is as good as it gets!

7 This is because looking at the company as a whole, on average, projects are likely to be halfway through their lives.

of more than 15 per cent. But if those projects are too slow to generate positive cash flows, they might fail a 12 per cent cost of capital hurdle.

There is no clear relationship between a company's return on capital employed and their cost of capital to be used for DCF.

Price/Earnings Ratio

A company's P/E ratio is a good indication of shareholders' expectations about the future profits of a company. Where a company's profits are expected to grow substantially, the share price is likely to be high in relation to the current level of profits: the P/E ratio is high. Where growth in earnings is expected to be low, then the company's share price is likely to be low in relation to the current level of profits: the P/E ratio is relatively low. Although the P/E ratio is a good indicator of shareholders' expectations, there is no easy way to convert the P/E ratio into a cost of capital figure.

Dividend Growth Model

A company's share price in relation to the last known level of dividends is also a good indicator of shareholders' expectations. If a company has a low dividend yield, this means that the share price is high in relation to the last known level of dividends; shareholders' expectations are high, and future dividends are expected to grow at a relatively high rate. The growth rate in dividends over recent years can be calculated, and incorporated into a 'model', or formula, that indicates the cost of a company's equity capital.

The cost of share capital is assumed to be the dividend yield on the shares (dividend expressed as a percentage of share price), adjusted for an assumed rate of growth.

Illustration 14.11

Last year's dividend per share: 20p
Current share price £5
Assumed rate of dividend growth: 15% per annum

1 Calculate next year's dividend: 20p + 15% = 23p

2 Express next year's dividend as a percentage of current share price

$$\frac{23}{500} \times \frac{100}{1} = 4.6\%$$

3 Add assumed rate of growth.   15% + 4.6% = 19.6%

Cost of capital is assumed to be 19.6%.

Capital Asset Pricing Model (CAPM)

The cost of capital is based on:

(a) a 'risk free' interest rate; to this is added

(b) an extra return to allow for the risk of investing in shares generally; this second element is adjusted to allow for

(c) the specific risk of a given company.

It is easy to find the 'risk free' interest rate: it is the interest yield on government bonds, currently about 4 per cent.

The second element is more difficult to estimate, but we might say that in recent decades investors in ordinary shares have had returns of about, say, 8 per cent over and above the rate on government bonds.

The specific risk of a given company may be measured as a 'beta', which might be average (1.0), or above average (say 1.2), or below average (say 0.8).

The cost of capital of a company with high risk might be:

$$4\% + (8\% \times 1.2)$$
$$= 4\% + 9.6\% = 13.6\%$$

The cost of capital of a company with low risk might be:

$$4\% + (8\% \times 0.8)$$
$$= 4\% + 6.4\% = 10.4\%$$

Evaluation of Different Approaches to Cost of Capital

It is difficult to establish the cost of ordinary shareholders' funds with any certainty, and without making a variety of questionable assumptions. Average returns on ordinary shares for the twentieth century can be calculated, and shareholders might expect this level of returns to continue. But in the first three years of the twenty-first century they have been disappointed: returns on ordinary shares have been negative, and share prices have fallen. If companies assumed a cost of capital based on returns in the first three years of this century, the figure would be negative, and this would not be acceptable as a basis for investment appraisal: companies would be planning to lose money!

Estimates of the cost of borrowing are likely to be more accurate; and the cost of borrowing is likely to be lower than the cost of ordinary shareholders' funds because it is seen as being lower risk, and because interest is an allowable expense for corporation tax purposes.

Given that the cost of borrowing is likely to be lower than the cost of equity, it is worth calculating a weighted average cost of capital figure. But this approach incorporates a dangerous assumption: the more a company relies on borrowing, the lower its cost of capital is likely to be. But if a company relies too much on borrowing, the amount of risk increases; and increased risk is likely to increase the cost of capital.

In practice many companies do not bother with the more sophisticated approaches to determining a 'correct' cost of capital figure. It is acceptable to choose a reasonable rate, and stick to it. For low risk projects 10 per cent is acceptable. For higher risk projects it could be increased up to about 15 per cent.

14.4 Uncertainty and Risk

All investment is based on assumptions about the future and there is usually some uncertainty about our forecasts, and a degree of risk. There are some 'risk free' investments, such as lending money to the government by buying 'gilts'. But managers are more likely to be involved in evaluating projects where there is some uncertainty and risk in estimating:

1 The initial cost of the project. With major projects the initial capital expenditure often turns out to be much higher than was originally planned.

2 The cash inflows that the project will generate. Forecasts may prove to be much too high, or much too low.

3 The cash outflows, including costs, that will be involved.

4 The timing. A project may take longer to be completed and to generate cash flows than was anticipated. And it is difficult to be sure how long a project will last. It is easy to 'assume' a five year life, but difficult to know how long it will really continue.

There are various ways of dealing with risk and uncertainty, all of which involve quite a bit of subjectivity, but which help to give some credibility to forecasts and appraisals.

One approach is to use a higher discount rate for projects which are seen as involving more risk than others. Such an approach may be theoretically sound; the problem is knowing how much extra risk there is, and by how much the discount rate should be increased.

A second approach, where there are several possible outcomes, is to apply probability theory to arrive at an 'expected value'. For example, if there is a 20 per cent chance that a cash flow will be £10,000, a 45 per cent chance that it will be £20,000, and a 35 per cent chance that it will be £30,000, the 'expected' cash flow can be calculated as follows:

20% × £10,000 =	£2,000
45% × £20,000 =	£9,000
35% × £30,000 =	£10,500
Expected cash flow	£21,500

The actual cash flow for a particular project is unlikely to be the 'expected' figure calculated in this way. But if probabilities can be applied in this way to a number of different projects, on average the actual results are likely to be in line with what is expected. The problem is, of course, knowing what the probability is for any particular outcome.

A third approach is to recognize that a range of different outcomes is possible, and to produce one appraisal based on rather pessimistic assumptions, one based on rather optimistic assumptions, and one 'realistic' appraisal between these two extremes. This may be attractive in terms of saying (a) this is the worst that is likely to happen; this is the downside risk; (b) this is what is most likely to happen; and (c) this is the best that is likely to happen. If (a) looks pretty dreadful, then a pretty good (c) is likely to be needed to make the risk look worthwhile. This may give a useful 'feel' for a project, and provide a basis for considering other likely outcomes. It may not be too difficult to get agreement on a range of likely outcomes, which can help to get decisions made. But it is all, of course, very subjective. There is no way of determining how dreadful the pessimistic assumptions should be, or how brilliant the optimistic assumptions should be.

A fourth approach is to use 'sensitivity analysis' to consider a wide range of different possible outcomes. The appraisal can be done again and again, using different assumptions, to see how sensitive it is to particular changes. It may be unsure whether a project will last for 5 years, or 10 years, or somewhere in between. Sensitivity analysis might show that it is brilliant if it lasts for 10 years, but it is still viable if it lasts for only 5 years. It may be unsure whether the initial project cost will be £1 million, or £2 million, or somewhere in between. Sensitivity analysis might show that it is a brilliant project if it costs only £1 million; a waste of money if it costs £2 million; and that, provided it does not cost more than £1.6 million, it is viable. Wherever there is uncertainty, the proposal can be recalculated to see how sensitive it is to a change in assumptions. This approach does not remove subjectivity, but it enables the financial effects of particular uncertainties to be quantified to provide a basis for judgement and decision making.

Summary

In theory managers use investment appraisal techniques to ensure that a company's funds are used in ways which maximize shareholders' wealth.

In practice managers may have their own agendas, favouring particular projects, seeking to impress their superiors, enhancing their reputation, increasing their personal remuneration packages, and getting promotion by claiming credit for all that goes well, and blaming others for all that goes badly. It is easy to gain approval for a pet project by producing forecasts and appraisals which meet the company's criteria and show it as being viable. It is important that companies have 'post investment appraisal' procedures in place that check if actual results are in line with the figures that were included in the appraisal which the company approved. Successful managers will have done some, or all, of the following:

1 Made sure that actual results are in line with the original appraisals.

2 Been promoted and transferred so that they are no longer around to take the blame.

3 Kept a careful record of all the forecasts that made up the appraisal, and made sure that someone else is responsible for each element that made up the total appraisal. If the project does not come up to expectations, it is Bill's fault because the sales forecasts were wrong; or Jane's fault because she underestimated the original cost; or Jo's fault because actual costs were way out of line.

Successful investment projects are the key to the financial success of a company, and to maximizing shareholder value. Management cannot avoid the results of their investment activities being assessed by the outside world through their published financial statements. For individual managers, taking credit for successful investment projects is important in success. All managers need to understand investment appraisals if they are to be the ones who take the credit, and not the ones who end up taking the blame. Good managers ensure that decisions are taken on the basis of information that is as honest as possible, with risks and uncertainties specified and taken into account. Good decisions are taken by responsible groups of managers who understand the limitations of the data, and of the techniques used for appraising the data.

Review of Key Points

- The ROI of a project is calculated using profits, not cash flow, and is comparable with the return on capital employed for the company as a whole

- The payback period is calculated using cash flows, not profits, and tells us how quickly a project is likely to pay for itself

- DCF properly allows for the timing of cash flows

- The net present value method of DCF is the preferred method of investment appraisal

- It is necessary to know the company's cost of capital to use NPV

- DCF calculations can be no better than the underlying data which are based on estimates, and there is always some risk and uncertainty

Self-testing Questions

1 How is ROI calculated?

2 The most recent annual report and accounts of the Row Sea Company shows that they made profit after tax of £1 million last year, and the balance sheet shows total shareholders' funds of £10 million. They are considering buying a ship which will cost £2 million and which will generate profits (after charging interest and depreciation) of £180,000 a year.

    Would the investment increase the company's return on capital employed?

3 The PBP company has £1 million to invest, and are considering the following two projects:
    Project A will generate annual net cash flows of £200,000 for 8 years;
    Project B will generate cash flows of £400,000 in year 1, £350,000 in year 2, £300,000 in year 3, £100,000 in year 4, £50,000 in year 5, and then about £5,000 a year for another few years.
    On the basis of this information, and without considering DCF, which of the two projects is better?

4 What are the main advantages and disadvantages of using the following methods of investment appraisal:
    (a) ROI
    (b) Payback period

5 Is there a case for investing in the following project?
    A new machine costs £200,000 and will have a 5 year life with no residual value at the end. It is expected to generate profits of £35,000 a year for 5 years.
    What is the highest cost of capital at which the project would be acceptable?

Self-testing Questions (continued)

6 The Peel Company is considering two alternative investment opportunities, a Kippering Project, and a Queenies Project. Each would involve an initial outlay of £50,000 and is expected to have a 5 year life with no scrap value at the end. The additional cash flows (before deducting depreciation) that each project is expected to generate are as follows:

Year	Kippering £	Queenies £
1	25,000	5,000
2	20,000	15,000
3	15,000	25,000
4	10,000	25,000
5	5,000	20,000

You are required to calculate the following for each project, and suggest how a decision should be made between the two projects:

(a) Average annual profits
(b) Return on initial capital employed
(c) Return on average capital employed
(d) Payback period
(e) Net present value using 10 per cent discount factor
(f) Net present value using 25 per cent discount factor
(g) An approximate internal rate of return

7 The Maroc Production Company is considering manufacturing and selling an economy video camera for use by small retailers for security purposes. A firm of management consultants has carried out a feasibility study for them at a cost of £25,000, which has not yet been paid. There would be two requirements for machinery:

(i)   Some existing machinery could be modified at a cost of £100,000 to undertake the first stage of production
(ii) For the second stage of production the company already has suitable machinery which is not in use; it has a book value of £80,000; it would be difficult to dismantle and dispose of, and its net realizable value at present is zero.

If the project goes ahead, maintenance costs of the machinery would be £10,000 per annum; there would be additional working capital requirements of £50,000 at the beginning of the project, which would be recovered at the end of 4 years; initial marketing costs, to be paid for as soon as soon as the project is approved, would be £60,000, and annual marketing costs would be £20,000 per annum for the full 4 years.

The cost and selling price per unit is expected to be:

	£	£
Selling price		60
Materials	11	
Direct labour	6	
Variable overheads	13	
General fixed overheads	12	
Interest	2	
		44
Profit		16

The management consultants have suggested that the product would have a 4 year life before being superseded by better cameras, and that the pattern of sales would be:

	(Sales in units)
Year 1	3,000
Year 2	7,000
Year 3	4,000
Year 4	1,000

The company's cost of capital is assumed to be 20 per cent per annum.

Making careful use of the above information, calculate the net present value of the project. Ignore taxation. Make and state appropriate assumptions where necessary.

Assessment Questions

1 How is the payback period calculated? Why is it widely used although it can suggest wrong decisions?

2 The Leongwei Company decided that there would be no additional purchases of fixed assets unless they had been subject to investment appraisal and showed a positive net present value when discounted at 10 per cent. The policy was implemented 5 years ago, but the company's return on capital employed is still only 7 per cent per annum.

Explain the apparent inconsistency.

3 A project with an initial cost of £200,000 is expected to make profits of £44,000 per annum for 5 years, at the end of which it will have a scrap value of £20,000.

Calculate:

a Average annual depreciation charge

b Average annual cash flows

   c   Payback period
   d   Total profits made during the five years
   e   Return on initial investment
   f   Return on average investment
   g   Net present value assuming a cost of capital of 20 per cent
   h   Internal rate of return

4 Respirer Limited is a small company that specializes in the manufacture of electronic devices for surveillance purposes. Recently they have been involved in producing devices to detect drugs, and the presence of live animals or humans, in import and export consignments. They have designed and produced a prototype of a device which they are calling the 'Kensington' and which can be worn by lorry drivers.

A report from a large firm of management consultants suggests that, in order to produce the device the company will need to set up a new production line at a cost of £600,000, and that an old assembly shop could be used. The assembly shop originally cost £500,000 and depreciation on it of £350,000 has been charged, but it has not been used for a number of years. The company was planning to sell it for £120,000, but the consultants' report recommends that it is used to produce the new device; modifications to the workshop for this purpose will cost £80,000.

The expected costs and selling price per unit of the Kensington are as follows:

	£	£
Selling price		110
Materials	18	
Labour	12	
Variable overheads	15	
General fixed overheads	8	
Interest	4	57
Profit		53

Anticipated sales, in units are 5,000 in year 1; 10,000 in year 2; 16,000 in year 3; 12,000 in year 4 and 7,000 in year 5.

Additional working capital requirements will be £250,000 which will be recovered at the end of the project. An initial advertising campaign costing £400,000 will be required at the beginning of the project; continuing marketing costs will be £130,000 per annum.

It cost £80,000 to produce the prototype and those costs have been paid; the consultants' report cost £120,000, but those costs have not yet been paid.

The company's cost of capital is 15 per cent

Making careful use of the above information, calculate the net present value of the project. Ignore taxation. Make and state appropriate assumptions where necessary.

Assessment Questions (continued)

5   The Bitchwood Company is considering two alternative investment proposals, details of which are as follows:

		Proposal 1 £	Proposal 2 £
Initial investment		100,000	120,000
Cash inflow	Year 1	35,000	30,000
	Year 2	30,000	30,000
	Year 3	30,000	35,000
	Year 4	25,000	50,000
	Year 5	15,000	40,000

Assume that the amount of the initial investment will be depreciated on a straight line basis over five years, and that there will be no residual value.

(a) Calculate for each proposal

(i)   Payback period
(ii)   Average annual profits
(iii) Return on initial investment
(iv) Net present value using discounted cash flow and assuming a cost of capital of 10 per cent
(v)   Internal rate of return

(b) Which of the two projects would you recommend, and why?

Group Activities and Discussion Questions

1   'The acceptability of an investment proposal depends on the company's cost of capital; a project that is acceptable to one company may not be acceptable to another.'

'Accurate assessments of cost of capital are not possible; choosing a figure of between 10 per cent and 15 per cent is a reasonable approximation.'

Explain, contrast, and attempt to reconcile these statements.

2   With many well-publicized projects it seems that proper investment appraisal techniques were not applied, were not possible or appropriate, or were ignored. Discuss this statement with reference to projects such as:

(a) The Millennium Dome
(b) Fees paid by telecommunications companies for third generation licences
(c) The building for the Scottish Assembly in Edinburgh.

3   To what extent is the proper use of investment appraisal techniques likely to stop the development of projects that are for the benefit of society?

Group Activities and Discussion Questions (continued)

4 Assess the role of cost benefit analysis.

5 Post-investment appraisal is essential to ensure that a company's investment appraisal techniques have been properly applied. But it is likely to reveal some uncomfortable facts. Discuss.

6 Sophisticated investment appraisal techniques are no substitute for sound judgement (or good luck). Discuss.

7 Effective managers usually succeed in getting approval for the projects that they want. A knowledge of the company's investment appraisal procedures enables them to produce figures that ensure that projects will be approved. It does nothing to ensure that projected results are actually delivered. Discuss.

References and Further Reading

Brealey, R.A., S.C. Myers and A.J. Marcus (2003), *Fundamentals of Corporate Finance*, 4th edn, McGraw-Hill.

Dayananda, D., R. Irons, S. Harrison, J. Herbohn and P. Rowland (2002) *Capital Budgeting: Financial Appraisal of Investment Projects*, Cambridge University Press.

Lumby, S. and C. Jones (2003) *Corporate Finance: Theory and Practice*, 7th edn, Thomson Learning.

Samuels, J.M., F.M. Wilkes and R. Brayshaw (1996) *Management of Company Finance*, 6th edn, Thomson Learning.

15

Conclusion: Financial Accounting and Assessing Company Performance

Chapter contents

15.1 **Strengths and Weaknesses of Financial Accounting**

15.2 **Other Approaches to Assessing Performance**

Learning objectives

After studying this chapter you should be able to:

- Evaluate some of the strengths and weaknesses of financial accounting as a system for providing information about companies and other organizations

- Synthesize your understanding of material from earlier chapters

- Understand different ways of looking at companies' performance

- Distinguish between efficiency and effectiveness

- Comment on the use of performance indicators

- Appreciate the idea of a balanced scorecard

- Discuss some possible future developments in financial accounting

Introduction

This chapter draws together some of the themes of earlier chapters to form an overall view of the strengths and weaknesses of financial accounting. Undue emphasis is probably given to single measures such as earnings per share, and there is no shortage of different ways of evaluating company performance. The provision of additional information which enables a fuller analysis of a company's financial position and performance to be made is to be welcomed. Approaches which would have the effect of emphasizing different aspects of performance should be treated with caution. It is probably better to improve and supplement financial accounting as it now operates than to attempt major changes.

15.1 Strengths and Weaknesses of Financial Accounting

It is easy to criticize financial accounting and this book is intended to provide a 'warts and all' coverage of the subject, emphasizing its potential usefulness, and its weaknesses.

Almost all information that we receive is incomplete, biased and inaccurate, with the uncomfortable parts edited out by those who have the power to get across a particular message. Information published by governments may be subject to all sorts of spin and editing so that most people do not know what to believe, and have limited trust in government information. Sometimes it seems more like propaganda. Anyone who has been closely involved in an event which comes to be reported in newspapers will know that there are very often inaccuracies in these reports. Sometimes misreporting is deliberate; sometimes reporters are unaware of their own biases; and sometimes there are innocent mistakes.

These weaknesses apply to all information, and there are particular criticisms of accounting. There seems to be no end to creative accounting; the independence of auditors is, to say the least, questionable; and some people can make a lot of money by bending accounting rules, or by outright criminal deception. But governments, regulatory authorities and the accountancy profession are only too aware of these problems, and much is done to overcome them. The problems can never be completely solved, and there is always room for improvement. But, as a system for providing information, financial accounting is rarely surpassed. There may be occasions when other information systems are more reliable, and there are cases where financial accounting is seriously questioned. But it is a pretty robust and reliable system on which hundreds of thousands of businesses (in the UK alone) and others rely every day.

However accurate we are with numerical work, there will always be mistakes. In the press wrong, incomplete or misleading figures are often reported; radio and television reports often confuse millions with billions; and the use of percentages is one of the most fertile grounds for misreporting, distortion and errors. Anyone working with accounting information or any figure work is likely to make mistakes: £345,000 can easily be typed in as £354,000, and a column of figures can easily be added up incorrectly. But bookkeeping and accounting systems, and the requirement to balance the figures, lead to most such errors being corrected. The work done by auditors (and the knowledge that they will be coming) leads to most other errors being found. In terms of arithmetic accuracy, financial accounting systems are probably the best information systems that we have.

Newspapers, the media generally, and governments seem to report whatever information they want, and in whatever form they want, to give whatever impression they may. To some extent companies do this too. They have investor relations departments, and public relations departments; and they can pad out their annual reports and accounts with whatever information they wish to give whatever impression they want. But there are also standardized disclosure requirements for financial accounting. Companies Acts and the requirements of accounting standards specify a great deal of information that is disclosed in ways that make it comparable with other companies and from year to year. Any additional claims made by management can be compared with the official story contained in the official accounting statements. In most other situations where information is disclosed we are totally dependent on those who have power over the information to disclose it in an appropriate way. There is no 'official story' with which to compare the versions that they choose to present to us.

We can criticize auditors for lack of independence. But at least there is some check on the information that is disclosed. Published financial statements are more thoroughly checked and verified than most other information available to us.

There are theoretical problems about exactly what we mean by profit. If we decide that profit is an increase in the net assets of a business (after allowing for new capital introduced, and withdrawals of capital), then we have the problems of definition and measurement of assets. If we decide that profits are the difference between revenues and expenses, we have comparable problems of definition and measurement. Whatever basis we decide, we cannot get away from the problems of asset valuation.

Accounting is based on the recording and summarizing of transactions, and transactions are recorded at cost – the price that was agreed at the time the transaction took place. Such historic cost figures are generally a matter of fact: properly recorded, easily verified, and not much open to debate or manipulation. Balance sheets, profit and loss accounts and cash flow statements are traditionally based on such historic cost information. But we cannot avoid the need to put a value on some assets, and the idea of 'value' is very different from cost: it cannot be traced back to the recording of transactions; it is not easily verified; and it can be very subjective. Value is in the eye of the beholder, and it can be established with certainty only at one point in time when a transaction takes place.

The traditional, prudent approach to accounting is based on historic cost. Net realizable value is used where historic cost figures are too high: where it would not be prudent to use historic cost figures because the assets concerned would not realize that amount if they were sold. Stocks are routinely written down to 'net realizable value' where necessary.

The practice of financial accounting has always been pragmatic rather than being developed from a theoretical framework. There are dangers in current trends which emphasize a theoretical framework such as the ASB's *Statement of Principles* as the basis of accounting; this may be seen as justifying a move towards an increasing use of current values rather than historic cost in accounting statements.

There is wide agreement on the need to 'improve' financial accounting, but the ways in which it should be improved are more open to debate. One approach would be to do what we have always done, but to do it better: rules could be stricter, choices of accounting practice could be reduced or eliminated, auditors' independence could be strengthened, and increased disclosures could be required. A different approach would be to decide that financial accounting is really a sub-branch of economics; its role is to establish the economic value of all assets; and profit is based on increases in these values.

Traditional accounting has sometimes been characterized as being reliable and accurate, but not very relevant to the needs of users. Most sensible users have accepted the limitations of financial statements, and have been glad to have some reliable information. In the quest for greater 'relevance' – to produce information that is designed to meet the needs of users – there is a danger that reliability will be sacrificed. Accounting information is not, of course, completely reliable, and there is plenty of scope for improvement. But it may be worth maintaining and increasing reliability rather than risking it in the pursuit of greater relevance.

Company Performance

Financial accounting can be criticized for not telling us what we really want to know. Most users of accounts are interested in knowing about the future prospects of the company. Will it get into financial difficulties, overwhelmed by its debts, and collapse? Will it be very profitable, and will those who buy the company's shares find that they increase in value substantially?

It is perhaps unreasonable to expect accountants, or their financial statements, to be able to predict the future. They can only report on the past. But it is probably the case that a careful examination of financial statements is likely to provide as sound a basis for predicting the financial prospects of a company as is available anywhere. There are always people who offer 'tips' on which shares to buy – sometimes for questionable financial reasons of their own. But a careful, fundamental analysis of a company's financial statements may be more reliable. This has been well documented in relation to Z-scores and predictions of financial distress.

15.2 Other Approaches to Assessing Performance

Financial accounting is based around the idea that measuring and reporting a company's profit is central to performance assessment. It is not the *amount* of profit that is most important. It is the amount of profit made in relation to the amount of capital employed that matters. The company's return on capital employed is the key ratio, and expressing profits in terms of earnings per share is the basis of a lot of investment analysis. But not everyone accepts that profit is the key to companies' performance.

Cash Flow

Some argue that cash flow is more important than profit. A company cannot survive without a healthy cash flow, and cash flow figures are seen as being more reliable and objective than accruals-based profit figures where there may be a suspicion of manipulation or creative accounting. Annual reports and accounts include cash flow statements which reconcile profit with cash flow, and users of accounts can evaluate both profit and cash flow, and consider the relationship between them. But it is rather pointless to argue whether cash flow or profit are more important: both are essential.

EBITDA

Earnings before interest, taxation, depreciation and amortization acquired a reputation as a performance measure in the late 1990s. Rapidly expanding telecommunications, media, technology and dot com companies were generating neither profits nor cash flows, but boasted substantial 'EBITDA'. Some financial commentators accepted it as being a good indicator of the performance of a company, almost as if it had the advantages of both profit and cash flow. Profit plus depreciation is often seen as being a simple measure of cash flow; and amortization can also be added back to profit – as it is in a cash flow statement. It is quite legitimate to argue that profit plus depreciation and amortization is a good indicator of cash flow. But it is quite misleading to ignore interest and taxation; they can be serious outflows of cash.

Those who made investments in companies with 'healthy' EBITDA figures, and ignored the traditional measures of cash flow and profit, had their fingers badly burned when the share prices of their chosen companies collapsed at the beginning of this century. When new and fashionable measures of performance are advocated by particular companies it is worth being a little suspicious.

Value Added

In the 1970s Value Added Statements were a fashionable addition to annual reports and accounts. Value added seemed to be a good measure of what a company contributed to the economy, and took the emphasis away from profit. If a company buys in goods and services for £60, and sells them for £100, then the company has added value of £40. The £40 was then distributed among the workers (wages), the lenders (interest), the government (taxation) or reinvested (retained profits and depreciation), with just a little going in dividends to shareholders.

Fashions have changed and these statements have disappeared. But value added may yet return as a measure of performance.

Performance Indicators: Economy, Efficiency and Effectiveness

For some organizations and individuals, emphasis on profit measurement is inappropriate or unacceptable and various other methods can be used to assess different aspects of performance. In companies it is usually assumed that profit is one of the main objectives, and that in measuring their profitability we are also measuring their efficiency and effectiveness.

Efficiency is concerned with the relationship between inputs and outputs. If inputs are costs, and outputs are sales or revenues, then profit is the difference between the two, and maximizing profits is identified with maximizing efficiency.

If we consider an organization such as a university, the issues are rather different. The 'output' is more debatable: it could be the number of graduates, or the number of graduates with particular degree classifications. If we define output as being the number of graduates produced, then the most 'efficient' university is the one that produces graduates at the minimum cost per graduate. But universities have other outputs, such as research, and contributions to learning and scholarship, and to local communities.

Effectiveness is concerned with achieving objectives. If a company's objective is to maximize profitability, then it is relatively easy to measure effectiveness. But it is hard to define what the objectives of universities are, and so it is hard to measure their effectiveness in achieving those objectives.

Governments are concerned about achieving 'economy, efficiency and effectiveness': they do not want to be seen to be wasting taxpayers' money. 'Value for money auditing' was introduced to a wide range of local government and public sector operations with a range of performance indicators designed to measure and monitor the achievement of value for money, or the 'three E's': economy, efficiency and effectiveness. The definition of economy is not as clear as the definition of efficiency and effectiveness. It is concerned with doing what is required 'economically', or without using too many resources.

The selection and measurement of performance indicators in public sector and not-for-profit organizations is not a neutral process. Determining what an organization's outputs and objectives are supposed to be is a political matter. There are usually several outputs and several objectives, and it is a matter of opinion which are most important. Even where they can be defined satisfactorily, it is often very difficult to measure them satisfactorily; usually it is necessary to use some surrogate measure. The process seems to lead to those outputs which are easiest to measure being given most importance.

The idea of being able to assess performance in a neutral and objective way is appealing. There may be a demand for some sort of balance, a generally agreed way of scoring different aspects of performance in a standardized way – like a score card for some kind of sport or game. If we accept that profitability is the main objective, then financial accounting plays a key role in producing a balanced set of ratios that assess financial position and performance and provide valuable indicators of how improvements can be made. But for many people and organizations that is too simple: there are many different social and environmental aspects of performance that need to be taken into consideration.

Social and Environmental Impacts

Some argue that the performance of companies should not be judged mainly in relation to investors and profits. What matters is companies' overall impact on society and many different groups in society: employees, customers, suppliers, local communities, the government and so on. There are also concerns about the impact of companies on the environment: the performance of companies should be assessed on the basis of their environmental impact. Are they using only sustainable resources? Are they polluting the atmosphere and the environment? Are they contributing to global warming?

Companies are increasingly providing information in their annual reports on the social and environmental impacts of their activities, and there may be a correlation between what companies do and what they disclose. Many companies make voluntary disclosures, and it is likely that additional compulsory disclosures on the social and environmental performance of companies will be introduced. Such disclosures may modify companies' behaviour when they want their performance in these areas to be seen in a favourable light. For example, companies are now required to disclose how long they take to pay creditors, and the requirement to make this disclosure may encourage a more responsible (i.e. prompt) approach to making such payments.

A Balanced Scorecard

The idea of an organization achieving a balanced performance that would please everyone, rather than the narrow objective of profit, would be appealing. Financial accountants would be the servants of society in ensuring that companies worked to please everyone, and that their results are monitored in broad terms, not just in terms of profitability or earnings per share.

One defence of financial accounting is that it ultimately reflects all of the efforts of management. Everything eventually shows up in 'the bottom line': earnings per share.

Earnings per share, and most measures of performance are typically measured on an annual basis. Performance in terms of share price is often assessed on a more short-term basis. But, as seen in Chapter 14, successful management and investment of funds should take a longer-term view than one year. Most strategies take more than a year to bear fruits in terms of improved results.

Kaplan and Norton (1992) have developed the idea of the *balanced scorecard*, which is intended to convert an organization's aims, visions and strategies into practical ways of achieving them, and monitoring their success. In many ways this is what accounting was always intended to do, but conventional accounting may be criticized for taking a view that is too short term, and too narrow. Investors on the stock market are often criticized for 'short termism' – the pursuit of short term gains – and companies often seem to respond to such demands. Too much concentration on the earnings per share figure for the next period can affect a business's priorities: the need to increase short-term earnings can distort strategies for long-term survival, growth and success.

The balanced scorecard approach starts by identifying the organization's vision for the future and converts these into strategies which can be communicated and measured. Financial measures are only part of it. Typically there are four aspects to achieve the balance required:

1 Financial perspective: how do we perceive our shareholders?

2 Customer perspective: how do we perceive our customers?

3 Process perspective: in what processes do we need to excel in order to succeed?

4 Learning and innovation perspective: how will we sustain our ability to change and improve?

The idea is to translate strategies for each of these four areas into action, defining the critical success factors, setting targets, and measuring performance in relation to each of these, using relevant and measurable indicators.

In many ways the balanced scorecard approach is comparable with a more enlightened view of traditional budgetary control, or the (now largely forgotten) 'Management by Objectives' approach. It does not change the fact that companies are assumed to be trying to maximize profitability and shareholders' wealth. But it takes a broader, less short-term view, and concentrates on how management achieves what it sets out to do. The financial perspective is still important, but no less important than the three other perspectives, which emphasize customers, internal processes, and learning and innovation. All of these approaches give more prominence to communication, training, and the importance of an organization's employees being valued and trained to participate more effectively in implementing strategies and achieving the targets that are established. The balanced scorecard approach may be seen as being more about management, and management accounting, than it is about financial accounting. But it does suggest directions in which financial accounting is likely to evolve as reporting on broader aspects of companies' performance is increasingly required.

Summary and Conclusion

We do not live in a perfect world, and there are no perfect information systems. The survival and performance of companies is central to the lives of millions of people, and financial accounting provides as good a guide to their financial position and performance as we can reasonably expect. Many of us will continue to criticize it, and we can hope for and anticipate continuing improvement.

Financial accounting information provides the basis for assessing and improving companies' solvency and profitability; it makes the important distinction between profits and cash flows; it helps to identify requirements for additional financing and provides the basis for raising additional funds; it shows how working capital can be managed and controlled more effectively; it plays an important role in appraising investments where predicted cash flows are more relevant than predicted profits. It has a central role in how shares are assessed by stock markets and investors – who also make use of a wide range of other information and predictions of varying degrees of reliability.

An understanding of how financial accounting evolved and developed, together with a critical appraisal of how it operates today, can help ensure that we do not have unrealistic expectations of it. It has many flaws, and there is plenty of room for improvement. But we ignore it at our peril.

A knowledge of financial accounting is an essential basis for understanding the financial position and performance of organizations, for planning and implementing improvements, and for assessing future performance. Managers may be mainly interested in the company's activities in areas such as marketing, production, quality, human resource management, and information systems. But strategies in all of these areas are related to the company's past financial position and performance, and to their plans and strategies for the future. The results of all managers' work is, in due course, reflected in and assessed through financial accounting information. Those who ignore, avoid, misunderstand or underestimate financial accounting information are making a serious mistake.

Review of Key Points

♦ Financial accounting provides an effective information system for monitoring a company's financial position and performance

♦ There are many ways in which financial accounting can be improved, including increased auditor independence, more effective accounting standards, and additional disclosures

♦ Many suggestions for improving financial accounting are political and intended to emphasize different aspects of the position and performance of companies

♦ A range of different ratios and performance indicators can be calculated and used to highlight different aspects of an organization's performance

♦ Efficiency and effectiveness are more difficult to assess in not-for-profit organizations than in companies

♦ The balanced scorecard approach encourages broader and longer-term perspectives on an organization's performance than concentrating on earnings per share

Self-testing Questions

1 What are the main strengths of financial accounting as an information system?

2 Why does profitability appear to be the main measure of a company's performance?

3 What is EBITDA? What are its attractions and weaknesses?

4 Is cash flow a better measure of performance than profit?

5 What is value for money auditing?

6 What are the four main perspectives of a balanced scorecard?

Assessment Questions

1 Why does there seem to be a lot of criticism of financial accounting?

2 What is meant by *efficiency* and *economy*?

Assessment Questions (continued)

3 How would you measure the outputs of a hospital, a church, and a local authority? How useful is it to assess the efficiency of such organizations? Why is it more difficult to measure their effectiveness?

4 What are the main limitations of relying on a single earnings per share figure to assess the performance of a company?

5 How would you like to see financial accounting develop in the future? Give your reasons.

Group Activities and Discussion Questions

1 Examine the case for requiring additional disclosures of a company's social and environmental performance.

2 Obtain the annual reports of about four companies. How many pages are devoted to disclosing information that is required by law and accounting standards? How many additional pages are there? How much of (a) the required disclosure, and (b) the voluntary disclosure appears to be social and environmental rather than being directly relevant to the balance sheets, profit and loss accounts, and cash flow statements? Why do the companies choose to disclose such information?

3 Based on textbooks, general knowledge, the financial press, and published annual reports, compile a list of accounting ratios that may be seen as being 'performance indicators'. Exclude the most conventional ones (e.g. those that are explained in this book), and evaluate the usefulness of the others.

4 To what extent can financial accounting information be made more 'relevant' without becoming less 'reliable'?

5 Can a group of students agree on what the objectives are of two of the following?
   (i) a church
   (ii) a trade union
   (iii) a fire brigade
   (iv) a GP (doctor)'s surgery
   (v) a local authority
   (vi) a police force

   How can the effectiveness of these organizations be measured?

6 Financial accounting is ill-suited to the needs of not-for-profit organizations. The application of financial accounting thinking to such organizations is likely to change their nature. Discuss.

7 While financial accounting as it exists may be criticized, and there is room for modification and improvement, there is no serious alternative. Discuss.

References and Further Reading

Kaplan, R.S. and D.P. Norton (1992) The Balanced Scorecard: Measures that Drive Performance, *Harvard Business Review*, January–February.

Kaplan, R.S. and D.P. Norton (2000) *The Strategy-focused Organization: How Balanced Scorecard Companies Thrive in the New Business Environment*, Harvard Business School Press.

Perks, R.W. (1993) *Accounting and Society*, Chapman and Hall (Chapters 4 and 5).

Appendix

Basic Accounting Procedures and Statements

Double Entry Bookkeeping

The rules for double entry bookkeeping are really very straightforward; a few rules, consistently applied, is all that is needed. There are lots of detailed rules for anyone who wants to be a bookkeeper, but the basic principles are quite straightforward.

Rule 1

A cash account shows all receipts of cash on the left-hand side, and all payments of cash on the right-hand side, as shown below.

Catherine Fox
Cash Account

Receipts				Payments		
Date	Description	Amount £		Date	Description	Amount £
2004				2004		
1 Jan	Capital – Catherine Fox	100,000		4 Jan	Rent	2,000
3 Jan	Loan from HSBS	50,000		5 Jan	Vehicle	20,000
8 Jan	Sales	3,300		6 Jan	Purchases of books	4,000

From the above it can easily be inferred what has happened.

Catherine Fox started a business as a bookseller on 1 January 2004 with £100,000 of her own capital which she paid into a business bank account. The money was 'received' into the business cash or bank account. She then borrowed £50,000 from HSBS. The next day she paid rent of £2,000; then paid £20,000 to buy a vehicle; then she paid £4,000 to buy some books. The next day she sold some books for £3,300.

Anyone with no training in accountancy would soon devise a system of record keeping such as the above. Recording receipts and payments is essential to keep track of the business's money.

A professional bookkeeper would separate 'petty cash' (notes and coins) from money in the bank; but this need not trouble us here. It is all money, and will be called cash.

But the above is too simple; and it is not double entry bookkeeping.

Rule 2

Every transaction must be recorded twice: on the left-hand side of one account, and the right-hand side of another account.

The next steps should follow naturally. Payments must be on the right-hand side of the Cash Account; payments are usually to pay for assets, or expenses, or purchases of goods for resale. Separate accounts are needed for each of these, and the amounts will be recorded on the left-hand side of the Asset, Expense and Purchases Accounts.

Receipts must be on the left-hand side of the Cash Account; receipts may be from the original capital provided, or from borrowings, but mainly from sales. Separate accounts are needed for each of these, and the amounts will be recorded on the right-hand side of the Capital, Loan and Sales Accounts.

These are illustrated below.

Capital Account

Date	Description	Amount £	Date	Description	Amount £
2004			2004		
			1 Jan	Cash	100,000

HSBS Loan Account

Date	Description	Amount £	Date	Description	Amount £
2004			2004		
			3 Jan	Cash	50,000

Sales Account

Date	Description	Amount £	Date	Description	Amount £
2004			2004		
			8 Jan	Cash	3,300

Rent Account

Date	Description	Amount £	Date	Description	Amount £
2004					
4 Jan	Cash	2,000			

Vehicle (Fixed Asset) Account

Date	Description	Amount £	Date	Description	Amount £
2004					
5 Jan	Cash	20,000			

Purchases Account

Date	Description	Amount £	Date	Description	Amount £
2004					
6 Jan	Cash	4,000			

There should be no difficulty in deciding what description to put for a transaction: it is simply the name of the account where the other half of the double entry is to be found. Payments for purchases are shown on the right-hand side of the Cash Account, and labelled as purchases; the transaction also appears on the left-hand side of the Purchases Account, labelled as cash.

But many, or most business transactions are not conducted on a cash basis. Purchases are typically made on credit, and the payment is made a month or so later. Sales to other businesses are normally made on credit, and the money is received a month or so later. Purchases and sales which take place on a credit basis must not be shown on the cash account when the transaction first takes place. Entries in the cash account will be made when the cash is received or paid. But there is a need to record the sales and purchases as soon as they are made – not least because there is a need to keep track of how much is owed to suppliers, and how much is owed to the business by customers.

Rules 3 and 4 seem to follow naturally from what we have already seen.

Rule 3

The Purchases Account records all purchases that have been made, whether they are on a cash basis, or are on credit.

Rule 4

The Sales Account records all sales that have been made, whether they are on a cash basis, or on credit.

Catherine Fox specializes in buying remaindered books on credit from UK publishers and selling them, on credit, to overseas colleges. Her Purchases Account and Sales Account for the rest of January appear as shown below.

Purchases Account

Date	Description	Amount £	Date	Description	Amount £
2004					
6 Jan	Cash	4,000			
18 Jan	Pinwin Publishers	8,000			
22 Jan	Grohill Publishers	7,000			

Sales Account

Date	Description	Amount £	Date	Description	Amount £
2004			2004		
			8 Jan	Cash	3,300
			10 Jan	College A	5,500
			27 Jan	College B	8,500

It is clear what has happened: she has bought books on credit from Pinwin Publishers and from Grohill Publishers; and she has sold books on credit to College A and to College B. No cash has changed hands in respect of these transactions (yet) and so the Cash Account is not affected. But she does need to keep track of her creditors and debtors. She must also follow Rule 2, and complete the double entry, as shown below.

Purchases made on credit are shown on the left-hand side of the Purchases Account, and on the right-hand side of the Creditors Account.

Pinwin Publishers (Creditors) Account

Date	Description	Amount £	Date	Description	Amount £
2004			2004		
			18 Jan	Purchases	8,000

Grohill Publishers (Creditors) Account

Date	Description	Amount £	Date	Description	Amount £
2004			2004		
			22 Jan	Purchases	7,000

Sales made on credit are shown on the right-hand side of the Sales Account, and on the left-hand side of the Debtors Account.

College A (Debtors) Account

Date	Description	Amount £	Date	Description	Amount £
2004					
10 Jan	Sales College A	5,500			

College B (Debtors) Account

Date	Description	Amount £	Date	Description	Amount £
2004					
27 Jan	Sales College B	8,500			

Catherine Fox will, in due course, pay some of what she owes to her suppliers, and these payments (like all payments) must be recorded on the Cash Account, as shown below:

Cash Account

Date	Description	Amount £	Date	Description	Amount £
2004			2004		
1 Jan	Capital – Catherine Fox	100,000	4 Jan	Rent	2,000
3 Jan	Loan from HSBS	50,000	5 Jan	Vehicle	20,000
8 Jan	Sales	3,300	6 Jan	Purchases of books	4,000
			24 Feb	Pinwin Publishers	6,000
			25 Feb	Grohill Publishers	6,500

She also needs to complete the double entry bookkeeping by recording the transactions on the left-hand side of her suppliers' accounts, as shown below.

Pinwin Publishers (Creditors) Account

Date	Description	Amount £	Date	Description	Amount £
2004			2004		
25 Feb	Cash	6,000	18 Jan	Purchases	8,000

Grohill Publishers (Creditors) Account

Date	Description	Amount £	Date	Description	Amount £
2004			2004		
25 Feb	Cash	6,500	22 Jan	Purchases	7,000

The balance on Pinwin's account now shows that Catherine Fox owes them £2,000. The balance on Grohill's account now shows that Catherine Fox owes them £500.

The money owed to Catherine Fox by her credit customers should, in due course be received. These receipts, like all receipts, must be recorded on the left-hand side of the cash account, as shown below.

Cash Account

Date	Description	Amount £	Date	Description	Amount £
2004			2004		
1 Jan	Capital – Catherine Fox	100,000	4 Jan	Rent	2,000
3 Jan	Loan from HSBS	50,000	5 Jan	Vehicle	20,000
8 Jan	Sales	3,300	6 Jan	Purchases of books	4,000
26 Feb	College A	3,000	24 Feb	Pinwin Publishers	6,000
28 Feb	College B	8,500	25 Feb	Grohill Publishers	6,500

Again it is necessary to complete the double entry by recording the amount that has been received on the right-hand side of the Debtors' Accounts, as shown below.

College A (Debtors) Account

Date	Description	Amount £	Date	Description	Amount £
2004			2004		
10 Jan	Sales	5,500	26 Feb	Cash	3,000

College B (Debtors) Account

Date	Description	Amount £	Date	Description	Amount £
2004			2004		
27 Jan	Sales	8,500	28 Feb	Cash	8,500

The balance on the College A Account shows that they still owe £2,500. College B has paid in full and so there is no balance remaining on their account.

The above example shows most types of transactions. There may be dozens of different types of expenses (rent, rates, insurance, postage, stationery, telephone, wages, salaries and so on), but in principle they are all the same. They are shown on the left-hand side of an expense account, such as Electricity, and on the right-hand side the Cash Account when it is paid.

It is not difficult to understand the words left and right. But the words 'debit' and 'credit' often seem to cause problems. But they are just more difficult words for the same simple idea.

Rule 5

Recording a transaction on the left-hand side of an account is called debiting it. Recording a transaction on the right-hand side of an account is called crediting it. If an account has more debited to it than credited to it, it is said to have a debit balance. If an account has more credited to it than debited to it, it has a credit balance.

Enough transactions have been illustrated above to be able to make the following generalizations:

- A Sales Account has a credit balance

- A Purchases Account has a debit balance

- An Expenses Account has a debit balance

- An Asset Account has a debit balance

- A Creditors Account has a credit balance (unless we have paid our suppliers too much by mistake!)

- A Debtors Account has a debit balance (unless our customers have paid us too much by mistake)

- A Cash or Bank Account has a debit balance, provided more has been received than paid out. If more has been paid out than received it will have a credit balance; that is an overdraft.

If every transaction is recorded twice, on the debit side of one account, and on the credit side of another account, the totals of all the debits must equal the totals of all the credits. This can be checked and summarized in the form of a trial balance, as shown below;

		Debit	Credit
	Capital		100,000
	Loan		50,000
	Vehicle	20,000	
(£164,800 – £38,500)	Cash	126,300	
	Pinwin (Creditor)		2,000
	Grohill (Creditor)		500
	College A (Debtor)	2,500	
	Rent	2,000	
	Purchases	19,000	
	Sales		17,300
		169,800	169,800

It is called a 'trial' balance because we are trying to see if it balances, or if there are errors and omissions. If it does not balance, there is definitely something wrong. If it does balance, there could still be some errors: items completely missing, or 'compensating errors', such as where a debit item and a credit item for the same amount have been omitted.

The trial balance is also useful in summarizing all transactions. Even if there have been hundreds of sales, we just have one figure for the total. A Cash Account may have hundreds of debits and credits, but on the trial balance we just show the one figure. In the above trial balance there are two creditors; a normal business might have hundreds, but the trial balance would show just one figure for the total.

The trial balance provides most of the information that is needed to produce a balance sheet and a profit and loss account, but some additional information is usually needed. Each 'adjustment' to the trial balance must involve a debit and a credit, otherwise it would not balance.

In the case of Catherine Fox the figure for closing stock (the amount of unsold books at the end of the period) must be added to the trial balance. It will appear on the balance sheet as a current asset; and it will be deducted from purchases to arrive at the cost of goods sold on the profit and loss account. If her closing stock is £6,000, her profit and loss account and balance sheet can be prepared as follows;

Catherine Fox

Trading and Profit and Loss Account for the two months ending 28 February 2004

	£	£
Sales		17,300
Cost of goods sold		
Opening stock	0	
Purchases	19,000	
	19,000	
Less closing stock	6,000	
		13,000
Gross profit		4,300
Expenses – Rent		2,000
Net profit		2,300

Balance Sheet as at 28 February 2004

	£	£
Fixed assets – Van		20,000
Current assets		
Stocks	6,000	
Debtors	2,500	
Cash	126,300	
	134,800	
Current liabilities		
Creditors	(2,500)	
		132,300
		152,300
Long-term liability		(50,000)
		102,300
Capital		100,000
Profit for year		2,300
		102,300

When looking at a balance sheet and profit and loss account like this for the first time it is a good idea to check where each item has come from.

It is important to note that the profit figure calculated at the end of the profit and loss account is added to the capital figure on the balance sheet. In a company's profit and loss account any amount for dividends that shareholders will receive is deducted to arrive at a 'retained' profit for the year, which is shown after share capital on the balance sheet.

The above statements are in a reasonably standardized form, but instead of referring to current liabilities and long-term liabilities, company accounts show 'Creditors: amounts falling due within a year'; and 'Creditors: amounts falling due after more than one year'.

A practice question, Carlos, is provided as a Self-testing Question at the end of this Appendix, and the answer is available at the end of the book. An additional practice question, A Florist, is provided as an Assessment Question.

Adjustments to the Trial Balance

All adjustments to the trial balance require a debit and a credit. Typically (but not always), one is shown on the balance sheet, and one on the profit and loss account.

1 Closing Stock

- Shown as a debit on the balance sheet, as a current asset

- Shown as a credit on the profit and loss account, deducted from purchases

2 Accruals

There are usually some expenses (e.g. electricity) that have not yet been recorded or paid at the end of the year.

- Shown as a debit on the profit and loss account, increasing the amount of expenses that have already been recorded

- Shown as a credit on the balance sheet, as a current liability.

3 Prepayments

There are usually some expenses (e.g. rent) that have been paid in advance at the end of the year, so part of the amount that has been recorded as an expense is in respect of the following year.

- Show as a debit on the balance sheet, as a current asset 'prepayments', alongside debtors

◆ Show as a credit on the profit and loss account, reducing the amount shown as an expense.

4 Depreciation

Fixed assets are 'written off' (charged as an expense) in the profit and loss account each year over their effective useful life.

◆ Show the current period's depreciation as an expense (a debit) in the profit and loss account

◆ There should be a 'provision for depreciation' shown on the balance sheet (a credit balance); this year's depreciation is added to (credited to) that provision, which normally increases each year

◆ The balance sheet then shows fixed assets in three stages: (i) at cost; (ii) less provision for depreciation; (iii) net book value

5 Provision for Bad Debts

When there is an *increase* in a provision for bad debts *the amount of the increase* is shown as an expense (a debit) on the profit and loss account.

The increase is added to (credited to) any existing provision for bad debts. This credit balance is then shown on the balance sheet as a deduction from debtors.

6 Bad Debts Written Off

It is easier to treat any bad debts written off separately from the provision for bad debts.

◆ Show as a debit (an expense) on the profit and loss account

◆ Treat as a credit on the balance sheet by reducing the amount of debtors (which are shown as a current asset)

7 Corporation Tax

In company accounts there is usually a charge for corporation tax that will be payable at a later date.

◆ Show as a debit on the profit and loss account (after all expenses have been charged)

◆ Show as a credit on the balance sheet, a current liability

8 Proposed Dividends

◆ Show as a debit on the profit and loss account – the last item before showing retained profit for the year (the figure which is added to previous years' retained profits which are shown, in total, on the balance sheet)

- Show as a credit on the balance sheet, a current liability

The application of these adjustments to a trial balance can be practised in the Self-testing Question, Ellie's Limited, at the end of this Appendix. The answer to this question is provided at the end of the book. An additional practice question, Faraway Retailers Limited, is provided as an Assessment Question.

Sales of Fixed Assets

A company should maintain two types of accounts for fixed assets. Companies usually have a number of categories of fixed assets (e.g. land and buildings; plant and machinery; fixtures and fittings; vehicles), and the two types of account are kept for each category.

1 Fixed assets at cost (or valuation). This shows all fixed assets that the company has, usually at the original cost price; the account has a debit balance. Sometimes a fixed asset is revalued; then the amount on the fixed asset is changed: if it is an increase in value the fixed asset account is debited; and the increase is credited to capital reserves, which is shown alongside retained profits, on the balance sheet.

2 Provision for depreciation. This shows the cumulative (or aggregate) depreciation that has been built up over a number of years; the account has a credit balance. Each year the depreciation charge is debited to the profit and loss account, and credited to the Provision for Depreciation Account. The credit balance on the Provision for Depreciation Account increases each year, until some fixed assets are sold.

On the balance sheet the amount shown for fixed assets is the net book value. The cumulative depreciation figure is deducted from the cost (or revalued amount) to give the net book value.

When a fixed asset is sold it is necessary to remove it from both of the above accounts: the original cost must be taken from the Fixed Asset at Cost Account; and the amount of depreciation that has been charged for it must be taken from the Provision for Depreciation Account. Both amounts are transferred to a 'Disposal of Fixed Asset Account', or a 'Sale of Fixed Asset Account', as shown in the Appendix Illustration 1.

As can be seen in that illustration, the machine which is disposed of has to be removed from the Machinery at Cost Account and transferred to the Disposal of Fixed Asset Account. This is done by crediting the Machinery at Cost Account, and debiting the Disposal of Fixed Asset Account.

Appendix Illustration 1

The Salov Company bought a machine some years ago for £20,000; cumulative depreciation in respect of the machine amounts to £16,000. The machine was sold last week for £5,500. The company's Fixed Asset Account, and their Provision for Depreciation Account had balances brought forward as shown below immediately before the disposal.

Machinery at Cost Account

Balance brought forward	£85,000

Provision for Depreciation on Machinery Account

Balance brought forward	£55,000

The accumulated depreciation in respect of the machine which is sold has to be removed from the Provision for Depreciation on Machinery Account and transferred to the Disposal of Fixed Asset Account. This is done by debiting the Provision for Depreciation on Machinery Account, and crediting the Disposal of Fixed Asset Account.

The effect of these two transactions is shown below.

Machinery at Cost Account

Balance brought forward	£85,000	Disposal of fixed asset	£20,000

Provision for Depreciation on Machinery Account

Disposal of fixed asset account	£16,000	Balance brought forward	£55,000

Disposal of Fixed Asset Account

Fixed asset at cost	£20,000	Provision for depreciation on machinery	£16,000

After these two transfers the balance on the Disposal of Fixed Asset Account is a debit of £4,000. This is the net book value of the machine. As the machine was sold for £5,500, a profit on sale of £1,500 was made. This profit is credited to the profit and loss account, and debited to the Disposal of Fixed Asset Account. The cash received is debited to the Cash Account, and credited to the Disposal of Fixed Asset Account. The effect of these two transactions is shown below.

Disposal of Fixed Asset Account

Fixed asset at cost	£20,000	Provision for depreciation on machinery	£16,000
Profit and loss account	£ 1,500	Cash	£ 5,500
	£21,500		£21,500

The effects of a sale of fixed assets is shown in Self-testing Question 6 (Ellie's Limited).

Cash Flow Statements

A company's balance sheet shows how much cash (bank) they have. Comparing this year's balance sheet with last year's shows whether they have more or less cash now than a year ago – or whether their overdraft has gone from bad to worse. It is worth comparing what has happened to their cash balances with the profit for the year. Maybe the company has made good profits, but they have run out of cash.

In the (very much simplified) illustration below, the company started the year with £160,000 in the bank, and ended the year with only £40,000 in the bank. Where did it all go?

The company is profitable: operating profit for the year was £100,000. Somehow they made £100,000 profits, but lost £120,000 cash. If you expect operating profit to turn up as cash, we have a difference of £220,000 to explain.

But all of the operating profit did not end up as cash: interest had to be paid; taxation had to be paid; dividends were paid. We do not know exactly how much was paid, or when. But those three items on the profit and loss account, added together, amount to £80,000.

The balance sheet also shows what has happened to some of the money. The company has more fixed assets (£50,000), and more stocks and debtors (£40,000). They have also reduced the amount that they owe to creditors (£10,000), and paid off part of their long-term loans (£40,000).

All of these differences added together explain the £220,000 difference between operating profit and the decrease in the company's cash balance during the year. We could each work this out for ourselves, in our own way. But there is a standardized way of presenting this information as a cash flow statement, as shown below. Cash flow statements are explained and illustrated more fully in Chapter 7. The example below is oversimplified[1] to give a general idea.

One way of interpreting a cash flow statement is to look at it in two parts. The first part shows how much was generated from operations (£50,000), but much of this was committed to paying interest and taxation (£37,000) which left £13,000 that the company could choose how to spend. This is rather like a 'free cash flow'. They chose to spend £50,000 on fixed assets; £40,000 repaying loans; and £43,000 on dividends for their shareholders. The net effect was to reduce their cash balances by £120,000.

---

1   The simplified statement here ignores depreciation, and the timing of the payment of tax and dividends.

Simplified Balance Sheet of Stuagra Company as at

	1 January Year 1 £000		31 December Year 1 £000	
Fixed assets		200		250
Stocks and debtors	100		140	
Cash	160		40	
	260		180	
Creditors	(40)	220	(30)	150
		420		400
Long-term loans		(70)		(30)
		350		370
Share capital		200		200
Retained profits		150		170
		350		370

Simplified Profit and Loss Account of Stuagra Company for Year to 31 December Year 1

Operating profit	100
Interest payable	(7)
Profit before tax	93
Tax payable	(30)
Profit after tax	63
Dividends	(43)
Retained profit	20

Simplified Cash Flow Statement of Stuagra Company for Year to 31 December Year 1

		£000
Operating profit		100
Increase in stocks and debtors		(40)
Decrease in creditors		(10)
Cash inflow from operating activities		50
Interest	(7)	
Taxation	(30)	(37)
		13
Additional fixed assets	(50)	
Loan repayment	(40)	
Dividend	(43)	(133)
Decrease in cash during year		120

Self-testing Questions

1 Complete the double entry for each of the following transactions:
   (a) Sales made for cash are credited to the Sales Account and debited to the _____
   (b) Sales made on credit to Smith are debited the Smith Account, and credited to the _____
   (c) Purchases made for cash are credited to the Cash Account, and debited to the _____
   (d) Purchases made on credit from Anirroc Company are debited to the Purchases Account and credited to the _____
   (e) Smith, a debtor, pays us part of what he owes; the amount is credited to the Smith Account and debited to the _____
   (f) The Provision for Bad Debts is increased by £30. This amount is debited to the Profit and Loss Account as an expense, and credited to the _____

2 Which of the following accounts normally have a credit balance (as shown on a trial balance)
   Sales, Purchases, Debtors, Creditors, Fixed Assets, Share Capital, Share Premium?

3 Which of the following accounts normally have a debit balance (as shown on a trial balance)
   Expenses, Fixed Assets, Debtors, Cash at Bank?

4 Which of the following statements is true?
   (a) Accounts for assets and expenses have credit balances
   (b) Accounts for liabilities, share capital, retained profits, and overdrafts have credit balances

5 Record the following transactions of Carlos using double entry bookkeeping; summarize them in the form of a trial balance; and prepare a profit and loss account for the three-month period, and a balance sheet as at the end of the period

1 July	Carlos started a business dealing in second-hand cars and opened a business bank account with £40,000
3 July	Carlos borrows £15,000 from the Spano Bank
5 July	Pays £5,000 to rent premises
8 July	Buys furniture and equipment for £11,000
13 July	Buys cars on credit from Motosales Ltd, £50,000
19 July	Pays general expenses, £2,500
27 July	Sells one car for £4,000 cash
3 Aug	Sells cars on credit to Minki Cabs for £18,000
10 Aug	Buys one car for cash, £3,300
16 Aug	Buys cars on credit from Motosales Ltd for £22,000
30 Aug	Pays £40,000 to Motosales Ltd
6 Sept	Pays general expenses £3,300
14 Sept	Receives £15,000 from Minki Cabs
21 Sept	Sells cars for cash, £24,000

The stock of unsold cars remaining at the end of September was £38,100 at cost. Ignore depreciation.

Self-testing Questions (continued)

6 The trial balance of Ellie's Ltd at 31 December Year 1 was as follows:

	Dr £	Cr £
Stocks at 1 Jan Year 1	19,500	
Debtors	61,000	
Creditors		13,400
Share capital: 100 £1 shares		100
Share premium		11,600
Retained profits at 1 Jan Year 1		17,100
Printing and stationery	2,400	
Provision for bad debts		600
Wages and salaries	12,300	
Purchases	167,000	
Sales		248,300
Cash at bank	450	
Rent	1,500	
Electricity	1,100	
Fixtures and fittings at cost	12,000	
Fixtures and fittings: Provision for depreciation at 31 Dec Year 0		2,000
Van at cost	8,400	
Van: Provision for depreciation at 31 Dec Year 0		4,200
Van: disposal proceeds		4,750
Car at cost	20,000	
Car: Provision for depreciation at 31 Dec year 0		5,000
General expenses	1,400	
	307,050	307,050

Additional information

(i)   Closing stock at 31 December Year 1 was £21,000

(ii)   Rent prepaid at 31 December Year 1 was £400

(iii) Accrued electricity at 31 December Year 1 was £200

(iv)   A debtor of £500 is to be written off

(v)   The provision for bad debts is to be increased to £650

(vi)   Depreciation is to be provided for the year as follows
         Fixtures and fittings: 25 per cent per annum on a reducing balance basis
         Vehicles: 25 per cent per annum on a straight line basis

(vii) The company's accounting policy is to charge no depreciation in the year that a fixed asset is sold

(viii) Corporation tax of £15,000 is to be provided

(ix)   The directors propose a dividend of £20 per share

You are required to prepare a profit and loss account for the year ended 31 December Year 1 and a balance sheet as at that date.

Assessment Questions

1 Complete the double entry for each of the following transactions:

(a) The owner of a business pays additional capital to the company; the Cash Account is debited and it is credited to the _____

(b) A business repays a loan; the Cash Account is credited, and it is debited to the _____

(c) The provision for bad debts is reduced by £50; the Provision for Bad Debts Account is debited and it is credited to the _____

(d) Dividends paid are credited to the Cash Account and debited to the _____

(e) A loss arising on the sale of a fixed asset is debited to the profit and loss account and credited to the _____

(f) Closing stock is shown as a debit item on the balance sheet and is credited to the _____

(g) A supplier allows a cash discount of £24; this is credited to the profit and loss account and debited to the _____

(h) Costs of delivering goods to customers of £123 are incurred with Rodo Transport Ltd. This amount is credited to the Rodo Transport Ltd Account and debited to the _____

(i) A customer returns goods as being unsatisfactory; the amount is debited to the Sales Returns (or Returns Inwards) Account, which is eventually deducted from sales on the profit and loss account. It is credited to the _____

(j) The cost of buying a new fixed asset (a car costing £20,000) has inadvertently been debited to the account for travelling expenses. To correct this error the Travelling Expenses Account is credited, and it is debited to the _____

(k) How would the answer to (j) differ if the car had been bought on credit from BWM Garages Ltd?

2 Record the following transactions of A Florist using double entry bookkeeping; summarize them in the form of a trial balance; and prepare a profit and loss account for the month of January, and a balance sheet as at the end of the period.

1 Jan	Started business with £10,000 capital, paid into the bank
2 Jan	Bought second-hand van; paid £4,000 by cheque
3 Jan	Bought flowers on credit from Miss Daisy, £700
4 Jan	Sold flowers for cash, £120
5 Jan	Bought flowers, paying by cheque, £456
6 Jan	Paid one month's rent £408
7 Jan	Sold flowers on credit to the University of Eastminster, £999
14 Jan	Sold flowers in Berwick Street Market for cash, £236
20 Jan	Paid Miss Daisy £400
28 Jan	Received a cheque from University of Eastminster for £899

At the end of January the closing stock of flowers amounted to £210, at net realizable value.

Assessment Questions (continued)

3 The trial balance of Faraway Retailers Limited at 31 December Year 1 is as follows

	Dr £000	Cr £000
Stock as at 1 Jan Year 1	545	
Debtors	705	
Creditors		600
Share capital: £1 shares		1,500
Share premium		750
8% Debentures		1,200
Retained profits at 1 Jan year 1		190
Printing and stationery	750	
Provision for bad debts		40
Wages and salaries	890	
Distribution costs	100	
Bad debt written off	20	
Purchases	3,350	
Sales		7,900
Cash at bank	51	
Rent and rates	320	
Electricity	55	
Debenture interest	48	
Land and buildings at cost	3,000	
Land and buildings provision for depreciation at 31 Dec Year 0		90
Fixtures and fittings at cost	1,500	
Fixtures and fittings provision for depreciation at 31 Dec Year 0		600
Plant and machinery at cost	2,800	
Plant and machinery provision for depreciation at 31 Dec Year 0		1,264
	14,134	14,134

Additional information

(i) The stock take on 31 December Year 1 revealed the following:

	Cost £000	Net realizable value £000
Home furnishing	500	1,000
Clothing	440	410

(ii) Rent and rates includes a rent payment of £144,000 for the period 1 April Year 1 to 31 March Year 2

(iii) Electricity for the three months ended 31 January Year 2 of £18,000 was paid in February Year 2

(iv) A debtor of £5,000 is to be written off

Assessment Questions (continued)

(v)   The provision for bad debts is to be adjusted to be 5 per cent of debtors

(vi)   Depreciation is to be provided for the year as follows:
         Land and buildings: 2 per cent per annum, straight line
         Fixtures and fittings: 20 per cent per annum, straight line
         Plant and machinery: 25 per cent per annum, reducing balance

(vii)   A full year's debenture interest is payable

(viii)   Corporation tax of £615,000 is to be provided

(ix)   The directors propose a dividend of 40 pence per share

You are required to prepare a profit and loss account for the year ended 31 December Year 1, and a balance sheet as at that date.

Answers to Self-testing Questions

Chapter 1

1 A balance sheets shows assets, liabilities and share capital. Expenses, sales and profit for the year are shown on the profit and loss account (or 'income statement').

2 A fixed asset is intended to be retained and used by the business for more than a year.

Current assets are cash and things that are intended for conversion into cash within a year.

3 Land and buildings; plant and machinery; furniture, fixtures and fittings; vehicles, ships and aircraft.

Furniture owned by a furniture shop and intended for sale is a current asset. Vehicles owned by a garage and intended for sale are a current asset.

4 Assets minus Liabilities equals Equity.

5 Individual assets may be worth more or less than the balance sheet value.

A successful business as a whole (including unrecorded goodwill) should be worth more than the balance sheet shows because of the profits that it now produces, and expectations for the future.

6 (a) Current ratio = Current Assets : Current Liabilities
                    45,000 : 22,000   2.05 : 1

(b) Liquidity ratio = Current assets excluding stock : Current liabilities
                    21,000 : 22,000   0.95 : 1

(c)

			Existing		Revised	
		£	£	£	£	£
Fixed assets			50,000			50,000
Current assets						
Stocks (at cost)		24,000			20,000	
Debtors		12,000			12,000	
Cash		9,000			17,000	
		45,000			49,000	
Creditors		22,000	23,000	22,000	27,000	
			73,000		77,000	
Share capital			50,000		50,000	
Retained profits			23,000		27,000	
			73,000		77,000	

(d) Current ratio = 49,000 : 22,000   2.2 : 1
     Liquidity ratio = 29,000 : 22,000   1.3 : 1
     As the business now has £4,000 less stock, and £8,000 more cash, both the current ratio and the liquidity ratio have improved, or become stronger.

7 (a) £83,000, being the increase in shareholders' funds
  (b) £83,000 + £10,000 − £20,000 − £30,000 = £43,000

8

	Domer Castle	Warmer Castle
Current ratio	34 : 17 = 2 : 1	34 : 17 = 2 : 1
Liquidity ratio	26 : 17 = 1.5 : 1	15 : 17 = 0.88 : 1
$\dfrac{\text{Debentures}}{\text{Debentures} + \text{Equity}}$	100 ÷ 331 = 30.2%	200 ÷ 331 = 60.4%
EBIT ÷ Interest payable	31,000 ÷ 10,000 = 3.1 times	32,000 ÷ 20,000 = 1.6 times

Warmer appears to be weaker. The two companies have the same current ratio, but a large part of Warmer's current assets is stocks and so they have a much lower liquidity ratio. Warmer also has much higher capital gearing and their interest cover is low.

9 (a) (i)   Fixed assets   −£80,000
                Cash   +£100,000
                Retained Profits   +£20,000

(ii)   Stocks   −£30,000
        Debtors   +£80,000
        Retained profits   +£50,000

(iii)   Cash   −£40,000
        Creditors   −£40,000

			Existing		Revised
(b)	Fixed assets		158,000		78,000
	Current assets				
	Stocks (at cost)	110,000		80,000	
	Debtors	120,000		200,000	
	Cash	20,000		80,000	
		250,000		360,000	
	Creditors	120,000	130,000	80,000	280,000
			288,000		358,000
	Share capital		250,000		250,000
	Retained profits		38,000		108,000
			288,000		358,000

Chapter 2

1 The balance sheet is *as at* a particular date. A profit and loss account is
   for a particular *period*, such as for a year.
       A balance sheet shows assets, liabilities, and equity (which includes all
   retained profits.
       An income statement (or profit and loss account) shows revenues,
   expenses, and the current year's profit

2 An expense is the cost incurred in earning the revenues of a particular
   period. Some assets become expenses. Assets such as unsold stocks and
   fixed assets may be seen as stores of value which have not yet been used
   up in generating revenues. Fixed assets become recognized as expenses
   as they are depreciated. Stocks become expenses when they are sold. A
   debtor becomes an expense if it is written off as a bad debt.

3 Closing stock is shown at the lower of cost and net realizable value. The
   valuation of closing stock has a direct effect on profits. If closing stock is
   overstated by £1million, then profits are overstated by £1 million.
       If closing stocks were shown at selling price the company would be
   taking credit for profits before sales are made; it is not a good idea to
   claim profits that have not yet been earned.

4 Depreciation is charged to write off the cost of the fixed asset over a number of years, depending on its economic life. If an asset is shown at a revalued amount rather than at cost, then the revalued amount is written off in the same way.

5 Capital expenditure adds to fixed assets which are then written off (as an expense) over a number of years. Examples would include a retail shop buying a new delivery vehicle, having an extension to the shop built, and buying new tills. Revenue expenditure is written off during the period in which it is incurred. Examples include lighting, heating, cleaning. (Some revenue expenditure is included in closing stocks which is carried forward and written off in the period in which they are sold.)

6 Profit after tax for the year, £12,000. This is because:

(a) it is the amount that has been earned for them after charging all expenses and taxation; and

(b) it is the basis for dividend decisions; dividends are the amounts actually paid to shareholders.

7

	Delivery Van	Boring Machine
	£	£
Cost	25,000	25,000
Year 1 Depreciation	6,250	2,500
Net book value at end of year 1	18,750	22,500
Year 2 Depreciation	4,688	2,500
Net book value at end of year 2	14,062	20,000
Year 3 Depreciation	3,516	2,500
Net book value at end of year 3	10,546	17,500
Year 4 Depreciation	2,636	2,500
Net book value at end of year 4	7,910	15,000

8

Product	Cost Price	Mark-up	Selling price	Gross profit
	£	%	£	%
Fargs	100	25	125	20
Gargs	100	10	110	9.09
Hargs	50	100	100	50
Jargs	40	100	80	50
Kargs	80	50	120	$33\frac{1}{3}$
Largs	50	20	60	$16\frac{2}{3}$
Margs	30.77	30	40	23.1
Nargs	45	11.11	50	10
Pargs	75	$33\frac{1}{3}$	100	25

9 Banterbury Company Ltd:

Income Statement for the Year Ended 31 December

	Year 3 £000	Year 3 %	Year 4 £000	Year 4 %
Turnover	100	100	120	100
Cost of sales	60	60	73	60.83
Gross profit	40	40	47	39.17
Distribution costs	(12)	12	(14)	11.67
Administration expenses	(9)	9	(12)	10
Operating profit	19	19	21	17.5
Interest payable	(3)	3	(3)	2.5
Profit before taxation	16	16	18	15
Tax on profit for year	(4)	4	(3)	2.5
Profit after tax for the year	12	12	15	12.5
Dividends paid and proposed	(5)	5	(6)	5
Retained profit for year	7	7	9	7.5

Turnover has increased by 20 per cent, but most costs have increased by a larger percentage than sales. Expressing all items as a percentage of sales we can see that cost of sales has increased slightly, and so gross profit has gone down. There has been an increase in operating costs as a percentage of sales,[1] and so operating profit as a percentage of sales has gone down. There has been no change in interest costs, and the company is fortunate that the amount of tax payable has gone down: the effect of these two is that there has been an increase in profit after tax as a proportion of sales.

The small improvement in profit as a percentage of sales is mainly due to the lower tax charge. Cost of sales and operating costs have both increased by a bigger proportion than sales. These results suggest that management have not been very successful in getting more profits out of the increase in sales.

Shareholders' funds are £300,000, and the profit after tax earned for them is £15,000, a return on shareholders' capital employed of only 5 per cent.

Chapter 3

1 The main users are investors and creditors. These include existing shareholders and those who are considering investing in the company. Creditors include trade creditors and short- and long-term lenders.

---

[1] A reduction in the percentage of sales taken up by distribution costs has been more than offset by an increase in administration expenses.

They want to know about the company's financial position, including its solvency and ability to survive; its financial performance, including its profitability; and its cash flows.

There may be many other potential users with wide information needs; but most of financial accounting concentrates on those specified above.

2 Creditors are interested in a company's ability to repay them. They are interested in assets as security, the total amount of debt, interest cover and cash flows.

Shareholders are more interested in prospects for future dividends and increases in the market price of their shares. They are particularly interested in profitability and growth.

3 The main framework is laid down by the Companies Act 1985. Additional requirements are specified by 'accounting standards'. A few Statements of Standard Accounting Practice still remain, but these are rapidly being superseded by Financial Reporting Standards of which 19 have been issued. International Financial Reporting Standards will, by 2005, become predominant. The remaining differences between UK and International Financial Reporting Standards are steadily being reduced and eliminated.

4 There is a lot of criticism of auditors partly because financial scandals receive a lot of publicity. Most such scandals are not the fault of the auditors; it is often the auditors who first draw attention to a problem. When something has gone wrong it seems to be easy to blame the auditors, and even to sue them and hope to get financial compensation. Some criticism of arrangements for auditing is justified, particularly in relation to their questionable independence. There is also the problem that rules for defining and valuing assets are not totally clear-cut, and if directors choose to adopt their own methods it is difficult for auditors to prevent them.

5 The main influences on the development of accounting in the UK have been companies and directors and the need for accountability; accountants, auditors, the professional accountancy bodies, and standards setters; governments and company law. In addition stock markets and the requirements of bankers and creditors have been influential. In recent years the role of theory has been increasingly emphasized.

Chapter 4

1 (a) Current assets : Current liabilities   e.g. 1.8 : 1
  (b) Current assets minus stocks : Current liabilities   e.g. 0.9 : 1

(c) Capital requiring a fixed return (e.g. Debentures) as a percentage of total long-term capital (equity plus debentures). This is often expressed as $\dfrac{D}{D+E}$ e.g. 35%

It may also be expressed as $\dfrac{D}{E}$

It is usually calculated using balance sheet values. It may be calculated using market values. Preference shares and all borrowings may be included with D.

(d) Earnings before interest and taxation ÷ interest payable e.g. 5 times

2 It might take a long time to convert stocks into cash; they are not a very 'liquid' asset.

3 Net profit for the year, after taxation, as a percentage of ordinary shareholders' funds (including all reserves and retained profits) as shown on the balance sheet.

4 The 'return' is earnings before interest and taxation. If debentures are included as part of capital employed, the interest payable on them should be included as part of the return on capital employed. It is important that the numerator and the denominator are consistent: where borrowings are included in the denominator, the interest on those borrowings should be included in the numerator. Return on ordinary shareholders' capital employed is usually measured after charging taxation for the year. If borrowings are included in capital employed, and EBIT is used as the numerator, it is taken before charging taxation; this is a matter of convenience, not a matter of principle.

5 An increase in the gross profit does not tell us anything for sure about sales. They may have increased; selling prices may have increased. But an increase in the gross profit ratio may be entirely attributable to a reduction in cost of sales as a percentage of sales, which could be due to more effective buying, or reductions in purchase prices. [2]

6 The company's financial position looks reasonably strong with some improvement in Year 2. The current ratio is lower, but the liquidity ratio has increased. The gearing looks rather high, but has reduced; the company has reduced its long-term borrowing slightly; shareholders' funds have increased slightly; and interest has increased.

   The company's current assets look rather high, and this can have an effect on profitability. They have generated substantial amounts of cash,

---

2 It could even be due to an excessive write down in last year's closing stocks. Think about it.

and the cash balance is now excessive and should be used profitably. It may be the company's intention to further reduce its long-term borrowing.

The company has managed to increase its profitability slightly: both measures of return on capital employed have improved. But they appear to be struggling with sales and costs. Sales have increased slightly (5 per cent), but the gross profit margin has gone down a little. Operating costs have been kept under control (a slight decrease); and because of reduced borrowings there has been a significant reduction in interest payable. After taxation there has been an improvement in net profit as a percentage of sales.

Overall utilization of capital employed has hardly changed, but there have been improvements in the management of stocks and debtors. Stock turnover looks very slow, but has been improved substantially. The length of time that debtors take to pay has also been reduced substantially.

More detailed analysis of each item of expense as a percentage of sales could be undertaken; more detailed analysis of each item of assets and liabilities in relation to sales could be made. But the analysis shown below brings out the main points outlined above. The overall impression might be of reasonably successful financial management struggling to improve financial performance in difficult market conditions.

Solvency

	Year 1	Year 2
Current ratio	1,868 : 434	2,100 : 600
	4.3 : 1	3.5 : 1
Liquidity ratio	688 : 434	1,100 : 600
	1.6 : 1	1.8 : 1
Gearing ratio	1,000/2,434	900/2,400
	41%	37.5%
Interest cover	295/100	305/90
	2.95 times	3.39 times

Profitability

Return on ordinary shareholders' capital employed

	135/1,434	150/1,500
	9.4%	10%

EBIT as a percentage of long-term capital employed

	295/2,434	305/2,400
	12.1%	12.7%
Gross profit ratio	375/3,600	384/3,780
	10.42%	10.16%

Operating profit/sales	295/3,600	305/3,780
	8.19%	8.07%
Net profit after tax/sales	135/3,600	150/3,780
	3.75%	3.97%
Sales/Net assets	3,600/1,434	3,780/1,500
	2.51 times	2.52 times
Stock turnover (days)	1,200/3,225 × 365	1,000/3,396 × 365
	136 days	107 days
Debtors ratio (days)	600/3,600 × 365	500/3,780 × 365
	61 days	48 days

Chapter 5

1 Profit is measured as a guide to dividend decisions; to indicate how successful or otherwise the management of the company is; as a basis for taxation; to guide investors in making decisions to buy, sell or hold shares; to guide creditors; to indicate the economic efficiency of the company and so to contribute to the efficient allocation of resources in the economy. It is also used for many different purposes, for example in relation to wage claims, price controls. It does not really indicate how much cash a company has generated.

2 The balance sheet can show the amount of profit made during a year by comparing the net asset value (or shareholders' funds) on the balance sheet at the beginning of the year with the equivalent figure on the balance sheet at the end of the year. If the amount has increased the difference is profit; but two adjustments have to be made. Any dividends paid must be added to the amount of the increase; any additional share capital subscribed must be deducted.

This approach differs from using income statements because it is based on asset valuation (rather than measurement of income and expenses).

3 Turnover and profit figures are shown separately for continuing operations, discontinued operations and acquisitions.

Exceptional items are separately disclosed, including profits or losses on the sale or termination of an operation; costs of a fundamental reorganization or restructuring; profits or losses on the disposal of fixed assets.

Segmental reports show sales, operating profit and assets for each segment in which the business operates.

Information is also available on the performance of investments; the performance of subsidiaries, associates and joint ventures, and simple investments can be monitored.

4 The calculation of profit requires a cost of sales figure which uses a closing stock figure; closing stock is shown at the lower of cost and net realizable value. Net realizable value requires prediction of how much the stock would sell for.

   Profit calculation also requires figures for depreciation; this necessitates estimates of the future life of a fixed asset, and its residual value.

5 CPP uses a general price index. CCA deals with specific price changes.

   CPP is based on maintaining capital in general purchasing power. CCA is based on maintaining the operating capability of the business.

6 (a) Mary's Opening Balance Sheet

Stocks 100 @ £10	£1,000
Capital	£1,000

   (b) Income Statement for Year

Sales 1,000 @ £15		£15,000
Cost of goods sold		
Opening stock 100 @ £10	1,000	
Purchases 1,000 [3]	11,000	
	12,000	
Closing stock 100 @ £12	1,200	10,800
Gross profit		£4,200

   (c) Balance Sheet at end of Year

Stocks 100 @ £12	£1,200
Cash (£15,000 – £11,000)	£4,000
	£5,200
Capital	£1,000
Profit	£4,200
	£5,200

   (d) The business has only £4,000 cash available to give to charity. Profits of £4,200 have been made, but part of these were required to finance the additional cost of replacing stocks. If all of the profit was given to charity, either the business would have to borrow money, or reduce its operating capability (i.e. hold less stocks).

   (e) If LIFO had been used, the most recently purchased items (at £12 each) would have been sold. Closing Stock would have been £200 less; cost of goods sold would have been £200 more; profit would have been £200 less. These are simplifying assumptions, but the profit for the year would have equalled the cash available to be paid

---

3 At varying prices. The most recent cost £12. On average they cost £11.

out to charity. But the closing stock figure on the balance sheet would have been unrealistic, and the business would not have been able to finance the existing level of stocks. LIFO is an inadequate solution to the problem.

7 (a) Jackie's Opening Balance Sheet

Vehicle	£30,000
Capital	£30,000

(b) Income statement for typical year

Sales		£40,000
Expenses	£20,000	
Depreciation	£ 3,000	£23,000
Profit		£17,000

(c) Jackie will take £17,000 out of the business each year. The business generates £20,000 cash a year. But profit is after charging depreciation of £3,000 a year. Each year £3,000 cash is retained in the business.

(d) Balance Sheet at end of nine years

Vehicle at cost	£30,000
Less provision for depreciation	27,000
	3,000
Cash	27,000
	30,000
Capital	30,000

(e) Jackie has maintained capital in terms of money: there is still £30,000 in the business at the end of nine years. The depreciation charge means that the annual £20,000 generated as cash was not taken out of the business. Only the £17,000 profit was taken out.

But, after nine years, the cost of replacing the vehicle has probably increased substantially; perhaps it has doubled. The business would then be able to buy only half a taxi. In terms of operating capability, the capital of the business has been halved over the 9-year period because no allowance has been made for the increase in prices of the fixed assets.

Chapter 6

1 The three ratios may be calculated on a 'per share' basis, or for the company as a whole. The results should be the same.

(a) The P/E ratio indicates whether the share price is expensive or cheap in relation to the most recent profits. It is calculated by dividing the share price by the earnings per share. A high P/E ratio (e.g. 30+) suggests that investors are optimistic about future increases in earnings. A low P/E ratio (e.g. 10 or less) suggest that investors are not very optimistic about future growth.

(b) The dividend yield indicates whether the share price is expensive or cheap in relation to the most recent dividends. It is calculated by dividing the most recent year's dividend per share by the share price. A high dividend yield (e.g. 5 per cent or more) suggests that shares are cheap in relation to the most recent dividend. A very high dividend yield (e.g. 8 per cent or more) suggests that there are serious concerns about the company: perhaps the share price has collapsed, and/or the level of dividends is not expected to be maintained at last year's level. A low dividend yield (e.g. 2 per cent or less) suggests that investors are optimistic about future growth.

(c) The dividend times cover relates the most recent year's dividends to the amount of profits earned in that period. It helps to indicate how 'safe' the dividends are. It is calculated by dividing the amount of earnings by the amount of dividends. A high cover (e.g. 2.5 or more) suggests that dividends are relatively safe. A low cover (e.g. 1.2, or even less than 1) suggests that the company would have difficulty maintaining the dividend, especially if there was a fall in earnings.

2 The market value of a successful company is likely to be higher than its balance sheet value. This is partly because balance sheet values may be understated. It is mainly because the market value of a business is largely influenced by its profitability, and expectations that it will be at least maintained, and will probably increase. The value of a successful business as a whole, as a going concern, with internally generated goodwill which is unrecorded, is normally higher than the value of a collection of dead assets.

Sometimes the market value of a company falls below the net asset value, especially when the company is doing badly. In these circumstances the company may unwittingly attract an asset stripping takeover bid. Another company may be attracted to buy up the assets of the company at a low price, and then split up the various parts of the company and sell them at a profit.

In some companies (e.g. property companies) assets may be fully valued, and prospects for growth in earnings are limited; the market value may then be lower than the net asset value.

3 The dividend yield refers to the last known dividend. The next dividend may be lower, or it may be zero. High dividend yields are associated with

low share prices, and question marks about how likely the dividend is to be maintained. At the time the United Utilities figure was quoted in Illustration 6.1 their share price had fallen following their announcement that they needed substantial additional capital and that they would make a large rights issue; their dividend cover was only 1; and there was uncertainty about the extent to which water companies would be allowed to increase their charges for water.

4 The figures are shown in full below.

	Alemouth plc	Beermouth plc
Share capital (20 pence shares)	£1,600,000	£ 2,000,000
Reserves	£3,200,000	£18,000,000
	£4,800,000	£20,000.000
Net profit after tax for year	£3,520,000	£1,200,000
Dividends for year	£3,200,000	£ 800,000
Number of shares	8,000,000	10,000,000
Market price of shares	£4.40	£1.80
Market capitalization	£35,200,000	£18,000,000
Earnings per share	£0.44	£0.12
Dividend per share	£0.40	£0.08
Price/earnings ratio	10	15
Dividend times cover	1.1 times	1.5 times
Dividend yield	9.09%	4.44%
Net assets per share	£0.60	£2.00

5 The dividend yield of Alemouth plc is very high, which is associated with a low share price (the P/E ratio is only 10), a low dividend cover (1.1 times), and pessimism about future prospects.

6 The market capitalization of Beermouth is only £18 million although their net asset value is £20 million. In most companies the market value is higher than the net asset value. There could something seriously wrong with Beermouth's balance sheet: perhaps the assets are overvalued, or there is a significant unrecorded liability – perhaps the company is about to be sued for something. It is more likely that the market value of the company is very low because the company is expected to be making losses. The company's return on capital employed (£1,200,000 ÷ £20,000,000) was only 6 per cent last year. If the company makes losses of more than £2 million in the current year, the net asset value would soon fall below the current market capitalization (which might then rise or fall, depending on investors' expectations).

Chapter 7

1 A very successful business will have serious cash shortages if their profits are poured into additional assets. This may be healthy expansion of stocks and debtors in line with sales; and investment in additional fixed assets, and buying shares in other companies. It may be unhealthy if poor control results in too many assets being bought, excessive stock levels, and fixed assets that are not profitably utilized.

   The situation could also arise if substantial loans are repaid, and if the company pays out more as dividends than it earns as profits.

2 If a company's depreciation charge is greater than its losses, it can still produce a positive cash flow. If a business is declining, additional cash could come in from reducing asset levels (stocks are sold off, debtors pay up, and excess fixed assets are sold). But this could not continue indefinitely. Eventually fixed assets will be fully depreciated and/or sold off, leaving little more than a cash shell.

3 The answer is shown as Illustration 7.2.

4 The answer is shown as Illustration 7.5.

5 **Penuham: Cash Flow Statement for Year 1**

Operating profit		170
Depreciation		51
		221
Increase in working capital		
Stocks	20	
Debtors	24	
Creditors	(8)	(36)
Net cash inflow from operating activities		185
Less profit on sale of vehicle		8
		177

Interest paid		(10)	
Taxation paid		(40)	
Purchase of machinery	(40)		
Proceeds from sale of vehicle	13	(27)	
Dividends paid		(30)	
Redemption of debentures		(80)	(187)
Net reduction in cash			10

6 <u>Leong</u>

Cash sales		10,000
Receipts from debtors		142,000
Deduct opening debtors	(9,000)	
Add closing debtors	7,000	
Sales		150,000

Opening stock	16,000		
Payments to creditors	91,000		
Deduct opening creditors	(8,000)		
Add closing creditors	11,000		
Purchases	94,000		
	110,000		
Deduct closing stock	(12,000)		
Cost of goods sold		98,000	
Gross profit		52,000	
Expenses	35,000		
Depreciation	10,000	(45,000)	
Net profit		7,000	

7 Free cash flow is the amount of cash flow that a company has generated during a period which it is free to spend as it wishes. It is based on cash flow from operations after deducting non-discretionary payments such as interest and taxation (and including any dividends received). The company is free to spend as much of this free cash flow as it wishes on additional investments in fixed assets, paying dividends and repaying loans. The figure should be reduced to allow for the fact that there is usually some *essential* replacement of fixed assets.

Ted Baker £3.215 m less (say) £1.215 m = £2 m
Tate & Lyle £303 m less (say) £25 m = £278 m

8 Jack Kit

Income Statement for Year Ended 31 December Year 3

Sales			
Receipts from debtors		120,000	
Less: from previous year		(10,000)	
Plus: this year's debtors		12,000	
Cash sales		60,000	182,000
Cost of sales			
Opening stock		14,000	
Payments to creditors	125,000		
Less: from previous year	(15,000)		
Plus: this year's creditors	17,000		
Purchases		127,000	
		141,000	
Deduct closing stock		16,000	125,000
Gross profit			57,000
Wages	25,000		
Expenses	20,000		
Depreciation	1,800		46,800
Net profit			10,200

Balance Sheet as at 31 December Year 3

Fixtures and fittings		
(18,000 – 1,800)		16,200
Premises		187,000
Stocks		16,000
Debtors		12,000
Cash		13,000
Creditors		(17,000)
Loan		(170,000)
		57,200
Capital		47,000
Retained profit		10,200
		57,200

Opening balance sheet

Fixtures and fittings	18,000
Stocks	14,000
Debtors	10,000
Cash	20,000
Creditors	(15,000)
	47,000
Capital	47,000

Jack Kit made a profit of £10,200 during the year, but his cash balance fell from £20,000 to £13,000. The business did much better than the cash figures suggest. Indeed, he managed to pay a deposit of £17,000 and buy new premises.

Cash flow statement for Jack Kit		£
Operating profit		10,200
Depreciation		1,800
		12,000
Increase in stocks	2,000	
Increase in debtors	2,000	
Increase in creditors	(2,000)	(2,000)
Cash flow from operations		10,000
Purchase of premises		(187,000)
Loan		170,000
Decrease in cash		£7,000

Chapter 8

1 Depreciation, stock valuation, the distinction between capital expenditure and revenue expenditure, provisions for bad debts, other provisions, amortization of goodwill.

2 Low depreciation figures; profits/losses on sales of fixed assets; other exceptional items; provisions; asset (re)valuations; capitalizing items in the grey area between capital and revenue expenditure; showing alternative earnings per share figures.

3 There is no agreed definition of creative accounting. At the moderate end of the spectrum of creative accounting practices, some exercise of judgment is perfectly legal. At the other extreme, deception is illegal.

4 Accounting standards could reduce or eliminate choices of accounting policy, and require additional disclosures. More effective systems for monitoring and enforcement could also be developed.

5 There may be a conflict of interest between the auditors' wish to earn additional fees from consultancy and their need to remain independent from directors. Many of the problems are criticisms of the arrangements for auditing rather than of the auditors themselves.

Chapter 9

1 Current ratio; liquidity ratio; capital gearing; interest cover. Profits, quality of assets, and cash flows are also important. Z scores take into account various combinations of similar information including working capital, total gross assets, retained profits, earnings before interest and tax, market value of equity and book value of debt.

2 Turnover, operating profit, net assets, for each class of business and for each geographic sector.

3 The key ratios are

	Year 2	Year 3
Operating profit/Operating assets	100/700	115/800
	14.286%	14.375%
Operating profit/Sales	100/1,000	115/1,100
	10%	10.45%
Sales/Operating assets	1,000/700	1,100/800
	1.43 times	1.375 times

There has been a small increase in return on capital employed, which is due to an increase in the operating profit/sales ratio. But there has been a deterioration of asset turnover, which has slowed down. It is tempting to simplify this and to say that reducing the company's operating assets would increase their return on capital employed.

This ignores several important matters such as:

(a) Some costs may be excessive, notwithstanding the fact that there has been a small increase in the operating profit/sales ratio. Attention should be given to all costs.

(b) Arithmetically, the alternative to reducing operating assets is to increase sales. There is no problem with operating assets increasing, provided sales increase by a bigger proportion than the increase in operating assets.

4 The key ratios for Gobbiediggan International plc are calculated as follows:

Segment	UK		Africa		South America	
	Year 1	Year 2	Year 1	Year 2	Year 1	Year 2
Operating profit/	80/900	78/760	40/200	44/175	20/40	21/60
Operating assets	8.9%	10.26%	20%	25.1%	50%	35%
Operating profit/	80/800	78/860	40/300	44/270	20/100	21/180
Sales	10%	9.1%	13.3%	16.3%	20%	11.7%
Sales/	800/900	860/760	300/200	270/175	100/40	180/60
Operating assets	0.89	1.13	1.5	1.54	2.5	3.0

It is true that profits in the UK are declining, in spite of a modest increase in sales. However, the UK produces the bulk of the company's profits; the amount of capital employed has declined, and the profitability of the UK (in terms of ROCE) has increased. The UK may be a mature market, with limited long-term prospects, but for the foreseeable future it is still very important and profitable to the company.

It is true that sales are declining in the Africa market; but profits are increasing; profitability (in terms of ROCE) is higher than the UK and is increasing. The decline in sales may be a one-off blip, and the company should investigate its causes, and try to increase sales before abandoning the market.

It is true that the South America market has had additional investment of £20,000; but this sum is small compared with the substantial increase in sales, and the high level of profitability. The ROCE declined, but this may be because it will take a little while for the additional investment to generate substantial additional profits.

The ratios may suggest that the company has a reasonable balance of different markets. It may also suggest priorities for developing each of the markets.

Chapter 10

1 The ASB's *Statement of Principles* defines assets as 'rights or other access to future economic benefits controlled by an entity as a result of past transactions or events'. Their definition of liabilities is 'obligations of an entity to transfer economic benefits as a result of past transactions or events'.

2 The purposes of asset measurement and reporting of fixed assets are:

(a) To complete the double entry system, and check on its accuracy, and to produce a list of balances to be transferred to a new ledger.

(b) To account for what has happened to the funds subscribed by shareholders by showing the assets in which they are invested.

(c) To give creditors information indicating the creditworthiness of the firm – showing that it has assets worth more than the amount that the firm owes.

(d) To provide up-to-date asset values so that the company does not have 'secret reserves', and to avoid unwelcome takeover bids based on hidden asset values.

(e) To provide up-to-date asset values as a basis for increased borrowing.

(f) As a basis for measuring profit – with profit measurement based on the increase in equity.

3 Methods of asset valuation include:

(i)   Historic cost

(ii)   Historic cost less depreciation.

(iii)   Net realizable value

(iv)   Economic value, or net present value

(v)   Replacement cost

(vi)   Face value

(vii)   Face value less a provision

(viii) Market price

(ix)   Directors' estimate of market value

(x)   Valuer's report

(xi)   Insurance values

(xii)   Historic cost adjusted for inflation

(xiii) Various combinations

4 Historic cost accounting requires fixed assets to be depreciated so that a proper charge is made against profits for the asset being 'used up'.

Stocks should be shown at the lower of cost and net realizable value; if they were always shown at cost, profits would be overstated if the assets could be sold only at a price significantly lower than cost.

Various other provisions, such as provisions for bad debts, are also created.

5 (a) Fixed assets: intangible.
Examples: deferred development expenditure; concessions, patents licences, trade marks; goodwill; payments on account.

(b) Fixed assets: tangible
Examples: land and buildings; land and machinery; fixtures and fittings; tools and equipment.

(c) Fixed assets: financial

Examples include investments in shares, debentures and government securities.

(d) Current assets

Examples include stocks of raw materials and consumables; work in progress; finished goods and goods for resale.

(e) Debtors and prepayments

(f) Investments (which may be held as fixed assets or as current assets).

(g) Cash and bank

6 (a) Creditors: amounts falling due within one year

Examples include debentures and loans; bank loans and overdrafts; payments received on account; trade creditors; bills of exchange payable; other creditors including taxation and social security; accruals and deferred income.

(b) Creditors: amounts falling due after more than one year

Examples are the same as with short-term creditors.

(c) Provisions for liabilities and charges

Examples include pensions and similar obligations; taxation including deferred taxation.

7 The main 'liabilities' that do not seem like other liabilities are provisions. Provisions for depreciation and for bad debts do not seem to be like obligations to transfer economic benefits. They are more an estimate of what has happened, and an appropriate charge against profits.

A provision for deferred taxation may not result in any payment in the foreseeable future. Provisions for pensions may seem to have been inappropriate if made at a time when the value of the pension fund's investments is very low; subsequent increases in the value of investments may mean that the provision is no longer required.

Sometimes provisions are created, and partly reversed at a later date.

Chapter 11

1 Any additional share capital is an increase in ownership interest, but is not revenue. Revaluations of assets, and restatements of amounts invested overseas in foreign currencies, can increase ownership interest, but would not usually be regarded as revenues. Other credits to the profit and loss account, such as reductions in provisions, would increase ownership interest, but it is more debatable whether or not they should be regarded as revenues.

2 The payment of dividends, and reductions in share capital (e.g. the company buying back its own shares on the stock market) are decreases in ownership interest, but are not expenses. Ownership

interest is also reduced when assets and investments are revalued downwards, and when provisions are created or increased; these may be more debatable, but prudence would suggest that they should be regarded as expenses.

3 (a) The small effects are with expenses like rates which are paid in advance, and it is necessary for the profit and loss account to include only those expenses which relate to the period of the profit and loss account. There are also usually some 'accruals' at the end of the year: expenses which belong to the period which has just ended, but which have yet to be recorded.

(b) A much bigger effect is with fixed assets. These are not regarded as an expense when they are purchased; the cost is charged to the profit and loss account over a number of years as depreciation.

(c) Another large effect is with closing stocks. The expense for the period is the cost of the goods that were sold. The cost of goods that were bought, or manufactured, but not sold, is carried forward and charged as an expense in the next period.

4 Cost of sales; distribution costs; administrative expenses; interest.

5 Exceptional items are 'material items which derive from events or transactions that fall within the ordinary activities of the reporting entity and which individually or, if of a similar type, in aggregate, need to be disclosed by virtue of their size or incidence if the financial statements are to give a true and fair view' (FRS 3). The main non-operating exceptional items are profits or losses on the sale or termination of an operation; costs of a fundamental reorganization or restructuring; and profits or losses on the disposal of fixed assets.

Exceptional items are separately disclosed; all are taken into account in calculating the basic earnings per share figure.

6 They could claim that the life of the fixed asset is so long that depreciation or amortization would be immaterial; that the asset is maintained; and that an annual impairment review takes place to ensure that this is the case.

Chapter 12

1 (i) Owners' capital, which is share capital in the case of a company
(ii) Borrowing, which may be short term (e.g. overdraft) or long term (e.g. debentures)
(iii) Retained profits

In addition, expansion can be funded in a variety of ways such as factoring debtors, sale and leaseback of premises.

2   Preference shareholders receive a fixed rate of dividend. No dividend can be paid to ordinary shareholders unless the preference dividend has been paid. There is no fixed rate of dividend for ordinary shareholders: they may receive very substantial dividends, or none at all.

Preference shares are usually *cumulative*, which means that if their dividend is not paid for one or more years, all arrears of preference dividends must be paid before any ordinary dividends are paid.

3   The main advantages of gearing (or borrowing) are that, if the company is successful, it can 'gear up' the return to ordinary shareholders. If a company can borrow money at, say 7 per cent, and invest it to earn, say, 10 per cent, the whole of the extra profits belongs to the ordinary shareholders. The more the company borrows, the more profit it will make. Such borrowing also has the advantage that it enables companies to finance expansion relatively quickly, and at relatively modest cost. Interest is an allowable expense for corporation tax purposes. If the alternative to borrowing is to issue ordinary shares, the issue costs of shares is likely to be higher, and shareholders are likely to expect a higher return in due course.

The main disadvantage of gearing is the risk of borrowing too much, and the company getting into difficulty. If a company has excessive borrowing, suppliers and lenders may be reluctant to do business with them. As long as a company has to pay only, say 7 per cent for its borrowing, and is able to earn, say 10 per cent, they should be all right. But if interest rates rise very much, or (more likely) if earnings are significantly reduced – or the company has no earnings – in particular years, they are likely to get into serious financial difficulties. Substantial borrowing is usually secured on some of the company's assets, and if the company is unable to meet the repayments, the lenders may require the assets to be sold, and the company could be forced into liquidation.

High gearing exaggerates the effects of changes in earnings before interest and taxation on earnings for ordinary shareholders. When EBIT is good, it is very, very good for the ordinary shareholders. But when EBIT is bad, it can be horrid for the ordinary shareholders – there may be no dividends and the share price may collapse. High gearing is associated with high risk.

4   (a)

		TimeBall Co		DownsPier Co	
		Year 6	Year 7	Year 6	Year 7
	Debentures	100	140	100	50
	Debentures + Equity	300	342.2	300	284.1

(i) Capital gearing

ratio[4]	$33\frac{1}{3}$%	40.9%	$33\frac{1}{3}$%	17.6%
Operating profit	20/	21.6/	20/	17.5/
÷ Interest	9	12.6	9	4.5
(ii) Interest cover	2.2 times	1.7 times	2.2 times	3.9 times
Profit after tax	7.7	6.3	7.7	9.1
Dividend	4	4.1	4	5
(iii) Dividend cover	1.9 times	1.5 times	1.9 times	1.8 times
(iv) Proportion of profit paid as dividend	36%	46%	36%	38%

(b) (i)   The capital gearing ratio shows the proportion of net assets financed by borrowing.

The TimeBall Company increased its fixed assets plus current assets less current liabilities; a small part of this was financed by retained profits; it was mainly financed by additional borrowing. It became a higher risk company.

The DownsPier Company reduced its fixed assets plus current assets less current liabilities; this was needed, plus an issue of additional shares, and a small amount of profit retained during the year, to provide enough to pay off half of the borrowing. The company's risk was reduced.

(ii)   The interest times cover shows how much the company is earning in relation to the amount of interest payable. In Year 6 the interest cover of both companies was very low (2.2 times) which means that nearly half of their EBIT was committed to interest payments. A serious dip in EBIT could make it very difficult for the company to pay the necessary interest.

In Year 7 the TimeBall Company's interest cover was lower, meaning that the situation became more risky. The DownsPier Company's interest cover increased significantly (though it is still on the low side), and risk was reduced.

(iii)   The dividend cover shows how much profit after tax was available to pay the dividend that the company chose to pay. The TimeBall Company's profit after tax was lower in Year 7 than in Year 6, and there was a very small increase in dividend, both of which reduced the cover.

The DownsPier Company's profit after tax increased significantly (by 18 per cent), but the increase in dividend was more substantial (25 per cent) and so the dividend cover was reduced.

---

4   Here the capital gearing ratio is measured as D ÷ (D + E). It is acceptable to measure it as D ÷ E (both expressed as a percentage).

(iv) The proportion of profits paid out as dividend is the same information as in (iii) above, but expressed the other way around (the reciprocal expressed as a percentage).

(c)

	TimeBall Co		DownsPier Co	
	Year 6	Year 7	Year 6	Year 7
Return on shareholders' capital employed				
Profit after tax	7.7	6.3	7.7	9.1
Shareholders'				
Capital employed	200	202.2	200	234.1
ROSCE	3.85%	3.1%	3.85%	3.9%
Return on total long-term capital employed				
Operating Profit	20	21.6	20	17.5
Debentures +				
Equity	300	342.2	300	284.1
Return	6.7%	6.3%	6.7%	6.2%

In year 7 the TimeBall Company increased their operating profit, but because of extra debenture interest, their profitability was reduced.

In Year 7 the DownsPier Company managed a small increase in the return on ordinary shareholders capital employed; although their operating profit was lower than in the previous year, their debenture interest was halved. The ordinary shareholders had put more money into the company, and they earned just enough to make it worthwhile.

Gross profit/Sales %	40%	40%	40%	43%
Operating profit/Sales %	20%	19.6%	20%	18.4

The TimeBall Company maintained the same gross profit ratio from Year 6 to Year 7, but their operating profit as a percentage of sales declined; this must have been due to operating expenses increasing more than sales.

The DownsPier Company's gross profit ratio increased from Year 6 to Year 7; perhaps they concentrated on their most profitable lines, and the total amount of sales declined. Their operating profit as a percentage of sales declined – although the gross profit had increased. This was because operating expenses had increased, both as a percentage of sales, and in total.[5]

---

5 Although the amount of operating expenses increased

	Year 6	Year 7
Gross profit	40	41
Operating profit	20	17.5
Operating expenses	20	23.5

470 ANSWERS TO SELF-TESTING QUESTIONS

The TimeBall Company expanded sales and borrowing in Year 6, and their financial position was weaker, as shown by the gearing ratio and interest times cover. But the expansion was not (yet?) worthwhile, and profitability declined. They managed a small increase in dividends, but this was not justified by profits.

The DownsPier Company seems a little safer. Sales declined, and borrowing was reduced, and the gross profit ratio increased, and the amount of net profit increased. The return on ordinary shareholders' capital increased very slightly and there was a substantial increase in dividend – more than was justified by the increase in profits.

Chapter 13

1 High levels of working capital makes life easier for managers. Sales can be made to anyone without worrying about collecting the money in. Having large amounts of stock is convenient to satisfy all demands. Having substantial sums of money in the bank is also very convenient – there is no need to plan it properly, and there is always money available. High levels of working capital also lead to high current ratios which make the company look financially stronger in terms of their ability to pay their creditors as they fall due.

2 Debtors can be reduced to little or nothing (or even negative) if customers are required to pay in advance. Some businesses have no stocks, or ensure that deliveries are 'just in time'. If there is a significant creditors figure, then working capital can be negative. This is not unusual with retailers.

3 At first it arises with attempts to expand with insufficient long-term capital. There might be significant increases in fixed assets, stocks and debtors; but then the business finds that it is unable to finance these. Creditors increase; current and liquidity ratios fall; and the company runs out of money. It may then have to operate on a cash only basis, and start to sell off assets.

4 Prompt paperwork, with invoices and reminders; follow up letters and telephone calls; personal visits. Threatening to cut off supplies and/or legal action. Implementing threats. Offering cash discounts for early payment. Charging interest on late payment.

A company might deliberately increase the length of time that customers are allowed to pay if this is likely to lead to increases in sales, and to generate additional profits greater than the cost of financing the additional debtors.

5 Stock holding costs; and the costs of ordering (which may include placing the order, monitoring receipt, and payment of invoice). It also considers the volume of usage during the year, and the price per unit.

6 By careful planning and monitoring of cash receipts and payments; ensuring that there are sufficient funds to meet all planned requirements; and not authorizing unplanned payments.

7 *Congle*

Applying the EOQ formula the ordering quantity will be the square root of

$$\frac{2 \times 40,000 \times £20}{1.25 \times 0.32} = \sqrt{\frac{1,600,000}{0.4}} = \sqrt{4,000,000} = 2,000$$

The number of orders placed each year will be 40,000 ÷ 2,000 = 20.
The annual ordering cost = £20 × 20 times per annum = £400.
Goods will be delivered (365 ÷ 20 =) every 18 days.
The average stock level will be half of the amount delivered, i.e.

$$\tfrac{1}{2} \times 2,000 \times £1.25 = £1,250$$

The annual stock holding cost is £1,250 × 32% = £400.

8 *Fleshwick Traders*

Annual cost of debtors now: £90,000 × 17% = £15,300.
Annual sales are £365,000, i.e. £1,000 per day.
Existing debtors figure is £90,000, i.e. 90 days.
Expected reduction in debtors applies to one-third of debtors, i.e. £30,000.
Reduction is from 90 days to 10 days, i.e. a reduction of $\tfrac{8}{9}$ (eight-ninths).
Eight ninths of £30,000 is £26,667.
Annual interest saved is 17% of £26,667 = £4,533.
Annual cost of discount on one-third of annual sales is £121,667 × 2.5% = £3,042.

(a) It is worth offering the discount because the amount of interest saved is greater than the cost of the discount offered.

(b) The annual interest saved is £4,533; discount costing up to £4,533 could be offered without reducing profits. £4,533 as a percentage of (one-third of annual sales) £121,667 is 3.726%.

(c) 5% discount to one-third of existing customers would cost £6,085.
The annual interest saved would be £4,533.
The additional cost would be £6,085.
The additional contribution required £1,552.
Additional annual sales to achieve this contribution (contribution is one-fifth of sales) is 5 × £1,552 = £7,760.

This is near enough for most purposes, but for the mathematically inclined it is rather simplistic. A more accurate calculation would be as follows:

Let I = the increase in sales required to finance the discount.

The cost of the discount is $\frac{1}{3}$ (365,000 + I) × 0.05, less the interest saving, which is 17% of eight-ninths of one-third of (365,000 + I). This will be equal to the amount of the additional contribution required, which is 20% of the additional sales. We can say, therefore, that

$$[\tfrac{1}{3}(365,000 + I) \times 0.05] -$$
$$[0.17 \times \tfrac{8}{9} \times \tfrac{1}{3} \times \tfrac{90}{365}(365,000 + I)] = 0.2 \times I$$

The amount of the additional contribution required (solving the above equation) is £7,913.

9 Stokeypokey

(i) Trading and Profit and Loss Account

		£000
Sales		6,180
Cost of sales		4,944
Gross profit		1,236
Rent	400	
Other expenses	165	
Depreciation	10	575
Net profit		661

(ii) Balance Sheet as at End of Year

Fixed assets at cost		100
Less provision for depreciation		10
		90
Current assets		
Stocks	560	
Debtors	1,400	
Prepayment	100	
Cash	71	
	2,131	
Creditors	(560)	1,571
		1,661
Loan from Stokeypokey		1,000
		661
Retained profit		661

(iii)

	Jan £000	Feb £000	Mar £000	Apr £000	May £000	Jun £000	Jul £000	Aug £000	Sep £000	Oct £000	Nov £000	Dec £000
Receipts from debtors	–	–	100	200	300	400	480	560	640	700	700	700
Payments for purchases		240	240	320	384	448	512	560	560	560	560	560
Rent	100		100			100			100			100
Fittings	50								50			
Expenses	10	10	10	10	15	15	15	16	16	16	16	16
Opening balance	1,000	840	590	340	210	111	(52)	(99)	(115)	(201)	(77)	47
Net receipts	(160)	(250)	(250)	(130)	(99)	(163)	(47)	(16)	(86)	124	124	24
	840	590	340	210	111	(52)	(99)	(115)	(201)	(77)	47	71

Workings

	Jan	Feb	Mar	Apr	May	Jun	Jul	Aug	Sep	Oct	Nov	Dec
Sales	100	200	300	400	480	560	640	700	700	700	700	700
Purchases	240	240	320	384	448	512	560	560	560	560	560	560

(iv) The business looks highly profitable. Stokeypokey plans to put £1 million into the Northern Ireland branch and expects to earn £661,000 profit: a return on capital of just over 66 per cent per annum.

The gross profit ratio is expected to be 20 per cent. The net profit/sales ratio is expected to be 10.7 per cent. The main reason for the high return on capital employed is that capital employed is fairly low, partly because the premises are rented.

Although profits look very good, it will take a little longer to generate cash flows to match. Rapid expansion in sales means that cash receipts from debtors tend to lag behind payments. A rapidly expanding and profitable business is often 'cash hungry' in the early stages. In this venture the branch pays out more cash than it receives in each of the first 9 months, and the initial £1 million will not be sufficient to avoid an overdraft by September.

By careful planning it might be possible to avoid an overdraft. Perhaps they could arrange to delay some payments in September, such as for the additional fittings, or make an extra effort to get debtors to pay more quickly in August.

Depreciation is an expense in calculating profit, but it is not a cash payment.

Chapter 14

1 ROI takes the average annual profits during the life of a project and expresses them as a percentage of the capital employed in the project. It

is sometimes based on the initial capital employed, and sometimes on the average capital employed over the life of the project.

2 The company's return on capital employed is 10 per cent (£1 million as a percentage of £10 million)

   The ROI of the proposed project is 9 per cent (£180,000 as a percentage of £2 million).

   The project would probably lower the company's return on capital employed to 9.83 per cent (£1.18 million as a percentage of £12 million). (It could increase the ROCE if it was financed by low cost borrowings, or from surplus cash that was earning only a modest return.)

3 Cash Flows

Year	Project A £000	Project B £000
0	(1,000)	(1,000)
1	200	400
2	200	350
3	200	300
4	200	100
5	200	50
6	200	5
7	200	5
8	200	5
Total	1,600	1,215

The payback period of Project A is 5 years. The payback period of Project B is just less than 3 years.

   Project A produces substantially more cash flows than Project B. If the time value of money is not considered Project A is much better.

   If DCF was used whether or not it is worth waiting for the extra money would depend on the discount rate used.

4 (a) ROI is based on profits and so is compatible with financial accounts. The answer is expressed as a percentage which appears to be easy to understand. It is relatively easily calculated and understood.

      However, the approach ignores the timing of the cash flows. A project may have a good ROI but not be worthwhile if the delay in receiving it is too long.

   (b) Payback period is easy to understand and easy to calculate. It uses cash flows rather than profits, and the emphasis is on getting back the money quickly.

      But Payback period ignores cash flows received after the end of the payback period. Use of payback period could lead to a project being accepted that makes very little money, but pays back quickly; and a very profitable project could be rejected because it takes a little longer to pay back.

5 The project will generate £35,000 profits a year for 5 years, giving total profits of £175,000. This looks poor.

But, profits are measured after charging depreciation, which amounts to £40,000 a year. Annual cash flows are therefore £75,000 a year.

Using a discount rate of 10 per cent, the project gives a net present value of about £84,300 as follows:

Year 1	$0.909 \times 75,000 = 68,175$
Year 2	$0.826 \times 75,000 = 61,950$
Year 3	$0.751 \times 75,000 = 56,325$
Year 4	$0.683 \times 75,000 = 51,225$
Year 5	$\underline{0.621 \times 75,000 = 46,575}$
	$3.790 \times 75,000 = 284,300$[6]

After deducting the initial cost of the investment (£284,300 – £200,000) the net present value of the project is £84,300 which makes it acceptable if the company's cost of capital is 10 per cent.

The project would still be just about acceptable with a cost of capital of 25 per cent (£75,000 × 2.689[7] = £201,675) because the net present values of the future cash flows would still be slightly above the initial cost.

				Kippering		Queenies	
6	(a) Average annual profits			£		£	
	Total cash flows			75,000		90,000	
	Total depreciation			50,000		50,000	
	Total profits			25,000		40,000	
	Average annual profits			5,000		8,000	
	(b) Return on initial capital employed			10%		16%	
	(c) Return on average capital employed			20%		32%	
	(c) Payback period			$2\frac{1}{3}$ years		3.2 years	
				£000		£000	
	(e) NPV using 10%	1	0.9091	25	22,727	5	4,545
		2	0.8264	20	16,528	15	12,396
		3	0.7513	15	11,269	25	18,782
		4	0.6830	10	6,830	25	17,075
		5	0.6209	5	3,105	20	12,418
					60,459		65,216
					(50,000)		(50,000)
	Net present value				10,459		15,216

----

6 Slight differences are due to roundings.

7 The cumulative present value factor for five years at 25 per cent (which can be looked up in a table, or found by adding together the 25 per cent discount factors for 5 years).

(f) NPV using 25%

	1	0.800	25	20,000	5	4,000
	2	0.640	20	12,800	15	9,600
	3	0.512	15	7,680	25	12,800
	4	0.410	10	4,100	25	10,250
	5	0.328	5	1,640	20	6,560
				46,220		43,210
				(50,000)		(50,000)
Net present value				(3,780)		(6,790)

(g) Approximate internal rate of return

10% plus a proportion of 15%	$\dfrac{10,459}{(10,459 + 3,780)}$	$\dfrac{15,216}{(15,216 + 6,790)}$
	0.735×15	0.691×15
	11.02	10.36
+10	21.02%	20.36%

7 If it is decided to go ahead with the proposal the additional cash outflows at the beginning of the project would be:

Modifications to existing machinery	£100,000
Additional working capital	£ 50,000
Initial marketing costs	£ 60,000
	£210,000

The book value of the other machine is irrelevant; it has no alternative use or disposal value and so there is no 'opportunity cost'.

The cost of the consultants' report has already been incurred whether the project goes ahead or not, and so is irrelevant.

The cash flows generated by each unit of sales are

Selling price		£60
Variable costs		
Materials	11	
Labour	6	
Variable overheads	13	£30
		£30

The costs of general fixed overheads and of interest will be incurred whether or not the project goes ahead and so they are not relevant.

	Year 0	Year 1	Year 2	Year 3	Year 4
Sales (units)	–	3,000	7,000	4,000	1,000
'Contribution' at £30 per unit		90,000	210,000	120,000	30,000
Machinery	(100,000)				
Working capital	(50,000)				50,000
Marketing	(60,000)	(20,000)	(20,000)	(20,000)	(20,000)
Maintenance		(10,000)	(10,000)	(10,000)	(10,000)
Net cash flow	(210,000)	60,000	180,000	90,000	50,000
20% discount factor	1.0	0.833	0.694	0.579	0.482
Present value	(210,000)	50,000	124,920	52,110	24,100

The net present value of the project discounted at 20% is (£251,130 − £210,000 =) £41,130

Chapter 15

1 It is numerically accurate because bookkeeping systems require balancing, and because it is audited. Where it is based on historic cost it reliably reflects the results of transactions and it is verifiable; it does not depend on subjective opinions about value. There is an 'official story' determined by company law and accounting standards: financial accounts are not just what a company chooses to disclose. It is a system which is widely used and understood.

2 Companies are owned by shareholders who are mainly interested in profits (or perhaps in their wealth being maximized, which is largely a product of profits being generated). Profit is also assumed to be a measure of efficiency and effectiveness.

3 Earnings before interest, taxation, depreciation and amortization. Rapidly expanding companies that have paid a lot for goodwill, and perhaps for fixed assets may generate little or no (or negative) profits and cash flows. A positive EBITDA may give a better impression. But companies still have to pay interest and taxation, and positive EBITDA is not a good sign unless it is soon backed up by positive cash flows and profits.

4 Cash flow is not a better measure of performance than profit. Both cash flow and profit are essential measures. Generating lots of cash is not necessarily a healthy sign if it is done by diminishing the value of the company. If a company has good profits, but lacks cash (perhaps because it is expanding), it should not be difficult to rectify cash shortages by borrowing.

5 Value for money auditing involves checking that an organization has proper systems for achieving economy, efficiency and effectiveness.

6 Financial, Customer, Process, and Learning and Innovation.

Appendix

1 (a) Cash Account
  (b) Sales Account
  (c) Purchases Account
  (d) Anirroc Account (Anirroc is a creditor)

(e) Cash Account

(f) Provision for Bad Debts Account

2 Sales, Creditors, Share Capital and Share Premium.

3 All of them.

4 Statement (b) is true.

5

Carlos Cash Account

Date 2004	Description	Amount £	Date 2004	Description	Amount £
1 July	Capital	40,000	5 July	Expenses (Rent)	5,000
3 July	Spano Bank	15,000	8 July	Furniture and equipment	11,000
27 July	Sales	4,000	19 July	Expenses	2,500
14 Sept	Minki Cabs	15,000	10 Aug	Purchases	3,300
21 Sept	Sales	24,000	30 Aug	Motosales	40,000
			6 Sept	General expenses	3,300

Carlos Capital Account

Date	Description	Amount £	Date	Description	Amount £
			2004		
			1 July	Cash	40,000

Spano Bank (Loan) Account

Date	Description	Amount £	Date	Description	Amount £
			2004		
			3 July	Cash	15,000

General Expenses Account

Date	Description	Amount £	Date	Description	Amount £
2004					
5 July	Cash (Rent)	5,000			
19 July	Cash	2,500			
6 Sept	Cash	3,300			

Furniture and Equipment Account

Date	Description	Amount £	Date	Description	Amount £
2004					
8 July	Cash	11,000			

Purchases Account

Date	Description	Amount £	Date	Description	Amount £
2004					
13 July	Motosales Ltd	50,000			
10 Aug	Cash	3,300			
16 Aug	Motosales	22,000			

Motosales Ltd (Creditor) Account

Date	Description	Amount £	Date	Description	Amount £
2004					
30 Aug	Cash	40,000	2004		
			13 July	Purchases	50,000
			16 Aug	Purchases	22,000

Sales Account

Date	Description	Amount £	Date	Description	Amount £
2004			2004		
			27 July	Cash	4,000
			3 Aug	Minki Cabs	18,000
			21 Sept	Cash	24,000

Minki Cabs (Debtors) Account

Date	Description	Amount £	Date	Description	Amount £
2004			2004		
3 Aug	Sales	18,000	14 Sept	Cash	15,000

Trial Balance as at 30 September

	Debit	Credit
Capital		40,000
Spano Bank Loan		15,000
Cash	32,900	
General expenses	10,800	
Furniture and equipment	11,000	
Purchases	75,300	
Creditor (Motosales)		32,000
Sales		46,000
Debtors (Minki Cabs)	3,000	
	133,000	133,000

Carlos: Profit and Loss Account for the three months ending 30 September

		£
Sales		46,000
Cost of sales		
Opening stock	0	
Purchases	75,300	
Deduct closing stock	38,100	
Cost of goods sold		37,200
Gross profit		8,800
General expenses		10,800
Loss		2,000

Carlos: Balance Sheet as at 30 September

Fixed Assets		£
Furniture and equipment		11,000
Current Assets		
Stocks	38,100	
Debtors	3,000	
Cash	32,900	
	74,000	
Creditors	(32,000)	
		42,000
		53,000
Loan		(15,000)
Net assets		38,000
Capital		40,000
Loss		(2,000)
		38,000

6   ## Ellie's Limited: Profit and Loss Account for Year 1 to 31 December

	£	£
Sales		248,300
Cost of goods sold		
Opening stock	19,500	
Purchases	167,000	
	186,500	
Less closing stock	21,000	165,500
Gross Profit		82,800
Printing and stationery	2,400	
Wages	12,300	
Bad debt written off	500	
Increase in provision for bad		
debts (650 – 600)	50	
Rent (1,500 – 400)	1,100	
Electricity (1,100 + 200)	1,300	
Depreciation on F and F		
(25% × 10,000)	2,500	
Depreciation on cars		
(25% × 20,000)	5,000	
Profit on disposal of van		
(8,400 – 4,200 – 4,750)	(550)	
General expenses	1,400	26,000
Operating profit		56,800
Corporation tax		15,000
Profit after tax		41,800
Proposed dividend (100 × £20)		2,000
Retained profit for year		39,800

Ellie's Limited: Balance Sheet as at 31 December Year 1

Fixed assets	Cost	Accumulated Depreciation	Net Book Value
	£	£	£
Fixtures and fittings	12,000	4,500	7,500
Vehicles	20,000	10,000	10,000
	_____	_____	17,500
Current assets			
Stocks		21,000	
Debtors (61,000 – 500)	60,500		
Less Provision			
for bad debts	(650)	59,850	
Prepaid rent		400	
Cash		450	
		81,700	
Current liabilities			
Creditors	13,400		
Accruals	200		
Taxation	15,000		
Dividend	2,000		
		30,600	51,100
			68,600
Share capital			100
Share premium			11,600
Retained profits as at 31 December Year 0		17,100	
For year to 31 December 01		39,800	56,900
			68,600

Index